SPANISH THE EASY WAY

Second Edition

By

RUTH J. SILVERSTEIN
ALLEN POMERANTZ, Ph.D.
HEYWOOD WALD, Ph.D.

General Editor
NATHAN QUIÑONES

BARRON'S EDUCATIONAL SERIES, INC.

All inquiries should be addressed to:
Barron's Educational Series, Inc.
250 Wireless Boulevard
Hauppauge, New York 11788

Library of Congress Catalog Card No. 88-39440

International Standard Book No. 0-8120-4204-2

Library of Congress Cataloging in Publication Data

Silverstein, Ruth J.
    Spanish the easy way, book 1 / by Ruth J. Silverstein, Allen
Pomerantz, Heywood Wald. — 2nd ed.
        p.   cm.
    Adaptation of: Spanish now!
    Continued by: Spanish the easy way, book 2 / by Christopher
Kendris.
    Includes index.
    ISBN 0-8120-4204-2
    1. Spanish language—Self-instruction. I. Pomerantz, Allen.
II. Wald, Heywood. III. Silverstein, Ruth J.   Spanish now!
IV. Kendris, Christopher. Spanish the easy way, book 2.   V. Title.
PC4112.5.s5 1989   88-39440
468.2'421—dc19   CIP

PRINTED IN THE UNITED STATES OF AMERICA

234 410 14 13 12 11 10

Table of Contents

Part One: Structures and Verbs

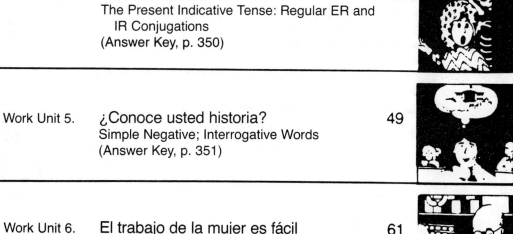

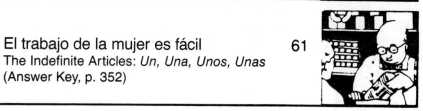

Part Two: Idioms and Dialogues

About the Authors

Ruth J. Silverstein is Chairperson of the Department of Foreign Languages at Richmond Hill High School, New York City. A specialist in Spanish and its teaching, she has been Assistant Professor of Applied Linguistics, NDEA; Assistant Professor of Spanish (Adjunct), New York University; and Lecturer of Foreign Language Methodology at Hunter College and of Spanish at Queens College, City University of New York. She has also taught secondary-school students of Spanish from beginners to Advanced Placement in both the Junior High School and Senior High School Divisions. Her postgraduate course work was taken at Teachers College, Columbia University, and at the University of Mexico, Mexico. She has lived and traveled in Mexico, Puerto Rico, and Spain; and has participated in innovative programs for teaching Spanish, and in writing foreign language syllabi for the New York City Board of Education.

Prof. Allen Pomerantz, Ph.D., is Coordinator of the Audio-Laboratory and Modern Language Workshop at Bronx Community College, CUNY, where he teaches basic Spanish, Advanced Spanish Conversation, and Peninsular and Latin-American Civilization and Literature. Committee activities and grant proposals involve him in computer-aided, independent, and interdisciplinary instruction; curriculum development, and multimedia learning. Professor Pomerantz completed graduate studies at New York University, and while teaching at the University of Wisconsin and working for the U.S. Armed Forces Institute. He studied at the Universidad de Valladolid, Spain, as a Fulbright-Hayes recipient, taught several years in local high schools, and served as translator-recorder for Region II, H.E.W. He is a Special Examiner in Spanish for the New York City Department of Personnel.

Heywood Wald, Ph.D., is the former Chairman of the Department of Foreign Languages and Bilingual Programs at the Martin Van Buren High School, New York City. He has served as center director of the Intensive Spanish Language Development Program of the New York City Board of Education to teach members of the teaching and administrative staff basic, functional Spanish. A foreign language specialist, Dr. Wald has taught Spanish, French, and Italian in both junior and senior high schools and is coauthor of *Aventuras en la ciudad*, an extremely popular supplementary reader currently in use throughout the United States and abroad, and of several other popular foreign language textbooks. Dr. Wald has done graduate work at the National University of Mexico and has studied at the universities of Madrid, Barcelona, and Havana.

General Editor

Nathan Quiñones is the former Chancellor of the New York City Board of Education. He was a member of the Board of Examiners in New York City. He served as Chairman of the Foreign Language Department at Benjamin N. Cardozo High School, New York City. He has also taught Spanish and Puerto Rican Orientation as Adjunct Professor at York College. He has served as consultant for textbooks and materials for secondary schools and college courses in the areas of foreign languages and bilingual education.

Note to the Student

SPANISH THE EASY WAY: BOOK 1 will give you a solid introduction to the basics of the Spanish language in the most interesting way. The preparatory lessons (Lecciones Preparatorias) are followed by twenty-eight Work Units consisting of enjoyable dramatized stories accompanied, of course, by vocabulary and practice material. A specific element of the Spanish language, with model sentences in Spanish and in English to illustrate the point, is presented in each Unit. Practice exercises, each with a sample answer in Spanish and English, are easy, interesting, and plentiful. Oral proficiency is encouraged with special practice material in each unit for speaking Spanish.

An end-vocabulary, Spanish-English and English-Spanish, offers a handy word reference. An Answer Key for all exercises in the book adds a very useful touch to SPANISH THE EASY WAY: BOOK 1, and an Index puts the contents of the book at your fingertips. A Pronunciation Guide is provided on pages xiii–xiv.

A Word About Oral Proficiency

Developing your ability to speak the beautiful Spanish language is easy when properly approached. Here are some suggestions that will show you how to take advantage of the many oral opportunities that SPANISH THE EASY WAY: BOOK 1 offers.

- Read aloud the Spanish Examples in your Pronunciation Guide on pages xiii–xiv. Practice these Spanish sounds daily at first.
- Try out your new ability to read Spanish aloud correctly using the Lecciones Preparatorias, which begin on page 1.
- Read aloud everything you see in Spanish in this book, including the stories, which you can dramatize alone or with a friend. Read aloud all models, examples, and rules. Say each answer before you write, then write and read it smoothly.
- Do the composition exercise orally before you write it. Oral composition is learning how to express several ideas in an organized, mature way. You can say it aloud again after you write the composition for smoother, more confident oral expression.
- Do the Oral Proficiency exercise at the end of each Work Unit to build your speaking power. You may do the Oral Proficiency practice alone, or you may invite a friend to take the minor role while you take the major role. Your friend may also prompt your responses by using the suggestions given in the exercise.
- Read aloud dramatically the idioms and dialogues, which begin on page 273, either alone or with a friend. Memorize the practical, short dialogues for daily use.
- Listen to Spanish being spoken whenever possible—by friends, on the radio, on television, on recordings, and in films.

Whether you want to study Spanish on your own or are a student who wishes to enrich your learning in a school or college, whether you are a native speaker seeking to improve your Spanish language ability or a beginner in Spanish, we hope that you will enjoy SPANISH THE EASY WAY and that you will continue your study of Spanish using other Barron's publications.

Ruth J. Silverstein
Allen Pomerantz, Ph.D.
Heywood Wald, Ph.D.

Introduction

¡ Hola !

Hola is a word that is used more than 225 million times a day. Yes, that's right. *Hola* is the Spanish word for *hello,* and millions of Spanish-speaking people use that word to greet their friends and relatives each day. Spanish is the native language for over 225 million people throughout the world. It is, in fact, one of the most widely used languages in the world. Spanish is a principal means of communication in Spain, Mexico, Central and South America, the Caribbean, and parts of Asia and Africa. It is also the first or the second language for over 14 million people in the United States.

Do you work for a multinational organization? Are you planning a career in international business? Are you preparing yourself in Spanish for government service here or abroad? Do you wish to travel? Are you interested in communicating with Spanish speakers? Would you like to broaden your knowledge of the world and of mankind?

Learning Spanish is a challenging and exciting experience!

SPANISH THE EASY WAY is a valuable instructional tool to help you achieve that goal. It offers a comprehensive presentation of all the essential elements of the first level of Spanish language study. SPANISH THE EASY WAY is for beginning students who need to learn the fundamental skills of the language. SPANISH THE EASY WAY is for more advanced students who need a refresher course in basic elements of the language. SPANISH THE EASY WAY is for students enrolled in bilingual programs designed to strengthen the native speaker's use of Spanish. SPANISH THE EASY WAY is for the student in the individualized classroom and for students following a program of self-instruction. SPANISH THE EASY WAY is for anyone seeking practice in the essentials of the language.

SPANISH THE EASY WAY gives you a natural and easy way to learn through "discovering and conceptualizing," that is to say, through "getting the idea yourself," from the numerous models in Spanish followed by their meanings in English. The rules need not always be memorized. You will understand almost immediately from the examples given in Spanish and English.

And now a word on how to use the book.

How to Use This Book

Part One

The Story

Step 1: Reading and Understanding

    a. Get interested in the topic. Imagine yourself in the same situation as the character(s) in the story, as described in English.

    b. Study the Palabras Nuevas or "New Words" a few at a time. Read one word at a time silently, and repeat it aloud. Try to associate its meaning with that of a similar word you know. Copy some of the words as you say them.

    c. Test your word memory. Cover the English first, then the Spanish.

    d. You are ready to read. Read silently, then aloud. Read as rapidly as you can to understand the main idea. Reread for details and for enjoyment.

    e. Consult the Palabras Nuevas and the Spanish-English Vocabulary given at the end of the book when you need to know the meaning of a word.

Step 2: Completing the Exercises (Ejercicios)

    a. Read the instructions carefully. Consult the story if you need to do so.

    b. Check your answers with the Answer Key provided at the back of the book when you finish each exercise. Write corrections in your exercise. Review the Palabras Nuevas and the story if you need to redo an exercise.

    c. Proceed to the next exercise when at least eighty percent of your writing is correct. You have done well!

The Structure of the Language (Estructuras de la Lengua)

Step 1: Studying

    a. Get interested in the topic. Read it to appreciate why it is important in order to understand what others communicate to you in Spanish, and in order for you to express your thoughts to them in Spanish.

    b. Carefully read each point of grammar, as well as the examples given in Spanish with their English meanings. Try to discover the forms, rules, and relationships as you study the examples.

    c. Learn the forms and uses in Section A, before you learn Section B, and learn those in Section B before you study Section C, etc.

    d. Now study the rules that follow the examples. Do they match your concepts?

    e. Restudy the points of grammar and the new forms. Reading model sentences silently and aloud and copying them are often helpful learning procedures.

    f. Review the complete presentation. Now you are ready to begin the exercises.

Step 2: Completing the Exercises

    a. Read the instructions. Study the sample sentences that illustrate how to do the exercise.

    b. Complete the exercise without referring to the material you have just studied.

    c. Consult the Spanish-English Vocabulary at the end of the book if a Spanish word used in the exercises interferes with your understanding the sentence.

    d. Check your answers with the Answer Key. Note the number of correct responses.

e. Cross out any incorrect answer, and write the correct one. If many of your responses are not correct, restudy the appropriate section of the lesson. Try to understand the reason for the errors, and redo the exercise.

f. Proceed to the next exercise when at least eighty percent of your writing is correct. You have done well!

CAUTION: Consult the Answer Key only when you have finished the exercise. In this way, you will find out whether you have really learned the lesson well.

Part Two

Idioms and Dialogues

Step 1: Studying

a. Enjoy reading the entire running dialogue of the unit, silently and carefully, then, aloud.
b. Study the smaller sections set off by the thicker black lines, one section at a time. Then, read them aloud.
c. Learn each section by heart. Copy it. Practice the dialogue with a friend.
d. Record the dialogue section on tape or on cassette if one is available. Replay it as often as needed in order to learn it.
e. Use the new expressions in your next conversation!

Step 2: Completing the Exercises

a. Read the instructions. Complete the exercise.
b. Check your answers with the Answer Key when you complete each exercise.
c. Proceed to the next exercise when at least eighty percent of your writing is correct. You have done well!

Pronunciation Guide

Read aloud both the English and the Spanish examples, pronouncing them carefully. The similarity between the English and the Spanish pronunciations is shown in bold type. (NOTE: English examples are the closest approximations possible.)

	English Example	Spanish Example
VOWELS		
a	**ma**ma, **ya**cht	**ca**ma
e	t**e**n, d**e**sk	t**e**le
i	tr**i**o, ch**i**c, el**i**te	s**í**, m**i**tin
o	**o**bey	s**o**lo
u	l**u**nar	**u**so
y (alone)	man**y**, penn**y**	**y**
COMMON DIPHTHONGS		
ai, ay	**i**ce	bail**ái**s, ¡**ay**!
ei, ey	v**ei**n	v**ei**nte, l**ey**
oi, oy	**oi**l, j**oy**	**oi**go, s**oy**
au	c**ow**, h**ow**	**au**to
CONSONANTS		
b and **v**	**b**at (at beginning of a breath group, and after *m* and *n*)	**b**amba, **v**amos un **b**eso un **v**als
	vat (between vowels)	e**v**itar, i**b**a
c before *a, o, u*	**c**at (*c* but without a puff of air)	**c**asa, **c**osa
c before *e, i*	**c**ent, **c**ity (in most of Spanish America)	**c**elos, **c**inco
	theater, **th**in (in a large part of Spain, especially in central and northern Spain)	**c**elos, **c**inco
ch	**ch**eck	**ch**ico
d	**d**o (at beginning of a breath group and after *l* and *n*—tongue touches back of upper teeth)	**d**onde, al**d**ea
	though (between vowels— with tongue between upper and lower teeth)	i**d**a
f	**f**ame	**f**ama
g before *a, o, u*	**g**as, **g**o, **g**un	**g**ala, **g**oma, **g**ustar
g before *e, i*	**h**ot (heavy aspirant *h*)	**g**esto, **G**il
h	silent as in **h**our, **h**onest, **h**onor	**h**asta
j before all vowels	**h**ot (heavily aspirated *h*)	**j**ota, **j**efe
k	**k**it (not used in words of Spanish origin)	**k**iosko (Russian origin; also, quiosco)

	English Example	Spanish Example
CONSONANTS (continued)		
l	similar, although not identical to English	lento
ll	million, bullion	llama, ella
m	similar in most articulations	mi
n	similar in most articulations	no
ñ	onion, union	uña, año
p	similar to English, but without puff of air	
qu used only before *e* or *i*	clique (similar to English **k**, but without puff of air)	**que**, **qui**en
r	"th**rr**ee"—trilled **r** (tongue tip flutters against boney ridge behind upper teeth)	aroma
rr and **R** at beginning of a breath group	doubly trilled **r**	arroz, Rosa
s	similar, although often not identical to English	sin
t	similar, although often not identical to English	tu
w	not used in words of Spanish origin	
x	similar, although not identical to English	excepto
z	**s** sound in most of Spanish America	zona
	th as in **th**in in a large part of Spain, especially in central and northern Spain	zona
COMMON SEMI-CONSONANTS		
i before *e*	**y**es	bien
u before *a, e, i*	**w**as, **w**ent, **w**ind	ag**ua**, b**ue**no, h**ui**r
y before *a, o*	**y**am	**y**a, **y**o

The Spanish alphabet, as you have probably noticed, consists of **a, b, c, ch, d, e, f, g, h, i, j, k, l, ll, m, n, ñ, o, p, q, r, rr, s, t, u, v, w, x, y, z.**

Where to Stress or Emphasize Spanish Words

Rule One: Spanish speakers normally emphasize the last syllable of the word when the word ends in a consonant, provided that it is not an **n** or an **s**. *Example:* alrede**dor**, pa**pel**, ac**triz**.

Rule Two: When the last syllable ends in **n**, **s**, or a vowel, the *next to the last syllable* receives the stress or emphasis. *Example:* re**su**men, **ro**sas, **ca**sa.

The Accent Mark: Some Spanish words do not follow Rule One or Rule Two. These words show us where to place the stress or emphasis by using a mark over the vowel in the stressed syllable. That mark is called an accent mark; it looks like this ´ . *Examples:* **lám**para, **lá**piz, de**trás**, reu**nión**.
    The accent mark has other uses. It distinguishes meanings between words that otherwise have the same spelling, for example, **el** (the) and **él** (he). The accent mark also causes **i** and **u** to be pronounced apart from the vowel near them, breaking the dipthong or semi-consonant, for example, pa**ís**, poli**cí**a, a**ún**. Finally, the accent mark appears on the stressed vowel of every question word (interrogative), for example, ¿**dón**de? (where), ¿**có**mo? (how).

LECCIONES PREPARATORIAS

Face of an Old Man.
Buff clay.
Teotihuacan III-IV.
Courtesy of the Art Institute of Chicago
Joseph P. Antonow Gift

I. La casa   The House (Home)   [El; la: The]

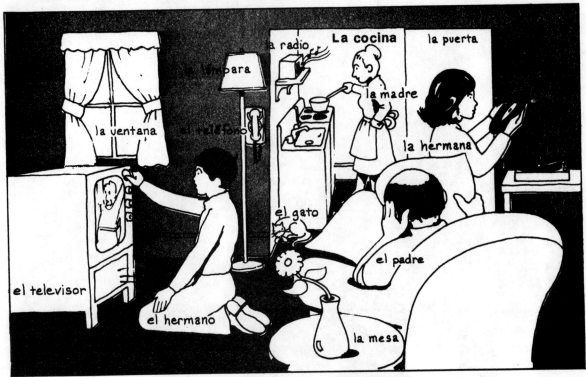

La sala   The living room

PREGUNTAS

Modelo:

*¿Es el televisor?

No, señor (señorita, señora), no es el televisor.
Es el gato.

1. ¿Es la puerta?

2. ¿Es la radio?

1. _____

2. _____

*¿Es. . .? Is it. . .?
Es. . . It is . . .

3. ¿Es la lámpara?   **4.** ¿Es el padre?   **5.** ¿Es la madre?   **6.** ¿Es el disco?

3. _____

4. _____

5. _____

6. _____

7. ¿Es la ventana?   **8.** ¿Es el teléfono?   **9.** ¿Es la cocina?   **10.** ¿Es la sala?

7. _____

8. _____

9. _____

10. _____

B. Draw pictures of as many items and people in your living room as you know how to label in Spanish. Label them in Spanish.

Remember these words in order to answer questions in the lessons that follow:

¿Qué? What?	**¿Quién?** Who?	**Dónde?** Where?	**¿Cómo es . . .?** What is . . .like?

II. Una escuela　A School　[Un; una: A; an]

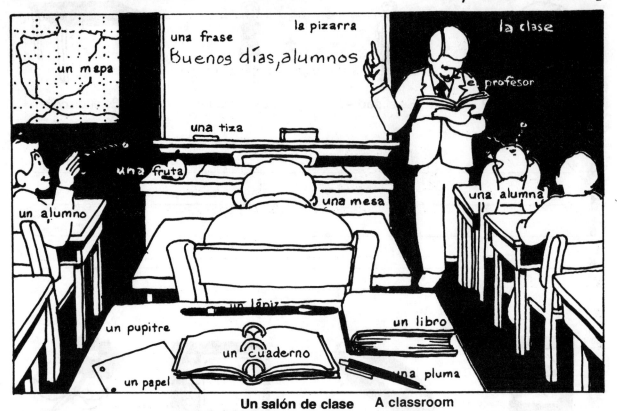

Un salón de clase　A classroom

PREGUNTAS

Modelo:

*¿Qué es esto?　　Es **una** fruta.

¿Qué es esto?　　Es **un** lápiz.

A.

1. ¿Qué es esto?　**2.** ¿Qué es esto?　**3.** ¿Qué es esto?　**4.** ¿Qué es esto?　**5.** ¿Qué es esto?　**6.** ¿Qué es esto?

1. _____

2. _____

3. _____

4. _____

5. _____

6. _____

　　*¿Qué?　What?

Modelo:

¿Es un disco?

Sí, señor (señorita, señora), es un disco.

B.

1. ¿Es un papel?   **2.** ¿Es un cuaderno?   **3.** ¿Es un pupitre?   **4.** ¿Es un lápiz?

1. _____

2. _____

3. _____

4. _____

C. Write an answer to the following question for each of the pictures seen below.
Modelo: ¿Qué es esto? Es un libro.

1.   **2.**   **3.** Buenos días, alumnos   **4.**

5.   **6.**   **7.**   **8.**

1. _____

2. _____

3. _____

4. _____

5. _____

6. _____

7. _____

8. _____

D. Draw a picture of the following in your notebook, and label the picture in Spanish.

1. una lámpara   **2.** un libro   **3.** un lápiz   **4.** el profesor   **5.** un disco   **6.** una flor

III. La ciudad   **The City**

[El; la: The]
[Un; una: A; an]

PREGUNTAS

Modelo:

¿Quién es?

Es un hombre.

A.

1. ¿Qué es?

2. ¿Quién es?

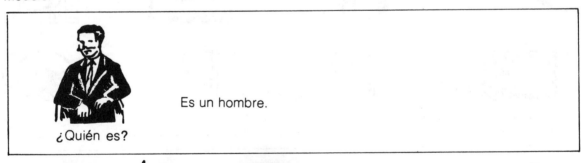

3. ¿Qué es?

4. ¿Qué es?

5. ¿Quién es?

1. _____

2. _____

3. _____

4. _____

5. _____

*¿**Quién?** Who?

Modelo:

¿Es un policía?   No es un policía. Es un ladrón.

B.

1. ¿Es una revista? **2.** ¿Es un hombre? **3.** ¿Es un coche? **4.** ¿Es el cine? **5.** ¿Es un profesor?

1. _____

2. _____

3. _____

4. _____

5. _____

Modelo:

*¿Dónde está la mujer?   La mujer está en el banco.

C.

1. ¿Dónde está   **2.** ¿Dónde está   **3.** ¿Dónde está   **4.** ¿Dónde está   **5.** ¿Dónde está
el muchacho?   el policía?   la madre?   la radio?   el hombre?

1. _____

2. _____

3. _____

4. _____

5. _____

7

*¿Dónde?   Where?

IV. Los alimentos   Foods   [Los; las:The]

El supermercado   The supermarket

PREGUNTAS

Modelo:

*¿Qué compra usted?   Compro alimentos.

A.

1. ¿Qué compra usted?

2. ¿Qué compra usted?

3. ¿Qué compra usted?

1. _____

2. _____

3. _____

*What **are you buying? I am buying** food.

4. ¿Qué compra usted?   **5.** ¿Qué compra usted?

4. _____

5. _____

B.

1. ¿Compra usted helado?   **2.** ¿Compra usted naranjas?   **3.** ¿Compra usted dulces?   **4.** ¿Compra usted flores?   **5.** ¿Compra usted una coca cola?

1. _____

2. _____

3. _____

4. _____

5. _____

C. Draw pictures of as many foods in your house as you know how to label in Spanish. Label them in Spanish.

V. Acciones

1. El alumno estudia la lección.

2. El padre mira la televisión.

3. La muchacha escribe la frase.

4. La alumna lee la revista.

5. El policía ve el accidente.

6. El hombre corre en la calle.

7. La mujer come helado.

8. El hermano bebe leche.

9. El profesor pregunta.

10. El alumno contesta mucho.

11. La señorita canta.

12. El señor escucha la radio.

13. La hermana baila.

14. El padre trabaja.

15 Las mujeres van a la tienda.

16. La madre compra alimentos.

17. María camina a la escuela.

18. Carlos descansa en casa.

19. Francisco sale de la casa.

20. Antonio pone la televisión.

PREGUNTAS:

A.

1. ¿Quién escribe en la pizarra?

2. ¿Quién come el pan?

3. ¿Quién sale de la escuela?

4. ¿Quién bebe la coca cola?

5. ¿Quién lee el periódico?

1. _____

2. _____

3. _____

4. _____

5. _____

B.

1. ¿Mira la mujer la televisión? **2.** ¿Canta la hermana? **3.** ¿Corre el policía? **4.** ¿Estudia Carlos? **5.** ¿Come María el queso?

1. _____

2. _____

3. _____

4. _____

5. _____

VI. Descripciones

1. fácil

2. difícil

3. grande

4. pequeño (a)

5. mucho (a)

6. poco

7. trabajador (a)

8. perezoso (a)

9. allí

10. aquí

11. tonto (a)

12. inteligente

13. bonito (a)

14. feo (a)

PREGUNTAS

Modelo:

 Fifí es bonita.

*¿Cómo es Fifí?

A.

1. ¿Cómo es el hombre?　**2.** ¿Cómo es la lección?　**3.** ¿Cómo es el profesor?　**4.** ¿Cómo es el alumno?　**5.** ¿Cómo es la madre?

1. _____

2. _____

3. _____

4. _____

5. _____

B.

1. ¿Es pequeño el elefante?　**2.** ¿Hay pocos alumnos en la clase?　**3.** ¿Está aquí la casa?　**4.** ¿Está deliciosa la manzana?　**5.** ¿Come mucho el hombre?

1. _____

2. _____

3. _____

4. _____

5. _____

Part One
STRUCTURES AND VERBS

Carlos, el hermano de Pepita,
pone la televisión.

Part One: Structures and Verbs

What's more important, TV or homework?
Let's see what Pepita does.

¡La televisión es muy importante!

Pepita Gómez es estudiosa. Ella estudia en la escuela y en casa. Esta noche Pepita estudia la lección de español en la sala. Estudia con el libro de gramática, el diccionario y el papel de vocabulario. Con su lápiz Pepita copia palabras y frases en su cuaderno.

El padre de Pepita lee el periódico en la sala. La madre escucha la radio en la cocina. Carlos, el hermano de Pepita, entra en la sala y pone la televisión.

Carlos:	Esta noche hay programas interesantes.
Pepita:	¡Ay, no, Carlos! Yo necesito estudiar. Mi examen de español es mañana.
Carlos:	¡Es posible estudiar mañana, muchacha!
Pepita:	¡Por favor, Carlos! El examen de español es muy importante. Yo necesito estudiar esta noche.
Carlos:	No es necesario estudiar el español. Es muy fácil. Yo quiero mirar la televisión.
El Padre:	¡No, Carlos! ¡La televisión no es importante! Es posible mirar la televisión mañana también.
La voz de la televisión:	Y ahora el programa: **El amor y la pasión.**
Pepita:	¡Ay, es mi programa favorito! ¡Ay, papá! ¡Sí, es posible estudiar mañana!

Palabras Nuevas

SUBSTANTIVOS *(NOUNS)*

el amor   *love*
Carlos   *Charles*
la casa   *the house*
   en casa   *at home*
la cocina   *the kitchen,*
   the cooking
el cuaderno   *the notebook*
el diccionario   *the dictionary*
la escuela   *the school*
el español   *the Spanish*
   language, Spanish
el examen   *the test*
   mi examen de español
   my Spanish test
la frase   *the sentence*
la gramática   *the grammar*
el hermano   *the brother*
   el hermano de Pepita   *Josie's*
   brother
el lápiz   *the pencil*
la lección   *the lesson*
   la lección de español   *the*
   Spanish lesson

el libro   *the book*
   el libro de gramática   *the*
   grammar textbook
la madre   *the mother*
la muchacha   *the girl*
la noche   *the night, the evening*
   esta noche   *tonight, this*
   evening
el padre   *the father*
   el padre de Pepita   *Josie's*
   father
el papel   *the paper*
   el papel de vocabulario   *the*
   vocabulary paper
la pasión   *the passion*
Pepita   *Josie*
el periódico   *the newspaper*
el programa   *the program*
   mi programa favorito
   my favorite program
la radio   *the radio*
la sala   *the living room*
la televisión   *the television*
la voz   *the voice*

ADJETIVOS (ADJECTIVES)

estudioso, a   *studious*
fácil   *easy*
favorito, a   *favorite*
importante   *important*
interesante   *interesting*
mi   *my*
necesario, a   *necessary*
posible   *possible*
su   *her*

VERBOS (VERBS)

copia   *(she) copies*
entra   *(he) enters*
es   *(it) is, (she) is*
   no es   *(it) is not*
escucha   *(she) listens to, is*
   listening to
estudia   *(she) studies, is*
   studying
estudiar   *to study*
hay   *there are*
lee   *(he) reads, is reading*
mirar   *to look at*
necesito   *I need*

---

*Adjectives that end in "**o**" describe masculine nouns.
   Adjectives that end in "**o**" change from "**o**" to "**a**" when describing feminine nouns.

pone la televisión *(he) turns on the television program*
quiero *I want*

OTRAS PALABRAS (OTHER WORDS)

ahora *now*

¡ay, papá! *Oh, Daddy!*
con *with*
de *of, in, from*
ella *she*
en *in, into*
mañana *tomorrow*
muy *very*

no *not, no*
por favor *please*
sí *yes; yes, indeed!*
también *also, too*
y *and*
yo *I*

EJERCICIOS

I. (A) Complete the sentence according to the story.

1. Pepita es muy _____.

2. Ella estudia la_____de español.

3. Ella copia palabras y frases en su_____.

4. El padre lee el_____en la_____.

5. La madre escucha la _____ en la _____.

6. El_____pone la televisión.

7. El examen de español es muy _____.

8. Carlos quiere _____ la televisión.

9. Es posible mirar la televisión _____.

10. El programa es "el _____ y la _____."

(B) Rewrite the sentence replacing the underlined word with a word that will make the sentence true.

1. Pepita estudia con el libro y el periódico.
2. Ella estudia el amor en la clase de español.
3. Pepita copia palabras con su voz.
4. No es posible estudiar y también mirar la radio.
5. Es necesario estudiar la lección de cocina.

1._____.

2._____.

3._____.

4._____.

5._____.

II. ¿Cómo se dice en español? Can you find these expressions in the story?

1. I need to study. _____

2. Tonight there are interesting programs. _____

_____

3. It is very easy. _____

4. It's my favorite program._____

_____

5. It is not necessary to study Spanish._____

III. Word Hunt — Find these 15 words in Spanish in the squares.

1. pencil
2. living room
3. book
4. notebook
5. sentence
6. brother
7. also
8. with
9. easy
10. now
11. there is
12. he looks at
13. night
14. he reads
15. this (f.)

C	A	A	F	B	S	C	N	L	L
U	H	E	R	M	A	N	O	A	I
A	O	H	A	Y	L	E	C	P	B
D	R	E	S	D	A	I	H	I	R
E	A	L	E	E	F	B	E	Z	O
R	G	H	I	J	K	M	I	R	A
N	L	M	N	O	F	A	C	I	L
O	R	T	S	E	S	T	A	P	Q

IV. Compositions: Oral or written.

(A) Look at the picture at the beginning of this Work Unit. Describe the scene in Spanish to a friend.

(B) Tell your friends about your evenings at home. Include the following:

En casa

1. What your favorite program is. 2. Where you want to watch television tonight. 3. Which brother or sister turns on the television. 4. Which brother or sister studies and listens to the radio. 5. What your father or mother reads.

ESTRUCTURAS DE LA LENGUA

The Noun (Persons, Things, Places, Ideas) and **the Definite Article** (Singular)

A. In Spanish, things as well as persons are of either masculine or feminine gender.

Examples:

Masculine Nouns

1. **El chico** es grande.
   The boy is big.

2. **El cuaderno** es grande.
   The notebook is large.

Feminine Nouns

3. **La chica** es grande.
   The girl is big.

4. **La pluma** es grande.
   The pen is large.

¿ Es el señor Gómez o la señorita Gómez?

17

Rules:

1. **El** means *the* before a masculine noun and is the masculine definite article.

2. **La** means *the* before a feminine noun and is the feminine definite article.

3. Masculine nouns often end in **o.** Feminine nouns often end in **a.** Feminine nouns also end in **-dad, -ción, -sión.** Learn: **la ciudad** (the city); **la canción** (the song); **la lección** (the lesson); **la nación** (the nation); **la televisión** (the television).

B. **El** and **la** indicate the gender of nouns that do not have the typical masculine ending **-o**, or the typical feminine endings: **-a, -dad, -ción, -sión.**

Examples:

Masculine Nouns	Feminine Nouns
El hombre usa **el lápiz** y **el papel.**	**La mujer** mira **la flor** en **la clase.**
The man uses the pencil and paper.	The woman looks at the flower in the class.

Rules:

1. Nouns should be memorized *with* their articles: **el** or **la.**

2. Learn these masculine nouns: **el avión** (the plane), **el coche** (the car), **el examen** (the test), **el hombre** (the man), **el hotel** (the hotel), **el lápiz** (the pencil), **el padre** (the father), **el papel** (the paper), **el profesor** (the teacher), **el reloj** (the clock, watch), **el tren** (the train).

3. Learn these feminine nouns: **la clase** (the class), **la frase** (the sentence), **la madre** (the mother), **la mujer** (the woman), **la noche** (the night).

4. The appropriate definite article must be used before *each* noun in a series: **el padre y la madre** (the father and mother); **el hombre y la mujer** (the man and woman).

C. Special uses of **el** and **la**

Special omissions of **el** and **la.**

Indirect Address (Narrative)	Direct address
1. **El señor Gómez** escucha *el programa.* Mr. Gomez listens to the program.	1. **Señor Gómez,** ¿escucha usted *la radio* todo *el día*? Mr. Gomez, do you listen to the radio all day?
2. **La señorita Molina** estudia *el idioma* y *el mapa.*	2. **Señorita Molina,** ¿estudia usted *el idioma* y *el mapa* de España?
Miss Molina studies the language and the map.	Miss Molina, do you study the language and the map of Spain?

Rules:

1. **El** or **la** is used *before a title* when talking *about* the person, but is *omitted* when talking *directly* to the "titled" person, in direct address.

2. A small number of masculine nouns end in **a** or **ma** and must be memorized with their articles: **el día** (the day), **el mapa** (the map), **el idioma** (the language), **el programa** (the program). But **la radio** (the radio) is feminine.

D. More uses of **el** and **la**   More special omissions of **el** and **la**.

---

1. **La escuela** está entre **la Avenida Arcos** y **la Calle Diez.**

   The school is between Arcos Avenue and Tenth Street.

2. Juan escucha **el español** y **el inglés.**

   John listens to Spanish and English.

1. Estudia **la lección de español** para hablar español bien.

   He studies the Spanish lesson in order to speak Spanish well.

2. Contesta **en español** en **la clase de español.**

   He answers in Spanish in the Spanish class.

Rules:

1. Use **la** before Avenida and Calle when identifying them by name or number.

2. Use **el** before all languages except when they directly follow **hablar, de, en.**

3. **De** indicates *concerned with* in expressions such as the following: **la clase de español** (the Spanish class), **la lección de español** (the Spanish lesson), **el profesor de inglés** (the English teacher), **el maestro de música** (the music teacher).

STUDY THE RULES, EXAMPLES, AND MODELS BEFORE BEGINNING THE EXERCISES!

Exercises

I. Rewrite the sentence, substituting the word in parentheses for the noun in *italics*. Make the necessary change in the definite article, **el** or **la**.

   Model: La *profesora* es interesante.   (libro) El libro es interesante.
            The teacher is interesting.   The book is interesting.

A. La *revista* es interesante.   The magazine is interesting.

1. (escuela)_____

2. (libro)   _____

3. (alumna)_____   **19**

4. (señorita)_____

5. (periódico)_____

B. El *profesor* estudia mucho.   The teacher studies a great deal.

1. (padre)_____

2. (madre)_____

3. (hombre)_____

4. (mujer)_____

5. (señor)_____

C. El *chico* es importante.   The boy is important.

1. (examen)_____

2. (lección)_____

3. (día)_____

4. (noche)_____

5. (televisión)_____

6. (nación)_____

7. (programa)_____

8. (ciudad)_____

9. (frase)_____

10. (idioma)_____

11. (mapa)_____

12. (cocina)_____

13. (calle)_____

14. (español)_____

15. (clase)_____

II. Rewrite as a simple statement. Use **el** or **la.** Omit **usted** and question marks.

Model: Señor Smith, ¿estudia usted el español?   El señor Smith estudia el español.
        Mr. Smith, do you study Spanish?   Mr. Smith studies Spanish.

1. Señor Moreno, ¿mira usted el programa de televisión?

_____

2. Profesora Mendoza, ¿lee usted el mapa de la ciudad?

_____

3. Presidente Guzmán, ¿entra usted en la capital de la nación?

_____

4. Señorita Gómez, ¿estudia usted el idioma toda la noche?

_____

5. Señorita Molina, ¿escucha usted la radio todo el día?

_____

III. Write two sentences using the name of language given in *italics.* Begin the first sentence with
Habla . . . Begin the second sentence with **Pronuncia bien** . . .

Model: El chico es de España. The boy is from Spain.
                el español **Habla español. Pronuncia bien el español.**
                He speaks Spanish. He pronounces Spanish well.

1. El hombre es de México.

el español
_____

2. La alumna es de Francia.

el francés
_____

3. El muchacho es de Italia.

el italiano
_____

4. Luis es de Inglaterra.

el inglés
_____

5. La muchacha es de Alemania.

el alemán
_____

21

IV. Rewrite the model sentence, substituting th noun in parentheses for the noun in *italics*. Make the necessary change in the definite article, **el** or **la.**

    A. Model: **El alumno estudia en** *la clase.*   The pupil studies in the classroom.
                 (dormitorio) El alumno estudia en el   The pupil studies in the bedroom.
                 dormitorio.

1. (hotel)_____

2. (clase de español)_____

3. (edificio)_____

4. (sala) _____

5. (escuela)_____

    B. Model: La alumna escucha *la frase.*   The pupil listens to the sentence.

1. (música)_____

2. (disco)_____

3. (inglés)_____

4. (reloj)_____

5. (radio)_____

    C. Model: Su hermano mira *el diccionario.*   Her brother looks at the dictionary.

1. (lápiz)_____

2. (pluma)_____

3. (papel)_____

4. (casa) _____

5. (libro)_____

6. (cuaderno)_____

7. (gramática)_____

8. (avión)_____

9. (tren)_____

10. (coche)_____   _____

V. Complete with an appropriate selection: **el** or **la.** Write a dash (—) if no article may be used.

$\overline{\underset{1}{}}$ muchacha entra en $\overline{\underset{2}{}}$ escuela en $\overline{\underset{3}{}}$ Avenida de Las Américas de $\overline{\underset{4}{}}$ ciudad de Nueva York. Su profesor, $\overline{\underset{5}{}}$ señor Valdés, lee $\overline{\underset{6}{}}$ español muy bien. $\overline{\underset{7}{}}$ clase estudia $\overline{\underset{8}{}}$ lección de $\overline{\underset{9}{}}$ español y escucha $\overline{\underset{10}{}}$ idioma en $\overline{\underset{11}{}}$ radio y en $\overline{\underset{12}{}}$ televisión. Su clase practica $\overline{\underset{13}{}}$ inglés también: — $\overline{\underset{14}{}}$ Profesor Brown, ¿lee usted $\overline{\underset{15}{}}$ periódico en $\overline{\underset{16}{}}$ casa? Sí, $\overline{\underset{17}{}}$ Profesor Brown lee mucho en $\overline{\underset{18}{}}$ tren también, y en $\overline{\underset{19}{}}$ casa por $\overline{\underset{20}{}}$ noche.

VI. Oral Proficiency. Respond orally to the situations described. (You may *later* write your responses for intensive practice.)

A. Situation: You are beginning your first Spanish studies. I am your friend. I ask what your impression is of the Spanish language:—*¿Cómo es el español?*

In **two** complete Spanish sentences tell me your impression. You may use your own ideas or ideas suggested by the following: *importante, interesante, fácil, necesario.*

B. Situation: I also ask what you need for your new Spanish studies:—*¿Qué es necesario?*

In two sentences tell me what kind of books or other items you need. You may use your own ideas or ideas suggested by the following: *yo necesito, yo quiero, es importante.*

C. Situation: Your friend wants to visit you this evening:—*¿Es posible esta noche?* You suggest another time. Tonight is not convenient.

Begin with: *Por favor, esta noche, no. Mañana es posible.* In **four** sentences tell how each member of the family is busy. You may use your own ideas or ideas suggested by the following: *pone la televisión, mira su programa favorito, lee su libro, escucha música, lee el periódico, estudia el español, yo necesito, yo quiero.*

D. Situation: Your older brother or sister wants you to study tonight because he or she does not want to have to watch your favorite television program with you. You give reasons for watching television *tonight.*

Hermano(a): El examen de español es mañana. Tú (You): *(Give a reason why you do not need to study for the Spanish test tonight.)*
Hermano(a): Es importante estudiar ahora. Tú: *(Suggest another time for studying.)*
Hermano(a): Es posible estudiar con la música de la radio. Tú: *(Tell what **you** want.)*
Hermano(a): Yo no quiero mirar "El amor y la pasión." Tú: *(Tell the name of another television program that is also your favorite.)*

María mira cómo los hombres y las mujeres van de prisa.

What a life! Work, work, work. And what does it all lead to?

Todo es rápido en la ciudad

María visita la ciudad grande de Nueva York. Su primo, Francisco, es de esta ciudad. Ella es de la pequeña aldea de Miraflores, y desea ver todas las cosas importantes en Nueva York. Francisco y María visitan los teatros, los museos y los parques. Los primos van por muchas calles y avenidas y miran los edificios altos y las tiendas grandes. En las calles María mira cómo los hombres y las mujeres van de prisa a los cines, a los restaurantes, a las oficinas y a sus casas. Para María, esta experiencia es interesante y nueva pero es extraña también.

María: Mira, Paco, aquí en la ciudad todo es muy rápido. ¿Por qué? ¿Por qué hay tanta prisa?

Francisco: Pues, María, todas las ciudades grandes son así. Es necesario comer de prisa, trabajar de prisa y vivir de prisa. Así ganamos mucho dinero, y después de veinte o treinta años es posible descansar en una pequeña aldea, mirar las flores y respirar el aire fresco.

María: ¡Ay, Paco! Eso es tonto. En Miraflores, ¡yo hago todas estas cosas ahora!

Palabras Nuevas

SUBSTANTIVOS (NOUNS)

el aire   *the air*
la aldea   *the town*
el año   *the year*
la avenida   *the avenue*
la calle   *the street*
el cine   *the movie theater*
la ciudad   *the city*
la cosa   *the thing*
el dinero   *the money*
el edificio   *the building*
la experiencia   *the experience*
la flor   *the flower*
Francisco   *Frank*
   Paco   *Frankie*
el hombre   *the man*
María   *Mary, Marie*
la mujer   *the woman*
el museo   *the museum*
Nueva York   *New York*
la oficina   *the office*
el parque   *the park*
el primo   *the cousin*
la prisa   *the hurry*
   de prisa   *in a hurry, in a rush*
el restaurante   *the restaurant*
el teatro   *the theater*
la tienda   *the store*

ADJETIVOS (ADJECTIVES)

alto,a   *tall, high*
estos,as   *these*
extraño,a   *strange*
fresco,a   *fresh*
grande   *big, large*
mucho,a   *a great deal of, much*
muchos,as   *many, a great many*
nuevo,a   *new*
pequeño,a   *small, little*
rápido,a   *fast, rapid*
sus   *their*
tanto,a   *so much*
todos,as   *every, all*
tonto,a   *foolish*

VERBOS (VERBS)

comer   *to eat*
descansar   *to rest*
desea   *(she) wishes, wants*
hago   *I do*
ir   *to go*
ganamos   *we earn*
¡mira!   *look!*
mira   *(she) looks at, watches*
miran   *they look at, watch*
respirar   *to breathe*

son   *they are*
trabajar   *to work*
van   *they go, walk*
ver   *to see*
visita   *(she) visits*
visitan   *they visit*
vivir   *to live*

OTRAS PALABRAS (OTHER WORDS)

a   *to*
aquí   *here*
así   *so, (in) this way, thus*
cómo   *how*
después de   *after*
eso   *that*
las (fem. pl.)   *the*
los (masc. pl.)   *the*
o   *or*
para   *for, in order to*
pero   *but*
por   *along, through*
¿por qué hay. . .?   *Why is there . . .?*
pues   *well, then*
todo   *everything, all*
treinta   *thirty*
una   *a*
veinte   *twenty*

EJERCICIOS

I. (A) Rewrite the sentence, using the expression that best completes it.

1.   El primo de María es de (a) Los Ángeles (b) San Antonio (c) Nueva York (d) Miami. _____

2. La aldea de María es (a) grande (b) alta (c) interesante (d) pequeña. _____

_____

3. Los primos van por (a) las aldeas (b) las calles (c) las escuelas (d) las casas. _____

_____

4. En la ciudad todo es (a) fresco (b) estudioso (c) necesario (d) rápido. _____

_____

(B) Rewrite the sentence, substituting a correct word for the underlined word.

1. Nueva York es pequeña. _____

2. Los parques son muy altos. _____

3. Los hombres y las mujeres van de prisa por las aldeas. _____

_____

4. Es posible descansar en las calles. _____

5. Para María es posible mirar las flores en su aldea mañana. _____

II. Match the following:

1. María visita _____ a. interesante y nueva.

2. Ella desea ver_____ b. de prisa.

3. Su experiencia es _____ c. en las aldeas.

4. Hay aire fresco_____ d. a su primo, Paco.

5. Los hombres y las mujeres van_____ e. todas las cosas
interesantes.

III. Juego de palabras—Translate these words to fill in the boxes of the puzzle below.

1. pencil
2. love
3. movies
4. important
5. a *(f.)*
6. money
7. now
8. to rest

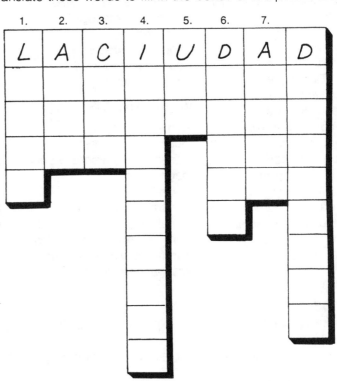

IV. Compositions: Oral or written.

(A) Look at the picture at the beginning of this Work Unit. Describe the scene in Spanish to a friend.

(B) Tell a visitor about your city. Include the following:

Mi ciudad

1. What kinds of buildings there are. 2. What interesting places it is possible to visit. 3. How fast it is necessary to work in order to earn money. 4. When it is possible to rest very well. 5. Why it is important to go to small towns.

ESTRUCTURAS DE LA LENGUA

The Noun and the Definite Article (Plural). Comparisons between singular and plural forms.

El libro

Los libros

Singular (one)	*Plural (more than one)*
1. **El chico** usa **el libro.** The boy uses the book.	**Los chicos** usan **los libros.** The boys use the books.
2. **La chica** usa **la pluma.** The girl uses the pen.	**Las chicas** usan **las plumas.** The girls use the pens.
3. **El hombre** y **la mujer** visitan **el hotel** en España y escuchan la canción. The man and woman visit the hotel in Spain and listen to the song.	**Los hombres** y **las mujeres** visitan **los hoteles** en España y escuchan las canciones. The men and women visit the hotels in Spain and listen to the songs.

Rules:

1. **Los** means *the* before a masculine plural noun and is the masculine plural article. **Las** means *the* before a feminine plural noun and is the feminine plural article. In summary, Spanish has *four* definite articles: **el** (masc. sing.), **los** (masc. pl.), **la** (fem. sing.), **las** (fem. pl.).

2. Add **s** to a noun of either masculine or feminine gender that ends in a *vowel: a, e i, o, u,* in order to form the plural, *e.g.* **el uso, los usos** (the uses); **la uva, las uvas** (the grapes).

3. Add **es** to a noun of either gender that ends in a *consonant* in order to form the plural, *e.g.* **el papel, los papeles** (the papers); **la flor, las flores** (the flowers)

4. Omit the accent mark from the final syllable when adding **es** to nouns ending in **ión,** *e.g. la lección, las lecciones* (the lessons), *la canción, las canciones* (the songs).

5. Change final **z** to **c** before adding **es,** *e.g.* **el lápiz, los lápices** (the pencils).

STUDY THE RULES, EXAMPLES AND MODELS BEFORE BEGINNING THE EXERCISES!
Exercises

I. Complete the sentence with the plural of the article and noun in *italics*, e.g., *el uso* **los usos.**

1. *el chico*_____ son estudiosos.

2. *la muchacha*_____ son necesarias.

3. *el hombre*_____ son extraños.

4. *la madre*_____ son importantes.

5. *la lección*_____ son interesantes.

6. *el lápiz*_____ son pequeños.

7. *el papel*_____ son muchos.

8. *la mujer*_____ son elegantes.

9. *el profesor*_____ son altos.

10. *el cine*_____ son nuevos.

11. *la frase*_____ son tontas.

12. *el tren*_____ son rápidos.

13. *la ciudad*_____ son grandes.

14. *el día*_____ son fáciles.

15. *la flor*_____ son atractivas.

II. Write this response in the *singular*, using the appropriate article and noun before the adjective **grande.   No. Solamente** _____ **grande.**

Model:—¿Son interesantes todos los libros?   —No. Solamente **el libro** grande.
          Are *all the books* interesting?   No. *Only the big book.*

1. ¿Son necesarios todos los restaurantes? _____

2. ¿Son buenos todos los museos? _____

3. ¿Son nuevas todas las aldeas? _____

4. ¿Son fáciles todas las clases?_____

5. ¿Son tontos todos los periódicos?_____

6. ¿Son interesantes todas las gramáticas? _____

7. ¿Son importantes todos los edificios? _____

8. ¿Son nuevos todos los hoteles? _____

9. ¿Son frescos todos los parques? _____

10. ¿Son rápidas todas las calles? _____

III. Write the following response: **Sí, todos los** _____ or **Sí, todas las** _____ according to the gender of the noun in the question.

Model: 1.—¿Desea usted libros?   —Sí, **todos los libros.**
         Do you want books?   Yes, all the books.

         2.—¿Desea usted plumas?   —Sí, **todas las plumas.**
         Do you want pens?   Yes, all the pens.

1. ¿Estudia usted libros? _____

2. ¿Necesita usted papeles? _____

3. ¿Usa usted gramáticas? _____

4. ¿Escucha usted canciones? _____

5. ¿Usa usted trenes? _____

6. ¿Escucha usted idiomas? _____

7. ¿Visita usted universidades? _____

8. ¿Necesita usted mapas? _____

9. ¿Estudia usted lecciones de español? _____

10. ¿Mira usted programas de televisión? _____

IV. Complete with the appropriate definite article: **el, la, los,** or **las.**

En _____ clases de español _____ alumnos escuchan _____ español y hablan español todos
    1   2   3
_____ días. _____ profesores de idiomas son _____ señorita Ruiz y _____ señor Martínez.
   4   5   6   7
Todos _____ chicos contestan bien en _____ escuela. Solamente _____ alumna Rosa no
        8   9   10
estudia _____ lecciones. Pero _____ alumno Juan estudia _____ libros todas _____ noches.
         11   12   13   14
Todas _____ muchachas desean escuchar _____ programas en español en _____ radio y en
        15   16   17
_____ televisión. _____ periódicos también son excelentes para practicar todos _____ idiomas.
  18   19   20

V. Oral Proficiency. Respond orally to the situation described. (You may *later* write your responses for intensive practice.)

Situation: Your cousin wants to buy a house but does not know whether to locate *en la ciudad o en la aldea.* You explain some advantages and disadvantages of each.

Begin with *Primo(a).* In **five** Spanish sentences, explain what one does **en la ciudad** and what one does **en la pequeña aldea.** You may use your own ideas or the ideas suggested by the following: *es necesario, es importante, es tonto, es interesante, es fácil, es posible.*

¡Felicidades, Joselito!
¡Feliz cumpleaños!

It's Joselito's birthday, but why is he so unhappy?

El cumpleaños de Joselito

Hoy es un día muy importante en la casa de la familia Hernández. ¿Pregunta usted por qué? Es importante porque es el cumpleaños de Joselito, el nene de la familia. Hoy el niño cumple cuatro años.

Todo el mundo está ocupado en las preparaciones para este día. Los padres compran la magnífica piñata típica en forma de pájaro. La piñata está llena de dulces y regalitos. Los hermanos de José preparan los juegos y las actividades para la fiesta. Sarita, la hermana que estudia música en la escuela, practica ahora porque ella va a bailar y cantar. La abuela prepara los refrescos y una torta deliciosa muy grande.

Joselito escucha y mira a todos. El pobre niño está triste porque todo el mundo trabaja y él también desea trabajar y ayudar.

Los padres invitan a todo el mundo. Todos los vecinos caminan a la casa Hernández. Cuando llegan a la casa y entran en la sala ellos preguntan:—¿Pero, qué pasa? ¿Dónde está Joselito? ¿Por qué no está aquí?

El pobre niño está solo en su cuarto. No está contento. Desea llorar.

Entonces el abuelo busca a Joselito y explica:—Joselito, hoy es tu día. Tú no necesitas trabajar. El día de tu cumpleaños tú ayudas con las cosas más importantes—soplar las velas, cortar la torta y tomar el pedazo más grande.

Joselito baja a la sala con el abuelo. En ese momento los padres entran en la sala. Ellos llevan una torta grande de chocolate con cuatro velas, y los amiguitos de Joselito llevan regalos para el niño.

Todo el mundo grita:—¡Felicidades, Joselito! ¡Feliz cumpleaños!

Ahora sí, Joselito está contento. Va a ayudar en la fiesta. Él también grita:—¡Vamos a gozar!

Palabras Nuevas

SUBSTANTIVOS

la abuela	*the grandmother*
el abuelo	*the grandfather*
la actividad	*the activity*
el amiguito	*the little friend*
el año	*the year*
la casa Hernández	*the Hernandez home*
el cuarto	*the room*
el cumpleaños	*the birthday*
el día	*the day*
los dulces	*the candy*
la familia	*the family*
la forma	*the shape, form*
la hermana	*the sister*
José	*Joseph*
Joselito	*Joey*
el juego	*the game*
la música	*the music*

el nene	*the baby, very young child*
el niño	*the child, the little boy*
los padres	*the parents*
el pájaro	*the bird*
el pedazo	*the piece*
la piñata	*the piñata (papier mâché figure filled with candies, etc.)*
los refrescos	*the refreshments*
el regalito	*the little present*
el regalo	*the present*
Sarita	*little Sarah*
todo el mundo	*everyone*
todos	*everybody, all*
la torta de chocolate	*the chocolate cake*
el vecino	*the neighbor*
la vela	*the candle*

VERBOS

ayudar	*to help*
bailar	*to dance*
bajar	*to go down*
caminar	*to walk, to stroll*
cantar	*to sing*
comprar	*to buy*
cortar	*to cut*
desear	*to wish, to want*
entrar (en)	*to enter*
escuchar	*to listen*
está	*he(she) is*
explicar	*to explain*
gozar	*to enjoy*
gritar	*to shout*
invitar	*to invite*
llegar	*to arrive*
llevar	*to carry*
llorar	*to cry*
necesitar	*to need*

pasar *to happen*	feliz *happy*	él *he*
practicar *to practice*	lleno,a (de) *filled (with)*	ella *she*
preguntar *to ask*	magnífico,a *magnificent*	ellos *they*
preparar *to prepare*	ocupado,a *busy*	entonces *then*
soplar *to blow (out)*	pobre *poor*	hoy *today*
tomar *to take*	su *his, her, your (formal)*	hoy cumple cuatro años
va (a) *he (she) is going*	típico,a *typical*	*today he is four years old*
¡vamos! (a) *let's*	triste *sad*	más *more, most*
	tu *your (familiar)*	que *who*
		¿qué? *what?*

ADJETIVOS

OTRAS PALABRAS

contento,a *happy*	solo,a *alone*
delicioso,a *delicious*	tú *you (familiar)*
ese *that (masc.)*	cuando *when*
este *this (masc.)*	cuatro *four*
	¿dónde? *where?*
	un,a *a*
	usted *you (formal)*

EJERCICIOS

I. (A) Complete the sentences according to the story.

1. Hoy es el _____ de Joselito. Él cumple cuatro _____ .

2. Todo el _____ está muy _____ .

3. Él está triste porque desea _____ y _____ .

4. Su hermana va a _____ y _____ en la fiesta.

5. La abuela prepara los _____ y la _____ .

(B) Preguntas. Write your answer in a complete Spanish sentence.

1. ¿Dónde está solo Joselito?

2. ¿Qué compran los padres?

3. ¿Qué llevan los amiguitos?

4. ¿Adónde caminan los vecinos?

5. ¿Por qué está contento Joselito?

1. _____

2. _____

3. _____

4. _____

5. _____

(C) Preguntas generales. Write your answer in a complete Spanish sentence.

1. ¿Cómo necesitan ayudar los niños?

2. ¿Cómo ayudan los hermanos?

3. ¿Qué quieres para tu cumpleaños?

4. ¿Está todo el mundo triste o contento en la fiesta?

5. ¿Qué gritan todos?

1. _____

2. _____

3. _____

4. _____

5. _____

II. Match the following.

1. Hoy es un día _____   a. a todo el mundo

2. La piñata está _____   b. llorar

3. Los padres invitan _____   c. ¡vamos a gozar!

4. El pobre niño desea _____   d. muy importante

5. Joselito grita _____   e. llena de dulces

III. Acróstico. Translate the words to fill in the boxes of the puzzle.

1. happy   1 F
2. to listen   2 E
3. to arrive   3 L
4. to invite   4 I
5. birthday   5 C
6. important   6 I
7. candy   '7 D
8. grandmother   8 A
9. to wish, want   9 D
10. school   10 E
11. to blow out   11 S

IV. Compositions: Oral or written.

(A) Look at the picture at the beginning of this Work Unit. Describe the scene to a friend.

(B) Tell us how to prepare for a birthday party.

El cumpleaños

1. What it is necessary to buy or prepare in the kitchen. 2. For whom the party is. 3. What activities it is important to prepare. 4. Who wants to help. 5. What everybody shouts.

ESTRUCTURAS DE LA LENGUA
The Present Indicative Tense; Regular AR Conjugation

A. The endings of the present tense tell who is doing the action; they change as the subject or "doer" changes. Subject pronouns are often unnecessary. Learn the set of personal endings for the **ar** infinitive.

	AR conjugation (I)
Infinitive:	**cantar** *to sing*
	I sing; do sing; am singing well.
Subject pronouns for emphasis	
Singular: 1. **Yo** *I*	Can**to** bien.
2. **Tú** *You* (fam.)	cant**as**
3. **Él** *He;* **Ella** *She* **Usted** *You* (formal)	cant**a**
Plural: 1. **Nosotros-as** *We*	cant**amos**
2. **Vosotros-as** *You* (fam.)	cant**áis**
3. **Ellos-as** *They* **Ustedes** *You* (formal)	cant**an**

Rules:

1. A Spanish verb has one of the following infinitive group endings: **ar, er,** or **ir.** These endings represent the English *to*. Examples: *cantar* to sing; *comer* to eat; *escribir* to write.

2. This unit deals with **ar** infinitives. When a subject is given, the infinitive group ending **ar** drops and is replaced by *personal endings* according to the subject.

   After removing the infinitive group ending **ar,** add the correct personal ending **o, as, a, amos, áis,** or **an,** according to the subject given.

3. The endings of the present tense tell us that an act or a state of being is taking place at present or that it occurs as a general rule. **Am, is, are, do, does** are included in the Spanish verb form of the present tense. Examples: *I am singing* **yo canto**; *she does sing* **ella canta.**

B. Subject pronouns (See page 34 for the list of subject pronouns.)

1. The subject pronoun is used *to stress* or *to emphasize* the subject. The subject pronoun *precedes* the verb in a statement. The subject pronoun must be used when no verb is given.

2. Excepting **usted** and **ustedes,** subject pronouns are *normally omitted* because the verb *ending identifies the subject,* provided that no emphasis is intended.

Normal unstressed subject.	*Stressed subject.*	*Without a verb.*
Cant**a**. He sings.	***El** canta y **yo** canto, también.	*¿**El**? Sí, **él** y **yo.**
Cant**o**. I sing.	*He* sings, and *I* am singing, too.	*He*? Yes, *he* and *I.*

3. Spanish subject pronouns show gender not only in **él** *he,* **ella** *she,* but also in **nosotros** *we* masculine, **nosotras** *we* feminine, and in **ellos** *they* masculine, **ellas** *they* feminine. ***Él** *he* commonly appears in print as **El** *without an accent mark when capitalized.*

4. Spanish has *four* subject pronouns meaning *you.* **Tú** addresses one person with familiarity, e.g., an intimate friend or someone younger. **Usted** (abbreviation: **Vd.**) addresses one person with formality, e.g., a teacher, the president, someone older than the speaker. **Ustedes** (abbreviation: **Vds.**), you *plural*, generally addresses two or more persons with either formality or familiarity in Latin America. In Spain **ustedes (Vds.)** addresses two or more persons only with formality. **Vosotros-as** is used chiefly in Spain to address two or more persons with familiarity. Since **vosotros-as** is *not* in general use in Latin America, it will receive limited treatment in this book.

C. Formation of yes-no questions:

Statement	*Question*
1. **Juan** canta aquí. John sings here.	¿Canta **Juan** aquí? *Does John* sing here?
2. **Vd.** canta también. You sing, too.	¿Canta **Vd.** también? *Do you* sing, too?

Rules:

1. The subject is generally placed *after* the verb to form a question.

2. An inverted question mark at the beginning of each written question informs the reader that a question is about to be asked. A final question mark punctuates the end of each question, like an English question.

---

*Capital letters may keep or may drop their accent marks.

STUDY THE RULES, EXAMPLES, AND MODELS BEFORE BEGINNING THE EXERCISES!

Exercises

I.   Learn these **ar** verbs in order to understand questions and answers.

   AR: **andar** *to walk;* **bailar** *to dance;* **cantar** *to sing;* **comprar** *to buy;* **contestar** *to answer;* **desear** *to want;* **entrar** *to enter;* **escuchar** *to listen;* **estudiar** *to study;* **hablar** *to speak;* **invitar** *to invite;* **llegar** *to arrive;* **necesitar** *to need;* **practicar** *to practice;* **preguntar** *to ask;* **preparar** *to prepare;* **regresar** *to return;* **tocar** *to play* (instrument); **tomar** *to take;* **trabajar** *to work;* **visitar** *to visit.*

A.   Rewrite the sentence, substituting ONE appropriate pronoun for the subject(s) in *italics*.

   Model: *Juanita y yo* hablamos español.   **Nosotros** hablamos español.
   Joan and I speak Spanish.   We speak Spanish.

   1. *Roberto* canta bien. _____

   2. *María* necesita papel. _____

   3. *Alberto y Tomás* caminan mucho. _____

   4. *Ana y Clara* buscan la casa._____

   5. *Ella y yo* entramos ahora. _____

B.   Rewrite the model sentence, substituting the subject in parentheses for the word(s) in *italics*. Make the necessary change in the verb.

   Model: *Pedro y yo* bailamos.   (Vosotros) **Vosotros bailáis.**
   Peter and I are dancing.   You (*fam., pl.*) are dancing.

   1. (Yo) _____   6. (Tú y yo) _____

   2. (Él) _____   7. (Ella)_____

   3. (Vd.) _____   8. (Ellas) _____

   4. (Tú) _____   9. (Ellos) _____

   5. (Vds.) _____   10. (Nosotros)_____

C.   Write affirmative answers in complete Spanish sentences. In answer (a) use **Sí.** In answer (b) use **también,** according to the model.

   Models: a. ¿Bailas *tú* en la fiesta?   a. **Sí, yo bailo** en la fiesta.
                 ¿Baila *Vd.* en la fiesta?   Yes, I dance at the party.
                 Do you dance at the party?
             b. ¿Y *Vds.*?   b. **Nosotros bailamos también.**
                 And do you (pl.)?   We dance, too.

   1. a. ¿Canta ella en la escuela?_____

      b. ¿Y nosotros? _____

   2. a. ¿Contestan ellos en la clase?_____

      b. ¿Y Pedro?_____

3. a. ¿Escuchan los amigos la música? _____

   b. ¿Tú y yo? _____

4. a. ¿Deseas tú la carta? _____

   b. ¿Juanita y Pablo? _____

5. a. ¿Andan ellos a casa? _____

   b. ¿Y Vd.? _____

D. Write an affirmative answer in a complete Spanish sentence according to the model.

   Model: ¿Toma *Vd.* café?   **Sí, yo tomo** café.
            ¿Tomas *tú* café?   Yes, I take coffee.
            Do you take coffee?

1. ¿Compra Vd. flores? _____

2. ¿Visitas tú la ciudad? _____

3. ¿Estudian Vds. el español? _____

4. ¿Necesitamos Juan y yo dinero? _____

5. ¿Respiro yo aire fresco? _____

E. Rewrite each of the following sentences as a question.
   Model: **Yo hablo mal.**   **¿Hablo yo mal?**
            I speak poorly.   *Do I speak poorly?*

1. Yo escucho la frase. _____

2. Carlitos visita a su madre. _____

3. Los niños desean la invitación. _____

4. El y yo andamos a las clases. _____

5. Pedro y yo tomamos café. _____

II. **Oral Proficiency.** Respond orally to the situation described. (You may *later* write your responses for intensive practice.)

   Situation: You and I are making plans for a party. I say:—¡*Vamos a gozar!* You agree.

   Begin with:—*Sí, ¡vamos a gozar!* In **four** Spanish sentences tell what we will do *para gozar.* You may use your own ideas or ideas suggested by the following: *nosotros/comprar; nosotros/ preparar; Nosotros/llevar; nosotros/escuchar (bailar, cantar, gritar, tomar).*

¡Qué horror!
Un fantasma abre la puerta.

Did you ever get a letter and not know where it was from? Juanita did and she's scared.

La carta misteriosa

Cuando Juanita Pacheco recibe una carta, está muy sorprendida. Ella abre la carta y lee:

—Pero, ¿quién escribe esta carta? ¿Quién invita a Juanita a esta reunión? ¿Y por qué a las once de la noche? Juanita no sabe y está loca de curiosidad.

El treinta y uno de octubre, Juanita sale de la casa. Es tarde y no hay nadie en las calles. Juanita corre a la Calle Treinta y Cinco. Ella busca los números en las puertas de las casas. —Sí, ¡aquí está el número noventa y nueve!

—Mmmmm. Es extraño.

En la casa no hay luz. Juanita está nerviosa, pero desea saber qué pasa. Ella toca a la puerta, y ¡qué horror! Un fantasma abre la puerta. Pero ¡qué sorpresa! No es un fantasma. Es su amigo Paco, con una máscara. ¡Oh, el amigo Paco vive aquí! Claro, es la víspera de Todos los Santos y hay una fiesta. Todos los amigos asisten. En las mesas hay dulces, helado y otras cosas buenas. Hay música, y todo el mundo canta y baila, come y bebe.

Palabras Nuevas

SUBSTANTIVOS
el amigo   *the friend*
la Calle Treinta y Cinco
    Thirty-fifth Street
la carta   *the letter*
el fantasma   *the ghost*
el horror   *the horror*
la invitación   *the invitation*
Juanita   *Janie, Jeannie*
la luz   *the light*
la máscara   *the mask*
la mesa   *the table*
el número   *the number*
la puerta   *the door*
la reunión   *the meeting*

la sorpresa   *the surprise*
el treinta y uno de octubre
    October thirty-first
la Víspera de Todos Los
    Santos   *Halloween*

VERBOS
abrir   *to open*
asistir   *to attend*
buscar   *to look for*
beber   *to drink*
comer   *to eat*
comprender   *to understand*
correr   *to run*
dice   *(she) says*

escribir   *to write*
están   *they are (with
    certain adjectives, and
    location)*
hay   *there is; there are*
leer   *to read*
no hay   *there is (are) no;
    there isn't (aren't) any*
pasar   *to happen*
recibir   *to receive*
saber   *to know*
salir (de)   *to leave*
tocar a la puerta   *to knock
    at the door*
vivir   *to live*

39

ADJETIVOS

bueno,a *good*
extrano,a *strange*
loco,a *crazy*
  de curiosidad *curiosity*
misterioso,a *mysterious*
nervioso,a *nervous*
otro,a *other*

sorprendido,a *surprised*

OTRAS PALABRAS

a las once de la noche
  at eleven P.M.
claro *of course*
¿de quién? *from whom?*
en *on*

nadie *nobody*
noventa y nueve
  ninety-nine
¡qué…! *what a…!*
¿quién? *who?*
tarde *late*

EJERCICIOS

I. (A) Complete the sentence according to the story.

1. Juanita _____ la carta pero ella no _____ la invitación.

2. Ella no _____ quién _____ la invitación.

3. Juanita _____ de su casa y _____ a la Calle Treinta y Cinco.

4. Un fantasma _____ la puerta; es su amigo Paco que _____ en

  esta casa.

5. Todos los amigos _____ a la fiesta de la Víspera de Todos Los Santos donde ellos

  _____ helados y dulces.

(B) Preguntas. Write your answer in a complete Spanish sentence.

1. ¿Quién lee la invitación?
2. ¿Por qué no hay nadie en las calles?
3. ¿Por qué está nerviosa Juanita?
4. ¿Cuándo es la reunión?
5. ¿Por qué es misteriosa la casa donde todos asisten a la fiesta?

1. _____

2. _____

3. _____

4. _____

5. _____

(C) Preguntas personales y generales. Write your answer in a complete Spanish sentence.

1. ¿Para qué es necesario escribir invitaciones?
2. ¿Qué hay para comer en las fiestas?
3. ¿Qué necesitamos para bailar y gozar?
4. ¿Qué escribe todo el mundo a los amigos?
5. ¿Por qué es misterioso el treinta y uno de octubre?

1. _____

2. _____

3. _____

4. _____

5. _____

II. Acróstico — Complete the story by filling in the boxes of the puzzle

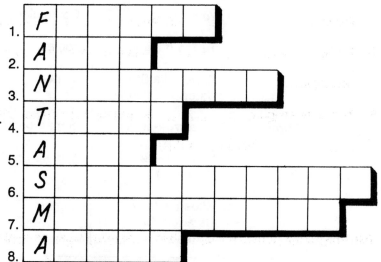

Hay una __1.__ en la casa.

__2.__ está el número 99.

Juanita está __3.__.

No hay personas porque es __4.__.

Un fantasma __5.__ la puerta.

Cuando recibe la carta está __6.__.

Es una carta __7.__.

Paco es el __8.__ de Juanita.

1. F
2. A
3. N
4. T
5. A
6. S
7. M
8. A

III. Compositions: Oral or written.

(A) Look at the picture at the beginning of this Work Unit. Describe the scene in Spanish to a friend.

(B) Tell a friend about a surprise party you are giving. Include the following:

Una fiesta

1. For whom the party is.   2. When the party is.   3. Where it is.   4. Whether there are good things to eat and drink.   5. What the friends do at the party.

ESTRUCTURAS DE LA LENGUA
The Present Indicative Tense: Regular ER and IR Conjugations

Just as the verbs of the **ar** conjugation change their endings to indicate the subject or "doer" of the action, so do those verbs of the **er** conjugation and **ir** conjugation. Learn the sets of personal endings for each of the **er** and **ir** infinitives.

	ER conjugation (II)	IR conjugation (III)
Infinitives:	**comer** *to eat*	**escribir** *to write*
	I eat; do eat; am eating well.	I write; do write; am writing well.
Subject pronouns for emphasis		
Singular: 1. **Yo** *I*	Com**o** bien.	Escrib**o** bien.
2. **Tú** *You* (fam.)	com**es**	escrib**es**
3. **Él** *He;* **Ella** *She* **Usted** *You* (formal)	com**e**	escrib**e**
Plural: *1. **Nosotros-as** *We*	*com**emos**	*escrib**imos**
*2. **Vosotros-as** *You* (fam.)	*com**éis**	*escrib**ís**
3. **Ellos-as** *They* **Ustedes** *You* (formal)	com**en**	escrib**en**

Rules:

1. When a subject is given, the infinitive group ending, **ar, er** or **ir**, drops and is replaced by personal endings according to the subject. This unit deals with **er** and **ir** infinitives.

   a. **ER** verbs: Remove the infinitive group ending **er**. Add the correct personal ending **o, es, e, emos, éis, en,** according to the subject given.

   b. **IR** verbs: Remove the infinitive group ending **ir**. Add the correct personal ending **o, es, e, imos, ís, en,** according to the subject given.

*2. Notice that the personal endings of verbs of the **er** conjugation and of the **ir** conjugation show a difference only when the subject is **nosotros-as** or **vosotros-as.**

STUDY THE RULES, EXAMPLES, AND MODELS BEFORE BEGINNING THE EXERCISES

Exercises

   I. ER verbs

      ER: aprender *to learn;* **beber** *to drink;* **comer** *to eat;* **comprender** *to understand;* **correr** *to run;* **creer** *to believe;* **leer** *to read;* **responder** *to answer;* **vender** *to sell.*

   A. Rewrite the sentence, substituting ONE appropriate pronoun for the subject in *italics.*

      Model: *Juanita* lee la carta.   **Ella** lee la carta.
                  Jeannie reads the letter.   She reads the letter.

    1. *La muchacha* aprende esto. _____

    2. *Mi primo* comprende el libro. _____

    3. *Ana y Laura* corren de prisa. _____

    4. *Él y yo* bebemos mucho. _____

    5. *Luis y Elena* comen bien. _____

   B. Rewrite the model sentence, substituting the subject in parentheses for the word(s) in italics. Make the necessary change in the verb.

      Model: *Alicia y yo* respondemos bien.   (Ella) Ella **responde** bien.
              Alice and I answer well.   She answers well.

    1. (Yo) _____   6. (Vd. y yo) _____

    2. (Vd.) _____   7. (Ellos) _____

    3. (Tú) _____   8. (Él) _____

    4. (Ella) _____   9. (Nosotras) _____

    5. (Vds.) _____   10. (Él y ella) _____

   C. Write affirmative answers in complete Spanish sentences. In answer (a) use **Sí.** In answer (b) use **también.**

      Models: a. *¿Crees tú* esto?   a. **Sí, yo creo** esto.
                ¿Cree *Vd.* esto?
                Do you believe this?   Yes, I believe this.
           b. ¿Y *ellos*?   b. **Ellos creen** esto **también.**
                And do they?   They believe this, too.

1. a. ¿Comemos rápido tú y yo? _____

   b. ¿Y la niña? _____

2. a. ¿Respondes tú bien? _____

   b. ¿Y María? _____

3. a. ¿Aprenden ellos el español? _____

   b. ¿Y Vds.? _____

4. a. ¿Lee José la gramática? _____

   b. ¿Y Vd.? _____

5. a. ¿Comprenden Vds. la frase? _____

   b. ¿Y los muchachos? _____

D. Write an affirmative answer in a complete Spanish sentence. Begin your answer with **Sí.**

1. ¿Corres tú en la calle? _____

2. ¿Venden Vds. limonada? _____

3. ¿Creemos María y yo el programa? _____

4. ¿Ponen las primas la televisión? _____

5. ¿Come Vd. bien aquí? _____

II. IR verbs

IR: **abrir** *to open;* **asistir** *to attend;* **cubrir** *to cover;* **describir** *to describe;* **escribir** *to write;* **omitir** *to omit;* **partir** *to leave;* **recibir** *to receive;* **subir** *to go up;* **vivir** *to live.*

A. Rewrite the sentence, substituting ONE appropriate pronoun for the subject in *italics.*

Model: *Mi amigo* abre la puerta.   **Él** abre la puerta.
       My friend opens the door.   He opens the door.

1. Mi madre parte hoy. _____

2. Juanita y Vd. reciben la invitación. _____

3. Isabel y Gloria escriben la carta. _____

4. El padre y la madre viven aquí. _____

5. Vd. y yo abrimos el cuaderno. _____

B. Rewrite the model sentence, substituting the subject in parentheses for the words in *italics.* Make the necessary change in the verb.

Model: *Carlos y yo* asistimos hoy.   (Ellas) **Ellas asisten** hoy.
       Charles and I are attending today.   They are attending today.

1. (Tú) _____   6. (Ellas) _____

2. (Vd.) _____   7. (Yo) _____

3. (Ellos) _____   8. (Él) _____

4. (Vds.) _____   9. (Ella) _____

5. (Ella y yo) _____   10. (Nosotras) _____

C. Write affirmative answers in complete sentences. In answer (a) use **Sí.** In answer (b) use **también.**

Models: a. *¿Describes tú* la ciudad?   a. **Sí, yo describo** la ciudad.
         ¿Describe Vd. la ciudad?
         Do you describe the city?   Yes, I describe the city.
      b. *¿Y nosotros?*   b. **Vds. describen** la ciudad **también.**
        And do we?   You describe the city, too.

1. a. ¿Recibe Carlos dinero? _____

   b. ¿Y las hermanas? _____

2. a. ¿Escriben los amigos cartas? _____

   b. ¿Y nosotros? _____

3. a. ¿Vives tú en esta aldea? _____

   b. ¿Y los primos? _____

4. a. ¿Cubro yo el libro? _____

   b. ¿Y Vds.? _____

5. a. ¿Suben Vds. la montaña? _____

   b. ¿Y Luis? _____

D. Write an affirmative answer in a complete Spanish sentence. Begin your answer with **Sí.**

1. ¿Abrimos Ana y yo los periódicos? _____

2. ¿Cubres tú la mesa? _____

3. ¿Parten Vds. ahora? _____

4. ¿Describe Vd. la clase? _____

5. ¿Omite el profesor la palabra? _____

6. ¿Asistes a la fiesta? _____

7. ¿Recibe Juanita la carta? _____

8. ¿Vives en un apartamiento? _____

9. ¿Escribimos en español? _____

10. ¿Suben ellos al automóvil? _____

Summary Diagram for AR, ER, and IŔ Conjugations

	AR conjugation (I)	**ER** conjugation (II)	**IR** conjugation (III)
Infinitives:	**cantar** *to sing*	**comer** *to eat*	**escribir** *to write*
	I sing; do sing; am singing well.	I eat; do eat; am eating well.	I write; do write; am writing well.
Subject pronouns for emphasis			
Singular: 1. **Yo** *I*	Cant**o** bien.	Com**o** bien.	Escrib**o** bien.
2. **Tú** *You* (fam.)	cant**as**	com**es**	escrib**es**
3. **Él** *He*; **Ella** *She* **Usted** *You* (formal)	cant**a**	com**e**	escrib**e**
Plural: 1. **Nosotros-as** *We*	cant**amos**	com**emos**	escrib**imos**
2. **Vosotros-as** *You* (fam.)	cant**áis**	com**éis**	escrib**ís**
3. **Ellos-as** *They* **Ustedes** *You* (formal)	cant**an**	com**en**	escrib**en**

Remember

1. All three conjugations use the ending **o** for the first person singular (*yo*).

2. Each set of endings has a vowel or vowels that dominate the endings, usually followed by personal endings that indicate who or what the subject is.

3. Subject pronouns are needed only for emphasis or clarification.

4. In the English translation, helping words like **am, is, are, do, does** are included in the Spanish verb form of the present tense.

III. AR, ER, IR verbs

A. Rewrite the sentence, using the name in parentheses and the formal address **Vd.** in place of the familiar **tú**. Note: Omit the **s** from the verb ending.

Model: *Tú* comes poco.   (Señor Ortiz) **Señor Ortiz, Vd.** com**e** poco.
You (fam.) eat little.   Mr. Ortiz, you (formal) eat little.

1. Tú entras en la sala. (Señor López)_____

2. Tú crees el libro. (Señora Gómez)_____

3. Tú vives aquí. (Profesor Ruiz) _____

4. Tú tocas bien. (Señorita Marín)_____

5. Tú escribes el inglés. (Doctor Muñoz)_____

B. Rewrite the sentence, using the name in parentheses and the familiar address **tú** in place of **Vd.**
Note: Add **s** to the verb ending.

Model: *Vd.* aprende bien.   (Felipe) **Felipe, tú** aprend**es** bien.
         You (formal) learn well.   Philip, you (fam.) learn well.

1. Vd. trabaja mucho. (Pepe)_____

2. Vd. contesta poco. (Ana)_____

3. Vd. aprende mal. (Carlos)_____

4. Vd. corre rápido. (niño)_____

5 Vd. lo describe bien. (niña)_____

C. Rewrite as a question, e.g., **Yo como mal.** *I eat poorly.*   **¿Como yo mal?** *Do I eat poorly?*

1. Yo comprendo la frase._____

2. Carlitos corre a su madre._____

3. Los niños desean la invitación. _____

4. El y yo asistimos a las clases._____

5. Pedro y yo tomamos café._____

IV. Oral Proficiency. Respond orally to the situation described. (You may *later* write your responses for intensive practice.)

Situation: I am a new student in the Spanish class, and I want to know why learning Spanish is easy. *¿Por qué es fácil aprender el español?* You tell me why.

State that Spanish is easy, and in **four** Spanish sentences tell what **we** do in the class that makes learning Spanish easy. You may use your own ideas or ideas suggested by the following: *para aprender; nosotros/asistir (poner atención, leer, responder, escribir); así comprender.*

¿Quién es el presidente de los Estados Unidos?

Do you like quiz shows? Here's one which might be embarrassing.

¿Conoce usted historia?

Para hacer interesante la clase de historia, el Profesor Fajardo decide usar otros métodos hoy. Todos los alumnos de la clase van a participar en un concurso. Luis, el muchacho más inteligente y más aplicado, va a ser el maestro de ceremonias. Otro muchacho, Jaimito, es perezoso. No estudia y no aprende mucho. Jaimito va a contestar primero.

Luis:　　Bueno, Jaimito. ¿Sabes mucho de la historia de los Estados Unidos?

Jaimito:　Claro. Ya estoy en esta clase de historia tres años.

Luis:　　Pues bien, ¿quién es el presidente de los Estados Unidos?

Jaimito:　Mmmmm. . . . No estoy seguro. Creo que es. . . . Creo que es Jorge Wáshington.

Luis:　　¿Jorge Wáshington? ¡Ay, qué tonto! ¿No sabes que Wáshington está muerto? Otra pregunta: ¿Dónde vive el presidente?

Jaimito:　Creo que vive en una casa blanca.

Luis:　　*Sí, claro. Vive en la Casa Blanca. Pero, ¿en qué ciudad?*

Jaimito:　¿En Los Ángeles?

Luis:　　No, tonto, en Wáshington.

Jaimito:　Pero, ¿cómo es posible? Wáshington está muerto. ¿No es verdad?

Luis:　　¡Ay, tonto! ¿Cuándo vas a aprender? ¿Para qué vas a la escuela? ¿Por qué no conoces la historia de los Estados Unidos?

Jaimito:　Pero, Luis, ésas ya son tres preguntas. ¿Cuántas debo contestar?

El profesor:　¡Ninguna! ¡Ninguna! Ya estoy enfermo. ¡Mañana hay una lección normal!

Palabras Nuevas

SUBSTANTIVOS

el alumno　*the pupil (masc.), the student*

la Casa Blanca　*the White House*

la clase　*the class*
el concurso　*the contest*

los Estados Unidos　*the United States*

la historia　*history*
　la clase de historia　*the history class*

Jaimito　*Jamie (little James)*

Jorge Wáshington　*George Washington*

Luis　*Louis*

el maestro de ceremonias　*the master of ceremonies*

el método　*the method*
el muchacho　*the boy*

la pregunta　*the question*
el presidente　*the president*
el profesor　*the teacher (masc.)*
el tonto　*the fool*

ADJETIVOS

aplicado,a　*studious*
　más aplicado,a　*most (more) studious*

blanco,a　*white*
enfermo,a　*sick*

inteligente　*intelligent*
　más inteligente　*Most (more) intelligent*

muerto,a　*dead*
normal　*normal*
otro,a　*another, other*
perezoso,a　*lazy*
seguro,a　*sure*
tres　*three*

VERBOS

aprender　*to learn*
¿Conoce . . .?　*Are you acquainted with. . .?*
contestar　*to answer*
creer　*to believe*
deber　*should, must, to have to, ought to*
decidir　*to decide*
estoy　*I am*
　no estoy　*I am not*
hacer　*to make, to do*
participar　*to participate*
saber　*to know*
　¿No sabe Vd.?　*Don't you know?*
ser　*to be*
usar　*to use*
van a　*they are going to; you (formal pl.) are going to*
¿vas a...?　*are you (fam.) going to...?*

49

PALABRAS INTERROGATIVAS	¿Para qué *For what purpose? Why?*	ninguna *none*
¿Cómo? *How*	¿Por qué? *Why?*	¿No es verdad? *Isn't it true? Right?*
¿Cuándo? *When?*	¿Quién *Who?*	primero *first*
¿Cuántos,as? *How many?*		pues bien *well, then*
¿Dónde? *Where?*	OTRAS PALABRAS	que *that*
	ésas *those*	ya *already, now*

EJERCICIOS

I. (A) Complete the sentences according to the story.

1. El señor Fajardo es profesor de _____.

2. Luis es un muchacho _____ y _____.

3. Jaimito no _____ y no _____.

4. Jaimito no sabe que Jorge Wáshington está _____.

5. El profesor ya está_____.

(B) Preguntas personales y generales. Write your answer in a complete Spanish sentence.

1. ¿Quién es el presidente de los Estados Unidos?
2. ¿Cómo está una persona que va al hospital?
3. ¿Para qué debe Vd. ir a la escuela?
4. ¿Cuántos alumnos perezosos están en la clase de español?
5. ¿En qué clase aprende Vd. mucho de los Estados Unidos?

1. _____

2. _____

3. _____

4. _____

5. _____

II. Mixed-up sentences. Can you put the words in the correct order to form complete sentences?

1. el usar métodos otros decide profesor.
2. primero a va contestar Jaimito.
3. en estoy esta historia clase de tres años.
4. ¿vive presidente el dónde?
5. ¿es presidente los Unidos quién el Estados de?

1. _____

2. _____

3. _____

4. _____

5. _____

III. Compositions: Oral or written.

(A) Look at the picture at the beginning of this Work Unit. Describe the scene in Spanish to a friend.

(B) Tell about your favorite class. Include the following:

Mi clase favorita

1. Which is your favorite class, and whether it is a smart class.   2. Whether anyone is lazy, and which student is very studious.   3. Whether the teacher is nice (**simpático, a**) and whether he or she uses interesting methods.   4. Whether you receive good marks (**notas**). 5. Where you study, and when.

ESTRUCTURAS DE LA LENGUA

Simple Negative; Interrogative Words

A. To form the simple negative place **no** before the verb.

Affirmative	*Negative*
1. Ellos cantan hoy. They are singing today.	Ellos **no** cantan hoy. They are not singing today.
2. ¿Cantas tú? Do you sing?	¿**No** cantas tú? Don't you sing?

Rule:

Place **no** before the verb in *both* statements and questions to form the negative.

B. Interrogative words request specific information. They begin the question.

1. **¿Cómo** come Juan? *How* does John eat?

2. **¿Cuándo** come Juan? *When* does John eat?

3. **¿Cuánto** come Juan? *How much* does John eat?

4. **¿Dónde** come Juan? *Where* does John eat?

5. **¿Para qué** come Juan? *For what purpose* does John eat?

6. **¿Por qué** come Juan? *Why* does John eat?

7. **¿Qué** come Juan? *What* does John eat?

8. **¿Quién come?** *Who* (sing. subject) *is eating*?
   ¿Quiénes comen? *Who* (pl. subject) *are eating*?

9. **¿A quién-es** ve? *Whom* does he see?
   ¿A quién-es corre él? *To whom does he run?*

Rules:

1. Interrogative words bear an accent mark on the stressed vowel.

2. **¿Cuánto?, ¿cuánta?, ¿cuántos?,** and **¿cuántas?** when followed by a noun are adjectives and must agree with the noun in gender and number.

3. **¿Quién?** is followed by a third person *singular* verb. **¿Quiénes?** is followed by a third person *plural* verb.

¿Cuánto dinero recibes?	How much money do you receive?
¿Cuánta fruta comes?	How much fruit do you eat?
¿Cuántos niños leen?	How many children read?
¿Cuántas chicas estudian?	How many girls study?

STUDY THE RULES, EXAMPLES AND MODELS BEFORE BEGINNING THE EXERCISES! ALSO REVIEW LESSONS 3 AND 4 — AR, ER, and IR Verbs

Exercises

I. a. Rewrite the sentence in the NEGATIVE by placing **no** before the verb.

b. Then rewrite the negative statement as a NEGATIVE QUESTION.

Model:	Ana come. Anne eats.	a. Ana **no** come. Anne doesn't eat.	b. **¿No come Ana?** Doesn't Anne eat?

1. Ellos hablan de la chica.   a. _____

   b. _____

2. Vd. canta en la fiesta.   a. _____

   b. _____

3. Tú escribes mucho.   a. _____

   b. _____

4. Nosotros vendemos periódicos.   a. _____

   b. _____

5. Yo vivo ꞁ la ciudad.   a. _____

b. _____

II. Write NEGATIVE answers in complete Spanish sentences according to the models.

Model: a. —¿Corre Vd. al parque?   Do you run to the park?
           —**Yo no corro** al parque.   I do not run to the park.
        b. —¿Y Juan?   And John?
           —**Juan no corre** al parque.   John does not run to the park.

1. a. ¿Come Vd. mucho en el café?_____

   b. ¿Y los amigos?_____

2. a. ¿Estudias tú por la noche?_____

   b. ¿Y Luis?_____

3. a. ¿Comprenden Vds. todo?_____

   b. ¿Y las alumnas? _____

4. a. ¿Asisten Rosa y tú a la clase?_____

   b. ¿Y Jorge y Elisa?_____

5. a. ¿Abrimos Juan y yo los libros?_____

   b. ¿Y Vds.?_____

III. a. Rewrite the sentence as a QUESTION (¿ ?) using the word in parentheses after **a.**
    b. Write a Spanish ANSWER to the question you formed using the word in parentheses after **b.**

Model: Estudia el español. a. (Quién)   a. —¿**Quién** estudia el español?
        He studies Spanish.   Who studies Spanish?
                  b. (Pablo)   b. —**Pablo** estudia el español.
                                  Paul studies Spanish.

1. Ana escribe la lección.   a. (Cómo)   b. (de prisa)

   a._____

   b._____

2. Luis toma el tren.   a. (Cuándo)   b. (ahora)

   a._____

   b._____

3. Leen la pregunta.   a. (Cuántos alumnos)   b. (tres alumnos)

   a._____

   b._____

4. La niña y su madre escuchan al Doctor Solar.   a. (Dónde)   b. (en el hospital)

a._____

b._____

5. Mi amigo y yo leemos.   a. (Qué)   b. (la pregunta)

a._____

b._____

6. Recibe la invitación.   a. (Quién)   b. (El chico)

a._____

b._____

7. Preguntan mucho.   a. (Quiénes)   b. (Las chicas)

a._____

b._____

8. Marta y yo escribimos.   a. (A quién)   b. (al padre)

a._____

b._____

9. La alumna aprende muchas cosas.   a. (Por qué)   b. (porque escucha bien)

a._____

b._____

10. Luis compra fruta.   a. (Para qué)   b. (para la fiesta de Ana)

a._____

b._____

IV. Rewrite the QUESTION substituting the subject in parentheses and making the necessary change in the verb.

Model: ¿Por qué **canta** ella "La Paloma"?   (yo) ¿Por qué **canto yo** "La Paloma"?
          Why does she sing "La Paloma"?   Why do I sing "La Paloma"?

A. ¿Cómo **prepara** ella la lección? 1. (tú) _____

2. (Vd.)._____   3. (ellos)_____

_____ 4. (nosotros)_____

¿Cuántas papas fritas comes?

B. ¿Qué **canta** Vd.? 1. (yo)_____ 2. (Vds.)_____

3. (Juan y yo)_____

C. ¿Dónde **beben** los animales? 1. (el animal)_____

_____ 2. (nosotros)_____

3. (tú)_____ 4. (Vd.)_____

D. ¿Cuántas papas fritas **comes** tú? 1. (Ana)_____

_____ 2. (ellos)_____

_____ 3. (tú y yo)_____

E. ¿A quién **escriben** ellos? 1. (Pepe)_____

2. (Vd. y yo)_____

3. (las niñas)_____

4. (Vd.)_____

I. STRUCTURES AND VERBS

F. ¿No **vive** Vd. en Los Ángeles? 1. (nosotros)_____

_____ 2. (¿Quién?)_____

_____ 3. (¿Quiénes?)_____

G. ¿Cuándo **toman** Vds. el tren? 1. (ella) _____

_____ 2. (su familia) _____

3. (nosotras)_____

H. ¿Para qué **aprende** Vd. el español? 1. (nosotros)_____

_____ 2. (yo)_____

3. (él y ella)_____

I. ¿Por qué **parte** Luisa? 1. (Vd. y yo)_____

_____ 2. (tú)_____

_____ 3. (Vds.)_____

V. A. Write the Spanish equivalent following the word order of the Spanish model.

1. **Ellos no andan a la escuela.**

   a. He is not walking to school. _____

   b. We are not walking to class. _____

   c. Who is not walking to class?_____

2. **¿Cuándo corre ella a casa?**

   a. When do I run home? _____

   b. Juanito, when do you (tú) run home?_____

   c. When does Mr. Torres run well? _____

3. **¿A quién escribo yo?**

   a. To whom (sing.) is she writing? _____

   b. To whom (pl.) are we writing? _____

   c. To whom (pl.) are they writing? _____

56

B. Write the Spanish equivalent following the word order of the Spanish model. Use the appropriate form of the verb cue given in parentheses.

1. **Aquí no venden periódicos.**

    a. Here they do not buy newspapers. _____
    (comprar)

    b. Here we do not read newspapers. _____
    (leer)

    c. Here you (tú) do not receive newspapers. _____
    (recibir)

2. **¿Cómo bailan Juan y tú?**

    a. How do you (tú) answer, John? _____
    (contestar)

    b. How does Mary understand? _____
    (comprender)

    c. How do we leave? _____
    (partir)

3. **¿Dónde cantas tú?**

    a. Where do we listen? _____
    (escuchar)

    b. Where do you (tú) learn, Anne? _____
    (aprender)

    c. Where do they attend? _____
    (asistir)

4. **¿Por qué describen ellos la ventana?**

    a. Why do you (Vd.) open the window? _____
    (abrir)

    b. Why do we cover the window? _____
    (cubrir)

5. **¿Cuánto dinero deseo yo?**

    a. How much money do we want? _____
    (desear)

    b. How much fruit (fruta) do we sell? _____
    (vender)

    c. How many books do they need? _____
    (necesitar)

6. **¿Quién no come en casa?**

    a. Who (sing.) is not living at home? _____
    (vivir)

    b. *Who (pl.) are not working at home?* _____
    (trabajar)

c. *Who (pl.) are not answering at home?* _____

(responder)

7. **¿Qué no preguntan ellos?**

a. What don't I ask?_____

(preguntar)

b. What don't we write?_____

(escribir)

c. What doesn't she practice?_____

(practicar)

VI. **Oral Proficiency.** Respond orally to the situation described. (You may *later* write your responses for intensive practice.)

Situation: You are a new student. I welcome you to the school with:—*¡Bienvenido(a)!* You ask me to give you information about the school.

Begin with *Amigo(a)*. Ask **five** Spanish questions using interrogative expressions such as *¿qué?, ¿quién(es)?, ¿dónde?, ¿cuántos(as)?, ¿cómo?, ¿por qué?, ¿a quién?, ¿cuándo?*. You may use your own ideas or the following: *how many students there are in the school; who the president of the school is; how the student participates in the life of the school; whom I know in the school; when and where there are contests; why there are not more.*

NO REBASE

NO PASSING

ANCHO LIBRE

HORIZONTAL CLEARANCE

PESO MAXIMO

MAXIMUM WEIGHT (METRIC TONS)

LÍMITE

PARKING LIMIT

UNA HORA

8 a 21 h DIAS HABILES

ONE-HOUR PARKING

NO

NO LEFT TURN

NO

NO PARKING

CONSERVE SU DERECHA

USE RIGHT LANE

INSPECCIÓN

INSPECTION

PEATONES A SU IZQUIERDA

PEDESTRIANS KEEP LEFT

MÁXIMA

SPEED LIMIT (IN K.P.H.)

CONTINÚA

CONTINUOUS TURN

Highway signs in Mexico

*Bueno, aquí tiene una docena
de huevos, una botella de leche,
un pan y una libra de mantequilla.*

Antonio thinks it's easy to be a housewife. Do
you agree with him?

El trabajo de la mujer es fácil

Esta mañana Alicia no está bien. Ella siempre compra las cosas para la casa. Pero hoy es imposible.

Alicia: Antonio, necesito unas cosas de la tienda de comestibles. ¡Por favor, mi amor! Ésta es una lista de las cosas necesarias.

Antonio: Mi amor, yo no necesito lista. Yo también compro cosas para la casa. Un tonto necesita una lista. Yo no.

Antonio va a la tienda de comestibles. Entra en la tienda y. . . . no sabe qué comprar. Sin la lista no sabe qué cosas necesitan en casa.

Dependiente: Buenos días, señor. ¿Qué desea?

Antonio: Mmmmm. . . La verdad es que no sé. Mi mujer está enferma y necesitamos unas cosas muy importantes en casa.

Dependiente: Sí, sí. . . . unas cosas importantes como. . . .una docena de huevos, una botella de leche, un pan y una libra de mantequilla.

Antonio: Ah, muy bien, Está bien.

Dependiente: Y. . . .un poco de queso, jugo de naranja, y unas frutas como estas manzanas. Todo esto es bueno para la casa.

Antonio: Muy bien. Y ¿cuánto es todo esto?

Dependiente: Doce dólares, cincuenta centavos.

Antonio: Gracias, adiós.

Antonio paga y regresa a casa. Entra en la casa con los comestibles.

Alicia: Oh, Antonio. . . . . ¡Exactamente las cosas que necesitamos! ¡Qué inteligente, mi amor!

Antonio: Oh, eso no es nada. ¡El trabajo de la mujer es tan fácil!

Palabras Nuevas

SUBSTANTIVOS

Alicia   *Alice*
Antonio   *Anthony*
la botella   *the bottle*
el centavo   *the cent*
los comestibles   *the groceries*
 la tienda de comestibles
  the grocery store
el dependiente   *the clerk*
la docena   *the dozen*
 la docena de huevos   *the*
  dozen eggs
el dólar   *the dollar*
la fruta   *the fruit*
el huevo   *the egg*
el jugo   *the juice*
 el jugo de naranja   *the*
  orange juice
la leche   *the milk*

la libra   *the pound*
la lista   *the list*
la mantequilla   *the butter*
la mañana   *the morning*
la mujer   *the wife, the woman*
el pan   *the bread*
un poco de   *a bit of, a little*
el queso   *the cheese*
el señor   *sir, mister*
el trabajo   *the work*
la verdad   *the truth*

VERBOS

comprar   *to buy*
pagar   *to pay*
regresar   *to return*
(yo) sé   *I know*
va   *he (she) goes; you (formal*
 sing.) go

OTRAS PALABRAS

adiós   *good-bye*
bien   *well*
 está bien!   *it's alright! OK.*
buenos días   *hello, good day*
cinco   *five*
cincuenta   *fifty*
como   *like*
¿cuánto,a?   *how much?*
exactamente   *exactly*
gracias   *thanks*
nada   *nothing, not. . .anything*
siempre   *always*
sin   *without*
tan   *so*
yo no   *not I*
un, una   *a, one*
unos,as   *some*

EJERCICIOS

I. Preguntas. Write your answer in a complete Spanish sentence.

1. ¿Por qué no va Alicia de compras hoy? _____

2. ¿Qué necesita Alicia? _____

3. ¿Adónde va Antonio? _____

4. ¿Qué compra Antonio en la tienda? _____

5. ¿Cuánto es todo eso? _____

6. ¿ Es Antonio tonto o inteligente? ¿Por qué? _____

II. Word Hunt – Find and circle these words in Spanish.

1.	dozen	9.	bread
2.	eggs	10.	three
3.	cheese	11.	pound
4.	dollars	12.	how much?
5.	cents	13.	things
6.	juice	14.	he leaves
7.	milk	15.	I know
8.	fruit		

D	O	C	E	N	A	H	C
O	L	E	C	H	E	U	U
L	I	N	P	A	N	E	A
A	B	T	R	E	S	V	N
R	R	A	J	U	G	O	T
E	A	V	Q	U	E	S	O
S	E	O	F	R	U	T	A
C	O	S	A	S	A	L	E

III. Compositions: Oral or written.

(A) Look at the picture at the beginning of this Work Unit. Describe the scene in Spanish to a friend.

(B) Tell what Emilio says.

Emilio goes into a store to buy some groceries. Complete the following dialogue.

Dependiente: Buenos días, ¿qué desea usted?

Emilio: _____

Dependiente: Aquí está, ¿Quiere algo más?

Emilio: _____

Dependiente: Bueno, son cinco dólares cincuenta.

Emilio: _____

Dependiente: Muchas gracias, señor. Adiós. El trabajo de la mujer no es muy difícil. ¿Verdad?

Emilio: _____

ESTRUCTURAS DE LA LENGUA

The Indefinite Articles: Un, Una, Unos, Unas.

Un chico canta

Unos chicos cantan

A. Uses of **Un** and **Una**

Un	Una
1. ¿Quiénes son los chicos? Who are the boys? **Un chico** es mi primo. *One* boy is my cousin. El otro es **un alumno** de mi clase. The other is *a* pupil in my class.	2. ¿Quiénes son las chicas? Who are the girls? **Una chica** es mi prima. *One* girl is my cousin. La otra es **una alumna** de mi clase. The other is *a* pupil in my class.

B. Uses of **Unos** and **Unas**

Unos	Unas
1. **Unos chicos** hablan español; otros hablan inglés. *Some (a few) boys* speak Spanish; others speak English.	2. **Unas chicas** estudian el español; otras estudian el inglés. *Some (a few) girls* study Spanish; others study English.

Rules:

1. **Un** and **una** single out *one* out of two or more.
   The English equivalents are *a, an, one.*
   Un precedes a masculine noun. **Una** precedes a feminine noun.

2. **Unos** and **unas** denote some samples of a class or a group.
   The English equivalents are *some, a few.*
   Unos precedes masculine nouns. **Unas** precedes feminine nouns.

3. **Unos pocos,** a few:

Unos pocos dulces A few candies	**Unas pocas** revistas A few magazines

STUDY THE RULES, EXAMPLES, AND MODELS BEFORE BEGINNING THE EXERCISES!

Exercises

I. Write the following response, using the appropriate form of **un** or **una** and the noun:
<< _____ **interesante.** >>

Model: ¿Qué libro desean?   **Un libro** interesante.
What book do they want?   An interesting book.

1. ¿Qué diccionario es? _____
2. ¿Qué revista desean?_____
3. ¿Qué profesor necesitan?_____
4. ¿Qué periódico prefieren?_____
5. ¿Qué ciudad visitan?_____
6. ¿Qué lección estudian?_____
7. ¿Qué pensión prefieren?_____
8. ¿Qué programa desean?_____
9. ¿Qué día es?_____
10. ¿Qué canción escuchan? _____

II. Write the following response, using the appropriate form of **un** and **una** and the noun in the singular: << **No. Solamente** _____ _____. >>

Model: ¿Deseas todos los libros?   No. Solamente **un libro.**
Do you want all the books?   No. Only _one book._

1. ¿Necesitas todos los cuadernos?_____
2. ¿Estudias todas las palabras?_____
3. ¿Escuchas todas las frases?_____
4. ¿Usas todos los lápices?_____
5. ¿Estudias todos los idiomas?_____

III. Write the following negative response, using the appropriate form of **unos** or **unas** and the noun in the plural: << **No. Solamente** _____ _____ . >>

  Model: ¿Deseas todos los dulces?   No. Solamente **unos dulces.**
      Do you want all the candy?   No. Only *some* candy.

1. ¿Usas todos los periódicos?_____

2. ¿Deseas todas las revistas?_____

3. ¿Estudias todas las lecciones?_____

4. ¿Escuchas todos los programas?_____

5. ¿Visitas todas las ciudades?_____

IV. Complete using the appropriate indefinite article: **un, una, unos,** or **unas.**

Entro en _____ tienda de comestibles. Compro _____ huevos, _____ botella
    1. (a)   2. (a few)   3. (one)

de leche, _____ pan y _____ manzanas.
    4. (one)   5. (some)

V. Complete using the appropriate indefinite article: **un, una, unos** or **unas.**

Asisto a _____ escuela grande. Hay _____ clases por la mañana y otras por la tarde. En _____
    1   2   3

pocos días no hay clases. Entonces, camino a _____ parque cerca de aquí donde paso _____
                4   5

horas al aire libre.

VI. Complete by writing the Spanish equivalent for the missing words.

Es _____ día muy bueno. Como _____ manzana. Tomo _____ vaso de leche.
  1. (a)   2. (one)   3. (a)
Charlo con _____ amigo muy bueno. Escuchamos _____ programas en _____
    4. (a)   5. (some)   6. (the)
radio. Paso _____ hora en _____ parque. Camino a la casa de _____ amigo
   7. (an)   8. (the)   9. (a)
donde bailo con _____ chica muy bonita. Ceno con _____ familia. Miramos _____
      10. (a)   11. (the)   12. (the)
televisión. Luego, estudio _____ lecciones fáciles. Prepara _____ libros para _____
      13. (some)   14. (the)   15. (the)
clases de mañana.

VII. Oral Proficiency. Respond orally to the situation described. (You may *later* write your responses for intensive practice.)

  Situation: You are working as an assistant in a grocery store. I am a customer who needs many grocery items, but left my shopping list at home. I say:—*No tengo mi lista.* You help me.

  Begin with *Buenos días.* In **five** Spanish questions or statements assist me by suggesting grocery items. You may use your own ideas or ideas suggested by the following: *siempre es necesario, es bueno para la casa, es importante, ¿necesita Vd.?, ¿quiere Vd.?, ¿desea Vd.?, gracias y adiós.*

*Los esposos, Marta y Miguel,
hacen sus planes de verano.*

Where would you like to go on your vacation?
Miguel thinks he's going to a tropical paradise.

Vamos a un país tropical

Es el mes de mayo. Los esposos Marta y Miguel hacen planes para las vacaciones de verano.

Marta: *Ay, Miguelito, este verano quiero descansar en una playa bonita,* y mirar el mar y un sol brillante.

Miguel: Bueno, mi amor. Yo prefiero tomar las vacaciones en el otoño o en la primavera cuando no hace calor. Pero si tú quieres, vamos a viajar a un país tropical. Allí nadamos y tomamos el sol.

Marta: Muy bien. Entonces mañana vamos a la agencia de viajes. Así, en junio pasamos cuatro semanas de vacaciones en una playa bonita.

Al día siguiente, a las nueve de la mañana, Miguel y su esposa están en la agencia de viajes. Hablan con el empleado.

Empleado: Bueno. ¿Cuándo y adónde desean Vds. ir?

Miguel: A Sudamérica en junio. Deseamos pasar un mes en Chile, en la famosa playa de Viña del Mar, para nadar y tomar el sol. ¿Qué tiempo hace? Hace buen tiempo. ¿Verdad?

Empleado: Pero … señores … Chile no es el Caribe. ¿Mucho sol y calor en junio en Chile? Señores, en junio es el invierno allí. ¿No saben Vds. que en muchos países de Sudamérica las estaciones son diferentes? Cuando hace calor aquí, hace frío allí. Pero, si Vds. desean *esquiar* en Chile, en junio es posible.

Palabras Nuevas

SUBSTANTIVOS

la agencia de viajes *the travel agency*
el calor *the heat*
el empleado *the clerk, the employee*
la esposa *the wife*
los esposos *the couple (husband and wife)*
la estación *the season*
el invierno *the winter*
junio *June*
el mar *the sea*
Marta *Martha*
mayo *May*
el mes *the month*
Miguel *Michael*
  Miguelito *Mike*
el otoño *the autumn*
el plan *the plan*

la playa *the beach*
la primavera *the spring*
la semana *the week*
señores *sir and madam*
el sol *the sun*
las vacaciones *the vacation*
el verano *the summer*
  las vacaciones de verano *the summer vacation*

ADJETIVOS

bonito,a *pretty*
brillante *brilliant, shiny*
cuatro *four*
diferente *different*
este (m. sing.) *this*
famoso,a *famous*

VERBOS

esquiar *to ski*

hace calor *it is hot*
hace frío *it is cold*
nadar *to swim*
pasar *to spend (time)*
prefiero *I prefer*
quieres *you (fam. sing.) want*
tomar el sol *to sunbathe*
vamos *we are going*
viajar *to travel*

OTRAS PALABRAS

a las nueve de la mañana *at 9 A.M.*
al día siguiente *on the following day*
allí *there*
¿Qué tiempo hace? *What is the weather like?*
si *if*

EJERCICIOS

I. (A) Preguntas. Write your answer in a complete Spanish sentence.

1. ¿Dónde desea Marta descansar?
2. ¿Quién prefiere pasar las vacaciones donde no hace calor?
3. ¿En qué país quieren nadar y tomar el sol en junio?
4. ¿Cuál es la estación en Chile en junio?
5. ¿Cuándo es posible esquiar en Chile?

1. _____

2. _____

3. _____

4. _____

5. _____

(B) Preguntas personales y generales. Write your answer in a complete Spanish sentence.

1. ¿Qué tiempo hace hoy?
2. ¿A qué país quiere Vd. viajar para pasar sus vacaciones?
3. ¿En qué país hace siempre sol y calor?
4. ¿Adónde va todo el mundo para nadar?
5. ¿En qué meses hace mucho frío?

1. _____

2. _____

3. _____

4. _____

5. _____

II. Unscramble the following words and place them in the proper boxes.

1. PRIAVREAM
2. SEM
3. ROMA
4. YOMA
5. INOVERIN
6. LOS

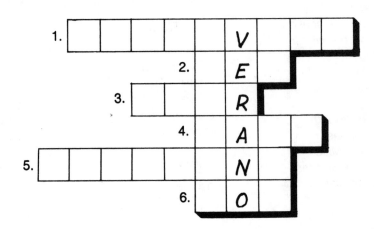

III. Place the following sentences in the order in which they occurred in the story.

1. Miguel prefiere el otoño.
2. Quieren pasar un mes en Chile.
3. Marta y Miguel hacen sus planes.
4. Los esposos van a una agencia de viajes.
5. Marta quiere ir a un país tropical.

1. _____

2. _____

3. _____

4. _____

5. _____

IV. Compositions: Oral or written.

(A) Look at the picture at the beginning of this Work Unit. Describe the scene in Spanish to a friend.

(B) Tell about your plans for vacation. Include the following:

Mis vacaciones

1. Where you always want to spend your summer vacation. 2. In what month it is good to go there. 3. What the weather is like there. 4. How much time you spend there and with whom. 5. What you do there.

ESTRUCTURAS DE LA LENGUA

Cardinal Numbers: 1-31; Time: Days, Months, Dates, Seasons

1. uno (un, una)	11. once	21. veinte y uno (un, una)
2. dos	12. doce	22. veinte y dos
3. tres	13. trece	23. veinte y tres
4. cuatro	14. catorce	24. veinte y cuatro
5. cinco	15. quince	25. veinte y cinco
6. seis	16. diez y seis	26. veinte y seis
7. siete	17. diez y siete	27. veinte y siete
8. ocho	18. diez y ocho	28. veinte y ocho
9. nueve	19. diez y nueve	29. veinte y nueve
10. diez	20. veinte	30. treinta
		31. treinta y uno (un, una)

A. Arithmetic Examples

1. **Quince y diez son veinte y cinco.**	15 plus 10 are 25.
2. **Treinta menos diez son veinte.**	30 minus 10 are 20.
3. **Seis por dos son doce.**	6 times 2 are 12.
4. **Veinte dividido por cinco son cuatro.**	20 divided by 5 equals 4.

69

B. One

1. **Un libro** está en la mesa.	*One* book is on the table.
2. Hay **veinte y un alumnos.**	There are *21* pupils.
3. El cuaderno tiene **treinta y una páginas.**	The notebook has *31* pages.

Rules:

1. **Uno,** indicating *one,* shortens to **un** before a masculine singular noun and changes to **una** before a feminine singular noun, whether alone or after **veinte** and **treinta.**

2. The numbers 16-19 are combinations of **diez.** Alternate forms are **dieciséis, diecisiete, dieciocho, diecinueve.**

3. **Veinte y uno** may be written as **veintiuno,** etc. Note the accent mark, however, on **veintidós** and **veintitrés.**

C. Telling Time

1. ¿Qué hora es?	What time is it?
2. **Es la** un**a.**	It is 1:00 o'clock.
3. **Es la** un**a** y diez (y cuart**o**; y medi**a**)	It is 10 minutes after 1:00 (a quarter past; half past).
4. **Son las** dos.	It is 2:00 o'clock.
5. **Son las** dos menos veinte y cinco.	It is 25 minutes to 2:00 o'clock *or* 1:35.
6. **Son las** dos menos quince.	It is 15 minutes to 2:00 o'clock *or* 1:45.

Rules:

1. One o'clock is feminine *singular;* 2 through 12 o'clock are feminine *plural.* **La** or **las** precede each hour. Use **es la** before **una,** and **son las** before **dos** through **doce** to express *it is.*

2. The hour is generally expressed *before* the minutes. Use **y** to *add* the minutes past the hour.

3. *After half past the hour,* the time is generally expressed in terms of *the next hour less the appropriate number of minutes.* Use **menos** to *subtract* the minutes.

4. Two forms of *P.M.* are used: For the afternoon and early evening until dinner, **de la tarde;** for the late evening, *de la noche.* A.M. is only **de la mañana.**

D. At What Time?

1. ¿A qué hora toma Vd. las comidas?   At what time do you take meals?

2. Tomo el desayuno a las siete de la mañana.   I eat breakfast at 7 A.M.

3. Tomo el almuerzo a las doce (al mediodía).   I eat lunch at 12 o'clock (at noon).

4. Llego a casa a las tres de la tarde y tomo café o leche.   I arrive home at 3 P.M. and take coffee or milk.

5. En casa tomamos la comida a las seis de la tarde.   At home we eat dinner at 6 P.M.

6. Vamos a la cama y dormimos a las diez de la noche.   We go to bed and sleep at 10 P.M.

Rule:

Use **a** to express *at* in telling time.

E. Days

1. Hoy es sábado. Mañana es domingo.   Today is Saturday. Tomorrow is Sunday.

2. Los días de la semana son: el domingo, el lunes, el martes, el miércoles, el jueves, el viernes, el sábado.   The days of the week are: Sunday, Monday, Tuesday, Wednesday, Thursday, Friday, Saturday.

3. Los sábados son para las tiendas. Los domingos son para descansar.   Saturdays are for shopping. Sundays are for resting.

F. Months and Dates

1. Los meses del año son: enero, febrero, marzo, abril, mayo, junio, julio, agosto, septiembre, octubre, noviembre, diciembre.
   The months of the year are: Jan., Feb., Mar., April, May, June, July, August, Sept., Oct., Nov., Dec.

2. ¿Cuál es la fecha de hoy?   What is today's date?
   Hoy es lunes el primero de mayo.   Today is Mon., May 1.
   Mañana es martes el dos de mayo.   Tomorrow is Tues., May 2.

G. Seasons

Las estaciones del año son **la primavera, el verano, el otoño, el invierno.**
The seasons are spring, summer, fall, winter.

Rules:

1. Days
   After forms of **ser** omit **el** before the day: **Es lunes.** *It is Monday.*
   Days are generally written in small letters entirely.

2. Months and dates.
   a. Months are generally written in small letters entirely.
   b. In writing the date, the number is generally given before the month: **el primero de enero.**
      Primero is used for the first of the month. The rest of the month is expressed in cardinal
      numbers: **el dos, el tres, etc.**

3. Seasons
   Seasons are generally written in small letters and generally require the use of the appropriate article, e.g., **la primavera,** *spring.*

STUDY THE RULES, EXAMPLES, AND MODELS BEFORE BEGINNING THE EXERCISES!

Exercises

I. Write the answers in Spanish words.

1. Cuatro y cinco son_____

2. Nueve y catorce son_____

3. Tres y siete son_____

4. Once y uno son_____

5. Trece y ocho son_____

6. Diez y siete y trece son_____

7. Ocho por dos son_____

8. Cuatro por dos son_____

9. Treinta y uno menos diez y seis son_____

10. Veinte y nueve menos dos son_____

11. Diez y nueve menos dos son_____

12. Veinte menos seis son_____

13. Diez y ocho dividido por tres son_____

14. Veinte dividido por cinco son_____

15. Quince por dos son_____

II. Write the following rejoinder telling what the *next* day is: << **Si hoy es** _____, **mañana es** _____ . >>

    Model: Hoy es martes.   Si hoy es martes, mañana es **miércoles.**
               Today is Tuesday.   If today is Tuesday, tomorrow is Wednesday.

1. Hoy es lunes. _____

2. Hoy es sábado. _____

3. Hoy es miércoles. _____

4. Hoy es jueves. _____

5. Hoy es viernes. _____

III. Complete in Spanish

Los meses de primavera son marzo, _____ y _____ . Los meses de verano son
                                  1   2

_____, julio y _____. Los meses de otoño son _____ , _____ ,
    3   4   5   6

y noviembre. Los meses de invierno son _____, _____ y febrero. Celebramos la
                                       7   8

Navidad (Christmas) en el mes de _____ . El Día de Año Nuevo (New Year's
                                        9

Day) es el _____ de enero.
          10

IV. Write the appropriate equivalent of *it is* to complete the sentence in Spanish: **Es la** or **Son las.** Then write the time in numbers within the parentheses.

    Model: _____**ocho menos diez.** (_____)
         Son las ocho menos diez.   **(7:50)**

1. _____una y quince. (_____)

2. _____dos y media. (_____)

3. _____doce y cuarto. (_____)

4. _____una menos veinte y cinco. (_____)

5. _____once menos cuarto. (_____)

V. Complete in Spanish according to the information given in parentheses.

1. Son las_____ (half-past three P.M.)

2. Regresa a la _____ (quarter to one A.M.)

3. Sale a las_____ (3:40 P.M.)

4. ¿Qué_____ (time is it?)

5. Llega_____ (at 1:15)

VI. Write the response using the time given in *italics* and the appropriate expression for A.M. **(de la mañana)** or for P.M. **(de la tarde** or **de la noche).**

    Model: —¿Estudiamos por la tarde?   (*a las tres*)   Do we study in the afternoon?

          —Sí, estudiamos a las tres **de la tarde.**   Yes, we study at 3 P.M.

1. ¿Estudiamos por la tarde?   *a las cinco*

2. ¿Tomamos el almuerzo por la tarde?   *a la una*

3. ¿Dormimos por la noche?   *a las once menos veinte*

4. ¿Toman el desayuno por la mañana?   *a las nueve y media*

5. ¿Estudian por la tarde?   *a la una menos cuarto*

VII. a. Write a *negative* response in a complete Spanish sentence.

    b. Then write a Spanish sentence stating the *next* day, hour, month, or season for each expression in *italics*.

    Model: ¿Es hoy *martes el treinta y uno de enero?*   Is today Tuesday, the 31st of January?

          a. Hoy **no es martes el treinta y uno de enero.**   Today is not Tuesday, the 31st of January.

          b. Hoy **es miércoles el primero de febrero.**   Today is Wednesday, the 1st of February.

1. ¿Es hoy *miércoles el treinta y uno* de *diciembre*?

    a.

    b.

2. ¿Es todavía (still) *la primavera* en el mes de *junio*?

    a.

    b.

3. ¿Son *las doce del mediodía* (noon)?

    a.

    b.

4. ¿Llegamos el *miércoles* el *treinta de septiembre*?

    a. _____

    b. _____

5. ¿Celebramos el día de la Navidad el *veinte y cuatro* de *noviembre*?

    a. _____

    b. _____

VIII. Complete the response.

1. ¿Cuáles son los días de la escuela?

    Son _____ (Monday
    through
    _____ Friday)

2. ¿Qué día es para las tiendas?

    _____ es para las tiendas. (Saturday)

3. ¿Qué día es para descansar?

    _____ es para descansar. (Sunday)

4. ¿Cuántos días hay en la semana?

    Hay _____ días en la semana. (seven)

5. ¿Cuántos días hay en el mes de agosto?

    En agosto hay_____ días. (thirty-one)

6. ¿Cuántas horas hay en un día?

    En un día hay _____ horas. (twenty-four)

7. ¿A qué hora entramos en la escuela?

    Entramos _____ (at half-past 8 A.M.)

8. ¿Cuántas alumnas hay en la clase?

    Hay_____ alumnas. (twenty-one)

9. ¿A qué hora regresamos a casa?

    Regresamos _____ (3:25 P.M.)

10. ¿A qué hora vamos a la cama?

    Vamos _____ (10:40 P.M.)

IX. Oral Proficiency. Respond orally to the situation described. (You may *later* write your responses for intensive practice.)

Situation: You and your friend have saved enough money to travel on your vacation. Your friend is hesitating now. He says:—*Ahora no sé si quiero viajar.* You telephone to persuade your friend to go.

Begin with *hola* and end with *hasta luego.* In **five** Spanish statements or questions persuade your friend to travel with you. You may use your own ideas or ideas suggested by the following: *a good season or month to travel, where you want to go, what you two are to see there, what you are going to do in the evening and in the daytime, does he or she want to spend the vacation there.*

Y-10

El Lancia Y-10 gusta a la gente de hoy, inquieta, joven, dinámica, como tú, a la gente que, como el Y-10, está de moda. Con un diseño que hace presente el futuro, el Y-10 en sus dos versiones —LX y Fila—, rompe con los moldes establecidos.

Agil en ciudad y potente en carretera, el Y-10 te acerca a las cosas que gustan.

P.V.P. **Fila 994.175 Ptas. LX 1.103.235 Ptas,** IVA incluido.

Gusta a la Gente que Gusta.

¿Estás ocupada esta noche,
o quieres ir al cine?

*Do girls really go for football players? Paco is
going to find out.*

Así es la vida

Paco Pérez sale de la clase de inglés, y allí, delante de él, ve a Josefina Jiménez, la muchacha más bella de la escuela. Ésta es la perfecta oportunidad para hacer una cita con ella. En este momento, el libro que Josefina trae, cae al suelo. ¡Perfecto! Paco pone el libro en la mano de Josefina y dice:

Paco: Perdone, señorita. ¿Es éste su libro?

Josefina: Ah, sí. Gracias, muchas gracias.

Paco: Vd. no me conoce. Soy Paco. . .Paco Pérez. ¿Tiene Vd. unos minutos para conversar?

Josefina: Gracias, no. Voy ahora a mi clase de álgebra.

Paco: Entonces, ¿después de las clases? ¿Tiene Vd. tiempo libre para tomar una Coca Cola?

Josefina: Gracias, pero tengo mucho trabajo esta tarde.

Paco: Pues, este sábado dan una película muy buena. Vengo en mi coche a las siete, si Vd. quiere.

Josefina: No, gracias. Voy a estudiar todo este fin de semana. Tengo muchos exámenes. Ésta es mi clase. Adiós.

Una hora más tarde, Alejandro Hombrón, capitán del equipo de fútbol, ve a Josefina en la cafetería.

Alejandro: ¡Hola, Josefina! ¿Qué tal? Oye, ¿estás ocupada esta noche o quieres ir al cine?

Josefina: Sí, por supuesto, Alejandro, con mucho gusto. ¡Tú eres tan amable!

Palabras Nuevas

SUBSTANTIVOS

Alejandro *Alexander*
la cafetería *the cafeteria*
el capitán *the captain*
el cine *the movie theater,
  the "movies"*
la cita *the appointment, the
  date*
la clase de álgebra *the
  algebra class*
la clase de inglés *the English
  class*
el coche *the car*
el equipo *the team*
los exámenes *the tests*
el fin de semana *the weekend*
el hombrón *the large man*
la hora *the hour, the time*
Josefina *Josephine*

el minuto *the minute*
la oportunidad *the opportunity*
la película *the film, the movie*
el sábado *(on) Saturday*
la tarde *the afternoon*
el tiempo *the time (period of
  time)*
la vida *the life*

ADJETIVOS

amable *kind*
bello,a *beautiful*
libre *free*
perfecto,a *perfect*

VERBOS

caer *to fall*
conocer *to be acquainted with*

Vd. no me conoce. *You
  don't know me.*
conversar *to converse, to
  chat*
dar *to give*
dice *he (she) says; you
  (formal sing.) say*
eres *you (fam. sing.) are*
estás *you (fam. sing.) are*
¡oye! *listen!, hear! (fam. sing.)*
¡perdone! *pardon (formal
  sing.)*
poner *to place, to put*
quiere *you (formal sing.)
  want; he (she) wants*
salir *to go out*
soy *I am*
tengo *I have*
tiene *you (formal sing.) have;
  he (she) has*

tomar *to drink*	al *to the (masc. sing.)*	en la mano de *in the*
traer *to carry, to bring*	al suelo *to the floor*	*hand of*
vengo *I come*	así es la vida *such is life*	esta tarde *this afternoon*
ver *to see*	con ella *with her*	¡hola! *hi!*
voy *I am going, I go*	con mucho gusto *with great pleasure*	más tarde *later*
		muchas gracias *many thanks*
	del *of the (masc. sing.)*	por supuesto *of course*
OTRAS PALABRAS	delante de él *in front of him*	¿qué tal? *how are things?*
	en este momento *at this moment*	
a las siete *at seven*		

EJERCICIOS

I. (A) Complete the sentences according to the story.

1. Paco _____ de la clase de inglés.   2. Él _____ a Josefina, la muchacha más

bonita de la escuela, y él desea una _____ con ella.   3. El libro de Josefina _____

al suelo, y Paco _____ el libro entre las manos de Josefina.   4. Paco invita a Josefina

al _____ pero ella dice que está ocupada todo el _____ de _____.

5. Josefina sale con Alejandro porque él es el capitán del _____ de _____.

B. Preguntas personales y generales. Write your answer in a complete Spanish sentence.

1. ¿Adónde va Vd. este sábado?
2. ¿Está Vd. ocupado(a) esta tarde o no?
3. ¿Qué películas dan en el cine?
4. ¿Adónde va Vd. después de su clase de español?
5. ¿Qué hace Vd. cuando tiene unos momentos libres?

1. _____

2. _____

3. _____

4. _____

5. _____

II. Each of the following sets of boxes contains a scrambled sentence. Can you figure the sentences out?

1.

Perdone	¿es	libro?
señorita	éste	su

2.

clase	de	a
voy	mi	álgebra

3.

Josefina	a	de
él	delante	ve

4.

película	dan	buena
este	una	sábado

1. _____

2. _____

3. _____

4. _____ _____

III. Write a summary of the story. Make complete sentences using the following words. You may change the verbs from the infinitive and add any other words you wish.

    Model: Paco Pérez/salir/clase/inglés.   Paco Pérez sale de la clase de inglés.

1. Paco/invitar/a Josefina cine _____

2. Josefina no/tener/tiempo libre _____

3. Alejandro/invitar/a Josefina a ver película _____

4. Josefina no/estar/ocupada y salir _____

5. Alejandro/ser/capitán equipo/fútbol _____

IV. **Compositions:** Oral or written.

(A) Look at the picture at the beginning of this Work Unit. Describe the scene in Spanish to a friend.

(B) Tell about a date or an appointment. Include the following:

Una cita

1. With whom you have the date or appointment. 2. At what time and for what day you have the appointment. 3. Where you are going. 4. Where you are going after that, or what you will do. 5. Why you are going home early.

ESTRUCTURAS DE LA LENGUA

Irregular Verbs of the Present Indicative Tense

A. Verbs that are *irregular* in *one person:* the first person singular, **yo.**

    (1) The irregularity is **go.**

hacer *to do, make*	**poner** *to put, place*	**salir** *to leave*
I do the homework.	I put the book here.	I'm leaving now.
Hago la tarea.	**Pongo** el libro aquí.	**Salgo** ahora.
haces	pones	sales
hace	pone	sale
Hacemos la tarea.	Ponemos el libro aquí.	Salimos ahora.
hacéis	ponéis	salís
hacen	ponen	salen

81

(2) The irregularity is **igo.**

caer *to fall*   **traer** *to bring*

I fall into the water.	I bring money.
Caigo al agua.	**Traigo** dinero.
caes	traes
cae	trae
Caemos al agua.	Traemos dinero.
caéis	traéis
caen	traen

(3) The irregularity is **oy.**

dar *to give*   ***ir** *to go*

I give thanks	I go there
Doy las gracias.	**Voy** allá.
das	**vas**
da	**va**
Damos las gracias.	**Vamos** allá.
dais	**vais**
dan	**van**

*****Ir,** *to go,* acquires the letter **v** at the beginning of each verb form. To the letter **v** are added endings like those of **dar: oy, as, a, amos, ais, an.**

*****Ir** is, therefore, irregular in all persons; and its forms in the present tense rhyme with those of the **ar** verb **dar.**

(4) The irregularity is **eo**   (5) The irregularity is **é**   (6) The irregularity is **zco**

ver *to see*   **saber** *to know* (facts)   **conocer** *to know* (persons, places)

I see everything.	I know a great deal.	I know John.
Veo todo.	**Sé** mucho.	**Conozco** a Juan.
ves	sabes	conoces
ve	sabe	conoce
Vemos todo.	Sabemos mucho.	Conocemos a Juan.
veis	sabéis	conocéis
ven	saben	conocen

B. Verbs that are *irregular* in *four persons*.

(1) The irregularities are **go** and **ie**

tener *to have*   **venir** *to come*

I have time.	I come home.
Tengo tiempo.	**Vengo** a casa.
tienes	**vienes**
tiene	**viene**
Tenemos tiempo.	Venimos a casa.
tenéis	venís
tienen	**vienen**

Rules for **tener** and **venir:**

1. **Tener** and **venir** have similar *stems*.

2. The *irregular* verb forms are in the first, second, and third persons singular and in the third person plural: **yo, tú, él, ella, Vd.** and **ellos-as, Vds.**

3. Regular verb forms are in the first person plural and in the second person plural: **nosotros-as** and **vosotros-as**

C. Verbs that have *speical irregularities* in *four persons*.

decir *to tell*   **oír** *to hear*

I tell the truth.	I hear the song.
Digo la verdad.	**Oigo** la canción.
dices	**oyes**
dice	**oye**
Decimos la verdad.	Oímos la canción.
decís	oís
dicen	**oyen**

Rules for **decir** and **oír:**

1. The *irregular* verb forms are in the first, second, and third persons singular, and in the third personal plural: **yo, tú, él, ella, Vd., ellos-as, Vds..**

2. The only regular verb forms are those for **nosotros-as** and **vosotros-as.**

STUDY THE RULES, EXAMPLES, AND MODELS BEFORE BEGINNING THE EXERCISES!

Exercises

I. Rewrite the model sentence using the appropriate form of the verb in parentheses.

Model: **Yo preparo la tarea.**   (escribir) **Yo escribo** la tarea.
I prepare the homework.   I write the homework.

1. (ver) _____   4. (hacer) _____

2. (traer) _____   5. (decir) _____

3. (tener) _____   6. (saber) _____

El habla mucho.

II. Write an affirmative answer in a complete Spanish sentence using **yo.**

Model: —¿Quién habla mucho?   **—Yo hablo mucho.**
Who speaks a great deal?   I speak a great deal.

1. ¿Quién sale ahora?_____

2. ¿Quién conoce a Manuel?_____

3. ¿Quién viene a su casa?_____

4. ¿Quién le trae dinero?_____

5. ¿Quién cae en la calle?_____

6. ¿Quién hace excusas?_____

7. ¿Quién pone el dinero en la mesa?_____

8. ¿Quién va al cine con Manuel?_____

9. ¿Quién oye la música allí?_____

10. ¿Quién le da las gracias?_____

III. Rewrite the model sentence, substituting the subject suggested in parentheses and making the necessary changes in each verb.

A. Model: Yo **vengo** a papá, le **digo** hola   (Vds.) Vds. **vienen** a papá, le
        y le **doy** un beso.   **dicen** hola y le **dan** un beso.

        I come to father, say hello   You come to father, say hello
        and give him a kiss.   and give him a kiss.

1. (tú)_____

2. (él)_____

3. (ellos)_____

4. (nosotros)_____

5. (Vd.)_____

6. (yo)_____

B. Yo **voy** a casa y **oigo** la canción que **tengo** que aprender.
        I go home and hear the song that I have to learn.

1. (tú)_____

2. (el chico)_____

3. (las chicas)_____

4. (tú y yo)_____

5. (Vds.)_____

6. (yo)_____

IV. Write an affirmative answer in a complete Spanish sentence. In **(a)** use **Sí.** In **(b)** use **también.**

Model: a. —¿Toman ellos café?   **—Sí. Ellos toman café.**
        Do they drink coffee?   Yes, they do drink coffee.

        b. —¿Y Vd.?   **—Yo también tomo café.**
        And do you?   I also drink coffee.

1. a. ¿Va Vd. a la escuela?_____

   b. ¿Y ellos?_____

2. a. ¿Oyen ellos el coche? _____

   b. ¿Y tú?_____

   c. ¿Y nosotros?_____

3. a. ¿Dices la verdad?_____

   b. ¿Y Vds.?_____

   c. ¿Y Luisa?_____

4. a. ¿Viene María mañana?_____

   b. ¿Y Vd.?_____

   c. ¿Y nosotros?_____

5. a. ¿Tenemos tiempo?_____

   b. ¿Y tú?_____

   c. ¿Y ellos?_____

6. a. ¿Ve Vd. el animal?_____

   b. ¿Y ellos?_____

7. a. ¿Da Vd. dinero?_____

   b. ¿Y yo?_____

8. a. ¿Trae Juan el periódico?_____

   b. ¿Y tú?_____

9. a. ¿Conoce Vd. al señor?_____

   b. ¿Juan y tú?_____

10. a. ¿Sabe Vd. la fecha?_____

    b. ¿Y ellas?_____

11. a. ¿Sale Vd. temprano?_____

    b. ¿Y nosotros?_____

12. a. ¿Pones tú el diccionario en la mesa? _____

    b. ¿Y tú y yo?_____

13. a. ¿Hace Vd. el ejercicio?_____

    b. ¿Y Vd. y Lola?_____

V. Complete the series telling about your day in school. Use **yo** with the appropriate form of the verb, and the vocabulary in parentheses.

 1. (salir de la casa ahora)_____

 2. (traer dos libros a la escuela)_____

 3. (venir a la clase a las nueve)_____

 4. (ver a mis amigos)_____

 5. (poner los libros en la mesa) _____

 6. (dar la tarea al profesor) _____

 7. (hacer los ejercicios)_____

 8. (decir el vocabulario)_____

 9. (saber bien las palabras)_____

10. (tener tiempo para conversar)_____

11. (conocer a un nuevo amigo)_____

12. (oír música) _____

13. (ir a la cafetería)_____

14. (caer en el corredor)_____

15. (decir: —¡Ay!)_____

VI. Oral Proficiency. Respond orally to the situation described. (You may *later* write your responses for intensive practice.)

Situation: Your friend invites you to go to the movies tomorrow if you are not busy then:— *¿Quieres ir al cine conmigo mañana?* You want to know some details about the plans.

Begin with *Con mucho gusto* and explain why you are not busy. In **four** Spanish questions ask for information about the date. You may use your own ideas or the following: *Does your friend know what movie you are seeing, what movie theater you are going to, at what time you are leaving the house, what you are doing after the movie, when you are coming home.*

Aquí tengo dos billetes para una excursión esta noche para visitar todos los cabarets.

*Who says women are the weaker sex? Ask
Diego about his wife.*

Una excursión por la ciudad

Diego y su mujer, Hortensia, visitan a los Estados Unidos por primera vez. Deciden tomar un autobús turístico para conocer una de las ciudades grandes. El primer autobús sale a las doce en punto. Diego y Hortensia toman asientos por delante para oír bien al guía. Escuchan con atención la voz del guía quien habla por micrófono.

Guía: Señoras y señores, bienvenidos a esta excursión. Esta tarde vamos a visitar varios sitios interesantes de esta gran ciudad. Primero, vamos al centro para conocer el barrio comercial, los hoteles y los grandes almacenes.

Hortensia: ¡Qué edificios tan altos! ¡Mira, Diego! Tienen al menos veinte pisos.

Diego: ¡Al menos! Ésta es una ciudad famosa por sus rascacielos.

Guía: Y ahora pasamos por el barrio cultural. A la derecha están la Biblioteca Central y el Museo de Arte. A la izquierda. . . .los edificios de la Universidad y varios teatros famosos.

Hortensia: ¡Cuánta gente! ¿Adónde va todo el mundo? ¡Mira! ¡Van debajo de la tierra!

Diego: ¡Claro! Van a tomar los trenes subterráneos. La entrada a la estación está allí.

Guía: Entramos ahora en el parque zoológico. Vamos a estar aquí media hora. Es posible caminar por el parque, mirar los animales, sacar fotografías y tomar un helado.

Después de cuatro horas en el autobús, marido y mujer regresan cansados al hotel.

Diego: Estas excursiones son muy interesantes. Pero estoy cansado. Gracias a Dios, podemos descansar un poco.

Hortensia: ¿Descansar? ¡Mira! Aquí tengo dos billetes para otra excursión esta noche. Vamos a visitar todos los cabarets.

Palabras Nuevas

SUBSTANTIVOS

el almacén *the department store*
el animal *the animal*
el autobús turístico *the tour bus*
el barrio *the district (of a city)*
la biblioteca *the library*
el billete *the ticket*
el centro *downtown; the shopping center*
Diego *James*
la entrada *the entrance*
la estación *the station*
los Estados Unidos *the United States*
la excursión *the short trip, the excursion*
la gente *the people*

¡Gracias a Dios! *Thank heaven! Thank God!*
el guía *the guide*
Hortensia *Hortense*
el marido *the husband*
el parque zoológico *the zoo*
el piso *the floor*
un poco *a little*
el rascacielos *the skyscraper*
señoras y señores *ladies and gentlemen*
el sitio *the place*
la tierra *the ground*
el tren subterráneo *the subway (train)*

ADJETIVOS

bienvenido,a *welcome*
cansado,a *tired*

central *central*
comercial *commercial*
cultural *cultural*
gran *great*
varios,as *various*

VERBOS

conocer *to become acquainted with, to know*
hablar por micrófono *to talk over the microphone*
oír *to hear*
poder *to be able to, can*
sacar fotografías *to take pictures*
tomar asiento *to take a seat*
tomar un helado *to eat (an) ice cream*

OTRAS PALABRAS

a la derecha *at the right*
a la izquierda *at the left*
¿adónde? *where?*
a las doce en punto *at twelve sharp*

por delante *in the front*
al menos *at least*
con atención *attentively*
¡Cuánta gente! *How many people!*
debajo de *under, beneath*

hasta *even*
media hora *a half hour*
por primera vez *for the first time*
quien *who*
todo el mundo *everybody*

EJERCICIOS

I. (A) Preguntas. Write your answer in a complete Spanish sentence.

1. ¿Qué país visitan Diego y Hortensia?
2. ¿Cuándo sale el primer autobús?
3. ¿Cuántos pisos tienen los edificios?
4. ¿Dónde es posible mirar los animales, caminar y sacar fotografías?
5. ¿Para qué tiene Hortensia billetes esta noche?

1. _____

2. _____

3. _____

4. _____

5. _____

(B) Preguntas personales y generales. Write your answer in a complete Spanish sentence.

1. ¿Qué hay en el centro de una ciudad?
2. ¿Dónde corre el tren subterráneo?
3. ¿En qué parte de la ciudad hay muchos rascacielos?
4. ¿Para ver bien una nueva ciudad es bueno tomar un autobús turístico o un tren subterráneo?
5. ¿Dónde es bueno descansar cuando Vd. está cansado?

1. _____

2. _____

3. _____

4. _____

5. _____

II. ¿Cómo se dice en español?

1. Welcome to this trip. _____

2. To the left . . . the buildings of the university _____

   _____

3. To the right . . . the Central Library _____

   _____

4. This is a city famous for its skyscrapers. _____

   _____

5. It is possible to walk and to have an ice cream. _____

   _____

III. Match with their definitions. Write the correct letter.

	A		B
1.	el rascacielos _____	a.	tienda muy grande
2.	el barrio _____	b.	sitio donde hay muchos libros
3.	la universidad _____	c.	edificio muy alto
4.	el almacén _____	d.	sitio para aprender
5.	la biblioteca _____	e.	sección de la ciudad

IV. Compositions: Oral or written.

(A) Look at the picture at the beginning of this Work Unit. Describe the scene in Spanish to a friend.

(B) Tell about a trip you are taking. Include the following:

Mi viaje

1. Where and when you are going. 2. Why you are going. 3. Where you are buying the tickets. 4. How much they cost. 5. What you want to see or do there.

ESTRUCTURAS DE LA LENGUA

Uses of the Preposition *a*

A. **A** indicates direction *toward* or *to*.

	To		*To the*
1.	Corre **a Pedro.** He runs *to* (toward) Peter.	1.	Corre **al chico.** He runs to (toward) *the* boy.
2.	Corre **a mi amiga.** He runs *to* (toward) my friend.	2.	Corre **a la chica.** He runs *to* (toward) *the* girl.
3.	Viaja **a España** y **a Francia.** He travels *to* Spain and France.	3.	Viaja **a los países.** He travels *to the* countries.
4.	Viaja **a Madrid** y **a París.** He travels *to* Madrid and Paris.	4.	Viaja **a las ciudades.** He travels *to the* cities.

Rules:

1. **Al** *to the*: **a** followed by **el** always combines as **al.**

2. **A la, a los, a las:** *to the* never combine.

3. **A** is repeated before each object noun in a series.

B. Personal **A** (Untranslated)

A indicates which person is the direct object. When there are two people, **A** precedes and clarifies the direct object.

	Personal object nouns		*Places and things as object nouns*
1.	José **visita a mi amiga.** Joe visits *my friend.*	1.	José **visita mi casa.** Joe visits *my house.*
2.	José **necesita al amigo.** Joe needs *the friend.*	2.	José **necesita el libro.** Joe needs *the book.*

Rules:

1. **A** precedes and dignifies object nouns that are *persons,* but **a** is *not* used to dignify object nouns that are *things.*

2. *Personal* **a** does *not* mean *to.* It has *no* meaning in Spanish or in English here other than to introduce personal nouns as objects of the verb.

C. Omission of **a** after **escuchar** *to listen to*, **mirar** *to look at*, and **tener** *to have*

Things:	1. Escucha **el disco.** He listens to the record.
Persons:	2. Escucha **al maestro.** He listens to the teacher.
	5. Tiene **un** hermano. He has a brother.

3. Mira **el reloj.**
He looks at the clock.

4. Mira **al chico.**
He looks at the boy.

Rules:

1. **Escuchar** *to listen to* and **mirar** *to look at* include *to* and *at* and do not require **a** when things or places follow. **A** will follow **escuchar** and **mirar** only to introduce a personal object noun.

2. **Tener** *to have* never takes a personal **a** after it.

STUDY THE RULES, EXAMPLES, AND MODELS BEFORE BEGINNING THE EXERCISES!

Exercises

I. Write an affirmative answer in a complete Spanish sentence, according to the model.

Model: –¿Caminas al parque hoy?   **–Sí, camino** al parque.
Are you walking to the park today?   Yes, I'm walking to the park.

1. ¿Caminas al centro?_____

2. ¿Viajas al almacén?_____

3. ¿Corres a la tienda?_____

4. ¿Hablas a la chica?_____

5. ¿Corres a los museos?_____

6. ¿Caminas a los parques?_____

7. ¿Regresas a las escuelas?_____

8. ¿Hablas a María?_____

9. ¿Viajas a España?_____

10. ¿Regresas pronto al amigo?_____

II. Rewrite the sentence, substituting the word in parentheses for the word in *italics*. Make necessary changes in the use of **a** and the definite article **el, la, los,** or **las.**

Model: Corro al *parque.*   (ciudad) Corro **a la ciudad.**   (Anita) Corro **a Anita.**
I run to the park.   I run to the city.   I run to Anita.

Regreso al *parque.*   I am returning to the park.

1. (oficina) _____

2. (subterráneo) _____

3. (escuelas) _____

4. (parques) _____

5. (casa) _____

6. (biblioteca) _____

7. (centro) _____

8. (autobús) _____

9. (museo) _____

10. (Pedro) _____

III. Rewrite the model sentence, substituting the words in parentheses for the words in *italics*. Make necessary changes in the use of **a** and in the definite article. (Note: **escuchar** means *to listen to*.)

Model: **Escucho** *al maestro* **con atención.** (la canción) Escucho la canción con atención.
I listen to the teacher attentively.   I listen to the song attentively.

1. (el piano) _____

2. (el alumno) _____

3. (las guitarras) _____

4. (las amigas) _____

5. (los discos) _____

6. (Luis) _____

7. (los señores) _____

8. (la música) _____

9. (la madre) _____

10. (Ana) _____

IV. Write two responses in complete Spanish sentences. Use cues where given.

Model: A. –¿Prefieres el helado?   **–Sí. Prefiero el helado.**
         Do you prefer the ice cream?   Yes, I prefer the ice cream.
         B. –¿A quién prefieres?   (el actor)**–Prefiero al actor.**
         Whom do you prefer?   I prefer the actor.

1. a. ¿Necesitas el lápiz?_____

   b. ¿A quién necesitas? (el amigo) _____

2. a. ¿Visitas los países? _____

   b. ¿A quiénes visitas? (los primos) _____

3. a. ¿Escuchas la radio? _____

   b. ¿A quién escuchas? (la madre) _____

4. a. ¿Prefieres las melodías?_____

   b. ¿A quiénes prefieres? (las niñas)_____

5. a. ¿Miras el programa?_____

   b. ¿A quién miras? (el chico)_____

V. Rewrite the sentence, substituting the word in parentheses for the word in *italics*. Make all necessary changes in the use of **a** and in the definite article *the*.

Model: *Vamos* **al concierto.**   We are going to the concert.
         (Escuchamos) Escuchamos **el concierto.**   We listen to the concert.

1. *Responden* a un profesor.
   (Tienen)_____

2. *Tengo* el libro.
   (Comprendo)_____

3. Escucho *la radio*.
   (profesoras) _____

4. Miras *al actor*.
   (cuadro)_____

5. *Viajan* a la ciudad.
   (Miran)_____

VI. Complete the narrative, with the correct word(s), or write a dash (—) on the blank line if no word is needed. Selection: **a, al, el, la, las, los.**

1. Por la mañana voy _____ escuela. 2. Miro _____ reloj y entro en _____

clase de español. 3. Escucho _____ las preguntas y escucho _____ profesor.

4. En otra clase tengo _____ un buen amigo. 5. Miro _____ mi amigo Juan

cuando él contesta _____ profesora. 6. Escribo _____ una carta _____

Luis y _____ su hermano. 7. No comprendo siempre _____ profesores. 8. Pero

admiro mucho _____ profesor de español. 9. Voy _____ parque con Juan.

10. En casa estudio _____ los libros.

VII. Write the equivalent in a *complete Spanish sentence*, using the vocabulary given.

1. At nine we look at the clock. _____

   A las nueve miramos/reloj _____

2. We go to class and listen to the teacher. _____

   Vamos/clase/escuchamos/profesor _____

3. We have a friend there and we speak to Louis. _____

   Tenemos/amigo allí/hablamos/Luis _____

4. We listen to the answers and copy the words. _____

   Escuchamos/respuestas/copiamos/palabras _____

5. We study the lessons and we understand the teachers. _____

   Estudiamos/lecciones/comprendemos/profesores _____

VIII. Oral Proficiency. Respond orally to the situation described. (You may *later* write your responses for intensive practice.)

Situation: You are a tourist in a large Spanish-speaking city. Your guide has given you a free afternoon without him. You need some information about the city. The guide asks you:—*¿Qué quiere Vd. saber, señor (señorita)?*

Begin with *por favor.* In **five** Spanish questions ask your guide about the city. You may use your own ideas or ideas suggested by the following: *Does he know the city and the people well? Is it necessary to know Spanish in order to speak to the people? Does the subway go to the museums? Is there an entrance to the right or to the left? Is it possible to take photos there? What bus goes to the department stores? Is there a nice place to eat in the shopping center? In what district (section) does everybody live?*

Toda Una Vida Creando Hogar.

Crear Hogar. Día a día.

Haciendo de cada detalle algo importante.
De cada rincón un mundo de confort.
Disfrutando de ese ambiente que has creado
a tu imagen. Que es como tú. A veces clásico,
a veces radicalmente nuevo.

Y cerca de ti, El Corte Inglés. Ayudándote
a crear el marco adecuado.

Decorando tu entorno. Amueblando y vistiendo
tu espacio, para hacer de cada momento un
acontecimiento feliz.

Ahora y siempre. A través del tiempo.

• Financiación hasta 24 meses.
  Sin entrada.
• Proyectos y presupuestos
  gratuitos.
• Entrega a domicilio.
• Instalación a cargo
  de especialistas.

El Corte Inglés

CREAR HOGAR

¿De quién es éste?

Everyone looks forward to Christmas. But
sometimes we don't get the presents we expect.

¿De quién es este hueso?

Comedia en un acto

Escena: La sala de la familia Fandango. Es la mañana del Día de Navidad. Debajo del árbol de Navidad están los regalos para cada uno de la familia. Toda la familia está en la sala, lista para abrir los paquetes.

Personajes: El abuelo – un viejo de ochenta años

La abuela – una vieja de setenta años

El padre, Ambrosio – padre de la familia

La madre, Berta – madre de la familia

El hijo, Esteban – un joven de diez y seis años

La hija, Rosalía – una muchacha de trece años

El nene, Gualterio – un nene de nueve meses que sólo dice: – Gu, gu, ga, ga.

El perro, Capitán – perro norteamericano que no habla español

Rosalía: ¡Feliz Navidad a todos! ¿Podemos abrir los regalos ahora?

Todos: ¡Feliz Navidad! Sí, sí, sí.

Madre: Pero, Ambrosio, ¿qué pasa aquí? No veo las etiquetas con los nombres de las personas.

Padre: ¡Mira, Berta! El nene, Gualterio, tiene todas las etiquetas entre las manos.

Gualterio: Gu, gu, ga, ga.

Esteban: ¿Qué vamos a hacer? No sabemos para quién es cada regalo.

Abuela: Tengo una idea. Cada uno va a tomar un paquete sin saber para quién es.

Abuelo: Muy bien, y la persona que abra paquete va a usar el regalo por un día. Así tenemos una buena sorpresa hoy, y mañana vamos a cambiar los regalos.

Todos: ¡Buena idea! ¡Buena idea!

Gualterio: ¡Gu, gu, ga, ga!

Cada uno toma y abre un paquete.

Abuelo: ¡Ay, Dios mío! Tengo una falda blanca de lana.

Abuela: ¡Y yo un guante de béisbol!

Ambrosio: ¡Yo tengo una blusa roja de algodón!

Madre: ¿Y yo? ¿Qué hago con esta navaja?

Esteban: ¡Oh, no! ¡Una muñeca de México!

Rosalía: ¡Ay! ¡Un cuchillo de explorador!

Abuelo: Pero, aquí hay un regalo más. ¿De quién es? (Abre el paquete.) ¡Es un hueso!

Capitán: Guao, guao. (Esto significa: ¡Ese hueso es mío, tonto!)

Palabras Nuevas

SUBSTANTIVOS

Ambrosio *Ambrose*
el árbol *the tree*
Berta *Bertha*
la blusa *the blouse*
el cuchillo *the knife*
  el cuchillo de explorador
  the boy scout knife
la escena *the scene*
la etiqueta *the label*
la falda *the skirt*
la familia Fandango *the Fandango family*
el fandango *the disorder*
Gualterio *Walter*
el guante *the glove*
  el guante de béisbol *the baseball glove*
la hija *the daughter*
el hijo *the son*
el hueso *the bone*
la idea *the idea*

el joven *the young man, the youth*
la muñeca *the doll*
la navaja *the razor*
la Navidad *Christmas*
  el Día de Navidad *Christmas Day*
  ¡Feliz Navidad! *Merry Christmas*
el nombre *the name*
el paquete *the package*
el perro *the dog*
el personaje *the character (in a play)*
Rosalía *Rosalie*
la vieja *the old woman*
el viejo *the old man*

ADJETIVOS

blanco,a *white*
cada *each*
de algodón *(of) cotton*

de lana *(of) wool, woolen*
esa *that (fem.)*
ese *that (masc.)*
listo,a *ready*
mío,a *mine*
norteamericano,a *North American (from the U.S.A.)*
rojo,a *red*

VERBOS

cambiar *to change, to exchange*
significar *to mean*

OTRAS PALABRAS

¿de quién? *from whom?*
¡Dios mío! *My heavens!*
¿para quién? *for whom?*
por *for*
sólo *only*
toda la familia *the whole family*

EJERCICIOS

I. (A) Write the correct word(s) in place of the underlined expression to make the statement true.

1. Los <u>personajes</u> de la familia Fandango están debajo del árbol. _____

2. Los paquetes van a ser una sorpresa porque no tienen <u>regalos</u>. _____

3. Cada uno va a usar el regalo por <u>una semana</u>. _____

4. Mañana la familia va a <u>abrir</u> los regalos. _____

5. El perro, Capitán, recibe un <u>cuchillo de explorador</u>. _____

(B) Preguntas personales y generales. Write your answer in a complete Spanish sentence.

1. ¿Qué expresión usa Vd. el Día de Navidad?
2. ¿Cuál es un buen regalo para un abuelo? ¿Una blusa roja de algodón?
3. ¿Para quién es la muñeca de México?
4. ¿Cuál es un buen regalo para una madre? ¿Una falda blanca de lana?
5. ¿Qué quiere Vd. recibir esta Navidad? ¿Un hueso?

1. _____

2. _____

3. _____

4. _____

5. _____

II. Crucigrama

Horizontales	Verticales
1. Christmas	1. razors
6. to the (m.)	2. he sees
8. he goes	3. to give
9. baby	4. same as 6 horizontal
12. the (m. sing)	5. grandparents
14. I	7. he reads
15. surprises	10. dog
16. old	11. to go
17. there is	13. to him
	14. already

III. Match columns *A* and *B* to form complete sentences.

A	B
1. En la sala	a. todas las etiquetas con los nombres.
2. Todo el mundo está listo	b. cambiar los paquetes
3. El nene tiene	c. para abrir los paquetes
4. Mañana vamos a	d. está el arbol de Navidad
5. ¿Qué voy a hacer con	e. una falda de lana?

1. _____

2. _____

3. _____

4. _____

5. _____

IV. Compositions: Oral or written.

(A) Look at the picture at the beginning of this Work Unit. Describe the scene in Spanish to a friend.

(B) Tell about Christmas. Include the following:

La Navidad

1. What the weather is like when Christmas comes. 2. Where and how you spend the vacation. 3. To what store(s) you are going in order to buy gifts. 4. What gifts you are buying and for whom. 5. To whom you wish love and a Merry Christmas.

ESTRUCTURAS DE LA LENGUA

Uses of the Preposition *de*

A. **De** indicates the place *from*: origin; the topic *of* or *about*

Origin: from	Topic: of, about

1. **¿De dónde** son Vds.?
   Where are you from?

2. **Somos de** México.
   We are from Mexico.

1. **¿De qué** hablan Vds.?
   What are you speaking of (about)?

2. **Hablamos de** Nueva York.
   We are speaking of (about) New York.

B. **Del:** *from the; of the; about the.* **De** followed by **el** is always combined as **del.**

1. **Son del** sur.
   They are from the south.

2. No **son de los** Estados Unidos.
   They are not from the United States.

3. **Hablan de** la patria.
   They speak of their country.

4. Hablan **de las** casas y **de las** comidas.
   They speak of the houses and meals.

Rules:

1. Although **de** followed by **el** must combine to form **del**, the following never combine: **de los, de la, de las.**

2. The preposition **de** in a series of nouns must be repeated before each noun.

> Hablamos **del** chico y **de la** chica.
> We speak of the boy and girl.

C. **De** indicates the owner (possessor) in Spanish just as **'s** indicates the owner in English.

de	del, de la, de los, de las

1. **Es de** Juan. No es **de Ana.**
   It's John's. It isn't Anna's.

2. **Es de** mi hermano.
   It is my brother's.

3. No **es de** su hermana.
   It isn't your sister's.

4. **Es del** chico. No es **de la chica.**
   It's the boy's. It isn't the girl's.

5. **Es de los** chicos.
   It is the boys'.

6. No **es de las** chicas.
   It isn't the girls'.

Rules:

1. **De** *precedes* the owner where English adds **'s** to the owner.

2. **De** is used instead of **'s** (single owner) or **s'** (most plural owners).

3. **Del, de la, de los, de las** are used when *the* precedes the owner.

D. Ownership word order:

The "possession" — the person, place, or thing owned — stands *before* **de** and the owner, unlike English.

la **chaqueta del chico**
the boy's jacket

el **reloj de la chica**
the girl's watch

Single owner

Plural owners

1. ¿**De quién** es el reloj?
Whose (sing.) watch is it?
Whose is the watch?

1. ¿**De quiénes es** la casa?
Whose (pl.) house is it?
Whose is the house?

2. Es el **reloj de Juan.**
It is John's watch.

2. Es la **casa de los vecinos.**
It is the neighbors' house.

3. El **reloj de la profesora** es **nuevo.***
The teacher's watch is new.

3. La **casa de los vecinos** es **nueva.***
The neighbors' house is new.

Rules:

1. ¿**De quién?** ¿**De quiénes?** *whose?* are followed by the Spanish *verb*. ¿**De quiénes?** anticipates more than one owner.

*2. The adjective describes and *agrees with the thing owned; not with the owner.* See Chart D above, #3 **nuevo, nueva.**

E. **De** indicates material (composition).

1. ¿**De qué** es el reloj?
What is the watch made of?

1. ¿**De qué** son los abrigos?
What are the coats made of?

2. El reloj **es de plata.**
The watch is silver.

2. Los abrigos **son de lana** y **de algodón.**
The coats are woolen and cotton.

Rules:

1. **¿De qué?** begins each question that asks *what a thing is made of.*

2. **De** must precede each material. No article follows **de**.

3. The material does *not* agree with the noun it describes in gender or in number.

4. Learn these materials:

1. **de algodón**	cotton	5. **de oro**	gold(en)
2. **de hierro**	iron	6. **de piedra**	stone(y)
3. **de lana**	woolen	7. **de plata**	silver(y)
4. **de madera**	wooden	8. **de seda**	silk(en)

F. **De** in special expressions:

1. ¿Va Vd. a **la clase de historia**? Are you going to the history class?	2. No. Voy a hablar al **profesor de español.** No. I'm going to speak to the Spanish teacher.

Rule:

De *about* indicates that the class, the teacher, etc., deal with a subject or with an organized body of knowledge. No article follows **de** in this use.

STUDY THE RULES, EXAMPLES, AND MODELS BEFORE BEGINNING THE EXERCISES!

Exercises

I. Rewrite the sentence, substituting the words in parentheses for the *italicized* expression. Make all necessary changes.

Model: Los sombreros son de *mi hermano.*   The hats are my brother's.

(el hombre) Los sombreros son del hombre.   The hats are the man's.

Los sombreros son del hombre.

1. (el chico) _____

2. (la abuela) _____

3. (el abuelo) _____

4. (Juan)_____

5. (mi padre)_____

6. (los hermanos)_____

7. (María / Pedro)_____

8. (sus amigos)_____

9. (las primas)_____

10. (el hermano/la hermana)_____

II. Rewrite the sentence changing each *owner* to the *singular*. Make all other necessary changes.

Model: Los guantes son de los **nenes.**   The gloves are *the babies'.*
          Los guantes son **del nene.**   The gloves are *the baby's.*

1. Las casas son de los profesores. _____

2. Ella es la madre de las muchachas._____

3. Somos los profesores de los chicos. _____

4. Es el padre de las alumnas._____

5. Es la clase de los alumnos de español._____

III. Write an affirmative answer in a complete Spanish sentence, using the words in parentheses.

Model: a. —¿De quién es el lápiz?   b. —¿De quiénes son los zapatos?
          Whose pencil is it?   Whose are the shoes?

(el chico) **—Es el lápiz del chico.**   (los chicos) **—Son los zapatos de los chicos.**
         It's the boy's pencil.   They are the boys' shoes.

1. ¿De quién es el libro? (la prima) _____

2. ¿De quiénes son las flores? (los muchachos) _____

3. ¿De quién son los cuadernos? (el chico) _____

4. ¿De quiénes es la casa? (mis padres) _____

5. ¿De quién es ella la madre? (el primo) _____

6. ¿De quiénes son ellas las primas? (Juan/Luisa) _____

7. ¿De quién son los papeles? (el hombre) _____

8. ¿De quiénes es la muñeca? (las hermanas) _____

9. ¿De quiénes es el regalo? (los chicos) _____

10. ¿De quién son las bicicletas? (el muchacho) _____

IV. Write an affirmative answer in a complete Spanish sentence, using the words in parentheses.

Model: —¿De qué es su sombrero?   (lana) — Mi sombrero es **de lana.**
            What is your hat made of?   My hat is *woolen.*

1. ¿De dónde es Vd.? (los Estados Unidos) _____

2. ¿En qué clase está Vd.? (historia) _____

3. ¿De qué es su casa? (piedra) _____

4. ¿De qué son las cortinas? (algodón) _____

5. ¿De dónde es su abuelo? (el otro país) _____

6. ¿De qué es su reloj? (plata/oro) _____

7. ¿De qué habla su hermanito? (el parque) _____

8. ¿A qué clase va su hermanita? (inglés) _____

9. ¿De qué son su blusa y su falda? (lana/seda) _____

10. ¿Qué profesora enseña aquí? (español) _____

V. Complete with the appropriate form: **de, del, de la, de los, de las**.

¿_____ quién es el mapa? Es _____ mis compañeros de clase. ¿Son los libros
      1   2

_____ chico? No. Son _____ chica. ¿Usa el profesor el lápiz _____ María?
      3   4   5

No. Usa el lápiz _____ alumno. ¿Mira los cuadernos _____ alumnos? No. Mira
                         6   7

los cuadernos _____ alumnas. ¿Está Vd. en la clase _____ español? No. Estoy
                      8   9

con el profesor _____ inglés. ¿_____ qué es su reloj? Es _____ plata.
                            10   11   12

No es _____ oro. ¿Son _____ madera las escuelas? No. Son _____ piedra.
             13   14   15

¿_____ dónde es Vd.? No soy _____Cuba. Soy _____ país _____ mis
    16   17   18   19

padres. Somos _____ Estados Unidos.
                    20

VI. Complete each sentence in Spanish. Use the vocabulary given below the line.

1. Where is your father's car? ¿Dónde está_____
                                         /coche/padre

2. It is near the girl's house. Está cerca de_____
                                         /casa/chica

3. She's in my history class. Ella está en_____
                                        mi clase/historia

4. What is her blouse made of? ¿_____
                                         /qué es/blusa

5. It's made of cotton and silk. Es_____
                                         /algodón/seda

6. Whose magazine is it?_____
                                         /quién es/revista

7. It is the boy's magazine. Es_____
                                         /revista/chico

8. I don't read Robert's magazines. No leo_____
                                         /revistas/Roberto

9. I look for the children's notebook. Busco_____
                                         /cuaderno/niños

10. I'm speaking about them to my Spanish teacher. Hablo de ellos a_____
                                         mi profesora/español

VII. Oral Proficiency. Respond orally to the situation described. (You may *later* write your responses.)

Situation: I am your friend. I live in Mexico. My family sent the members of your family gift packages, but we forgot to label the gifts. You call me long distance to determine *for whom* and *from whom* each gift is. I answer with:—*Hola, ¿quién habla?*

Greet me and tell me who you are. In **four** Spanish questions and statements explain what you need to know, naming each gift. You may use your own ideas or ideas suggested by the following: *necesitamos saber, ¿para quién?, ¿de quién?, ¿es para?, ¿es de?*

Cuando la profesora habla, Virgilio siempre
lee algo debajo del pupitre.

*Let's play "Who am I?" In Spanish it's not
that easy.*

¿Quién soy yo?

Virgilio Chupadedos es un alumno que no presta atención y no aprende mucho. Cuando la profesora habla, Virgilio siempre lee su libro de adivinanzas que él tiene abierto debajo del pupitre. Virgilio tiene un talento para las adivinanzas y sabe muchas.

Aquí tiene Vd. unas adivinanzas que Virgilio lee en su libro. Las respuestas están al pie de la página.

1. Soy un hombre o una mujer. Siempre hago preguntas. Soy amigo de los alumnos aplicados. Generalmente soy inteligente. ¿Quién soy yo?

2. Estoy en todos los edificios. Soy de madera o de otros materiales. Soy útil para entrar y salir. ¿Qué soy yo?

3. Tengo mucha información y muchas frases. Estoy en las casas, en las bibliotecas y en las escuelas. Soy de papel. ¿Qué soy yo?

4. Yo no soy muy grande. Soy negro, amarillo, azul, y de otros colores también. Soy útil para escribir en los cuadernos. ¿Qué soy yo?

5. Yo soy una parte de todas las personas. Tengo muchos usos: hablo, como, bebo. Tengo labios y dientes. ¿Qué soy yo?

6. Soy de madera. Estoy en todas las salas de clase. Hay uno para cada alumno. Los alumnos me usan para poner sus libros y para poner su papel para escribir. ¿Qué soy yo?

7. Yo soy muy grande. Estoy delante de la clase. El profesor escribe en mí. Así los alumnos pueden leer las frases importantes de la lección. ¿Qué soy yo?

8. Soy un animal. Soy grande o soy pequeño. Soy de varios colores. Dicen que soy el mejor amigo del hombre. No soy amigo de los gatos. ¿Qué soy yo?

9. Soy un edificio. Tengo varios cuartos. Los alumnos entran para aprender. Aquí todo el mundo trabaja y aprende. ¿Qué soy yo?

10. Soy para abrir y cerrar. Estoy en todos los cuartos. Soy necesaria para el aire y la luz. Soy de vidrio. ¿Qué soy yo?

11. Soy de un país grande donde hablamos inglés y aprendemos mucho español. ¿Quién soy yo?

1. el profesor o la profesora	4. la pluma, el lápiz	8. el perro
2. la puerta	5. la boca	9. la escuela
3. el libro	6. el pupitre	10. la ventana
	7. la pizarra	11. el norteamericano

I. STRUCTURES AND VERBS

Palabras Nuevas

SUBSTANTIVOS

la adivinanza   *the riddle*
la boca   *the mouth*
el color   *the color*
el diente   *the tooth*
el gato   *the cat*
la información   *the information*
el labio   *the lip*
el material   *the material*
la página   *the page*
la parte   *the part*
la pizarra   *the blackboard*
la pluma   *the pen*
el pupitre   *the (student's) desk*
la respuesta   *the answer*

la sala de clase   *the classroom*
el talento   *the talent*
la ventana   *the window*

ADJETIVOS

abierto,a   *open*
amarillo,a   *yellow*
azul   *blue*
mejor   *better*
  el mejor   *the best*
negro,a   *black*
útil   *useful*

VERBOS

chupar los dedos   *to be a simpleton*

prestar atención   *to pay attention*
pueden   *they can; you (formal pl.) can*
soy   *I am*

OTRAS PALABRAS

al pie de   *at the bottom of*
de madera   *wooden, of wood*
de papel   *of paper*
de vidrio   *of glass*
en mí   *on me*
generalmente   *generally*
me   *me*
que   *which, that*

EJERCICIOS

I. Preguntas. Write your answer in a complete Spanish sentence.

1. ¿A quién no presta atención Virgilio?
2. ¿Qué lee debajo del pupitre?
3. ¿Qué deja entrar aire en la clase? ¿De qué es?
4. ¿Qué usa Vd. para escribir en la pizarra? ¿En el cuaderno?
5. ¿Para qué es útil una puerta? ¿De qué es?

1. _____
2. _____
3. _____
4. _____
5. _____

II. Acróstico español

1. pupil
2. tooth
3. intelligent
4. window
5. information
6. black
7. attention
8. North American
9. blackboard
10. to open

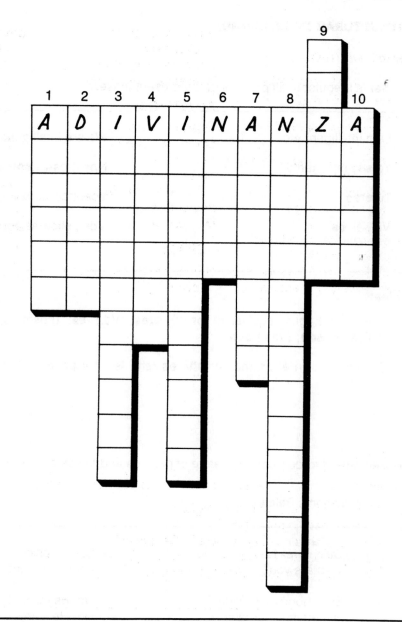

	1	2	3	4	5	6	7	8	9	10
	A	D	I	V	I	N	A	N	Z	A

III. Compositions: Oral or written.

(A) Look at the picture at the beginning of this Work Unit. Describe the scene in Spanish to a friend.

(B) Tell about a class in which you pay little attention. Include the following:

Una clase

1. In which class you pay little attention. 2. Why you pay little attention. 3. What you do in the class. 4. Why it is useful to study and to pay attention. 5. When you are going to study and to listen.

ESTRUCTURAS DE LA LENGUA

Ser *to be*

A. **Ser** is irregular in all persons of the present tense.

I am intelligent etc.	We are intelligent etc.
Yo **soy** inteligente.	Nosotros-as **somos** inteligentes.
Tú **eres**	Vosotros-as **sois**
Vd., él, **es** ella	Vds., ellos-as **son**

Rules:

1. *Are* is the English equivalent for (tú) **eres**; (Vd.) **es**; (nosotros) **somos**; (vosotros) **sois**; (ellos-as) **son**; (Vds.) **son**.

2. **Es** means *is* in **él es** (he Is); **ella es** (she Is); but **es** means *are* In **Vd. es** (you are).

B. Ser is used to describe the *nature of* persons and things as in A above. Other uses follow.

1. Identifications. Relationships.

a.	— ¿Quién eres tú? Who are you?	— Soy un chico norteamericano. I am an American boy.
b.	— ¿Es el hombre tu padre? Is the man your father?	— No. Es mi tío. Sus hijos son mis primos. No. He is my uncle. His children are my cousins.

2. *Profession.

a.	— ¿Qué es tu padre? What is your father?	— Es piloto. He is a pilot.
b.	— ¿Qué deseas ser? What do you want to be?	— Yo deseo ser actor. I want to be an actor.
c.	— ¿Es tu padre **un buen** piloto? Is your father a good pilot?	— Es **un** piloto **excelente.** He is an excellent pilot.

*Omit the articles *un* and *una* when describing profession. Use *un* or *una* only when the profession is accompanied by an adjective.

3. Origin and *nationality.

---

a. – ¿De dónde es tu amigo?
    Where is your friend from?

    – Es de Puerto Rico; es puertorriqueño.
    He is from Puerto Rico; he is (a) Puerto
    Rican.

b. – ¿Eres tú español?
    Are you a Spaniard?

    – Soy **un** español **sincero.**
    I am a sincere Spaniard.

---

*Omit the articles *un* and *una* when describing nationality. Use **un** or **una** only when the nationality is accompanied by an adjective.

4. Personality, nature, and characteristics.

—¿ Cómo son Vds.?

What are you like?

—Somos buenos, alegres, amables y
    generosos.
We are good, cheerful, kind and
    generous.

---

5. Characteristic appearance.

---

a. —¿ Cómo es su amigo?
    What is your friend like?

    —Es alto, moreno y guapo.
    He is tall, dark and handsome.

b. —¿ De qué color son sus ojos?
    What color are his eyes?

    —Sus ojos son negros.
    His eyes are black.

---

6. Possession and material.

---

a. —¿ De quién es ese reloj?
    Whose watch is that?

    —Es mi reloj. No es de María.
    It is my watch. It isn't Mary's.

b. —¿ De qué es su reloj?
    What is your watch made of?

    —Es de oro y de plata. No es de madera.
    It's (of) gold and silver. It isn't wooden.

---

7. Date and time.

---

a. —¿ Qué día es?
    What day is it?

    —Hoy es martes el dos de mayo.
    Today is Tuesday, May 2nd.

b. —¿ Qué hora es?
    What time is it?

    —Son las dos. No es la una.
    It is two o'clock. It isn't one o'clock.

STUDY THE RULES, EXAMPLES, AND MODELS BEFORE BEGINNING THE EXERCISES!

Exercises

I. Rewrite the sentence, substituting the new subject in *italics* and giving the correct form of the verb.

Model: **Yo soy** de los Estados Unidos.   **El muchacho es de los Estados Unidos.**
I am from the United States.   The boy is from the United States.
(El muchacho)

1. *La chica*_____

2. *Yo*_____

3. *Tú*_____

4. *Vd.*_____

5. *Ella*_____

6. *Roberto*_____

7. *Nosotros*_____

8. *Tú y yo*_____

9. *Vds.*_____

10. *Eduardo y Pablo*_____

¿ Es alto el chico?

II. Rewrite the sentence in the *singular* using the subject given in parentheses. Make all necessary changes.

Model: ¿Son altos los chicos?   (el chico) ¿**Es alto el chico**?
        Are the boys tall?   Is the boy tall?

1. Nosotros somos bonitos. (yo)_____

2. Vds. son actores. (Vd.)_____

3. Vds. son unos chicos aplicados. (tú)_____

4 ¿Son los relojes de oro? (el reloj)_____

5. Ellos no son de San Juan. (él)_____

III. Rewrite the sentence in the *plural* using the subject given in parentheses. Make all necessary changes for agreement.

1. Ella es cubana. (ellas)_____

2. ¿Es la una? (las dos)_____

3. ¿Es sábado el día? (sábado y domingo)_____

4. Yo no soy de España. (Juan y yo)_____

5. Vd. es mi primo. (Vd. y Luis)_____

IV. a. Write a factual answer in a complete Spanish sentence. **b.** Write a factual answer to the *second* question, adding **también.**

Model: a.—¿Eres de aquí o de Rusia?   Are you from here or from Russia?
        — **Soy de aquí.**   I am from here.
        b.—¿*Y tu padre?*   And your father?
        — **Mi padre es de aquí también.**   My father is from here, too.

1a. ¿Es Vd. de los Estados Unidos o de Oz?_____

b. ¿*Y el chico?*_____

2a. ¿Son Vds. americanos o españoles?_____

b. ¿*Y ellos?*_____

3a. ¿Somos tú y yo personas o cosas?_____

b. ¿*Y los hermanos?*_____

4a. ¿Eres profesor-a o alumno-a?_____

b. ¿*Y la chica?*_____

5a. ¿Somos yo y el Sr. Delibes maestros o alumnos?_____

_____ b. ¿*Y la señora?*_____

V. Write a complete Spanish sentence using all the cue words provided. Supply the appropriate form of SER in each sentence.

Model: _____
    Hoy / sábado (Today / Saturday)

Hoy es sábado. _____
(Today is Saturday.)

1. _____
    Hoy no / domingo.

2. _____
    Los días / largos.

3. _____
    Juan y María / inteligentes.

4. ¿_____?
    ¿ / yo inteligente?

5. ¿_____?
    ¿Por qué no / nosotros aplicados?

6. _____
    La chica / de los Estados Unidos.

7. _____
    Vd. / mi amigo.

8. _____
    Vds. / generosos.

9. ¿_____?
    ¿De qué color / los libros?

10. _____
    No / la una.

11. ¿_____?
    ¿Quién / tú?

12. _____
    Ellos / franceses.

13. ¿_____?
    ¿De quién / las casas?

14. ¿_____?
    ¿No / altos tú y yo?

15. ¿_____?
    ¿De qué / su sombrero?

VI. Write an affirmative answer in a complete Spanish sentence using the cue words given in italics.

Model: —¿Qué eres?
        What are you?

español —**Soy español.**
          I am Spanish.

1. ¿Quién eres tú? *alumno-a*_____

2. ¿Eres norteamericano-a? *sí*_____

3. ¿De qué color son sus ojos? *negros*_____

4. ¿Cómo eres? *inteligente y hermoso-a*_____

5. ¿De dónde son sus padres? *los Estados Unidos*_____

6. ¿Qué es su padre? *capitán* _____

7. ¿De qué color es su casa? *azul*_____

8. ¿De quién son Juan y tú alumnos? *del Sr. López*_____

9. ¿De qué son su mesa y su silla? *de madera*_____

10. ¿Qué deseas ser? *profesor-a* _____

VII. Oral Proficiency. Respond orally to the situation described. (You may *later* write your responses for intensive practice.)

Situation: You and your friends are playing riddle games. It is your turn to invent a riddle. Your friends say:—*Y ahora tú.*

In **five** Spanish statements lead your friends to the answer *un alumno estudioso.* You may use your own ideas or ideas suggested by the following: *yo soy, tengo, asisto, voy, traigo, hago.*

117

¡Mamá, estoy mejor!

*It's no fun to be stuck in bed all day. Would
you prefer that to going to school?*

Una enfermedad imaginaria

Hoy Ramón Tramposo no va a la escuela. Dice que es imposible bajar de la cama porque está enfermo. Su madre está muy triste y preocupada por la salud de su hijo. Cuando llega el Doctor Humberto Matasanos, la madre va con el médico al cuarto de Ramón. El muchacho está sentado en la cama. Todas las ventanas están cerradas.

Médico: ¡Ah! Aquí está el enfermo. ¿Qué tiene el chico?

Madre: Oh, doctor, mi hijo no quiere comer. No quiere beber. Sólo quiere guardar cama todo el día.

Ramón: Ay, ay, ay. Estoy enfermo. Tengo dolor de cabeza, dolor de estómago, dolor de garganta. Es horrible.

Madre: ¡Ay, mi pobre Ramoncito!

Médico: Bueno, bueno joven. (El médico lo examina al chico.) Mmmmm. . . .El pulso está normal. Ramón, ¡abre la boca y saca la lengua!

Ramón: Aaaaaaaaah.

Madre: Mi pobre hijo. ¡Cómo sufre!

Médico: Yo no veo nada. La temperatura está normal. No tiene fiebre.

Ramón: Ay, tengo tanto dolor. Es terrible.

En ese momento suena el teléfono. Es Enrique, el amigo de Ramón.

Ramón: Hola, Enrique. ¿Qué hay?. . . . . . .¿Cómo?. . . .¿No hay examen de matemáticas? (Ramón salta de la cama.) ¡Mamá, mamá, estoy mejor! ¡Quiero comer! ¡Tengo hambre, mucha hambre!

Palabras Nuevas

SUBSTANTIVOS

la cabeza   *the head*
la cama   the bed
el chico   *the boy*
la clase de matemáticas   *the mathematics class*
el Doctor Humberto Matasanos   *Dr. Humbert Quack*
el dolor   *the pain, the ache*
   el dolor de cabeza   *the headache*
   el dolor de estómago   *the stomachache*
   el dolor de garganta   *the sore throat*
la enfermedad   *the sickness*
el enfermo   *the patient, the sick person*
Enrique   *Henry*
la fiebre   *the fever*

el hambre (fem.)   *the hunger*
la lengua   *the tongue*
el médico   *the doctor*
el pulso   *the pulse*
Ramón   *Raymond*
   Ramoncito   *little Ray*
la salud   *the health*
el teléfono   *the telephone*
la temperatura   *the temperature*

ADJETIVOS

cerrado,a   *closed*
imaginario,a   *imaginary*
imposible   *impossible*
normal   *normal*
preocupado,a por   *worried about*
sentado,a   *seated*
terrible   *terrible*
tramposo,a   *tricky*

VERBOS

bajar de   *to get off*
guardar cama   *to stay in bed*
puede(s)   *you can*
sacar   *to stick out, to take out*
saltar   *to jump*
suena   *it rings*
sufrir   *to suffer*
tener hambre   *to be hungry*

OTRAS PALABRAS

¿Cómo?   *What do you mean?*
nada   *nothing*
porque   *because*
¿Qué hay?   *What's up? What's new? What's the matter?*
¿Qué tiene el chico?   *What is the matter with the boy?*
sólo   *only*
todo el día   *the whole day*

119

EJERCICIOS

I. (A) Preguntas. Write your answer in a complete Spanish sentence.

1. ¿Por qué no sale Ramón?
2. ¿Cómo está su madre?
3. ¿Dónde está sentado el muchacho cuando entra el médico?
4. ¿Qué dolor tiene Ramón?
5. ¿Por qué salta de la cama y desea comer?

1. _____

2. _____

3. _____

4. _____

5. _____

(B) Preguntas personales y generales. Write your answer in a complete Spanish sentence.

1. ¿Quién está preocupado por su salud?
2. ¿Cuándo guarda Vd. cama?
3. ¿Qué dice Vd. cuando saca la lengua?
4. ¿En qué clase sufre Vd. mucho?
5. ¿Qué toma Vd. cuando tiene mucha hambre?

1. _____

2. _____

3. _____

4. _____

5. _____

II. Unscramble the sentences in the boxes.

1.
su	y	triste
está	preocupada	madre

2.
hambre	comer	tengo
quiero	estoy	mejor

3.
mi	como	hijo
ay	pobre	sufre

4.
suena	teléfono	en
ese	momento	el

1. _____

2. _____

3. _____

4. _____

III. Compositions: Oral or written.

(A) Look at the picture at the beginning of this Work Unit. Describe the scene in Spanish to a friend.

(B) Complete the dialogue about a visit from your doctor, and act it out with another student:

Una visita del médico

1. Médico: ¿Qué tiene Vd.?

   Vd.: _____
   (Say that you have a headache.)

2. Médico: ¿Tiene Vd. otro dolor?

   Vd.: _____
   (Say that you have a fever, too.)

3. Médico: Vd. debe guardar cama y no debe comer hoy.

   Vd.: _____
   (Say that that is terrible.)

4. Médico: ¿Tiene Vd. apetito?

   Vd.: _____
   (Say that you want to eat.)

5. Médico: Mañana su mamá le da una hamburguesa.

   Vd.: _____
   (Say that you are better NOW!)

ESTRUCTURAS DE LA LENGUA

Estar *to be;* Contrasting Uses of **Estar** and **Ser.**

A. Forms of **estar**—used in greetings—contrasted with forms of **ser.**

Estar *to be*	**Ser** *to be*
¿Cómo **está** Vd.? How are you?	¿Cómo **es** Vd.? What are you like?
Yo **estoy** bien. I am well.	Yo **soy** bueno. I am good.
Tú **estás**	Tú **eres** . . . .

Vd., él **está** . . . .
    ella
	Vd., él **es** . . . .
	    ella

Nosotros-as **estamos** . . . . We are well.	Nosotros-as **somos** buenos. We are good.
Vosotros-as **estáis**	Vosotros-as **sois** . . . .
Vds., ellos-as **están**	Vds., ellos-as **son** . . . .

Rules:

1. **Estar** is used for greetings. For the uses of **ser** see Work Unit 11.

2. **Estar** is irregular in four verb forms: **estoy, estás, está, están.** An accent mark is written on each **a** except **estamos.**

3. **Está** means *is* in the following: **él está** (he is); **ella está** (she is); but **está** means *are* in **Vd. está** (you are).

B. Estar *to be* is also used to describe 1) location, 2) health, 3) mood, and 4) results of actions.

1. Location: with **¿dónde?** *where*; **aquí** *here*; **allí** *there*; **en** *on, in*; **ausente** *absent*; **presente** *present.*

—¿Dónde está Juan?   —Juan está aquí en casa; no está en la escuela.
Where is John?   John is here at home; he is not in school.

---

2. State of health: with **bien, bueno**—*well*; **enfermo, *mal, malo**—*sick.*

—¿Cómo está Juan, bien o enfermo?   —Está bien (bueno); no está enfermo (*malo)
How is John, well or ill?   He is well; he is not sick.

---

*Mal *is preferred to indicate "sick" in several Hispanic countries.*

3. Mood: with **contento, alegre**—*happy,* *cheerful*; **triste**—*sad.*

—¿Está él contento o triste?   —Está muy alegre hoy.
Is he happy or sad?   He is very cheerful today.

---

4. Results of actions: with **abierto-a** *open*, **cansado-a** *tired*, **cerrado-a** *closed*, **descansado-a** *rested*, **ocupado-a** *busy*, **sentado-a** *seated.*

---

1. —¿Está sentado?   —Sí. Está cansado y ocupado en leer.
   Is he seated?   Yes. He is tired and busy reading.

2. —¿Está cerrado su libro?   —No. Su libro está abierto.
   Is his book closed?   No. His book is open.

C. Agreement:

Only the adjectives which end in **o** change **o** to **a** when they describe a feminine noun. Adjectives ending in **o, a** or **e** add **s** when describing plural nouns.

---

1. Juan está content**o** pero María no está content**a**.
   John is happy but Mary is not happy.

2. El está alegr**e** pero ella está trist**e**.
   He is cheerful but she is sad.

3. Están present**es** y sentad**os**.
   They are present and seated.

D. Review: Contrasted uses of **ESTAR**—*to be;* **SER**—*to be* [Work Unit 11].

---

1. Juan **está en** Puerto Rico.
   John is in Puerto Rico.
   Location

   Juan **es de** Puerto Rico.
   John is from Puerto Rico.
   Place of origin

2. Juan **está bueno** (*or* **bien**).
   John is well.
   Health
   Juan **está malo** (**mal** *or* **enfermo**).
   John is sick (*or* ill).

   Juan **es bueno.**
   John is good (a good person).
   Character (or identification)
   Juan **es malo.**
   John is bad (a bad person).

3. Juan **está alegre** (*or* **contento**).
   John is cheerful (*or* happy).
   Mood

   Juan **es alegre. Es feliz.**
   John is jolly. He is a happy person.
   Personality type (identification)

4. El **está sentado** y **está cansado.**
   He is seated and he is tired.
   Results of actions

   El **es alto** y **joven.**
   He is tall and young.
   Characteristic appearance
   Other uses: See lesson 7, Part Two.

STUDY THE RULES, EXAMPLES, AND MODELS BEFORE BEGINNING THE EXERCISES!

I. Rewrite the sentence substituting the new subject and giving the appropriate form of the verb.

Model: (ellos) **Ellos están muy bien hoy.**   (Vd.) **Vd. está muy bien hoy.**
             They are very well today.   You are very well today.

1. (Yo)_____

2. (María)_____

3. (El chico)_____

4. (Tú)_____

5. (Vd.)_____

6. (Nosotros)_____

7. (Los chicos)_____

8. (Ellas)_____

9. (Juan y Pedro)_____

10. (Tú y yo)_____

II. Rewrite the sentence, substituting the cue words in parentheses for the expression in *italics*. Make the necessary changes in the verb and the adjective.

> Model: *El libro* está abierto.   (las revistas) **Las revistas están abiertas.**
>   The book is open.   The magazines are open.

1. *Los libros* están abiertos. (la puerta)

_____

2. *Las niñas* están tristes. (el profesor)

_____

3. *Manuela* está contenta hoy. (Felipe y Pedro)

_____

4. *Mi primo* está sentado. (Elisa y su prima)

_____

5. *Yo no estoy ausente.* (Tú y yo)

_____

III. Write a factual answer in *two* complete sentences according to the model. Give the NEGATIVE sentence *first*.

> Model: —¿Está Vd. en <u>América</u> o en   Are you in America or in Europe?
>   <u>Europa</u>?
>   —**No estoy en Europa. Estoy en**   I'm not in Europe. I'm in America.
>   **América.**

1. *¿Está Vd. en la <u>tierra</u> o en <u>otro planeta</u>?*_____

_____

2. ¿Estás <u>triste</u> o <u>alegre</u> cuando recibes dinero?_____

_____

3. ¿Están tú y los amigos ausentes o presentes en la clase los sábados?_____

_____

4. ¿Están los alumnos sentados o de pie cuando escriben en los cuadernos?_____

_____

5. ¿Están las escuelas abiertas o cerradas los domingos?_____

_____

6. ¿Están los profesores ocupados o sentados todo el día?_____

_____

7. ¿Está la gente en el hospital enferma o bien?_____

_____

8. ¿Está la gente allí cansada o descansada al fin del día?_____

_____

9. ¿Estás contenta o triste en el hospital?_____

_____

10. ¿Deseas estar en casa o en el hospital?_____

_____

IV. Write an answer in a complete Spanish sentence. Use the cue words in *italics*.

1. ¿Cómo estás? *bien*_____

2. ¿Por qué estás sentado-a? *porque escribo*_____

_____

3. ¿Dónde estoy yo ahora? *en la calle*_____

4. ¿Cuándo están abiertas las tiendas? *los sábados*_____

_____

5. ¿Están tú y los amigos alegres los sábados? *sí*_____

_____

V. Write a complete Spanish sentence using the word cues provided. Supply the appropriate form of **estar** or **ser**. (Review **ser** in this unit and in Unit 11.)

    Model: Los niños/bien.   Los niños están bien.   The children are well.

1. Los niños/sentados_____

2. Mi madre/mexicana_____

3. Nosotros/inteligentes_____

4. Yo/médico_____

5. No es la una. Ahora/las tres_____

6. Las mesas/de madera_____

7. Hoy/el primero de junio_____

8. La casa/de mi abuela_____

9. Tú y yo/en San Francisco_____

10. Tú/de Chicago_____

11. La escuela/abierta_____

12. Yo/aquí_____

13. ¿/tú cansada?_____

14. Juana/enferma_____

15. Los alumnos/ausentes_____

VI. Oral Proficiency. Respond orally to the situation described. (You may *later* write your responses for intensive practice.)

Situation: Your friend is sick. You have not seen him or her for two days. You telephone to find out how he or she is, and to socialize. Your friend asks:—*¿Por qué estás muy preocupado(a)?*

State that you are worried. In **four** Spanish questions try to obtain information about your friend's state of health. You may use your own ideas or ideas suggested by the following: *what ails him/her, whether he/she has to stay in bed and in the house many more days, when he/she is going to be better; is he/she tired or busy.*

RESTAURANTE
LA HABANA

RESTAURANTE HISPANO-AMERICANO

Menú

Aperitivos/Sopas

Sardinas en Aceite con Huevos	2.75
Entremés Variado	2.75
Coctel de Camarones	2.25
Jugo de Naranja . . . . .50 y	.70
Coctel de Langosta	3.95

Sopa de Cebollas	.75
Fabada Asturiana	1.50
Potaje de Chícharos y Lentejas . . .	1.50

Aves

Medio Pollo a la Cubana	3.95
Medio Pollo a la Parrilla	3.95
Pollo Fricasé	3.95
Pollo en Cacerola	3.95
Chicharrón de Pollo	3.95
Asopao de Pollo	3.75

Mariscos

Pescado en Escabeche	3.75
Filete de Pescado	3.75
Filete de Pescado Empanizado	3.75
Rueda de Serrucho Frita	3.75
Bacalao a la Vizcaína	3.95
Camarones Enchilados	4.75
Langosta a la Catalana	6.95
Camarones Rebozados Fritos	4.75
Langosta Enchilada	6.95
Calamares en su Tinta con Arroz . .	2.75

Carnes y Asados

Hígado a la Italiana	2.95
Bistec de Palomilla	4.85
Filete Mignon	7.25
Chuletas de Puerco	4.75
Bistec Empanizado	4.75
Bistec de Jamón, Habanera	3.90
Bistec de Hígado	2.95
Lechón y Moros, Vier., Sáb. y Dom.	5.50
Boliche Mechado	4.25

Bebidas

Café Expreso	.30
Café Americano	.25
Café con Leche	.40
Té	.25
Malta Hatuey	.60
Sodas Variadas	.40

Postres

Flan de Calabaza	.80
Pudín Diplomático	.80
Pudín de Pan	.80
Flan de Huevos	.80
Tocino del Cielo	.90
Coco Rallado con Queso	.85
Casco de Guayaba con Queso	.85
Casco de Naranja con Queso	.85
Fruta Bomba con Queso	.85
Helados Varíados	.70

*Estoy enamorado de una
chica alta y flaca.*

Every newspaper has an advice to the lovelorn
column. What would you advise this
heartbroken young man?

El consultorio sentimental

¿Tiene Vd. un problema romántico? Gertrudis ayuda a muchas personas, y puede ayudarlo a Vd. Si Vd. le escribe su problema al consultorio de Gertrudis, Gertrudis le responde con una solución.

Querida Gertrudis,
Quiero a una muchacha alta y delgada. Es una muchacha española muy interesante y simpática. Tiene el pelo negro y los ojos verdes. Es una chica alegre y yo quiero salir con ella. Tengo un coche nuevo y soy muy generoso y trabajador. Pero ella dice que no quiere salir conmigo porque soy bajito y muy gordo. Además, dice que tengo mucho pelo como un mono. Pero yo no deseo ir a la barbería. ¿Qué voy a hacer? No puedo dormir. No puedo comer. Necesito su ayuda.

Desesperado

Querido "Desesperado,"
La solución no es difícil. Es muy fácil. Vd. dice que no tiene apetito y que no come. Bueno. Así, tarde o temprano Vd. va a estar tan flaco como ella. Luego, si Vd. lleva un sombrero alto, Vd. puede parecer alto, y además, va a cubrir todo su pelo.

Buena suerte.

Gertrudis

Palabras Nuevas

SUBSTANTIVOS

el apetito   *the appetite*
la ayuda   *the aid, the help*
la barbería   *the barbershop*
el consultorio   *the clinic*
  el consultorio sentimental
  advice to the lovelorn
Gertrudis   *Gertrude*
el mono   *the monkey*
el ojo   *the eye*
el pelo   *the hair*
el problema   *the problem*
la solución   *the solution*
el sombrero   *the hat*
la suerte   *the luck*
  ¡Buena suerte!   *Good luck!*

ADJETIVOS

alegre   *lively, happy, cheerful*
alto,a   *tall*

bajo,a   *short*
  bajito,a   *quite short*
delgado,a   *slender*
desesperado,a   *desperate*
difícil   *difficult*
español,a   *Spanish*
flaco,a   *skinny, thin*
generoso,a   *generous*
gordo,a   *fat*
querido,a   *dear*
romántico,a   *romantic*
simpático,a   *nice, pleasant*
  (persons)
su   *your*
trabajador,a   *hard-working*
verde   *green*

VERBOS

cubrir   *to cover*
dormir   *to sleep*

estar   *to be (health, location)*
llevar   *to wear*
parecer   *to seem*
puede   *he (she) can, is able*
  to, you (formal sing.) can,
  are able to
puedo   *I can, am able*
querer a   *to love*
responder   *to answer*

OTRAS PALABRAS

además   *besides*
conmigo   *with me*
le   *(indirect object of verb)*
  you, to you
luego   *then*
tan...como   *as...as*
tarde o temprano   *sooner or*
  later

129

EJERCICIOS

I. Preguntas. Write your answer in a complete Spanish sentence.

1. ¿Cómo es la chica española?
2. ¿Cómo es el "querido desesperado"?
3. ¿Para qué va a llevar un sombrero alto?
4. Si él no come ¿cómo va a estar?
5. ¿Cómo es la persona a quien Vd. quiere mucho?

1. _____
2. _____
3. _____
4. _____
5. _____

II. Word Hunt — Find the following words in Spanish.

1. dear
2. skinny
3. tall
4. fat
5. eyes
6. besides
7. hair
8. monkey
9. barber shop
10. to eat
11. all
12. a *(m.)*
13. your *(pl.)*
14. (he) says
15. if

Q	U	E	R	I	D	O	F
G	C	O	M	E	R	J	L
O	D	S	T	E	P	O	A
R	I	U	O	S	E	S	C
D	C	S	D	A	L	T	O
O	E	M	O	N	O	U	N
A	D	E	M	A	S	S	I
B	A	R	B	E	R	I	A

III. Construct sentences, using the 3 words given. You may change the form of the verb as needed.

1. estar   enamorado   chica _____
2. tener   pelo   ojos _____
3. decir   querer   salir _____
4. desear   ir   barbería _____
5. tener   apetito   comer _____

IV. **Compositions:** Oral or written.

(A) Look at the picture at the beginning of this Work Unit. Describe the scene in Spanish to a friend.

(B) Tell how you feel about a person you love. Include the following:

Mi amor

1. Who this person is.   2. Why you love him or her (appearance, character and personality traits).   3. Whether you eat more or less now.   4. Describe yourself.   5. When you want to speak to this person about a date and what you are going to say.

ESTRUCTURAS DE LA LENGUA

Descriptive Adjectives and Limiting Adjectives.

A. *Descriptive adjectives* generally *follow* the person, or thing described, *unlike* English.

Limiting adjectives tell *how many*; they appear *before* the person, or the thing limited, as in English.

Descriptive (What kind?)

1. Juan es un **chico alto, inteligente y popular.**
   John is a *tall, intelligent, and popular* boy.

2. Es **una revista bonita, interesante y fácil.**
   It is a *nice, interesting, and easy* magazine.

Limiting (How many?)

1. **Muchos otros chicos** son altos, inteligentes y populares.
   Many other boys are tall, intelligent, and popular.

2. **Varias revistas** son bonitas, interesantes y fáciles.
   Several magazines are nice, interesting, and easy.

Rules:

1. In a series, **y** *and* is placed before the last descriptive adjective.

2. Limiting adjectives *showing quantity* and *preceding* the noun are: **bastante(s)** *enough*; **mismo-a-s,** *same*; **muchos-as** *many*; **otros-as,** *other*; **pocos-as,** *few*; **todos los; todas las,** *all*; **varios-as,** *several*. They agree with their nouns in gender and number.

Pocos chicos estudian.
Few *boys* study.

Todas las chicas estudian.
All the *girls* study.

B. Descriptive adjectives, too, *agree* with their nouns (person, place, or thing) in *gender* (masculine or feminine) and in *number* (singular or plural).

1. To form the *feminine adjective,* substitute feminine **a** for the masculine **o** ending.

Pedro es **rico.** Tiene **un coche nuevo.**
Peter is rich. He has a new car.

Ana es **rica.** Tiene **una casa nueva.**
Anna is rich. She has a new house.

I. STRUCTURES AND VERBS

2. Adjectives which do *not* end in **o** are the *same* in both masculine and feminine forms.

Masculine	Feminine
Es **un joven interesante** y **popular.**	Es **una joven interesante** y **popular.**
He is an interesting and popular young man.	She is an interesting and popular young woman.

3. To form the *plural* of an adjective that ends in a vowel — **a, e,** or **o** — add the letter **s:** **alto — altos; alta — altas; amable — amables.**

Los habitantes de Nueva York son **generosos** y **amables.**	Sus avenidas son **anchas** y **agradables.**
The inhabitants of New York are generous and kind.	Its avenues are wide and pleasant.

4. To form the *plural* of an adjective that ends in a consonant — a letter that is not **a, e, i, o,** or **u** — add **es: azul — azules; gris — grises; popular — populares.**

Prefiero un cielo **azul** a un cielo **gris.**	Los cielos están **azules** y no **grises.**
I prefer a blue sky to a gray sky.	The skies are blue and not gray.

C. Adjectives of nationality are made feminine by changing final masculine **o** to feminine **a,** e.g., **italiano — italiana.** But adjectives of nationality which end in consonants need to *add* **a: alemán — alemana; español — española; francés — francesa; inglés — inglesa.**

1. Juan es **un alumno español.** John is a Spanish (native) pupil.	3. Pedro es **un amigo inglés.** Peter is an English friend.
2. Juana es **una alumna española.** Joan is a Spanish (native) pupil.	4. Ana es **una amiga inglesa.** Anna is an English friend.

D. Adjectives of nationality form their plurals like all other adjectives.

1. En la clase hay **chicos españoles, ingleses** y **norteamericanos.**	2. También hay **chicas españolas, inglesas** y **norteamericanas.**
In class there are Spanish, English, and American boys.	There are also Spanish, English, and American girls.

Rules:

1. Adjectives of nationality, like other descriptive adjectives, *follow* their nouns.

2. Adjectives of nationality form their plurals by adding **s** to vowels and **es** to consonants.

3. **Alemán, francés, inglés** drop the accent mark for the feminine singular, and for both masculine and feminine plural forms.

E. Adjectives which bear accent marks on *other than* the final syllable *keep the accent mark* on all singular and plural forms.

---

difícil difíciles (difficult)   práctico-a prácticos-as (practical)

fácil fáciles (easy)   rápido-a rápidos-as (fast)

STUDY THE RULES, EXAMPLES, AND MODELS BEFORE BEGINNING THE EXERCISES!

Exercises

I. Rewrite the sentence, substituting the adjectives given in parentheses for the words in *italics*. Make all necessary changes in the new adjectives.

> Model: María es una chica *inteligente* y *bonita*.   Mary is an intelligent and pretty girl.
> (alegre/simpático)
> María es una chica **alegre** y **simpática**.   Mary is a cheerful and likable girl.
>
> María es una chica *inteligente* y *bonita*.

1. (alto/elegante)_____

2. (inglés/rubio)_____

3. (español/moreno)_____

4. (sincero/agradable)_____

5. (alemán/práctico)_____

II. Rewrite each sentence in the *plural*. Make all necessary changes. (Omit **un** and **una**.)

> Model: El niño es un alumno cubano.   **Los niños son alumnos cubanos.**
> The child is a Cuban pupil.   The children are Cuban pupils.

1. El niño es un alumno aplicado._____

2. El primo es un chico inglés._____

3. La ciencia es un estudio fácil._____

4. La cosa es una tiza azul._____

5. La abuela es una señora española._____

6. La madre es una mujer inteligente._____

133

7. La tía es una persona liberal. _____

8. El señor es un profesor alemán. _____

9. La muchacha es una chica francesa. _____

10. El tío es un hombre español. _____

III. Rewrite each sentence in the singular. Make all necessary changes for agreement. (Add **un** or **una**.)

Model: Son chicas alegres.   Es **una** chica alegre.
        They are happy girls.   She is a happy girl.

1. Son hombres inteligentes. _____

2. Son mujeres tristes. _____

3. Son maestros españoles. _____

4. Son cines alemanes. _____

5. Son periódicos franceses. _____

IV. Rewrite the sentence, using the word in parentheses in its proper position in the sentence.

Model: **Trabajan hoy.** They work today.
        a. (muchos) _____   c. (buenos) _____
        Muchos trabajan hoy.   Muchos alumnos **buenos** trabajan hoy.
        Many work today.   Many good students work today.

        b. (alumnos) _____   d. (alegres) _____
        Muchos **alumnos** trabajan hoy.   Muchos alumnos buenos y **alegres** trabajan hoy.
        Many students work today.   Many good and happy students work today.

1. Contestan bien.

   a. (muchas) _____

   b. (alumnas) _____

   c. (lindas) _____

   d. (amables) _____

134

2. Hablan hoy.

   a. (los muchachos)_____

   b. (todos)_____

   c. (españoles)_____

   d. (inglés)_____

   e. (poco)_____

3. Lee aquí.

   a. (mi amiga)_____

   b. (revistas)_____

   c. (varias)_____

   d. (interesantes)_____

   e. (cómicas)_____

4. Escribe ahora.

   a. (el muchacho)_____

   b. (mismo)_____

   c. (bueno)_____

   d. (aplicado)_____

   e. (ruso)_____

   f. (bastante)_____

V. Write affirmative answers in complete Spanish sentences. Include in *both* your answers all *adjectives* used in the first *question*, changing adjective endings as needed.

Model: ¿Son los *otros* alumnos *aplicados*?   Are the *other* pupils *diligent*?
           Los **otros** alumnos son **aplicados.**   The *other* pupils are *diligent*.
           ¿Y las otras alumnas también?   And the other girl pupils, too?
           Las **otras** alumnas son **aplicadas.**   The *other* girl pupils are *diligent*.

1. ¿Trabajan *todos* los chicos *españoles*? ¿Y todas las chicas también? _____

   _____

2. ¿Compran ellas sombreros *bonitos* y *baratos*? ¿Y muchas faldas también? _____

   _____

   _____

3. ¿Tiene la familia *otro* coche *nuevo* y *lindo*? ¿Y otra casa también? _____

_____

_____

4. ¿Ven los chicos *pocas* ciudades *grandes* y *hermosas*? ¿Y pocos países también? _____

_____

_____

5. ¿Visitan *varios* señores *ingleses bastantes* ciudades *interesantes*? ¿Y varias señoras tam-

bién? _____

_____

VII. Oral Proficiency. Respond orally to the situation described. (You may *later* write your responses for intensive practice.)

Situation: Your friends have arranged a blind date for you. You telephone before the date to introduce yourself. Your date asks you to describe yourself:—¿*Cómo es usted?*

After greeting your date and stating who you are, in **four** Spanish sentences describe yourself. You may use your own ideas or ideas suggested by the following: *how you look, what kind of a person you are, what you will be wearing to the date (for recognition), what is he/she like, until then.*

LOS NIÑOS TERRIBLES DE GAD

—Bueno, bueno. Por lo pronto, me gustaría saber quién eres tú, de qué vives, qué porvenir tienes, cuáles son tus intenciones . . .

—¡Claro! Usted, que tiene más años que Matusalén, ya se ha olvidado del amor y todas esas cosas . . .

LLEGA EL AMOR

—No se enfade usted, señorita. El amor no tiene edad . . ., el amor desprecia los obstáculos . . . ¿Podemos salir juntos esta tarde?

—Déjame que te acompañe hasta tu casa. Este barrio es peligroso, ¿sabes?

Es un gran honor y placer
poder hablar con Vd.

How would you like to live more than a
thousand years? It might be interesting.

El hombre más viejo del mundo.

Ahora, queridos amigos de este programa, el canal cincuenta y cinco tiene el gran privilegio de presentar una entrevista con el hombre más viejo del mundo. Tiene cuatro mil años.

Locutor: Bienvenido, señor. Es un gran honor hablar con Vd.

Viejo: Bueno. ¿Quiere Vd. hacer unas preguntas? Tengo prisa.

Locutor: Sí, sí. Claro. . .Vd. no parece tan viejo. ¿Cuál es su secreto?

Viejo: Pues, duermo mucho, como poco y no miro la televisión.

Locutor: Ah, ya comprendo. ¿Hay una gran diferencia entre el presente y el pasado?

Viejo: No hay mucha. Los chicos de hoy llevan el pelo largo como los hombres prehistóricos, y la música de hoy es similar a la música de las cavernas.

Locutor: ¿Qué come Vd.?

Viejo: En el pasado. . .carne cruda de tigre o de elefante.

Locutor: ¡Ay! ¡Es muy diferente de la comida de hoy! ¿Verdad?

Viejo: No. Es muy similar a las comidas congeladas T.V. que las mujeres de hoy sirven a sus familias.

Locutor: Y, ¿quién es el hombre más famoso que Vd. ha conocido?

Viejo: Es el primer profesor de español en América. Lo conocí en el año mil cuatrocientos noventa y dos.

Locutor: ¡Su nombre, por favor!

Viejo: Cristóbal Colón.

Locutor: ¿Cristóbal Colón, un profesor de español?

Viejo: Claro, un profesor de español para los indios del Nuevo Mundo. Bueno. Me voy. Tengo una cita con una joven.

Locutor: ¿Una joven? ¿Cuántos años tiene ella?

Viejo: Solamente cuatrocientos, si ella dice la verdad. Adiós.

Locutor: Adiós, señor. Buena suerte en su cita.

Palabras Nuevas

SUBSTANTIVOS

el canal   *the channel*
la carne   *the meat*
　la carne de elefante   *the elephant meat*
　la carne de tigre   *the tiger meat*
la caverna   *the cave*
la comida   *the food*
　la comida congelada T.V.   *the frozen T.V. dinner*

Cristóbal Colón   *Christopher Columbus*
la diferencia   *the difference*
la entrevista   *the interview*
el honor   *the honor*
el locutor   *the commentator, the announcer*
el mundo   *the world*
　el Nuevo Mundo   *the New World*
el pasado   *the past*
el presente   *the present (time)*
el privilegio   *the privilege*

el profesor de español   *the Spanish teacher*
el secreto   *the secret*

ADJETIVOS

crudo,a   *raw*
largo,a   *long*
poco,a   *little (small amount)*
prehistórico,a   *prehistoric*
primer(o),a   *first*
similar   *similar, same*
viejo,a   *old*

VERBOS

duermo   *I sleep*

ha conocido   *you (formal sing.) have known; he (she) has known*

hacer una pregunta   *to ask a question*

lo conocí   *I met him*

presentar   *to present*

sirven   *they serve; you (formal pl.) serve*

tener. . .años   *to be. . .years old*

tener prisa   *to be in a hurry*

OTRAS PALABRAS

cincuenta y cinco   *fifty-five*

¿Cuál es. . .?   *What is . . .?*

cuatrocientos   *four hundred*

el hombre más viejo del mundo   *the oldest man in the world*

mil   *one thousand*

mil cuatrocientos noventa y dos   *1492*

solamente   *only*

EJERCICIOS

I. (A) Complete the sentences according to the story.

1. El canal 55 presenta una _____ con el hombre más viejo.

2. Este hombre tiene _____.

3. El secreto del hombre es que _____ poco, _____ mucho y no

    _____ la televisión.

4. Los chicos de hoy llevan el _____.

5. Las mujeres de hoy sirven _____ a sus familias.

(B) Preguntas personales y generales. Write your answer in a complete Spanish sentence.

1. ¿Quién es la persona más famosa del mundo?
2. ¿Cuál al es una diferencia entre el pasado y el presente?
3. ¿Cuál es su comida favorita?
4. ¿Cuántos años tiene Vd.?
5. ¿Con quién tiene Vd. una cita este sábado?

1. _____

2. _____

3. _____

4. _____

5. _____

II. Write the letter of the expression that best completes the sentence.

A		B	
1. Tenemos el gran privilegio ____		a)	que ha conocido.
2. Hay mucha diferencia ____		b)	no es similar.
3. Es el hombre más famoso ____		c)	de presentar una entrevista.
4. Me voy porque ____		d)	tengo una cita.
5. La comida ____		e)	entre el pasado y el presente.

III. Compositions: Oral and written.

(A) Look at the picture at the beginning of this Work Unit. Describe the scene in Spanish to a friend.

(B) You are being interviewed by a T.V. announcer because you are over 100 years old. What would you say?

Locutor — Bienvenido a nuestro programa. Es un privilegio hablar con Vd.

Usted — _____

Locutor — ¿Quiere usted decirnos el secreto de su larga vida?

Usted — _____

Locutor — Muy interesante. ¿Come usted algo especial?

Usted — _____

Locutor — Muy bien. Usted es una inspiración para nosotros. ¡Buena Suerte!

Usted – _____

ESTRUCTURAS DE LA LENGUA

Cardinal Numbers: 31-1000

A. Learn these paired sets of numbers:

One ending only for the decades 20-100		*Masculine or feminine endings* for 200-900	
20	veinte	200	doscientos, -as
30	treinta	300	trescientos, -as
40	cuarenta	400	cuatrocientos, -as
50	cincuenta	500	quinientos, -as
60	sesenta	600	seiscientos, -as
70	setenta	700	setecientos, -as
80	ochenta	800	ochocientos, -as
90	noventa	900	novecientos, -as
100	ciento (cien)	1000	mil
101	ciento uno		

Rules:

1. **Y** is placed after the decades *20 through 90* before adding *one through nine*, e.g., **veinte y uno** (21); **treinta y dos** (32); **cuarenta y tres** (43); **cincuenta y cuatro** (54); **sesenta y cinco** (65); **setenta y seis** (76); **ochenta y siete** (87); **noventa y ocho** (98).

2. **Uno** (1) in compound numbers shortens to **un** before a masculine noun, and becomes **una** before a feminine noun. See the examples below:

treinta y un chicos y **veinte y una chicas**
thirty-one boys and twenty-one girls.

141

3. **Ciento** (100) shortens to **cien** before *both masculine and feminine nouns*, but remains **ciento** directly before a smaller number followed by a noun of either gender. *One* is *not* expressed before **cien(to). Y** *never* follows **cien(to).**

---

cien dólares por **cien revistas**
one hundred dollars for one hundred magazines

ciento noventa dólares por **ciento noventa revistas**
one hundred (and) ninety dollars for one hundred (and) ninety magazines.

---

4. **Doscientos** through **novecientos** (200-900) change their endings to **as** when describing feminine nouns, e.g.,

---

doscientas tres chicas y **quinientas mujeres**
two hundred and three girls, and five hundred women

---

5. **Quin**ientos, -as (500), **sete**cientos, -as (700), **nove**cientos, -as (900) have special stems.

6. **Mil** (1,000): *One* is *not* expressed before **mil. Y** is *not* generally used after **mil.**

---

1. Hay casi **mil escuelas** en Nueva York.
There are almost *one thousand* schools in New York.

2. **¿Mil setecientas?**   3. No. **Mil.**
   Seventeen hundred?   No. *A thousand.*
   (one thousand seven hundred)

B. La fecha (The date). — Two ways.

What is today's date?   Today is April 1st (2nd), nineteen (hundred) seventy-one.

---

1. **¿A cuántos estamos?**   **Estamos a primero (dos) de abril de mil novecientos setenta y uno.**

2. **¿Cuál es la fecha de hoy?**   **Hoy es el primero (dos) de abril, mil novecientos setenta y uno.**

Rules:

1. **Estamos a** and **Hoy es el** represent *today is*; **el** never follows **estamos a.**

2. **De** or a comma appear between the month and the year.

3. *Nineteen hundred* and other hundreds above one thousand must be expressed as *one thousand nine hundred*: **mil novecientos,** for example.

C. Study the following models which *contrast the numbers below one hundred* with numbers from *200* to *900.*

Questions	Answers
1. ¿Cuántos chicos hay en las clases de gimnasia?	1. **Sesenta y uno.** Tenemos clases de **sesenta y un chicos** o de **sesenta y una chicas.**
How many pupils are there in the gym classes?	*Sixty-one.* We have classes of *sixty-one* boys or *sixty-one* girls.
2. ¿Cuántos alumnos hay en su escuela?	2. Hay **mil doscientos: seiscientos chicos y seiscientas** chicas.
How many pupils are there in your school?	There are *twelve hundred.* There are *six hundred* boys and *six hundred* girls.
3. a. ¿Hay **cincuenta** o **quinientas revistas** allí?	3. a. Hay **quinientas revistas** y **quinientos** libros.
Are there *fifty* or *five hundred* magazines there?	There are *five hundred* magazines and *five hundred* books.
b. ¿Hay **setenta** o **setecientas páginas?**	b. Hay **setecientas páginas.**
Are there *seventy* or *seven hundred* pages?	There are *seven hundred* pages.
c. ¿Hay **noventa** o **novecientas gramáticas?**	c. Hay **novecientas** gramáticas.
Are there *ninety* or *nine hundred* grammars?	There are *nine hundred* grammars.
4. ¿Cuánto paga Vd. por un coche? **¿Cien pesetas?**	4. No pago **cien pesetas.** Pago **cien dólares** ahora y **mil ciento cincuenta dólares** después.
How much do you pay for a car? One hundred pesetas?	I don't pay *one hundred* pesetas. I pay *one hundred dollars* now and *one thousand one hundred fifty* later.

STUDY THE RULES, EXAMPLES, AND MODELS BEFORE BEGINNING THE EXERCISES!

Exercises

I. Write an answer in a complete Spanish sentence, *writing out* in Spanish words the number given in parentheses.

Model: ¿Es **once** o **uno**?   Is it eleven or one?
(11) Es **once.**   It is eleven

1. ¿Es **setenta** o **setecientos?** (700)_____

2. ¿Es **cincuenta** o **quinientos?** (500)_____

3. ¿Es **noventa** o **novecientos?** (900)_____

4. ¿Es **sesenta y siete** o **setenta y seis?** (67)_____

5. ¿Es **mil quinientos** o **ciento cincuenta?** (150)_____

6. ¿Es **ciento quince** o **mil quinientos** (1500)_____

7. ¿Es **ochocientos nueve** o **novecientos ocho?** (908)_____

8. ¿Es **trescientos treinta** o **mil trescientos?** (330)_____

9. ¿Es **quinientos once** o **ciento quince?** (115)_____

10. ¿Es **quinientos cinco** o **cincuenta y cinco?** (505)_____

II. Write the complete example and the answer in Spanish. Use **y** for +; **menos** for —; *por* for X; **dividido por** for ÷.

Model: 20 y 10 son_____ Veinte y diez son treinta.

1. (30 + 10 son)_____

2. (80 — 20 son)_____

3. (100 X 2 son)_____

4. (1,000 ÷ 2 son)_____

5. (35 + 36 son)_____

6. (300 — 150 son)_____

7. (600 ÷ 3 son)_____

8. (444 — 40 son)_____

9. (700 — 200 son)_____

10. (700 + 200 son)_____

III. Write the number in Spanish with the noun. Make the number agree with the noun as needed.

Model: 21 diccionarios **veinte y un** diccionarios. 101 casas **ciento una** casas.

1. (41 periódicos)_____

2. (51 sillas)_____

3. (101 mesas)_____

4. (100 estantes)_____

5. (115 papeles)_____

6. (691 tarjetas)_____

7. (200 lecciones)_____

8. (261 alumnos)_____

9. (371 chicos)_____

10. (481 alumnas)_____

IV. Write the number out in Spanish using **Cuentan** _____ **personas** according to the model.
Model: **601** Cuentan **seiscientas una personas.**   They count *601 people.*

1. 555_____

2. 777_____

3. 991_____

4. 1,000_____

5. 1717_____

V. Write each date in Spanish according to the model.

Model: ¿Cuál es la fecha de hoy?   What is today's date?

Hoy es . . .   **Hoy es el trece de febrero de**

Feb. 13, 1973   **mil novecientos setenta y tres.**

A. ¿Cuál es la fecha de hoy?   What is today's date?

Hoy es . . . (rewrite)   Today is . . .

1. Mar. 1, 1999 _____

_____

2. Jan. 31, 1888 _____

_____

B. ¿Cuál es la fecha de mañana?   What is tomorrow's date?

Mañana es . . . (rewrite)   Tomorrow is . . .

3. August 11, 1666 _____

_____

C. ¿A cuántos estamos?   What is today's date?

Estamos a . . . (rewrite)   Today is . . .

4. October 15, 1555 _____

_____

5. Dec. 14, 1777 _____

_____

VI. Complete the composition by writing the word(s) or numbers in italics.

Tengo_____años. Mi cumpleaños es   I am *14* years old. My
         1   1
_____. Vivo en   birthday is *May 31*. I
               2   2
la calle_____,número   live on *115th* Street,
                    3   3
_____. Gano entre   number *1,171*. I earn
               4   4
_____ y _____   between *40* and *50*
          5   6   5   6
dólares semanales. Ya tengo en el banco_____   dollars a week. I now
                                                              7   have *999* dollars in
_____dólares. Tengo_____   7
               7   8   the bank. I have *100*
amigos pero solamente_____madre. Nací en   8
                                        9   friends but only *one*
_____   9
                    10   mother. I was born in
                                                                    19 . . . .
10

VII. Oral Proficiency. Respond orally to the situation described. (You may *later* write your responses for intensive practice.)

Situation: You are the public address announcer for your school or club. They asked you to announce *Fiestas Y Eventos*, the dates of the major holidays and other events:—¿*Cuáles son los más importantes?*

After introducing yourself, in **five** Spanish sentences announce holidays and events with their dates for the current year. You may use your own ideas or ideas suggested by the following: *El Día De La Acción De Gracias, La Navidad, El Año Nuevo, La Pascua Florida, El Día De La Independencia, reuniones, bailes, festivales.*

*He comido tres helados y
tengo dolor de estómago.*

It's nice to be able to get away for the summer.
What happens to Federico after a week?

Queridos mamá y papá

Federico Caracoles es un muchacho de nueve años. No tiene hermanos y está muy aburrido en el verano. Todos sus buenos amigos pasan las vacaciones lejos de la ciudad. Pobre Federico está solo los veranos. Este año, los padres de Federico deciden enviar al chico a un buen campamento de verano. Así Federico va a pasar un mes al aire libre con otros muchachos de su edad. Es una nueva experiencia. Federico escribe una carta a sus padres todos los días con una descripción de sus actividades.

Primer día:	¡Este campamento es una maravilla! Hay árboles, flores y hierba por todas partes. Hay un lago en el centro con muchos botes. Hugo, el consejero, dice que vamos a hacer algo nuevo todos los días. Podemos jugar al béisbol, al fútbol y al básquetbol. Hay mucho que hacer, pero por la noche pienso en Vds.
Segundo día:	Hay cinco muchachos en nuestro grupo — Jaime, Adelberto, Arnaldo, Inocencio y yo. Adelberto es mi mejor amigo. Es muy gordo y siempre come de día y de noche. Hoy Adelberto ha comido tres platos de macarrones. El dice que tiene mucha hambre.
Tercer día:	Hoy todo el grupo va a tener una fiesta. Hay muchos problemas porque no hay mesas y es necesario poner la comida en la hierba. Adelberto ha comido tres hormigas con la ensalada de papas y dice que la ensalada está buena.
Cuarto día:	Hoy vamos al lago para nadar. Hay una isla en el lago. Vamos allá en botes. Regresamos con sólo cuatro muchachos. Hugo, el consejero, está muy enojado porque Inocencio está todavía en la isla.
Quinto día:	Hoy es el cumpleaños de Arnaldo y tenemos una buena fiesta. Hay dulces, helado y otros refrescos. Adelberto está muy contento, porque dice que el helado es una de sus cosas favoritas. Yo he comido tres helados y tengo dolor de estómago.
Sexto día:	Es sábado y vemos una película. Todo el mundo grita y tira cosas por el aire. Nadie escucha cuando los actores hablan. Adelberto recibe un golpe en la cabeza. Hugo, el consejero, dice que nunca vamos a ver otra película.
Séptimo día:	¡Una semana aquí! El campamento es una maravilla. Tengo muchos amigos, hago muchas cosas. . .pero. . . ¡Quiero regresar a casa!

Palabras Nuevas

SUBSTANTIVOS

Adelberto *Adelbert*
Arnaldo *Arnold*
el bote *the boat*
el campamento (de verano)
   the (summer) camp
el caracol *the snail*
el consejero *the counselor*

la descripción *the description*
el dolor de estómago *the stomachache*
la edad *the age*
la ensalada de papas *the potato salad*
Federico *Frederick*

el golpe en la cabeza *the blow to the head*
el grupo *the group*
la hierba *the grass*
la hormiga *the ant*
Inocencio *Innocent*
la isla *the island*

Jaime   *James*
el lago   *the lake*
los padres   *the parents*
el plato de macarrones   *the dish of macaroni*
la maravilla   *the marvel, the wonder*
el refresco   *the snack*

ADJETIVOS
aburrido,a   *bored*
contento,a   *happy*
enojado,a   *angry*
solo,a   *alone*

VERBOS
enviar   *to send*
estar bueno   *to taste good*
ha comido   *he (she) has eaten; you (formal sing.) have eaten*
he comido   *I have eaten*
jugar al básquetbol (al béisbol, al fútbol)   *to play basketball (baseball, football)*
tener mucha hambre   *to be very hungry*
tirar   *to throw*

OTRAS PALABRAS
al aire libre   *in the open air*
de día y de noche   *night and day*
nunca   *never*
sólo   *only*
todavía   *still*
todos los días   *everyday*

EJERCICIOS

I. Preguntas. Write your answer in a complete Spanish sentence.

1. ¿Por qué está aburrido Federico?_____

2. ¿Adónde va Federico este año? _____

3. ¿Qué hace el muchacho todos los días?_____

4. ¿Qué quiere hacer Federico después de una semana en el campo?_____

_____

II. ¿Cómo se dice en español?
1. They're going to spend their vacation far from the city.
2. We're going to do new things everyday.
3. He's always eating, day and night.
4. Everybody shouts and throws things.

1 . _____

2 . _____

3 . _____

4 . _____

III. El mensaje secreto — Inocencio has written a secret message to Federico by leaving out all the letters *o* and *a* from the words. Can you put back these vowels and decipher the code?

Querid__   Federic__,

V__m__s __l l__g__ est__ n__che.   P__dem__s ir __ l__ isl__

c__n un__ de l__s b__t__s. Si el c__nsejer__ s__be, v__ __ estar

muy en__j__d__.

Tu __mig__,

In__cenci__

IV. Compositions: Oral or written.

(A) Look at the picture at the beginning of this Work Unit. Describe the scene in Spanish to a friend.

(B) Tell what you are going to do this summer. Include the following:

Las vacaciones del verano
1. Whether you go to camp. 2. You swim and play baseball. 3. You eat ice cream. 4. You go to the movies in the evening. 5. Whether the camp or the city is more wonderful.

ESTRUCTURAS DE LA LENGUA

Ordinal numbers: Shortening of Adjectives **bueno** and **malo**.

A. *Ordinal* numbers tell the order or place of any item within a series:

1st **primero** –a first	6th **sexto** –a sixth
2nd **segundo** –a second	7th **séptimo** –a seventh
3rd **tercero** –a third	8th **octavo** –a eighth
4th **cuarto** –a fourth	9th **noveno** –a ninth
5th **quinto** –a fifth	10th **décimo** –a tenth

B. *Ordinal* numbers identify the noun by its place in a series. *Cardinal* numbers tell "how many."

1. –¿Estamos en la **Quinta** Avenida?
   Are we on **Fifth** Avenue?
   –Sí. Y tenemos **cinco** días para la visita.
   Yes. And we have **five** days for the visit.

2. –Es nuestro **primer** viaje.
   It is our **first** trip.
   –Hicimos **un** viaje antes.
   We made **one** trip before.

3. –El **tercer** edificio es muy alto.
   The **third** building is very tall.
   –Hay **tres** edificios y **un** parque allí.
   –There are **three** buildings and **a** park there.

Rules:

1. The ordinal numbers are widely used from **first** through **tenth** and agree in number and gender with the nouns they precede.

2. **Primero** and **tercero** drop their final **o** and become **primer** and **tercer** before a *masculine singular noun only. Feminine singular and all plural forms never shorten.*

C. Bueno *good,* **malo** *bad,* also drop their **o** *before* a masculine singular noun in common use.

Common Use	*Emphatic Use*
1. –¿Es un **buen** chico? Is he a good boy?	–Sí, es un chico muy **bueno**. Yes, he's a very *good* boy.
2. –Entonces no es un **mal** alumno. Then he's not a bad pupil.	–No es un alumno **malo**. He is not a *bad* pupil.

Rules:

1. **Bueno** and **malo,** being common adjectives, are usually placed *before* the noun, unlike most descriptive Spanish adjectives. In that position **bueno** shortens to **buen; malo** shortens to **mal.** Shortening occurs *only in the masculine singular* forms.

2. For *emphasis* only, **bueno** and **malo** may be placed *after* the noun. In that position **bueno** and **malo** never lose the **o.**

3. Buen**a,** buen**os,** buen**as;** mal**a,** mal**os,** mal**as** never shorten, being feminine or plural forms.

STUDY THE RULES, EXAMPLES, AND MODELS BEFORE BEGINNING THE EXERCISES!

Exercises

I. Rewrite the Spanish sentence in the singular. Make all necessary changes for agreement.

  Model: Veo los buenos libros.   I see the good books.
     Veo **el buen libro.**   I see the good book.

1. Veo los buenos sombreros. _____

2. Ahí van las buenas alumnas. _____

3. Paso los primeros días aquí. _____

4. Leo durante las primeras horas. _____

5. Tiene los malos pensamientos. _____

6. Cuenta las malas cosas. _____

7. Ocupan los terceros asientos. _____

8. Escribe las terceras líneas. _____

II. Rewrite the sentence placing the correct form of **bueno** or **malo** *before* the noun.

1. Francisco tiene un padre bueno. _____

2. María tiene unas ideas buenas. _____

3. Pablo lee un cuento malo. _____

4. Elena prepara una comida mala. _____

5. Paco tiene unos errores malos. _____

III. Write an answer in a complete Spanish sentence using the *next higher ordinal* number. Make the ordinal number agree with the noun. Use **No. Es_____** according to the model.

  Model: — ¿Es el segundo libro?   Is it the second book?
      — No. Es el **tercer** libro.   No. It's the third book.

1. ¿Es la novena canción?_____

2. ¿Es el quinto piso?_____

3. ¿Es la séptima avenida?_____

4. ¿Es el segundo alumno?_____

5. ¿Es la cuarta casa?_____

IV. Write the rejoinder using the appropriate *ordinal* number according to the model. Make the ordinal number agree with the noun in the *singular*. Begin with **Sí, es su _____**.

Model: — Escribe *tres* cartas.   He writes *three* letters.
       — **Sí, es su tercera carta.**   Yes, it's his *third* letter.

1. Hace cuatro visitas._____

2. Compra dos blusas._____

3. Hace siete viajes._____

4. Comete tres faltas._____

5. Come un helado._____

V. Write the most *logical* answer in a complete Spanish sentence. Use cue words.

1. ¿Desea Vd. *el primer dólar* o *el segundo centavo*? (Deseo)_____

_____

2. ¿Quieres ver *una mala película* o *un buen drama*? (Quiero)_____

_____

3. ¿Deseas *un buen examen fácil* o *un mal examen difícil*? (Deseo)_____

_____

4. ¿Es más fácil *la tercera hora* o *la décima hora* del trabajo? (Es más fácil)_____

_____

5. ¿Escribe Vd. ahora *la sexta frase* o *la quinta frase*? (Escribo)_____

_____

VI. Complete the paragraph about John, writing the appropriate form of the adjective. Make all necessary changes for agreement with the noun.

Juan ocupa la _____ silla en la _____ fila. Es un _____
               1. séptimo   **2. sexto**   **3. bueno**

amigo. Nunca hace cosas _____. En los _____ exámenes,
                             4. malo   **5. primero**

recibe unas _____ notas. Ahora, después del _____ examen,
                6. bueno   **7. tercero**

es el _____ alumno de la clase. Es uno de los estudiantes muy _____
     8. primero   **9. bueno**

de la escuela. Yo soy la _____ persona que lo admira; la primera es su mamá.
                    10. segundo

VII. Oral Proficiency. Respond orally to the situation described. (You may *later* write your responses for intensive practice.)

Situation: You are the president of the club. The members have asked you to announce a list of items to bring for an outing in the country:—*¿Qué necesitamos traer?*

After you announce the date for *un buen día en el campo,* list **ten** items in order of importance, using the ordinals *first, second, third,* etc., before each. You may use your own ideas or the following suggestions: *refrescos, helados, comida (ensalada de papas, hamburguesas), platos de papel, guantes de béisbol, botes, automóviles, un béisbol, un fútbol, deseamos, necesitamos.*

Helados. Ellos disfrutan y tú los alimentas.

¿Sabías que un helado tiene más vitamina A que las manzanas? ¿Y más proteínas que los plátanos? ¿Y hasta más calcio que el arroz con leche?

Se los puedes dar tranquilamente. ¡Son tan ricos! Y son super-agradecidos. Te van a comer a besos.

Asociación Española
de Fabricantes de Helados.

¡Vaya Vd. allá, y doble Vd. a la
izquierda en la esquina!

If you were lost in the city, what would you do?

Si está perdido, ¡llame a un policía!

—¿Qué voy a hacer ahora?, piensa Santiago Santurce. Tengo una cita a las ocho con mi jefe. Ya son las ocho menos cuarto y estoy completamente perdido.

En este momento pasa un coche con un policía sentado adentro. Santiago recuerda las palabras de su madre: — Si estás perdido, ¡llama a un policía!

—¡Qué suerte!, piensa, y comienza a gritar:

—¡Oiga, espere Vd. un momento!

—Sí señor, a sus órdenes.

—¿Puede Vd. ayudarme? Busco la avenida Cortés, número 58.

—Creo que está en esa dirección. ¡Siga derecho tres o cuatro cuadras!

—Pero eso es imposible. Vengo de allí, y no hay avenida Cortés.

—Ah, sí, ¿La avenida, dice Vd? ¡Venga conmigo! ¿Ve Vd. aquel edificio alto? ¡Vaya Vd. allá, y doble Vd. a la izquierda en la esquina! Allí puede Vd. tomar el tren que va hacia el norte.

—¡Hombre, yo no voy al norte! La Avenida Cortés está muy cerca.

—Bueno, en ese caso, ¡pregunte a ese hombre que vende periódicos! El debe saberlo.

—Gracias, pero dígame ¿cómo es posible? ¿Vd., un policía, no sabe absolutamente nada? Generalmente Vds. saben las direcciones.

—Claro, pero yo no soy policía de esta ciudad. Estoy aquí sólo para asistir a una reunión de policías.

Palabras Nuevas

SUBSTANTIVOS

el coche   *the car*
la cuadra   *the block*
la dirección   *the direction*
la esquina   *the street corner*
el jefe   *the chief, the boss*
el norte   *the north*
el policía   *the policeman*
Santiago   *James*

ADJETIVOS

aquel, aquella   *that*
perdido,a   *lost*

VERBOS

ayudarme   *to help me*

comienza (a)   *he (she) begins;
  you (formal sing.) begin*
deber   *should, ought*
  debe saberlo   *he (she)
  should know it; you (formal
  sing.) should know it*
¡dígame!   *tell me (formal sing.)*
¡doble!   *turn (formal sing.)*
¡espere!   *wait (formal sing.)*
¡llama!   *call (fam. sing.)*
¡llame!   *call (formal sing.)*
¡oiga!   *listen, hear (formal
  sing.)*
¡pregunte!   *ask (formal sing.)*
piensa   *he (she) thinks;
  you (formal sing.) think*
recuerda   *he (she) remembers;
  you (formal sing.) remember*

¡siga derecho!   *continue
  straight ahead (formal sing.)*
¡vaya allá!   *go there (formal
  sing.)*
vender   *to sell*
¡venga!   *come (formal sing.)*

OTRAS PALABRAS

a sus órdenes   *at your service*
absolutamente   *absolutely*
adentro   *inside*
cerca   *nearby*
completamente   *completely*
generalmente   *generally*
hacia   *toward*
¡hombre!   *(exclamation) man!*
ya   *already*

EJERCICIOS

I. (A) Complete the sentences according to the story.

1. Santiago tiene una cita a _____ con su _____.

2. El policía está _____ dentro del _____.

3. El policía dice: ¡Siga _____, tres o cuatro _____!

4. Puede tomar el _____ en la _____ que va al _____.

5. El policía asiste a una _____ de esta _____.

(B) Preguntas personales y generales. Write your answer in a complete Spanish sentence.

1. *Si está perdido, ¿a quién llama Vd.?*
2. ¿Cuántas cuadras hay entre su escuela y su casa?
3. ¿Qué diferencia hay entre una calle y una avenida?
4. ¿Qué hay en la esquina de su escuela?
5. ¿Quién es el alumno (la alumna) a su izquierda en la clase de español?

1. _____

2. _____

3. _____

4. _____

5. _____

II. Write complete sentences according to the story, using the following sets of words.

1. tener   cita   jefe
2. momento   pasar   policía
3. Si   perdido   llamar
4. esquina   tomar   tren
5. preguntar   hombre   periódico

1. _____

2. _____

3. _____

4. _____

5. _____

III. Compositions: Oral or written.

(A) Look at the picture at the beginning of this Work Unit. Describe the scene in Spanish to a friend.

(B) Tell what you can do if you are lost. Include the following:

Cuando estoy perdido(a)

1. Where you look for a policeman.   2. You call home.   3. You ask (*pregunta*) people on the street.   4. You ask for (*pide*) directions.   5. You look for a street number.

ESTRUCTURAS DE LA LENGUA

Formation and Use of the Direct Commands.

A. Regular Direct Commands are formed from the *stem* of the first person singular of the present tense but have special command *endings*.

cant**ar** **Canto** bien. I sing well.	¡Cante Vd. bien! Sing well!	¡Canten Vds. bien! Sing well!	¡Cantemos bien! Let's sing well!
vend**er** **Vendo** esto. I sell this.	¡Venda Vd. esto! Sell this!	¡Vendan Vds. esto! Sell this!	¡Vendamos esto! Let's sell this!
viv**ir** **Vivo** aquí. I live here.	¡Viva Vd. aquí! Live here!	¡Vivan Vds. aquí! Live here!	¡Vivamos aquí! Let's live here!

Rules:

1. Direct commands are orders addressed to the persons who are expected to carry them out: **Vd., Vds.,** and **nosotros.**

2. Remove the **o** from the first person singular of the present tense. Add **e, en, emos,** to stems which come from **ar** verbs. Add **a, an, amos,** to stems which come from **er** and **ir** verbs. In this way, **ar, er,** and **ir** verbs exchange their usual present tense endings to form commands.

3. **Vd.** and **Vds.** follow the command, but **nosotros** is not expressed.

4. Commands usually bear exclamation points before and after them.

B. See the following direct command forms of verbs which are irregular in the first person singular of the present tense.

decir *to say, to tell* Digo más. I say more.	¡Diga Vd. más! Say more!	¡Digan Vds. más! Say more!	¡Digamos más! Let's say more!

hacer *to do, to make* Hago la tarea. I do the chore.	¡Haga Vd. la tarea! Do the chore!	¡Hagan Vds. la tarea! Do the chore!	¡Hagamos la tarea! Let's do the chore!

oír *to hear* Oigo la música. I hear the music.	¡Oiga Vd. la música! Hear the music!	¡Oigan Vds. la música! Hear the music!	¡Oigamos la música! Let's hear the music!

poner *to put*
Pongo eso aquí.
I put that here.

¡Ponga Vd. eso aquí!	¡Pongan Vds. eso aquí!	¡Pongamos eso aquí!
Put that here!	Put that here!	Let's put that here!

salir *to leave*
Salgo pronto.
I leave soon.

¡Salga Vd. pronto!	¡Salgan Vds. pronto!	¡Salgamos pronto!
Leave soon!	Leave soon!	Let's leave soon!

tener *to have*
Tengo paciencia.
I have patience.

¡Tenga Vd. paciencia!	¡Tengan Vds. paciencia!	¡Tengamos paciencia!
Have patience!	Have patience!	Let's have patience!

traer *to bring*
Traigo dinero.
I bring money.

¡Traiga Vd. dinero!	¡Traigan Vds. dinero!	¡Traigamos dinero!
Bring money!	Bring money!	Let's bring money!

venir *to come*
Vengo a casa.
I come home.

¡Venga Vd. a casa!	¡Vengan Vds. a casa!	¡Vengamos a casa!
Come home!	Come home!	Let's come home!

ver *to see*
Veo el mapa.
I see the map.

¡Vea Vd. el mapa!	¡Vean Vds. el mapa!	¡Veamos el mapa!
See the map!	See the map!	Let's see the map!

Rule:

Form the **Vd., Vds.,** and **nosotros** commands for the verbs above, in the same way as the regular verbs in A. Remove the **o** from the first person singular of the present tense. Add **e, en, emos,** to **ar** verbs. Add **a, an, amos,** to **er** and **ir** verbs.

C. Irregular direct commands

dar *to give*
Doy gracias.
I give thanks.

¡Dé Vd. gracias!	¡Den Vds. gracias!	¡Demos gracias!
Give thanks!	Give thanks!	Let's give thanks!

estar *to be*
Estoy aquí.
I am here.

(location, health, result of action)		
¡Esté Vd. aquí!	¡Estén Vds. aquí!	¡Estemos aquí!
Be here!	Be here!	Let's be here!

ir *to go*
Voy ahora.
I go now.

¡Vaya Vd. ahora!	¡Vayan Vds. ahora!	*¡Vamos ahora!
Go now!	Go now!	Let's go now!

saber *to know*
Sé esto.
I know this.

¡Sepa Vd. esto!	¡Sepan Vds. esto!	¡Sepamos esto!
Know this!	Know this!	Let's know this!

ser *to be*
Soy bueno.
I am good.

¡Sea Vd. bueno!	¡Sean Vds. buenos!	¡Seamos buenos!
Be good!	Be good!	Let's be good!

Rules:

1. The **Vd., Vds.,** and **nosotros** commands of **dar, estar, ir, saber, ser,** are irregular and must be *memorized* because the first person singular of their present tense does not end in **o.**

2. *Let's go* or *let us go* uses **¡vamos!** instead of the **vay** stem of the **vaya Vd.** and **vayan Vds.** commands.

STUDY THE RULES, EXAMPLES, AND MODELS BEFORE BEGINNING THE EXERCISES!

Exercises

I. Write the appropriate command for each statement.

> Model: 1. Vd. baila. **¡Baile Vd.!**
> You are dancing. Dance!
>
> 2. Vds. bailan. **¡Bailen Vds.!**
> You (pl.) are dancing. Dance!
>
> 3. Nosotros bailamos. **¡Bailemos!**
> We are dancing. Let's (Let us) dance!

1. Vd. escucha bien._____

2. Nosotros escuchamos bien._____

3. Vds. comen poco._____

4. Nosotros comemos poco._____

5. Vd. vive mucho tiempo._____

6. Nosotros vivimos mucho tiempo._____

7. Vds. salen pronto._____

8. Nosotros salimos pronto._____

9. Vd. va al mercado._____

10. Nosotros vamos al mercado._____

11. Vds. son diligentes. _____

12. Nosotros somos diligentes. _____

13. Vd. está contento. _____

14. Nosotros estamos contentos. _____

15. Vds. dan las gracias. _____

16. Nosotros damos las gracias. _____

¡ Baile Vd. ahora!

II. Write a response using the appropriate affirmative command according to each model.

    A. Model: —¿Bailo ahora?   **—Sí, ¡baile Vd. ahora!**
                   Shall I dance now?   Yes, dance now!

1. ¿Canto ahora? _____

2. ¿Respondo ahora? _____

3. ¿Escribo ahora? _____

4. ¿Compro ahora? _____

5. ¿Leo ahora? _____

B. Model: —¿Bailamos ahora?   **—Sí, ¡bailen Vds. ahora!**
                  Shall we dance now?   Yes, dance now!

1. ¿Hablamos ahora?_____

2. ¿Aprendemos ahora?_____

3. ¿Comemos ahora?_____

4. ¿Andamos ahora?_____

5. ¿Corremos ahora?_____

C. Model: —¿Vamos a **bailar** pronto?   **—¡Bailemos ahora mismo!**
                  Are we going to dance soon?   Let's dance right now!

1. ¿Vamos a **estudiar** pronto?_____

2. ¿Vamos a **beber** pronto?_____

3. ¿Vamos a **asistir** pronto?_____

4. ¿Vamos a **entrar** pronto?_____

5. ¿Vamos a **leer** pronto?_____

III. Write a response using the appropriate affirmative command according to each model.

A. Model: —Deseo **salir temprano.**   **—Bueno, ¡salga Vd. temprano!**
                  I want to leave early.   Fine, leave early!

1. Quiero **venir tarde.**_____

2. Deseo **oír la música.**_____

3. Necesito **conocer a todos.**_____

4. Debo **hacer el trabajo.**_____

5. Voy a **poner la silla aquí.**_____

6. Me gusta **ser perezoso.**_____

7. Tengo que **dar una fiesta.**_____

B. Model: —Deseamos **salir hoy.**   **—Bueno, ¡salgan Vds. hoy!**

1. Queremos **saber la verdad.**_____

2. Me gusta **decir la palabra.**_____

3. Pensamos **traer flores.**_____

4. Tenemos que **estar allí a la una.**_____

5. Debemos **tener paciencia.**_____

6. Deseamos **ver esa película.**_____

7. Vamos a **salir pronto.**_____

8. Necesitamos **oír la respuesta.**_____

IV. Complete each sentence in which the teacher gives advice to a new student. Use the appropriate command of the infinitive given in parentheses.

1. Juan: —¿Es necesario estudiar mucho?

   La maestra: —¡_____todos los días! (estudiar / Vd.)

2. Juan: —¿Cuándo hago la tarea?

   La maestra: —¡_____la tarea por la tarde! (hacer / Vd.)

3. Juan: —¿Tengo clases todos los días?

   La maestra: —¡_____a las clases cinco días! (asistir / Vd.)

4. Juan: —¿Y en la clase?

   La maestra: —¡_____un buen alumno! (ser / Vd.)

5. Juan: —¿Y los libros?

   La maestra: —¡_____ siempre los libros! (traer / Vd.)

6. Juan: —¿Son difíciles las lecciones?

   La maestra: —¡_____las lecciones muy bien! (saber / Vd.)

7. Juan: —¿Y por la tarde?

   La maestra: —¡_____a hablarme un poco! (venir / Vd.)

8. Juan: —¿No es posible mirar la televisión por la noche?

   La maestra: —¡_____a la cama a las diez! (ir / Vd.)

9. Juan: —¿Y los domingos por la tarde?

   La maestra: —¡_____a muchos amigos! (conocer / Vd.)

10. La maestra: —¡_____paseos con ellos! (dar / Vd.) ¡Buena suerte!

V. Oral Proficiency. Respond orally to the situation described. (You may *later* write your responses for intensive practice.)

Situation: A Spanish-speaking person asks you for directions to a park that is in walking distance:—*¿Cómo llego al parque, por favor?*

After expressing your pleasure, *con mucho gusto*, use Vd. command forms to give **four** directions. You may use your own ideas or ideas suggested by the following: *how many blocks to walk directly ahead, when to turn to the right, when to the left.*

El Alcázar.

Alcázar de Segovia, nave anclada en el corazón de Castilla.

Llegue en pocas horas. Recuérdelo por muchos años.

Nuestro boleto le mostrará la austera Castilla, la brava Extremadura, la activa Cataluña, la dulce Galicia. Cualquier lugar de la arrebatadora geografía de España. Y por el costo de ida y vuelta a Barcelona, en Pan American,® usted podrá ver otras ciudades como Lisboa, Madrid, Sevilla, París, Amsterdam, Bruselas y Londres. Además un vuelo en Pan American a Europa significa la oportunidad de ver también Nueva York, donde usted puede quedarse hasta 5 días sin necesidad de visa. Llame al Agente de Viajes o a nuestra oficina. Tendrá la incomparable satisfacción de haber elegido lo mejor.

La línea aérea de mayor experiencia en el mundo PAN AM

Primera en América Latina   Primera sobre el Pacífico   Primera sobre el Atlántico   Primera Alrededor del Mundo

Pero Señora López,
su hija no es así.

Did you ever forget someone's name? Think what a job it must be for a teacher with so many pupils.

Su hija es una alumna excelente

Es el día de entrevistas entre padres y maestros. Una vez al año los padres vienen a la escuela para hablar con los profesores acerca del progreso de sus hijos. El profesor Yerbaverde es un joven en su primer año de enseñanza. El espera nerviosamente la visita de los padres. Pero, ¡atención! ahí viene una madre.

Profesor: Buenos días, señora. ¿En qué puedo servirla?

Madre: Buenos días. Yo soy la señora de López. Vd. tiene mi hija, Sonia, en su clase de biología.

Profesor: (Piensa un momento porque tiene muchas alumnas en sus clases.) Ah, sí. Sonia López. Es una alumna excelente. Siempre sale bien en los exámenes. Va a sacar una nota buena en mi clase.

Madre: ¡Ay, qué bueno! ¿Hace siempre mi hija su tarea?

Profesor: Sí, sí. Claro. En la escuela no hay muchas como ella. Siempre prepara sus lecciones y contesta mis preguntas. Trae sus libros y su pluma todos los días. Su trabajo es excelente.

Madre: ¡Oh, gracias a Dios! Vd. es el primer profesor que me dice eso. Todos los otros profesores dicen que mi hija es una tonta, que Sonia nunca quiere hacer nada, que ella pasa todo el día sin estudiar y que sólo piensa en los muchachos.

Profesor: No, señora, su hija no es así. Los otros profesores están equivocados.

Madre: Gracias, señor profesor. Muchísimas gracias. Adiós. (Ella se va.)

Profesor: Después de cinco minutos, entra otra madre.

Madre: Buenos días, señor. Yo soy la señora de Gómez. Mi hija, Sonia, está en su clase de biología.

Profesor: (completamente sorprendido) ¡Sonia Gómez! Ay, ¡Dios mío! ¡Es su Sonia la alumna excelente! El equivocado soy yo. ¡Hay dos Sonias en mis clases!

Palabras Nuevas

SUBSTANTIVOS

la clase de biología *the biology class*
el día de entrevistas entre padres y maestros *Open School Day*
la enseñanza *the teaching*
el equivocado *the one who made a mistake*
los hijos *the sons and daughters, the children*
el progreso *the progress*
la sala de clase *the classroom*
la Sra. de López *Mrs. Lopez*
la tarea *the homework*

la tonta *the fool*
la visita *the visit*

VERBOS

esperar *to wait for*
sacar una nota *to get a mark*
salir bien en los exámenes *to pass tests*
se va *he (she) leaves; you (formal sing.) leave*
traer *to bring*

ADJETIVOS

excelente *excellent*
sorprendido,a *surprised*

OTRAS PALABRAS

acerca de *about*
ahí viene una madre *there comes a mother*
¡atención! *attention*
como *like*
¡Dios mío! *Heavens!*
¿En qué puedo servirle? *What can I do for you?*
nerviosamente *nervously*
¡qué bueno! *how good! great!*
una vez al año *once a year*

EJERCICIOS

I. (A) Complete the sentences according to the story.

1. Una _____ al año, los padres vienen a _____ con los _____ .

2. El profesor es un joven en su _____ año de _____ .

3. La hija de la señora de López está en la clase de _____ .

4. El profesor dice que Sonia va a sacar una _____ _____ .

5. La señora de Gómez tiene una hija que se llama _____ también.

(B) Preguntas personales y generales. Write your answer in a complete Spanish sentence.

1. ¿Qué nota va Vd. a sacar en la clase de español?
2. ¿Qué dicen todos los profesores de Vd.?
3. ¿Cuántas veces al año viene su padre a la escuela?
4. ¿Quién siempre sale bien en los exámenes?
5. ¿Por qué debe Vd. hacer siempre su tarea?

1. _____

2. _____

3. _____

4. _____

5. _____

II. Acróstico

1. teach	1. E
2. mark	2. N
3. homework	3. T
4. thanks	4. R
5. test	5. E
6. time	6. V
7. always	7. I
8. to get (a mark)	8. S
9. so many	9. T
10. to appear	10. A

III. Compositions: Oral or written.

(A) Look at the picture at the beginning of this Work Unit. Describe the scene in Spanish to a friend.

(B) Tell about your work in school. Include the following:

Mi trabajo en la escuela

1. Whether you want to attend school. 2. What kind of marks you get. 3. Whether you always do the homework. 4. What kind of student you are. 5. Whether you parents are happy with (*contentos de*) your work.

ESTRUCTURAS DE LA LENGUA

Possessive Adjectives. The five possessive adjectives below tell who the owner is.

(A) Agreement with singular nouns:

With Masculine Singular Nouns

Mi cuarto es bonito.	*My room* is pretty.
Tu cuarto es bonito.	*Your room* (fam. sing. address)
Su cuarto es bonito.	*His room(her, its, their room).* *Your room* (formal sing. & pl. address)
Nuestro cuarto es bonito.	*Our room* is pretty.
Vuestro cuarto es bonito.	*Your room* (fam. pl. address – used in Spain)

Rules:

1. Possessive adjectives precede the noun.

2. **Su** has five meanings: *his, her, its, their, your.* **Su** meaning *your* is used when speaking to one or more persons ina formal way.

3. **Tu** *your* is distinguished from **tú** *you* by dropping the accent mark. **Tu(s)** is used when speaking to *one person* in a familiar way.

4. **Vuestro(s)** *your* is used largely in Spain when speaking to *more than one person* in a familiar way.

B. Agreement with plural nouns:

With Masculine Plural Nouns

Mis cuartos son bonitos.	*My rooms* are pretty.
Tus cuartos son bonitos.	*Your rooms* (fam. sing. address)
Sus cuartos son bonitos.	*His rooms (her, its, their rooms)* *Your rooms* (formal sing. & pl. address)
Nuestros cuartos son bonitos.	*Our rooms* are pretty.
Vuestros cuartos son bonitos.	*Your rooms* (fam. pl. address – used in Spain)

169

Rules:

1. Add **s** to each possessive adjective when the following noun is plural.

2. Adding **s** does not change the meaning of the possessive adjective; **su amigo** may mean *their friend*, **sus amigos** may mean *his friends.*

C. Agreement with feminine nouns:

Feminine Singular: **nuestra** and **vuestra**

Nuestra casa es bonita.	Our house is pretty.
Vuestra casa es bonita.	Your house (fam. pl. — in Spain)

Feminine Plural: **nuestras** and **vuestras**

Nuestras casas son bonitas.	Our houses are pretty.
Vuestras casas son bonitas.	Your houses (fam. pl. — in Spain)

Rules:

1. **Nuestro** *our* and **vuestro** *your* change **o** to **a** before a feminine singular noun. **Nuestra** and **vuestra** add **s** before a feminine plural noun.

2. The other possessive adjectives do *not* have distinctive feminine forms:

mi casa, tu casa, su casa

mis casas, tus casas, sus casas

D. De él, de ella, de Vd., de Vds., de ellos-as, instead of **su** and **sus.**

1. **¿Son sus amigas?** may mean: Are they *his, her, its, your,* or *their* friends?

2. For clarity, *instead* of **su** and **sus,** use the appropriate definite article **(el, la, los,** or **las)** *before* the noun, followed by **de** and the *personal pronoun* that represents the owner *clearly.*

Son **las** amigas **de él**	They are *his* friends.
. . . . **de ella.**	. . . . *her* friends.
. . . . **de Vd.**	. . . . *your* friends.
. . . . **de Vds.**	. . . . *your* friends.
. . . . **de ellos-as**	. . . . *their* friends.

Rule:

De él, de ella, de Vd., de Vds., de ellos-as, always *follow* the noun.

STUDY THE RULES, EXAMPLES, AND MODELS BEFORE BEGINNING THE EXERCISES!

Exercises

I. Rewrite the sentence giving the *plural* of the expression in *italics*.

    Model: Tengo *mi papel.*   Tengo **mis papeles.**
                 I have my paper.   I have my papers.

1. Tengo *mi cuaderno.* _____

2. Los vecinos venden *su casa.* _____

3. Invitas a *nuestra clase.* _____

4. Escribo *mi respuesta* _____

5. ¿Hablas a *tu tío?* _____

6. ¿Están los niños en *su cuarto?* _____

7. No tenemos *nuestro periódico.* _____

8. No preparas *tu comida.* _____

9. Juana aprende *su lección.* _____

10. Vds. miran *su programa.* _____

II. Write the response using the appropriate form of the possessive adjective **nuestro.** Use **No.**

    Model: —¿Es su escuela?   **— No. Es nuestra** escuela.
           Is it their school?   No. It's our school.

1. ¿Es su pluma? _____

2. ¿Es su sombrero? _____

3. ¿Son sus zapatos? _____

4. ¿Son sus hijas? _____

5. ¿Son sus amigos? _____

III. Write the affirmative response, *changing the possessive adjective appropriately.* Use **Sí.**

    Model: —¿Usas (fam.) mi reloj?   **—Sí. Uso tu (fam.)** reloj.
             Are you using my watch?   Yes. I'm using your watch.

            —¿Usa Vd. (formal) mi reloj?   **—Sí. Uso su (formal)** reloj.
             Are you using my watch?   Yes. I'm using your watch.

1. ¿Usas mi abrigo? _____

2. ¿Usa Vd. mis pantalones? _____

3. ¿Abre Vd. su puerta? _____

4. ¿Desea Vd. sus lecciones? _____

5. ¿Necesitas mis radios? _____

IV. Write the *double* response, using the clarifying possessives **de él** and **de ella** instead of **su** and **sus.** Use   **No son (es)** _____ **de él. Son (es)** _____ **de ella.**

   Model: —¿Son sus cuadernos?   —**No son** los cuadernos **de él.**   **Son de ella.**
   Are they his notebooks?   They are not *his* notebooks.   They are *hers*.

1. ¿Son sus lápices? _____

   _____

2. ¿Son sus camisas? _____

   _____

3. ¿Es su amiga? _____

   _____

4. ¿Es su reloj? _____

   _____

5. ¿Son sus hermanos? _____

   _____

V. Write the *double* rejoinder, using the clarifying possessives **de Vds.** and **de ellos.** See model.
   Model: —Es nuestro dinero.   —**No es** el dinero **de Vds.**   **Es** el dinero **de ellos.**
   It is our money.   It is not *your* money.   It's *their* money.

1. Es nuestro coche. _____

   _____

2. Es nuestra pelota. _____

   _____

3. Son nuestras chaquetas. _____

   _____

4. Son nuestros abrigos. _____

   _____

5. Es nuestra familia. _____

_____

VI. Rewrite the sentence, substituting the appropriate form of the possessive adjective given in parentheses in place of the word in *italics*.

Model: Compro *las* flores.   (our) Compro **nuestras** flores.
        I buy the flowers.   I buy our flowers.

1. Vendo *los* coches. (my)_____

2. Escribimos *las* cartas. (our)_____

3. Estudian *las* lecciones. (his)_____

4. Entran en *los* cuartos. (her)_____

5. Salen de *la* casa. (your *fam.*)_____

6. Explican *el* examen. (their)_____

7. Buscan *el* mapa. (our)_____

8. Deseas *la* respuesta. (their)_____

9. Miran *la* casa. (your *formal*) _____

10. Responden a *las* preguntas. (your *formal*) _____

VII. Complete the dialog between the brothers, Paul and Anthony. (Use the familiar **tu** for *your*.)

1. Pablo: –¿Tienes_____ fútbol?
                              (my)

2. Antonio: –¿Por qué dices_____fútbol?
                                    (your)

3. Pablo: –Tú sabes, el fútbol que nos dieron_____tías.
                                                                (our)

   Eres mi hermano y_____cosas son_____cosas.
                              (your)   (my)

4. Antonio: –Pues bien, ¡quiero en seguida "_____" diez dólares que las
                                                          (our)

   tías te dieron ayer!

VIII. Oral Proficiency. Respond orally to the situation described. (You may *later* write your responses for intensive practice.)

Situation: Your younger brother and sister are fighting over ownership of some toys, etc. The children come to you to settle the problem. You clarify the ownership:—*¿De quién son estos juguetes?*

Begin with *Niños*. In **five** Spanish sentences tell your brother and sister which toys, etc., belong to each, which belong to both, and which are theirs and yours, too. You may use your own ideas based on the following model: *Es tu (mi) guante de béisbol, muñeca, bicicleta, navaja de explorador, perro, pelota, trenes eléctricos, libros.*

¿No está interesado
en comprar esta casa?

The house seems like a good buy. Is Carlos interested in buying it?

Casa a la venta

Cuando pasa por la calle, Carlos ve este letrero delante de una casa.

Toca a la puerta y espera unos momentos. Pronto, un hombre viejo abre la puerta y lo saluda.

Hombre:　Buenos días señor, ¿en qué puedo servirle?

Carlos:　Veo que esta casa está a la venta. ¿Puedo verla?

Hombre:　Sí, cómo no. Pase Vd. Yo soy Pedro Piragua.

Carlos:　Mucho gusto en conocerlo. Me llamo Comequeso, Carlos Comequeso.

Hombre:　Bueno, señor Comequeso, Mire Vd. esta sala. Está recién pintada. Ahora vamos a pasar a la cocina. Ese refrigerador y esa estufa son nuevos.

Carlos:　Ya veo. Parecen estar en excelentes condiciones. ¿Dónde están los dormitorios?

Hombre:　Hay tres y están en el piso de arriba. Vamos allá ahora. . .

Carlos:　¡Qué hermosos! Estos cuartos son grandes y claros.

Hombre:　Además, hay otro cuarto de baño que es completamente nuevo.

Carlos:　Dígame algo del vecindario.

Hombre:　Es excelente. La casa está cerca de los trenes y autobuses y Vd. puede ir de compras en aquella próxima calle. Ahora, ¿quiere Vd. saber el precio? Es muy barato.

Carlos:　No, gracias.

Hombre:　¿Cómo que no? ¿No está Vd. interesado en comprar esta casa?

Carlos:　No. Es que voy a poner mi casa a la venta esta semana y quiero saber el mejor método de hacerlo.

Palabras Nuevas

SUBSTANTIVOS

el cuarto de baño　*the bathroom*
el dormitorio　*the bedroom*
la estufa　*the stove*
el letrero　*the sign*
Pedro　*Peter*
el piso de arriba　*the floor above, upstairs*
el precio　*the price*
el queso　*the cheese*
el refrigerador　*the refrigerator*
el vecindario　*the neighborhood*

ADJETIVOS

barato,a　*inexpensive, cheap*
claro,a　*light, clear*
hermoso,a　*beautiful*
interesado,a　*interested*
(recién) pintado,a　*(recently) painted*
próximo,a　*next*

VERBOS

ir de compras　*to go shopping*
pasar por la calle　*to walk*

along the street
¡pida informes!　*ask for information (formal sing.)*
saludar　*to greet*
ver　*to see*
　ya veo　*now I see, indeed I do understand*

OTRAS PALABRAS

a la venta　*for sale*
¡cómo no!　*of course*
¿Cómo que no?　*What do you mean by "no?"*

175

en aquella próxima calle *on that next street*
es que *the fact is that*

lo *him, it, you (masc.)*
mucho gusto en conocerlo *pleased to meet you*

pronto *soon*
¡Qué hermosos! *How beautiful!*

EJERCICIOS

I. (A) Preguntas. Write your answer in a complete Spanish sentence.

1. ¿Qué ve Carlos delante de una casa? _____

2. ¿Por qué quiere ver Carlos la casa? _____

3. ¿Qué hay en la cocina? _____

4. ¿Cómo son los dormitorios? _____

5. ¿Qué va a hacer Carlos esta semana? _____

(B) Preguntas personales y generales. Write your answer in a complete Spanish sentence.

1. ¿Qué hay generalmente en una cocina?
2. ¿Cuántas habitaciones hay en su casa o apartamiento? ¿Cuáles son?
3. Describa Vd. el vecindario donde vive Vd.
4. ¿Qué pone Vd. en un letrero para vender una casa?
5. ¿Qué dice Vd. para saludar a una persona?

1. _____

2. _____

3. _____

4. _____

5. _____

II. Write the words from group B that match the words in group A.

A

1. La ventana se usa para _____

2. La puerta se usa para _____

3. La sala se usa para _____

4. El tren se usa para _____

5. La estufa se usa para _____

6. El refrigerador se usa para _____

7. El dormitorio se usa para _____

8. El baño se usa para _____

B

a) lavarse
b) descansar y mirar la televisión
c) dormir
d) mantener fría la comida

e) entrar y salir
f) preparar la comida
g) dejar entrar el aire fresco
h) viajar

III. ¿Cómo se dice en español?
1. House for sale, inquire within.
2. He knocks on the door and waits a few minutes.
3. Good morning, what can I do for you?
4. I'm very pleased to meet you.
5. Tell me something about the neighborhood.

1. _____

2. _____

3. _____

4. _____

5. _____

IV. Compositions: Oral or written.

(A) Look at the picture at the beginning of this Work Unit. Describe the scene in Spanish to a friend.

(B) Tell about the place where you live. Include the following:

Mi casa

1. You live in a big (small) house (apartment). 2. There are __ rooms in your house. 3. You have a beautiful bedroom .4. The rooms are large and light. 5. You go shopping in the neighborhood.

ESTRUCTURAS DE LA LENGUA

Demonstrative Adjectives

A. *This, these:* The speaker uses the following to indicate a person, place, or thing (or persons, places, things) *close to himself,* i.e., *close to the speaker:*

Este (masc.); **esta** (fem.) — *this*

1. Este perrito cerca de mí es mono.
   This puppy near me is cute.

2. Esta rosa que tengo es roja.
   This rose which I'm holding is red.

Estos (masc.); **estas** (fem.) — *these*

1. Estos perritos aquí son más monos.
   These puppies over here are cuter.

2. Estas rosas que tengo son blancas.
   These roses which I have are white.

Rules:

1. **Este** (masc.) and **esta** (fem. sing.), *this*, are used respectively before a masculine singular noun and before a feminine singular noun.

2. **Estos** (masc. pl.) and **estas** (fem. pl.), *these,* are used respectively before masculine plural nouns and before feminine plural nouns. Note that **estos** is the irregular plural of **este.**

3. Closeness to the speaker may be indicated by additional expressions such as: **aquí,** *here;* **cerca de mí,** *near me;* **que tengo,** *which I hold (have).*

B. *That, those:* The speaker uses the following to indicate that a person, place, or thing (or persons, places, things) is (are) *close to the listener:*

Ese (masc.); **esa** (fem.) — *that*	**Esos** (masc.); **esas** (fem.) — *those*

1. Ese perrito está cerca de ti (Vd., Vds.).
   That puppy is near you.
	1. Esos perritos están cerca de ti (Vd., Vds.).
	   Those puppies are near you.

2. Esa rosa que tienes ahí es rosada.
   That rose which you have there is pink.
	2. Esas rosas que tienes ahí son rojas.
	   Those roses which you have there are red.

Rules:

1. **Ese, esa,** *that,* are formed by dropping the *t* from **este, esta** (*this*). **Esos, esas,** *those,* are formed by dropping the *t* from **estos, estas** (*these*).

2. **Ese** (masc. sing.) and **esa** (fem. sing.), *that,* are used respectively before a masculine singular noun and before a feminine singular noun.

3. **Esos** (masc. pl.) and **esas** (fem. pl.), *those,* are used respectively before masculine plural nouns and before feminine plural nouns. Note that **esos** is the irregular plural of **ese.**

4. Closeness to the listener may be indicated by additional expressions such as: **ahí,** *there near you;* **cerca de ti (Vd., Vds.),** *near you;* **que tienes (Vd. tiene; Vds. tienen),** *which you hold (have).*

C. *That, those;* indicating *distance from both the listener and the speaker.*

Aquel (masc.); **aquella** (fem.) — *that*	**Aquellos** (masc.); **aquellas** (fem.) — *those*

1. Aquel parque está lejos de ti y de mí.
   That park is far from you and me.
	1. Aquellos parques están lejos de nosotros.
	   Those parks are far from us.

2. Aquella casa allí es magnífica.
   That house over there is magnificent.
	2. Aquellas casas allí son magníficas.
	   Those houses over there are magnificent.

Rules:

1. Unlike English, the speaker of Spanish insists on making a distinction between *that, those,* **aquel,** etc., *distant from the listener;* and *that, those,* **ese,** etc., *near the listener.*

2. **Aquel** (masc. sing.) and **aquella** (fem. sing.), *that,* are used respectively before a masculine singular noun and before a feminine singular noun.

3. **Aquellos** (masc. pl.) and **aquellas** (fem. pl.), *those,* are used respectively before masculine plural nouns and before feminine plural nouns.

4. Distance from the listener may be indicated by additional expressions such as: **allí,** *over there, yonder,* and **lejos de nosotros-as,** *far from us.*

STUDY THE RULES, EXAMPLES, AND MODELS BEFORE BEGINNING THE EXERCISES!

Exercises

I. Rewrite each sentence, substituting the noun in parentheses for the noun in *italics*. Make all necessary changes in the demonstrative adjectives (*this, that,* etc.).

Model: Necesito este *libro.*   I need this book.
              (pluma) Necesito **esta pluma.**   I need this pen.

A. Compro este *papel.* I'm buying this paper.

1. (tiza)_____

2. (plumas)_____

3. (lápiz)_____

4. (papeles)_____

5. (diccionario)_____

B. ¿Deseas ese *libro* ahí? Do you want that book there (near you)?

1. (silla)_____

2. (peras)_____

3. (periódicos)_____

4. (libros)_____

5. (sombrero)_____

C. Miramos aquel *cuadro* allí. We look at that picture over there.

1. (rosa)_____

2. (pinturas)_____

3. (coche)_____

4. (cuadros)_____

5. (edificio)_____

I. STRUCTURES AND VERBS

II. Rewrite the sentence, changing the words in *italics* to the *singular*, e.g., *esos usos,* **ese uso.**

1. Reciben *estos papeles y aquellos libros.*

   _____

2. Estudian *estas palabras y esas frases.*

   _____

3. Contestan a *esos profesores* y a *aquellos alumnos.*

   _____

4. Abren *esas puertas y aquellas ventanas.*

   _____

5. ¿Admiran *estos pañuelos y esos zapatos?*

   _____

III. Rewrite the sentence changing the words in *italics* to the *plural,* e.g., *ese uso,* **esos usos.**

1. Leemos *este periódico y ese artículo.*_____

2. Deseamos *esta silla y aquella cama.*_____

3. Admiramos *este sombrero y aquel vestido.*_____

4. Preferimos *esa clase y aquel profesor.*_____

5. Queremos *ese vestido y aquella falda.*_____

IV. Write a response according to the model. Use the correct form of **este-a, estos-as.**

Model: –¿Es interesante **ese libro** suyo?   **–¿Este libro? Sí, gracias.**
         Is *that* book of yours interesting?   *This* book? Yes, thank you.

1. ¿Está contento ese amigo suyo?_____

2. ¿Es interesante esa revista suya?_____

3. ¿Son fantásticos esos cuentos suyos?_____

4. ¿Son excelentes esas fotos suyas?_____

5. ¿Es importante ese papel suyo?_____

V. Write a response according to the model. Use the correct form of **ese-a; esos-as.**

Model: –¿Desea Vd. [Deseas] **este** cuarto?   **–¿Ese cuarto? No, gracias.**
         Do you want *this* room?   *That* room (near you)? No, thanks.

1. ¿Desea Vd. este postre?_____

2. ¿Quieres esta gramática?_____

3. ¿Necesita Vd. estos libros?_____

4. ¿Prefiere Vd. estas manzanas?_____

5. ¿Invita Vd. a estos amigos?_____

VI. Complete in Spanish the dialogue between Luisita and her mother in which Luisita insists on having her brother's ice cream, candy, cookies, and soda.

Remember: Este _____aquí;	Ese _____ahí;	Aquel _____allí;
. . . cerca de mí;	. . . cerca de ti;	. . . cerca de él;
. . . que tengo.	. . . que tienes.	. . . que él tiene.

1. La mamá: ¿Qué prefieres _____ helado a vainilla que tengo o _____
                                 (this)   (that)
  helado a chocolate que tú tienes?

2. Luisita: Prefiero _____ helado que Juan tiene allí.
                     (that)

3. La mamá: Entonces, Juan te da su plato, ¿Y qué prefieres como dulces, _____
                                                                            (these)
  dulces aquí o _____ dulces que están cerca de ti?
                 (those)

4. Luisita: Quiero también _____ dulces que Juan come allí.
                             (those)

5. La mamá: ¿Lo mismo con _____ galleticas y _____ gaseosa que Juan
                                   (those)   (that)
  toma?

6. Luisita: Sí, lo mismo. No me gustan _____ galleticas ni _____
                                                (these)   (this)
  gaseosa mía.

7. La mamá: ¡Ay! ¡Qué difícil es _____ hija mía!
                               (that)

8. Luisita: ¡Ay! ¡Qué difíciles son _____ mamás de hoy!
                               (those)

VII. Oral Proficiency. Respond orally to the situations described. (You may *later* write your responses for intensive practice.)

Situation: I am looking for some clothing for myself and for a friend. You are the salesperson who shows me various items. Finally, you want to know which items I want to buy. I say:—*No es fácil decidir.*

In **five** Spanish questions using *this, these, that, those* before each item, ask me which I am thinking of buying. You may use your own ideas or ideas suggested by the following: *¿Cuál(es) desea Vd.? ¿Qué quiere Vd. comprar? ¿Cómo decide Vd.?; esta camisa, este sombrero, estas faldas, estos pantalones; ese..., esa..., esos..., esas...; Muy bien, gracias.*

El lobo también tiene los dientes grandes y blancos.

Sure, everybody's heard the story of Little Red
Riding Hood. But what happens to it on TV?

!Qué dientes tan grandes tienes!

Es la hora de los niños. Todos los chicos esperan impacientemente su programa favorito de televisión. Esta tarde van a ver una versión moderna del clásico "Caperucita Roja." Vamos a escuchar.

Locutor: Y ahora niños, vamos a ver el capítulo final. Como Vds. ya saben, Caperucita Roja va a la casa de su abuela, con una cesta llena de frutas y dulces. Ya es tarde y quiere llegar antes de la noche. La casa está lejos y dentro de un bosque oscuro. Caperucita Roja anda mucho por el bosque. Al fin llega a la casa de su abuela. Ella no sabe que el lobo ha comido a la abuela y está en su cama. Caperucita toca a la puerta y canta alegremente.

Lobo: ¿Quién es?

Caperucita Roja: Soy yo, abuelita, y te traigo unos dulces y unas frutas.

Lobo: Pasa, pasa, hija mía. La puerta está abierta. Yo estoy enferma y no puedo bajar de la cama.

Caperucita Roja: Oh, mi pobre abuelita. . . . Pero abuelita, ¡qué orejas tan grandes tienes!

Lobo: Para oírte mejor, hija mía. ¡Ven, ven cerca de la cama!

Caperucita Roja: Aquí tienes los dulces. . . . Pero abuelita, ¡qué ojos tan grandes tienes!

Lobo: Para verte mejor, hija mía. Pero ven más cerca, un poco más.

Caperucita Roja: Pero abuelita, ¡qué dientes tan grandes tienes!

Locutor: Sí, el lobo tiene los dientes grandes y blancos también. Y si Vds. quieren tener la sonrisa que encanta, usen nuestro producto, la pasta dentífrica — Blanco Fantástico — y Vds. van a notar la diferencia.

Palabras Nuevas

SUBSTANTIVOS

la abuelita   *the granny*
el bosque   *the woods*
Caperucita Roja   *Little Red Riding Hood*
el capítulo   *the chapter*
la cesta   *the basket*
el diente   *the tooth*
los dulces   *the candy*
la fruta   *the fruit*
la hora de los niños   *the children's hour*
el lobo   *the wolf*
el ojo   *the eye*
la oreja   *the ear*
la pasta dentífrica   *the toothpaste*

la sonrisa   *the smile*
la sonrisa que encanta   *the charming smile*

ADJETIVO

lleno,a de   *full of, filled with*

VERBOS

bajar de   *to get off, to go down from*
llegar   *to arrive*
notar   *to notice*
oírte   *to hear you (fam. sing.)*
pasar   *to enter, to pass*
  ¡pasa!   *enter! (fam. sing.)*
(no) puedo   *I can(not)*

soy yo   *it's I*
vamos a. . .   *let us. . .*
¡ven más cerca!   *come closer (fam. sing.)*
verte   *to see you (fam. sing.)*

OTRAS PALABRAS

alegremente   *cheerfully*
antes (de)   *before*
hija mía   *my child*
impacientemente   *impatiently*
¡Qué orejas (ojos, dientes) tan grandes!   *What big ears (eyes, teeth)!*
ya es tarde   *it's late now (already)*

EJERCICIOS

I. (A) ¿Cierto (true) **o falso** *(false)?*

1. Es el primer capítulo de Caperucita Roja.   _____
2. Caperucita lleva una cesta a la casa de su abuela.   _____
3. La chica pasa por unas calles oscuras.   _____
4. La abuela está en la cama porque ella ha comido al lobo.   _____
5. Caperucita dice: —¡Qué manos grandes tienes!   _____
6. El lobo tiene los dientes blancos porque usa una buena pasta dentífrica.   _____

(B) Preguntas personales y generales. Write your answer in a complete Spanish sentence.

1. ¿Qué contesta Vd. si la persona dentro de la casa pregunta: —¿Quién es?
2. Para tener los dientes blancos, ¿qué usa Vd. todos los días?
3. ¿Hay mucha diferencia entre las pastas dentífricas?
4. ¿Cuál es un buen nombre para una pasta dentífrica?
5. ¡Mencione Vd. un animal que tiene los dientes grandes!

1. _____

_____

2. _____

_____

3. _____

_____

4. _____

_____

5. _____

_____

II.   Compositions: Oral or written.

(A) Look at the picture at the beginning of this Work Unit. Describe the scene in Spanish to a friend.

(B) You are Little Red Riding Hood, and you meet the wolf. What would you say to him?

Lobo: Buenos días, señorita. ¿Adónde vas?

Cap. Roja: _____

Lobo: Oh, ¿está enferma la pobre vieja?

Cap. Roja: _____

Lobo: ¿Qué tienes en esa cesta?

Cap. Roja: _____

Lobo: Eres una niña muy buena. Adiós, Caperucita. Hasta pronto.

Cap. Roja: _____

III. Caperucita Roja has a number of things in her basket. Can you unscramble the words to find out what they are?

1. unas __ __ __ __ __ __ (tuarfs)

2. unos __ __ __ __ __ __ (selcud)

3. una __ __ __ __ (lorf)

4. un __ __ __ __ __ (vueho)

5. un __ __ __ __ __ __ (hadleo)

Buenos días, señorita.
¿Adónde vas tan de prisa?

ESTRUCTURAS DE LA LENGUA

Common Adverbs. Exclamatory ¡Qué!

A. Common adverbs of time, place, and manner.

Learn the following paired opposites.

1. **ahora**	now		6. **hoy**	today
más tarde	later		**mañana**	tomorrow
2. **allí**	there		7. **más**	more
aquí	here		**menos**	less
3. **antes**	before; previously		8. **mucho**	a great deal
después	afterwards		**poco**	little
4. **bien**	well		9. **siempre**	always
mal	badly		**nunca**	never
5. **cerca**	nearby		10. **temprano**	early
lejos	faraway		**tarde**	late

B. ¡Qué! in an exclamation.

How!   What a . . . . !

How!	What a . . . . !
1. **¡Qué bonita** es ella! How pretty she is!	1. **¡Qué chica!** What a girl!
2. **¡Qué bien** canta ella! How well she sings!	2. **¡Qué chica bonita!** What a pretty girl!

Rules:

1. Before adjectives and adverbs **¡qué!** means *How!* in an excited or exclamatory sense.

2. Before nouns **¡qué!** means *what!* or *what a . . . !* in an excited or exclamatory sense. Do *not* use **un** or **una** after **¡qué!**

3. When both a noun and an adjective are present, the *noun* is generally stated *first.*

4. Write an accent mark on **qué**, and place exclamation points *before* and *after* the statement.

5. The subject is placed *after* the verb in exclamations as in questions.

STUDY THE RULES, EXAMPLES, AND MODELS BEFORE BEGINNING THE EXERCISES!

Exercises

I. Write an affirmative answer in a complete Spanish sentence, using the adverbs in *italics.*

Model: –¿Trabaja Vd. *bien* hoy?   –Trabajo bien hoy.
¿Trabajas tú bien hoy?

Are you working well today?   I am working well today.

1. ¿Entra Vd. *tarde* hoy?_____

2. ¿Termina Vd. *temprano y bien*?_____

3. ¿Habla Vd. *poco allí*?_____

4. ¿Aprendes *mucho ahora*?_____

5. ¿Contestas *más después*?_____

6. ¿Comes *mal aquí*?_____

7. ¿Viajas *lejos mañana*?_____

8. ¿*Siempre* tomas café *antes*?_____

9. ¿*Nunca* llegas *más tarde*?_____

10. ¿Gritas *menos* cuando Ana está *cerca*?_____

II. Write a rejoinder that states the *opposite* of the expression in *italics.* See the paired opposites on p. 185.

Model: –Luis vive *cerca.*   –Luis vive **lejos.**
Louis lives nearby.   Louis lives far away.

1. Juan estudia *mucho.*_____

2. Mi amiga viene *más tarde.*_____

3. *Siempre* toman café._____

4. Gritan *más* en casa._____

5. La escuela está *lejos*._____

6. *Hoy* es otro día._____

7. La casa está *aquí*._____

8. Comemos *antes*._____

9. Regresamos *temprano*._____

10. María escribe *bien*._____

III. Complete the exclamation according to the Palabras Nuevas for this work unit.

   Model: How slowly you speak! ¡ _____ habla Vd! **¡Qué despacio** habla Vd!

1. How well you dance! ¡_____baila Vd.!

2. How badly they study! ¡_____estudian ellos!

3. How late John eats! ¡_____come Juan!

4. How near the house is! ¡_____está la casa!

5. How far the park is! ¡_____está el parque!

IV. Write an affirmative response beginning with **¡Qué!**. Make all necessary changes in word order according to the model. Use exclamation points.

   Model: –¿Trabajan ellos tarde?   –**¡Qué tarde** trabajan ellos!
            Do they work late?   How late they work!

1. ¿Llega ella tarde?_____

2. ¿Habla Vd. bien?_____

3. ¿Estudian ellos mal?_____

4. ¿Viene Rosa temprano?_____

5. ¿Vive Juan lejos?_____

6. ¿Vive Ana cerca?_____

7. ¿Está ella cansada?_____

8. ¿Es él pobre?_____

9. ¿Son ellos ricos?_____

10. ¿Es Luisa bonita?_____

187

V. Write two exclamations in response to each statement, according to the model. Make all necessary changes in word order, *omitting* the verb and the article.

Model: —La chica es inteligente. ¿Verdad?   **—¡Qué chica! ¡Qué chica inteligente!**
"The girl is intelligent. Isn't she?"   "What a girl! What an intelligent girl!"

1. —Las casas son altas. ¿Verdad?_____

2. —Su madre es buena. ¿Verdad?_____

3. —Los niños son lindos. ¿Verdad?_____

4. —El cielo está azul. ¿Verdad?_____

5. —Esta escuela es grande. ¿Verdad?_____

VI. Write the Spanish equivalent in the correct word order according to the model. Use cues.

Model: What a fine day!
        bonito / día   **¡Qué día bonito!**

1. What an interesting day!

   interesante / día_____

2. What an important year!

   importante / año_____

3. What a nice boy!

   simpático / muchacho_____

4. What kind teachers!

   amables / profesores_____

5. What good classes!

   buenas / clases_____

VII. Oral Proficiency. Respond orally to the situation described. (You may *later* write your responses for intensive practice.)

Situation: Your close friend admires your smile and asks how you maintain it:—*¡Tienes una sonrisa encantadora!*

After telling your friend that he or she also has a charming smile, in **four** sentences tell your friend what **you do** and what **you do not do** for your smile. You may use your own ideas or ideas suggested by the following: *nunca dulces, menos helados, más frutas, muchas legumbres, después de comer (antes de dormir), pasta dentífrica, dentista dos veces al año, nunca dolor de dientes (muelas).*

¿Sueñas con Cocina nueva?

FAGOR
Muebles de Cocina

PORCELANOSA
CERAMICA

Una cocina Fantástica FAGOR Completa. Totalmente equipada con la mejor y más actual gama de sus muebles de cocina y electrodomésticos integrales. Con la belleza y calidad en suelos y paredes de PORCELANOSA.

Si es esta la cocina con que sueñas, ahora puede ser tuya. AVECREM te la monta **completa:** *obra, electrodomésticos y muebles FAGOR.*

Avecrem te regala tu Cocina Soñada.

Porque tus sueños merecen hacerse realidad, AVECREM sortea cada semana la cocina de tus sueños. ¿Cómo...?

Muy fácil, tan fácil como enviar una cajita de AVECREM, de cualquier formato y sabor, al Apartado 200 de Barcelona - 08080, indicando tu nombre, dirección y teléfono.

Todas las cartas recibidas participarán en todos los sorteos semanales del 17 de octubre al 12 de diciembre de 1988.

Cuantas más cajitas envíes, más posibilidades de hacer realidad TU COCINA SOÑADA.

¡Te la mereces!

Gallina Blanca

La participación supone la aceptación de las bases depositadas ante notario.

8 Pastillas

CALDO DE
Pollo

AVECREM®

Es una carta urgente.

Do you believe in horoscopes? Sometimes they
contain surprises.

¿Qué dice el horóscopo?

¿Es Vd. una persona supersticiosa? ¿Es posible saber qué va a pasar en el futuro? Hay muchas personas en este mundo que creen en los horóscopos. Uno de ellos es nuestro héroe, Patricio Pisapapeles. Cuando recibe el periódico por la mañana, no empieza a mirar ni las noticias ni los deportes. Sólo le interesa su horóscopo. Así empieza a leer su fortuna y piensa en sus planes para el día. Busca su signo de Acuario.

Piscis: (20 febrero-21 marzo)
                ¡No pierda el tiempo! Su oportunidad está aquí ahora.

Aries: (22 marzo-20 abril)
                ¡Defienda sus derechos! ¡No sea tímido!

Tauro: (21 abril-21 mayo)
                Su fortuna comienza a cambiar. Va a tener suerte.

Géminis: (22 mayo-21 junio)
                Vd. puede hacer todo ahora. Su signo es favorable.

Cáncer: (22 junio-23 julio)
                Si encuentra algún dinero, ¡no lo gaste todo!

Leo: (24 julio-23 agosto)
                ¡Recuerde a sus amigos! Ellos pueden ayudarlo.

Virgo: (24 agosto-23 septiembre)
                ¡Vuelva a su casa pronto!

Libra: (24 septiembre-23 octubre)
                ¡No cierre los ojos a oportunidades nuevas!.

Escorpión: (24 octubre-22 noviembre)
                ¡Entienda sus deseos! ¡Tenga paciencia!

Sagitario: (23 noviembre-23 diciembre)
                Si llueve hoy, Vd. pronto va a ver el sol.

Capricornio: (23 diciembre-20 enero)
                La fortuna juega con nuestras vidas. Es necesario ser valiente.

Acuario: (21 enero-19 febrero)
                Hoy viene una noticia importante. Puede cambiar su vida.

¡Dios mío, una noticia imprtante! ¿Qué puede ser? ¡La lotería, quizás! Voy a ganar la lotería. Sí, sí, eso es. Voy a recibir dinero, mucho dinero.

En este momento suena el timbre. Patricio corre a la puerta. Es el cartero con una carta urgente. Es de la madre de su mujer. Patricio la abre en un segundo y lee:

Queridos Patricio y Alicia:
    Voy a tu casa para visitarlos la semana próxima. Pienso pasar tres semanas agradables con mis hijos favoritos.

                    Cariñosamente,
                    Mamá.

191

Palabras Nuevas

SUBSTANTIVOS

el cartero   *the letter carrier*
el deporte   *the sport*
el derecho   *the right*
el deseo   *the wish, the desire*
la fortuna   *the fortune*
el horóscopo   *the horoscope*
la lotería   *the lottery*
la noticia   *the news*
Patricio   *Patrick*
la persona   *the person*
el pisapapeles   *the paperweight*
el signo de Acuario   *the sign of Aquarius*
el timbre   *the bell*

VERBOS

cambiar   *to change*
cerrar (ie)   *to close*
comenzar (ie)   *to begin*
defender (ie)   *to defend*
empezar (ie)   *to begin*
encontrar (ue)   *to find, to meet*
entender (ie)   *to understand*
ganar   *to win*
gastar   *to spend (money)*
(le) interesa   *interests him*
jugar (ue)   *to play*
llover (ue)   *to rain*
perder (ie)   *to lose*
 perder el tiempo   *to waste time*
pensar (ie)   *to think, to intend*
poder (ue)   *to be able to, can*
recordar (ue)   *to remember*
¡sea!   *be! (formal sing.)*
sonar (ue)   *to ring*
tener paciencia   *to be patient*
tener suerte   *to be lucky*

ADJETIVOS

favorable   *favorable*
supersticioso,a   *superstitious*
tímido,a   *timid*
urgente   *urgent*
valiente   *brave, valiant*

OTRAS PALABRAS

algún dinero   *some money*
cariñosamente   *affectionately*
quizás   *perhaps, maybe*

EJERCICIOS

I. (A) Complete the sentences according to the story.

1. Hay muchas personas que creen en los horóscopos. Son personas _____.

2. El horóscopo dice la _____ de una persona.

3. Patricio no lee ni las _____ ni los _____ en el periódico.

4. La fortuna de Patricio está bajo el signo de _____.

5. Una persona que nace el 22 de junio no debe _____.

(B) Preguntas personales y generales. Write your answer in a complete Spanish sentence.

1. ¿Qué parte del periódico lee Vd. generalmente?
2. ¿Cuál es el día de su nacimiento (birth)?
3. ¿Cuál es su signo del Zodíaco?
4. ¿Cuánto dinero puede Vd. ganar en la lotería?
5. ¿Qué hace un cartero?

1. _____

2. _____

3. _____

4. _____

5. _____

II. Unscramble the letters in the boxes below and see the advice given in your horoscope.

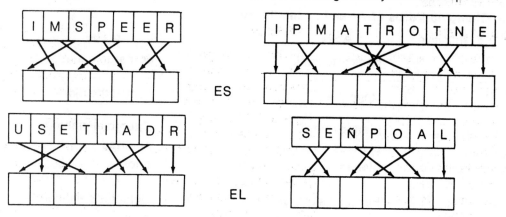

| I | M | S | P | E | E | R |

| | | | | | | |

| I | P | M | A | T | R | O | T | N | E |

ES

| | | | | | | | | | |

| U | S | E | T | I | A | D | R |

| | | | | | | | |

EL

| S | E | Ñ | P | O | A | L |

| | | | | | | |

III. Compositions: Oral or written.

(A) Look at the picture at the beginning of this Work Unit. Describe the scene in Spanish to a friend.

(B) Tell about a five-day horoscope, giving advice according to the word cues. Change *infinitives* to commands.

Su horóscopo

1. **lunes:** _____
   ¡No *perder* tiempo! Su oportunidad está aquí.

2. **martes:** _____
   ¡*Defender* sus derechos! ¡No sea tímido!

3. **miércoles:** _____
   ¡*Cambiar* su fortuna! Vd. tiene suerte.

4. **jueves:** _____
   ¡*Tener* Vd. paciencia! Su signo es favorable.

5. **viernes:** _____
   ¡No *gastar* Vd. mucho dinero!

Add two more horoscopes in Spanish: **El fin de semana:**

6. **sábado:** _____

7. **domingo:** _____

ESTRUCTURAS DE LA LENGUA

Stem-Changing Verbs of Ar and Er Infinitives

A. **ar** Infinitives e>ie o>ue

pensar to think contar to count

	I think so.	I count the money.
1. yo	**Pienso** que sí.	**Cuento** el dinero.
2. tú	**piensas**	**cuentas**
3. él, ella, Vd.	**piensa**	**cuenta**
4. nosotros-as	Pensamos que sí.	Contamos el dinero.
5. vosotros-as	pensáis	contáis
6. ellos-as, Vds.	**piensan**	**cuentan**
Commands	**¡Piense** Vd.!	**¡Cuente** Vd.!
	¡Piensen Vds.!	**¡Cuenten** Vds.!
	¡Pensemos!	¡Contemos!

B. **er** Infinitives e>ie o>ue

entender to understand volver to return

	I understand very well.	I'm returning home.
1. yo	**Entiendo** muy bien.	**Vuelvo** a casa.
2. tú	**entiendes**	**vuelves**
3. él, ella, Vd.	**entiende**	**vuelve**
4. nosotros-as	Entendemos muy bien.	Volvemos a casa.
5. vosotros-as	entendéis	volvéis
6. ellos-as, Vds.	**entienden**	**vuelven**
Commands	**¡Entienda** Vd.!	**¡Vuelva** Vd.!
	¡Entiendan Vds.!	**¡Vuelvan** Vds.!
	¡Entendamos!	¡Volvamos!

Rules:

1. **o>ue** The **o** in the stem of some **ar** and **er** infinitives changes to **ue** in the present tense, in persons 1, 2, 3, 6, and in the commands, **Vd.** and **Vds.**

2. **e>ie** The **e** in the stem of some **ar** and **er** infinitives changes to **ie** in the present tense, in persons 1, 2, 3, 6, and in the commands, **Vd.** and **Vds.**

C. Learn these stem-changing verbs:

ar infinitives

e>ie		o>ue	
cerrar	to close	**almorzar**	to lunch
comenzar	to begin	**contar**	to tell, count
empezar	to begin	**encontrar**	to meet, to find
pensar	to think;	**mostrar**	to show
	to intend	**recordar**	to remember
nevar	to snow	**volar**	to fly

er infinitives

e>ie		o>ue	
defender	to defend	**mover**	to move
entender	to understand	**poder**	to be able
perder	to lose	**volver**	to return
querer	to want	**llover**	to rain

D. Llover (ue) and **nevar (ie)** are meaningful only in the third person singular:

llueve it rains   **nieva** it snows

E. **Jugar** is the only verb which changes the infinitive stem's **u** to **ue** in persons 1, 2, 3, 6 of the present tense.

jugar to play (a game)

		I play football.
1. yo	**Juego** al fútbol.	
2. tú	**juegas**	
3. él, ella, Vd.	**juega**	
4. nosotros-as	Jugamos al fútbol.	
5. vosotros-as	jugáis	
6. ellos-as Vds.	**juegan**	

STUDY THE RULES, EXAMPLES, AND MODELS BEFORE BEGINNING THE EXERCISES!

Exercises

I. Rewrite the model sentence substituting the subject given in parentheses, and using the appropriate form of the verb.

A. Model: Yo pienso ir mañana.   (Ellos) **Ellos piensan ir mañana.**
                I intend to go tomorrow.   They intend to go tomorrow.

1. (Tú)_____

2. (Diego)_____

3. (Diego y María)_____

4. (Tú y yo)_____

5. (Vds.)_____

6. (Yo)_____

B. Model: ¿Almuerzas *tú* a las doce?   (Vds.) **¿Almuerzan Vds. a las doce?**
                Do you (fam. sing.) lunch at 12:00?   Do you (formal pl.) lunch at 12:00?

1. (Vd.)_____

2. (Vd. y yo)_____

3. (Las mujeres)_____

4. (Mi amiga)_____

5. (Yo)_____

6. (Tú)_____

II. Rewrite the sentence substituting the appropriate form of the verb given in parentheses. Keep the same subject.

   Model: Yo encuentro a mis amigos.   (perder) **Yo pierdo a mis amigos.**
            I meet my friends.   I lose my friends.

1. Ellos empiezan el examen. (comenzar)_____

2. ¿Cuentas tú el dinero? (encontrar)_____

3. Ana y él pierden el libro. (entender)_____

4. Él cierra la revista. (empezar)_____

5. Vds. no pueden leer. *(volver a)_____

*again

6. Ella quiere la música. (perder)_____

7. Vd. no lo piensa bien. (cerrar)_____

8. Yo encuentro el disco. (recordar)_____

9. ¿No lo comienzan ellas? (empezar)_____

10. Nosotros almorzamos mal. (contar)_____

III. Write an affirmative answer in a complete Spanish sentence using the words in *italics* and the appropriate form of the verb used in the question.

Model: ¿A dónde volvemos?   *Vds. / a casa* **Vds. vuelven a casa.**
        Where are we returning?   You are returning home.

1. ¿Cuándo comenzamos a estudiar?   *Vds. / a las cuatro*

_____

2. ¿A qué hora cerramos los libros?   *Vds. / a las diez*

_____

3. ¿Cuándo podemos venir a la casa?   *Vds. / venir temprano*

_____

4. ¿A dónde volamos mañana?   *Vds. / a Madrid*

_____

5. ¿Cómo quieren Vds. viajar?   *Nosotros / viajar en coche*

_____

6. ¿Entienden Vds. la novela?   *Nosotros no / la novela*

_____

7. ¿Dónde encuentran Vds. comida?   *Nosotras / en la cafetería*

_____

8. ¿Cuentas el dinero?   *Yo nunca / los dólares*

_____

9. ¿Cuánto dinero pierdes?   *Yo / dos dólares*

_____

10. ¿Con quiénes vuelvo yo a casa?   *Tú / a casa con nosotros.*

_____

IV. Write an answer in *two* complete Spanish sentences: a) a NEGATIVE answer using **Nosotros;** b) an affirmative answer using **Ella sí que . . .** according to the model.

Model: ¿Piensan Vds. leer?   **Nosotros no** pensamos leer.   **Ella sí que** piensa leer.
            Do you intend to read?   We don't intend to read.   She surely intends to read.

1. ¿Empiezan la comida ahora? _____

_____

2. ¿Almuerzan Vds. en un restaurante chino? _____

_____

3. ¿Entienden Vds. el chino? _____

_____

Barron's has been authorized to use the chart
"Consuma Diariamente Los Cuatro Alimentos Básicos"
by Del Monte Corporation, San Francisco, California, its creator.
DEL MONTE is the registered trademark of Del Monte Corporation."

4. ¿Comienzan Vds. a comer?_____

_____

5. ¿Mueven Vds. la boca? _____

_____

6. ¿Cierran Vds. la boca?_____

_____

7. ¿Quieren Vds. tomar un helado?_____

_____

8. ¿Pueden Vds. comer más?_____

_____

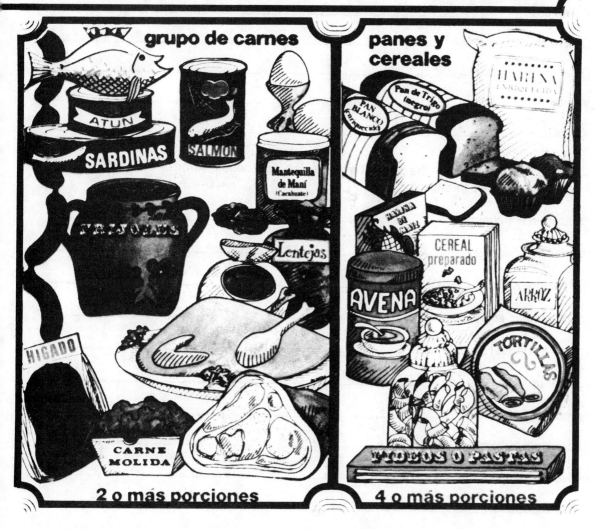

Los Cuatro Alimentos Básicos

grupo de carnes

panes y cereales

ATUN

SARDINAS

SALMON

Mantequilla de Maní (Cacahuate)

FRIJOLES

Lentejas

HIGADO

CARNE MOLIDA

HARINA ENRIQUECIDA

Pan de Trigo (negro)

PAN BLANCO Enriquecido

CEREAL preparado

AVENA

ARROZ

TORTILLAS

FIDEOS O PASTAS

2 o más porciones

4 o más porciones

9. ¿Vuelven Vds. a la escuela mañana cuando llueve? _____

_____

10. ¿Juegan Vds. en la calle cuando nieva? _____

_____

V. Write the appropriate NEGATIVE command in a complete Spanish sentence as a response to the question.

Models: ¿Pierde(n) Vd(s.) paciencia?   **¡No pierda(n) Vd(s.) paciencia!**
          Are you losing patience?   Don't lose patience!

          ¿Perdemos paciencia?   **¡No perdamos paciencia!**
          Are we losing patience?   Let us not lose patience!

1. ¿Pierde Vd.? _____

2. ¿Perdemos? _____

3. ¿Piensan Vds.? _____

4. ¿Pensamos? _____

5. ¿Cuenta Vd.? _____

6. ¿Contamos? _____

7. ¿Defienden Vds. al amigo? _____

8. ¿Defendemos a los amigos? _____

9. ¿Vuelve Vd.? _____

10. ¿Volvemos? _____

VI. Complete the series using the subject **yo** with the *appropriate form of the verb*, and the vocabulary provided in parentheses.

1. (pensar en el trabajo) _____

2. (comenzar el trabajo) _____

3. (no entender los ejercicios) _____

4. (perder la paciencia) _____

5. (cerrar los libros) _____

6. (querer una fruta) _____

7. (almorzar en la cocina) _____

8. (recordar el trabajo) _____

9. (volver al escritorio) _____

10. (mostrar paciencia) _____

VII. Oral Proficiency. Respond orally to the situation described. (You may *later* write your responses for intensive practice.)

Situation: We are at a party. You are telling fortunes. I ask you to tell me mine:—¿*Cómo cambia mi suerte?*

After asking me my birthday, and telling me my sign, in **four** Spanish sentences state how my luck is changing. You may use your own ideas or ideas suggested by the following: *la vida / comenzar, la suerte / empezer, encontrar / el amor, los amigos / entender, tú / tener buena suerte.*

Quiero casarme con una millonaria.

Teodoro thinks he's found a way to be rich and happy without working.
Do you agree?

Quiero ser rico

Este junio va a ser un mes especial para Teodoro Tacones. Después de pasar cinco años en la escuela secundaria, finalmente va a graduarse. Teodoro es un muchacho de poco talento pero de mucha ambición. Sabe que tiene que encontrar trabajo lo más pronto posible. Así va a la oficina de empleos de la escuela para pedir ayuda.

Consejero: ¿Qué tal, Teodoro? Al fin va a graduarse.

Teodoro: Sí, señor. Por eso estoy aquí. Necesito su consejo. Busco un empleo.

Consejero: Ah, bueno. ¿Qué clase de trabajo desea?

Teodoro: Pues, un puesto con buen sueldo. Quiero ganar mucho dinero; quiero ser rico.

Consejero: Entonces, Vd. debe ir a la universidad para estudiar más. Tiene que aprender una profesión como médico o como abogado.

Teodoro: No, eso es mucho trabajo. Quiero un empleo fácil. Así puedo descansar y no hacer nada. Quiero viajar por el mundo y ver a la gente de otros países.

Consejero: Entonces, ¿por qué no estudia para ser piloto? Así Vd. puede ganar un buen sueldo y puede viajar también.

Teodoro: No, tengo miedo de los aviones. Y además, los pilotos trabajan largas horas y tienen muchas responsabilidades.

Consejero: Bueno, tengo la solución. Vd. debe casarse con una millonaria.

Teodoro: ¡Perfecto! ¡Ésta es la solución ideal! ¿Para qué trabajar?

Consejero: Sí, pero sólo hay un problema.

Teodoro: ¿Cuál?

Consejero: Todas la chicas quieren casarse con millonarios.

Palabras Nuevas

SUBSTANTIVOS

el abogado   *the lawyer*
la ambición   *the ambition*
el avión   *the airplane*
la chica   *the girl*
el consejo   *the advice*
el empleo   *the job, the employment*
la escuela secundaria   *the high school, the secondary school*
la oficina de empleos   *the employment office*
el millonario   *the millionaire*
el piloto   *the pilot*
el puesto   *the job, the position*

la responsabilidad   *the responsibility*
la solución   *the solution*
el sueldo   *the salary*
el tacón   *the heel*
el talento   *the talent*
Teodoro   *Theodore*

VERBOS

casarse (con)   *to marry, to get married (to)*
ganar dinero   *to earn money*
graduarse   *to graduate*
pedir (i) ayuda   *to ask for help*
tener miedo   *to be afraid*

tener que   *to have to*
viajar   *to travel*

OTRAS PALABRAS

al fin   *finally*
¿Cuál?   *Which? What?*
finalmente   *finally*
lo más pronto posible   *as soon as possible*
¿Para qué?   *For what purpose? Why?*
por eso   *therefore, because of that*
¿Qué clase de?   *What kind of?*

203

EJERCICIOS

I. (A) Preguntas. Write your answer in a complete Spanish sentence.

1. ¿Por qué es un día especial para Teodoro Tacones? _____

2. ¿Cuántos años está en la escuela secundaria? _____

3. ¿Qué quiere ser el muchacho? _____

4. ¿Por qué no quiere ser piloto? _____

(B) Preguntas personales y generales. Write your answer in a complete Spanish sentence.

1. ¿Cuándo va Vd. a terminar la escuela?
2. ¿Cuál es su ambición?
3. ¿Quiere Vd. ser rico? ¿Por qué?
4. ¿En qué clase de trabajo va a recibir un buen sueldo?

1. _____

2. _____

3. _____

4. _____

II. ¿Cómo se dice en español?

1. He's finally going to graduate.
2. He wants to find work as soon as possible.
3. I want to earn a lot of money.
4. I want an easy job in order to rest.

1. _____

2. _____

3. _____

4. _____

III. Compositions: Oral or written.

(A) Look at the picture at the beginning of this Work Unit. Describe the scene in Spanish to a friend.

(B) You're looking for a job and are discussing the possibilities with the employment counselor.

Consejero—Bueno, ¿ qué clase de trabajo busca Vd?

1. Usted _____

Consejero—Para ese empleo, va a necesitar ir a la universidad.

2. Usted _____

Consejero—Es una posibilidad. ¿Cuánto quiere ganar por semana?

3. Usted _____

Consejero—En ese caso, creo que no hay ninguna dificultad. ¡Venga a verme mañana!

4. Usted _____

ESTRUCTURAS DE LA LENGUA

The complementary infinitive. The infinitive after **ir a, tener que,** and **para.**

A. The complementary infinitive completes the thought:

After verbs of mild obligation — **deber, necesitar**

1. —¿Qué debes hacer? What should you do?	—Debo saber la lección. I should know the lesson.
2. —¿Qué necesitas hacer? What do you need to do?	—Necesito estudiarla. I need to study it.

After verbs of wanting and planning — **desear, querer, pensar**

1. —¿Qué quieres (deseas) hacer? What do you want to do?	—Quiero (deseo) escuchar mis discos. I want to listen to my records.
2. —¿Qué piensas hacer? What do you plan (intend) to do?	—Pienso escucharlos ahora. I plan (intend) to listen to them now.

After verbs of being able — **poder, saber**

1. —¿No puedes andar hoy? Can't you walk today?	—Puedo andar un poco. I can (am able to) walk a little.
2. —¿Sabes leer el español? Do you know how to (can you) read Spanish?	—Sé escribirlo también. I know how to (can) write it, too.

Rules:

1. Only the first verb agrees with the subject.

2. **Deber, necesitar, desear, querer, pensar, poder, saber,** are completed by the infinitive form of the verb that follows. Infinitives end in **ar, er,** or **ir.**

3. **Poder** means *can, to be able* in a strictly physical sense. **Saber** means *can* or *to know how* in the sense of possessing a skill or talent.

205

Tengo que comer

B. The infinitive form of the verb follows **ir a** and **tener que.**

---

1. —¿Qué tienes **que** hacer?　　　　　—**Tengo que comer.** (strong obligation)
　　What do you have to (must you) do?　　I have to (must) eat.

2. —¿Cuándo vas **a** comer?　　　　　—**Voy a comer** ahora.
　　When are you going to eat?　　　　I am going to eat now.

Rules:

1. **Tener que** followed by the infinitive means *to have to* or *must* and indicates strong obligation. **Deber** (should, ought) is milder. **Tener** agrees with its subject. **Que** has no English translation in this idiomatic expression.

2. **Ir a** followed by the infinitive tells what you are going to do in the immediate future. **Ir** agrees with its subject. **A** has no translation here.

3. For the present tense forms of **ir** and **tener** see Work Unit 7.

C. **Para:** *in order (to)* indicates purpose and introduces a complementary infinitive.

---

1. —¿**Para** qué trabajas?　　　　　—**Trabajo para tener dinero.**
　　For what purpose do you work?　　I work to (in order to) have money.

2. —¿**Para** qué comen Vds.?　　　　—**Comemos para vivir.**
　　For what purpose (why) do you eat?　We eat to (in order to) live.

STUDY THE RULES, EXAMPLES, AND MODELS BEFORE BEGINNING TH EXERCISES!

Exercises

I. Rewrite the model sentence using the subject in *italics*. Make necessary changes in the verb. (Review the forms of **tener** in Work Unit 8.)

Model: **Nosotros tenemos que comer.**   *Ella.* **Ella tiene que comer.**
We have to eat.   She has to eat.

1. *Yo*_____   4. *Vds.*_____

2. *Tú*_____   5. *Vd.*_____

3. *Juan*_____   6. *Ana y yo*_____

7. *Juan y Ana*_____

II. Rewrite the model sentence using the subject in *italics*. Make necessary changes in the verb. (Review forms of **ir** in Work Unit 8.)

Model: **Yo no voy a leer esta noche.**   *Tomás.* **Tomás no va a leer esta noche.**
I'm not going to read tonight.   Thomas isn't going to read tonight.

1. *Los tíos*_____

2. *Susana*_____

3. *Tú*_____

4. *Vds.*_____

5. *Marta y yo*_____

6. *Yo*_____

7. *Él*_____

III. Rewrite the MODEL QUESTION substituting the verbs in parentheses for the verbs in *italics*.

Model: ¿*Comemos* para *vivir*?   (escribir / practicar) **¿Escribimos** para **practicar?**
Do we eat in order to live?   Do we write in order to practice?

1. (Estudiamos / comprender)_____

2. (Leemos / saber)_____

3. (Hablamos / practicar)_____

4. (Escuchamos / aprender)_____

5. (Trabajamos / comer)_____

IV. Rewrite the model sentence substituting the verb in parentheses for the one in *italics.* Use the appropriate preposition **(a, para,** or **que)** *if* one is necessary.

Model: *Quieren* hacerlo.   (Voy) **Voy a hacerlo.**
They want to do it.   I'm going to do it.

1. (Necesita)_____   6. (Tengo)_____

2. (Deben)_____   7. (Trabaja)_____

3. (Tiene) _____   8. (Quiero)_____

4. (Puedes)_____   9. (Vamos)_____

5. (Sé)_____   10. (Desean)_____

V. Complete the following. Insert the appropriate word **(a, para,** or **que)** if one is needed. Write a dash (—) if no additional word is needed.

1. Yo deseo _____ pasar un rato con mis amigos.   2. Uso el teléfono _____ invitarlos.

3. Los amigos, Pepe y Luisa, van _____ venir a mi casa.   4. Ellos tienen _____ llamar

a la puerta dos veces.   5. No pueden _____ esperar mucho tiempo.   6. Yo voy _____

abrir la puerta.   7. Queremos _____ escuchar música.   8. Pepe va al centro _____

comprar más discos.   9. Sabemos _____ bailar muy bien a la música popular.   10. No

tenemos mucho tiempo porque los amigos deben _____ regresar a casa a las diez.

VI. Complete with the correct form of an appropriate verb from those provided below.

1. Hoy _____ _____ estudiar para un examen. (I have to)   2. Yo _____ pasar

dos horas con mis libros. (I should)   3. Primero, _____ _____ comer una fruta.

(I'm going to)   4. Tomo mi pluma _____ _____ el vocabulario. (in order to write)

5. Mi madre me llama dos veces pero yo no _____ _____ ahora. (want to eat)

6. Ella _____ _____ esperar más. (cannot)   7. Finalmente ella _____ _____

gritar. (has to) 8. —Nosotros _____ _____ comer _____ _____. (need; in

order to live)   9. Respondo: —Voy porque ya _____ _____ todo el vocabu-

lario. (I know how to write)   10. Me gusta _____ y luego _____. (to study; to eat)

VOCABULARIO: **comer, deber, escribir, estudiar, ir a, necesitar, no, para, poder, querer, saber, tener que, vivir.**

VII. Write an affirmative response using the words given in parentheses.

Model: —¿Cuándo vas a llegar? (hoy) —**Voy a llegar hoy.**
When are you going to arrive? I'm going to arrive today.

1. ¿A qué hora tienes que llegar al trabajo? (a las tres de la tarde)

_____

2. ¿Qué sabes tú hacer allí? (vender ropa)

_____

3. ¿Cuántas horas tienes que trabajar? (tres horas después de la escuela)

_____

4. ¿Cuándo vas a casa a comer? (un poco antes de las seis)

_____

5. ¿Cuándo puedes salir temprano? (los sábados)

_____

6. ¿No deseas jugar por la tarde? (siempre)

_____

7. ¿Para qué trabajas? (tener dinero)

_____

8. ¿Para qué necesitas dinero? (ir a estudiar en la universidad)

_____

9. ¿Debe trabajar tu hermano? (sí, también)

_____

10. ¿Van Vds. a estudiar juntos? (sí, juntos)

_____

VIII. Oral Proficiency. Respond orally to the situation described. (You may *later* write your responses for intensive practice.)

Situation: You speak to me, your counselor, about your future career. I encourage you to tell me about your ideas:—¿*Qué ideas tienes?*

After telling me that you need advice, in **four** Spanish sentences tell me what talent(s) you have, and about one or two of your ambitions. You may use your own ideas or ideas suggested by the following: *tener talento (interés, ambición); voy a (quiero) ser; para ayudar (ganar, ser millonario[a]); tener que estudiar (graduarme).*

Yo creí que traías una mala noticia.

*We all love a sad story. It gives us a chance
to have a good cry.*

¡Qué vida tan cruel!

A las doce en punto, todas las mujeres de la ciudad ponen un programa de televisión, "La vida feliz de Alfonso y Adela." En este programa las personas sufren terriblemente. Todos los días hay un nuevo capítulo triste. Yolanda González está loca por este programa. Durante toda la hora, llora constantemente. Pero al día siguiente, lo mira otra vez. Vamos a escuchar el capítulo de hoy. Alfonso regresa de su trabajo y habla con su mujer.

Adela:	Ay, mi vida. Estás tan triste. ¿Qué te pasa?
Alfonso:	Adela, mi amor, tengo una mala noticia para ti. Ya no puedo trabajar. Cierran la oficina mañana y todos tenemos que buscar otro empleo.
Adela:	No es tan serio, Alfonsito. Pronto vas a encontrar trabajo.
Alfonso:	Imposible, mi cielo. Estoy muy enfermo y el médico dice que necesito una operación. Tengo que ir mañana al hospital.
Adela:	Oh, no. ¡Y mañana viene la abuela a vivir con nosotros porque ella no puede pagar su alquiler! ¡No tenemos más dinero! ¿Qué vamos a hacer?
Alfonso:	Es necesario ser valiente. ¿Dónde están nuestros hijos adorables, Raúl y Rodrigo? Quiero hablar con ellos.
Adela:	Oh, Alfonso. ¿No recuerdas? Están en la prisión por robar un automóvil.
Alfonso:	Sí, sí. Un coche patrullero con el policía adentro. Nuestros hijos son adorables pero estúpidos.
Adela:	¡Ay, qué vida tan miserable y cruel!

En ese momento, Gustavo González, el esposo de Yolanda, abre la puerta y entra en la sala. Completamente sorprendida, Yolanda le pregunta:

Yolanda:	Gustavo, ¿Qué te pasa! ¿Por qué vuelves a casa tan temprano?
Gustavo:	Yolanda, tengo una mala noticia para ti. Tengo un resfriado y no puedo trabajar más hoy. Además perdí mi cartera con veinte dólares. (Yolanda comienza a reír.) Pero, ¿estás loca? ¿Por qué ríes?
Yolanda:	¿Es eso todo? ¿Cuál es la mala noticia?

Palabras Nuevas

SUBSTANTIVOS

Adela *Adele*
Alfonso *Alphonse*
  Alfonsito *little Alphonse,*
  "Alfie"
el alquiler *the rent*
la cartera *the wallet*
(mi) cielo (vida, amor) *(my)*
  darling
el coche (patrullero) *the*
  (patrol) car
la operación *the operation*
la prisión *the prison, the jail*
el resfriado *the cold (illness)*

ADJETIVOS

adorable *adorable*
cruel *cruel*
estúpido *stupid*
miserable *miserable*
serio,a *serious*

VERBOS

llorar *to cry*
perdí *I lost*
reír *to laugh*
  ríes *you (fam. sing.) are*
  laughing

OTRAS PALABRAS

al día siguiente *on the*
  following day
constantemente *constantly*
durante toda la hora *for the*
  whole hour
estar loco,a por *to be crazy*
  about
otra vez *again*
para ti *for you (fam. sing.)*
¿Qué te pasa? *What is the*
  matter with you (fam. sing.)
terriblemente *terribly*

EJERCICIOS

I. (A) Write the word that makes the sentence correct, replacing the word in italics.

1. A las doce todas las mujeres escuchan un programa en *la radio*.   _____
2. Alfonso y Adela llevan una vida *feliz*.   _____
3. En el último cápitulo del programa, Alfonso trae una *buena* noticia.   _____
4. Raúl y Rodrigo están ahora en la *universidad*.   _____
5. Gustavo vuelve *tarde* a la casa.   _____

(B) Preguntas personales y generales. Write your answer in a complete Spanish sentence.

1. ¿Qué hace su papá cuando regresa del trabajo?
2. ¿Qué tiene Vd. que hacer si tiene un resfriado?
3. ¿Qué hay dentro de su cartera?
4. ¿Qué puede Vd. comprar con veinte dólares?
5. ¿Cuál es un ejemplo de una mala noticia?

1. _____

2. _____

    _____

3. _____

    _____

4. _____

    _____

5. _____

    _____

II. Unscramble the words in the boxes to form complete sentences.

1.

llora	durante	la
constantemente	hora	toda

2.

mala	para	noticia
ti	tengo	una

3.

nuestros	estúpidos	son
adorables	pero	hijos

4.

tenemos	empleo	buscar
que	todos	otro

1. _____

2. _____

3. _____

4. _____

III. Compositions: Oral or written.

(A) Look at the picture at the beginning of this Work Unit. Describe the scene in Spanish to a friend.

(B) Tell about watching television. Include the following:

La televisión

1. At night you always watch television.   2. There are many interesting programs.   3. Some programs are very stupid.   4. Your favorite program is _____.   5. It starts at _____.

ESTRUCTURAS DE LA LENGUA
Prepositional Pronouns

A. **After the prepositions a, para, sin, sobre, de,** and compounds of **de (cerca de,** etc.), use **mí, ti,** and forms that look like subject pronouns.

¡ Para ti !

Singular Persons	*Plural Persons*
1. El regalo es **para mí.** The present is for me.	4. Sale **sin nosotros, -as** He leaves without us.
2. Corre **a ti.** He runs to you (*fam. sing.*).	5. Vivo cerca de **vosotros, -as** I live near you (*fam. pl.*)
3. Habla **de él, de ella** y **de Vd.** I speak of him (it *masc.*), of her (it *fem*), and of you (*formal sing.*).	6. Estoy **con ellos -as** y **con Vds.** I am with them and you.

Rules:

1. Learn these prepositions: **a** *to*, **de** *from*, **sin** *without*, **con** *with*, **para** *for*, **cerca de** *near*.

2. Except for **mí** and **ti,** the pronouns that follow the above prepositions are identical with these subject pronouns: **él, ella, Vd., nosotros, -as, vosotros, -as, ellos, ellas, Vds.**

3. After a preposition **él, ella,** may mean *it*, as well as *her*, *him*. **Ellos, -as** mean *them* for things as well as persons.

4. **Mí** *me* is distinguished from **mi** *my* by the accent mark.

5. **De él** *of him* does not contract, unlike **del** *of the.*

B. The preposition **con** *with* combines with **mí** and **ti** to form **conmigo** *with me*, and **contigo** *with you.*

1. Trabajan **conmigo.**
   They work *with me.*

2. Estudian **contigo.**
   They study *with you* (fam. sing.).

3. Comen **con él, con ella, con Vd.**
   They eat *with him* (it *masc.*), *with her* (it *fem.*) *with you.*

4. Juegan **con nosotros, -as.**
   They play *with us.*

5. Hablan **con vosotros, -as.**
   They speak *with you* (fam. pl.).

6. Van **con ellos-as** y **con Vds.**
   They are going *with them* and *with you* (pl.)

Rule:

Con *must* combine to form **conmigo, contigo. Con** remains separate from the following: **él, ella, Vd., nosotros, -as, vosotros, -as, ellos, -as, Vds.**

STUDY THE RULES, EXAMPLES, AND MODELS BEFORE BEGINNING THE EXERCISES!

Exercises

I. Rewrite the sentence, substituting for each of the two expressions in *italics* the appropriate form of the word in parentheses. Use **con** and **para** in each sentence.

Model: Compran el regalo *conmigo* y es para *mí.*
They buy the present with me and it is for me.

(ella) Compran el regalo con **ella** y es para **ella.**
They buy the present with her and it is for her.

Compran el regalo *conmigo* y es para *mí.*

1. (él)_____

2. (ellos)_____

3. (ella)_____

4. (ellas)_____

5. (mí)_____

6. (ti)_____

7. (Vds.)_____

8. (nosotros)_____

9. (vosotros)_____

10. (Vd.)_____

II. Rewrite the sentence, substituting ONE appropriate prepositional pronoun for the expression in *italics*.

    Model: Están cerca de Luis y de mí.   Están cerca de **nosotros.**
                  They are near Louis and me.   They are near us. (*m.*)

1. Vivo cerca del *centro y del tren.* _____

2. Los niños vienen sin *su abuela y sin Juan.* _____

3. Compras dulces para *Luisa y para su amiga.* _____

4. Los perritos corren a *Pedro y a Vd.* _____

5. Las chicas bailan *conmigo y con mis amigos.* _____

III. Write an affirmative answer, substituting the appropriate prepositional pronoun for the expression in *italics*. Begin with **Sí**.

    Model: —¿Vive Vd. (Vives) en *la casa grande?*   **—Sí,** vivo en **ella.**
                  Do you live in the large house?   Yes, I live in it.

1. ¿Vive Vd. cerca de *la ciudad?* _____

2. ¿Lo prepara Vd. para *las fiestas?* _____

3. ¿Desea Vd. escribir sin *lápiz?* _____

4. ¿Estás sentado en *el banco?* _____

5. ¿Juegas cerca de *los árboles?* _____

IV. Write a response using the preposition and the appropriate prepositional pronoun suggested by the word(s) in *italics*: **¿_____? Gracias.**

    Model: —El regalo es *para Vd.*   **—¿Para mí? Gracias.**
                  The present is for you.   For me? Thanks.

1. Compro una bicicleta *para Vd.* _____

2. Vamos a estudiar *con Vd.* _____

3. Hacemos el trabajo *sin ti.* _____

4. Vamos a comer *cerca de Vds.* _____

5. ¡Coma Vd. *con nosotros!* _____

V. Write a rejoinder in a complete Spanish sentence. Use **con** and the appropriate prepositional pronoun in your answer. Begin with **Sí**.

    Model: —Van contigo, ¿verdad?   **—Sí. Van conmigo.**
                  They're going with you. Right?   Yes. They're going with me.

1. Asisten contigo, ¿verdad? _____

215

    2. Juegan con Vds., ¿verdad?_____

    3. Van con Vd., ¿verdad?_____

    4. Trabajan con nosotros, ¿verdad?_____

    5. Comen conmigo, ¿verdad?_____

VI. Write the equivalent in a complete Spanish sentence using the vocabulary provided.

    1. They buy the present for me and for him._____

                                   Ellos compran / regalo para / y para /

    2. The child plays with me and with my friend._____

                                   El niño juega con / y / mi amigo

    3. She runs to him, not to you (*formal*)_____

                                   Ella corre a /, no a /

    4. The man works without us and without her._____

                                   El hombre trabaja sin / y sin /

    5. She lives near you (*fam.*), Peter, and near them._____

                                   Ella vive cerca de /, Pedro, y cerca de /

VII. Oral Proficiency. Respond orally to the situation described. (You may *later* write your responses for more practice.)

Situation: You telephone me. You are sad because your friend's family is having bad luck. I encourage you to talk about them asking:—*¿Qué pasa?*. You tell me all their bad news.

After telling me that you are sad, in **four** Spanish sentences mention several bad things that are happening to them. You may use your own ideas or ideas suggested by the following: *The family lives near you, but cannot pay the rent. Your friend is going to live far from you. His girlfriend is not crazy about him (her boyfriend is not crazy about her) any more (ya no). Someone stole their car. You lost your wallet and do not have money for them with you. What bad news it is!*

La construcción de la casa
está terminada.

Some people are never satisfied. What could
Esmeralda want now?

¡Vamos a construir una casa!

¡Qué día tan triste! Esmeralda, una niña de seis años, está sola en casa con su abuelo. Su padre trabaja, sus hermanos mayores están en la escuela, y su madre está en la casa de una vecina enferma. Quiere ir a jugar afuera pero no puede porque hace mal tiempo. Hace frío y llueve. Esmeralda ya está cansada de jugar con su muñeca, Pepita, y está muy triste.

Esmeralda: Ay, abuelito, ¿qué vamos a hacer? Estoy tan aburrida.

Abuelo: Bueno, niña. Dime, ¿dónde vive tu Pepita?

Esmeralda: ¿Cómo? Pepita vive aquí, conmigo, por supuesto.

Abuelo: Ah, pero no tiene su propia casa, ¿verdad? ¡Vamos a construirla!

Esmeralda: Oh, ¡qué buena idea! Sí, vamos a construir una casa para Pepita.

Abuelo: Primero, necesitamos una caja, así.

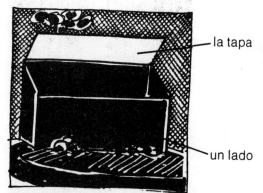

la tapa

una caja

un lado

Esmeralda: Sí, los lados de la caja pueden ser las paredes de la casa. ¡Haga Vd. un techo de la tapa y póngalo en la casa!

el techo

la ventana

Esmeralda: Ahora, ¡ponga una puerta en el frente de la casa y unas ventanas en las paredes!

219

Abuelo: ¿Qué más necesitamos?

Esmeralda: Bueno, ¡haga una chimenea y póngala en el techo! Necesitamos también un jardín con unos árboles de cartón.

Después de media hora, la construcción está terminada.

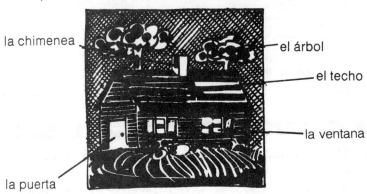

la chimenea — el árbol — el techo — la ventana — la puerta

Abuelo: Aquí tienes tu casa, niña. ¿No estás contenta ahora?

Esmeralda: No, abuelito, porque es la única casa en el vecindario y Pepita va a estar sola. Ahora, tenemos que hacer otra cosa necesaria. . . . ¡Construir más casas!

Palabras Nuevas

SUBSTANTIVOS

el abuelito   *the grandpa*
la caja   *the box*
el cartón   *the cardboard*
la construcción   *the construction*
la chimenea   *the chimney*
el frente   *the front*
el jardín   *the garden*
el lado   *the side*
la pared   *the wall*
Pepita   *Josie, little Josephine*

la tapa   *the cover*
el techo   *the roof, the ceiling*

ADJETIVOS

propio,a   *own*
terminado,a   *finished*
único,a   *only*

VERBOS

construir   *to build, to construct*
¡dime!   *tell me! (fam. sing.)*
hace frío   *it is cold (weather)*

hace mal tiempo   *it is bad weather*
¡haga!   *make! (formal sing.)*
¡póngalo(la)!   *put it (formal sing.)*
¡vamos!   *let's go!*

OTRAS PALABRAS

afuera   *outside*
después de media hora   *after a half hour*
por supuesto   *of course*

EJERCICIOS

I. (A) **Preguntas.** Write your answer in a complete Spanish sentence.

1.   ¿Cuántos años tiene Esmeralda?
2.   ¿Por qué está triste hoy?
3.   ¿Dónde está la familia de Esmeralda?
4.   ¿Por qué no puede jugar afuera?
5.   Después de ver la casa, ¿por qué no está contenta Esmeralda?

1. _____

2. _____

3. _____

4. _____

5. _____

(B) Preguntas personales y generales. Write your answer in a complete Spanish sentence.

1. ¿Qué hace Vd. en casa cuando hace mal tiempo?
2. ¿En qué clase está Vd. aburrido? ¿Por qué?
3. ¿Para qué sirve la puerta de una casa?
4. ¿Vive Vd. en un apartamiento o en su propia casa?
5. ¿Qué hay en las paredes de su clase?

1. _____

2. _____

3. _____

4. _____

5. _____

II. Fill in the missing words.

Instrucciones para construir una casa para muñecas.

Primero, es necesario encontrár una _____ de cartón. Los _____ de
$\qquad$ 1 $\qquad$ 2

la caja van a ser las _____ de la casa. Después, hacemos el _____ de la tapa de
$\qquad$ 3 $\qquad$ 4

la caja. En el frente de la casa, ponemos una _____ . Las personas _____ y
$\qquad$ 5 $\qquad$ 6

_____ de la casa por esta _____ . En las paredes ponemos dos _____ .
7 $\qquad$ 8 $\qquad$ 9

Así pueden entrar luz y _____ . Terminamos el trabajo con un jardín con hierba y con unos
10

_____ .
11

III. Compositions: Oral or written.

(A) Look at the picture at the beginning of this Work Unit. Describe the scene in Spanish to a friend.

(B) Tell about constructing something. Include the following:

Para construír algo

1. You want to build a _____. 2. You need _____, _____, and _____. 3. Afterwards, you have to build more _____. 4. You can do the work in _____ hours. 5. You are very happy with (*contento, a de*) your work.

ESTRUCTURAS DE LA LENGUA
Direct Object Pronouns

A. The direct object *pronoun* stands for the noun, and agrees with it in number and gender.

THINGS

The *noun* as object of the verb.   The *pronoun* used in place of the noun.

1. ¿Tiene Anita el libro? Does Anita have the book?	Anita **lo** tiene. Anita has *it*.
2. ¿Tiene Anita la tiza? Does Anita have the chalk?	Anita no **la** tiene. Anita does not have *it*.
3. ¿Aprende Juan los números? Does John learn the numbers?	Sí, Juan **los** aprende. Yes, John learns *them*.
4. ¿Aprende Luis las reglas? Does Louis learn the rules?	Luis no **las** aprende. Louis does not learn *them*.

Rules:

1. Meanings: **lo** (masc.), **la** (fem.) *it;* **los** (masc.), **las** (fem.) *them.*

2. **Lo, la, los,** or **las** (the direct object pronouns) are placed *before* the verb. When **no** is present, it is placed before **lo, la, los,** or **las.**

B. Direct Object Pronouns representing PERSONS.

Juan **me** ve	(a mí)	John sees	*me*
te ve	(a ti)		*you* (familiar sing.)
lo ve	(a él)		*him*
la ve	(a ella)		*her*
lo, la ve	(a Vd.)		*you* (formal: masc. sing., fem. sing.)
Juan **nos** ve	(a nosotros)	John sees	*us*
os ve	(a vosotros)		*you* (familiar pl.)
los ve	(a ellos)		*them* (masc.)
las ve	(a ellas)		*them* (fem.)
los ve	(a Vds.)		*you* (formal, masc.; plural)
las ve	(a Vds.)		*you* (formal, fem.; plural)

Rules:

1. *All* direct object pronouns are placed directly *before* the conjugated verb.

2. Multiple English meanings for **lo:** *him, you* (masc.), *it* (masc.); for **la:** *her, you* (fem.), *it* (fem.).

3. **A mí, a ti, a él, a ella, a Vd.; a nosotros, a vosotros, a ellos, a ellas, a Vds.**, are omitted under ordinary circumstances. They *are* used for *emphasis,* and to *clarify the meanings* of **lo, la, los,** and **las.**

4. **Le** is reserved for the indirect object pronouns *to him, to her, to you,* in this book.

C. Direct object pronouns *are attached to the end of*

Direct object pronouns are placed *before*

AFFIRMATIVE COMMANDS.	NEGATIVE COMMANDS.
1. **¡Cómalo** Vd. ahora! Eat it now!	1. **¡No lo coma** Vd. después! Don't eat it later!
2. **¡Apréndanla** Vds. bien! Learn it right!	2. **¡No la aprendan** Vds. mal! Don't learn it wrong!
3. **¡Comprémoslos** aquí! Let's buy them here!	3. **¡No los compremos** allí! Let's not buy them there!

Rules:

1. The accent mark is written after attaching the object pronoun to the end of the affirmative command. The mark is placed on the stressed vowel of the third syllable from the end of the combined word. This written accent preserves the original stress on the verb for the reader.

2. No attachment is possible on negative commands; no accent mark is needed.

No lo veo.

D. The position of object pronouns varies in the presence of a conjugated verb which is followed by an INFINITIVE.

---

1. Anita no **lo quiere comer.**   2. Anita no **quiere comerlo.**
   Anita does not want to eat it.

Rules:

1. Direct object pronouns may be placed either (1) before the conjugated verb or (2) attached to the infinitive, when both conjugated verb and complementary infinitive are present.

2. Direct object pronouns MUST be attached to the end of the infinitive when no conjugated verb is seen *before* it, e.g.,

---

Para **comerlo** necesito una cuchara.
In order *to eat it* I need a spoon.

---

3. No accent mark is written when attaching one object pronoun to an infinitive.

STUDY THE RULES, EXAMPLES, AND MODELS BEFORE BEGINNING THE EXERCISES!

Exercises

I. Rewrite the sentence, substituting the appropriate direct object pronoun for the noun in *italics*.

Model: Yo no tengo *los guantes.*   Yo no **los** tengo.
         I don't have the gloves.   I don't have them.

1. Yo no leo *los libros.* _____

2. Ellas no toman *el avión.* _____

3. Juan no tiene *la pelota.* _____

4. Mi amiga no sabe *las repuestas.* _____

5. Los niños no desean *helado.* _____

II. Write an affirmative answer in a complete Spanish sentence using the object pronoun before the verb and the emphatic phrase after.

Model: ¿A quién observan allí?   (lo/a él) **Lo** observan a **él** allí.
         Whom do they observe there?   They observe *him* there.

1. ¿A quién necesitan en el jardín?
   (me/a mí)_____

2. ¿A quién ven en el supermercado?
   (la/a Vd.)_____

3. ¿A quién visitan en aquel país?
   (lo/a Vd.)_____

4. ¿A quién observan en la calle?
(lo/a él)_____

5. ¿A quién permiten en la casa?
(te/a ti)_____

6. ¿A quiénes hallan en la sala?
(los/a Vds.)_____

7. ¿A quiénes describen en la foto?
(nos/a nosotros)_____

8. ¿A quiénes miran por la avenida?
(las/a ellas)_____

9. ¿A quién escuchan en su clase de historia?
(la/a ella)_____

10. ¿A quiénes comprenden en el cine?
(los/a ellos)_____

III. Write an affirmative response using the appropriate direct object pronoun and emphasizing phrase. Begin each response with **Sí que . . .** (certainly) or **Sí . . .** (yes), according to the models.

A. Model: —¿La observan a *María*?   —Sí que **la** observan **a ella.**
             Are they watching Mary?   They certainly are watching her.

1. ¿La invitan a *la niña*?_____

2. ¿Lo prefieren a *este profesor*?_____

3. ¿Las quieren a *Marta* y a *Luisa*?_____

4. ¿Los ven a *los hombres*?_____

5. ¿Los escuchan a *Ana* y a *Tomás*?_____

B. Model: —¿**Nos** invitan **a nosotros?**   —Sí, **los** invitan **a Vds.**
             Are they inviting *us*?   Yes, they are inviting *you* (pl.)

1. ¿Nos ven a nosotros?_____

2. ¿Me necesitan a mí?_____

3. ¿Te comprenden a ti?_____

4. ¿Los visitan a Vds.?_____

5. ¿La observan a Vd.?_____

IV. Rewrite the sentence, changing the position of the object pronoun according to the models.

A. Model: No lo debo estudiar.   I must not study it.
             No debo estudiarlo.

1. No lo deseo leer.   2. ¿No los quiere visitar?

_____   _____

3. No te vamos a comer.

_____

4. ¿No nos pueden ver?

_____

5. No me deben mirar.

_____

6. No la voy a construir.

_____

B. Model: No puedo estudiarlo. I cannot study it.
No lo puedo estudiar.

1. No esperamos verte.

_____

2. ¿No sabes hacerlas?

_____

3. No prefiere contestarla.

_____

4. ¿No pueden comprenderme?

_____

5. No van a escucharnos.

_____

V. Write the appropriate NEGATIVE command. Make all necessary changes in the position of the object pronoun and the use of the accent mark.

Model: ¡Cómprelo Vd.!   or   ¡Cómprenlo Vds.!   or   ¡Comprémoslo!
Buy it!   Buy it!   Let's buy it!

¡No lo compre Vd.!   ¡No lo compren Vds.!   ¡No lo compremos!
Don't buy it!   Don't buy it!   Let's not buy it!

1. ¡Enséñelo Vd.!_____

2. ¡Llámeme Vd.!_____

3. ¡Visítenla Vds.!_____

4. ¡Mírennos Vds.!_____

5. ¡Invitémoslos!_____

VI. Write the appropriate AFFIRMATIVE command. Make all necessary changes. (Study the affirmative models seen in Exercise V.)

1. ¡No lo visite Vd.!_____

2. ¡No nos miren Vds.!_____

3. ¡No la contestemos!_____

4. ¡No los use Vd.!_____

5. ¡No me imiten Vds.!_____

VII. Complete the dialog, using the Spanish vocabulary provided in parentheses. Be sure to supply the missing direct object pronoun where indicated by the slash.

Model: My father takes **us** to the park. (Mi padre/lleva al parque.)
Mi padre **nos** lleva al parque.

Luis: ¿La ve Vd. a María en la escuela?

1. Pablo:_____
Yes, I see her.　　(Sí, yo/veo)

Luis: ¿Lo saluda ella a Vd.?

2. Pablo:_____
No, she doesn't look at me.　　(No, ella no/mira)

Luis: ¿A quién saluda ella entonces? ¿A Jorge?

3. Pablo:_____
Yes. She greets him *(emphatic).*　　(Sí. Ella/saluda/)

Luis: ¡No me digas! ¿Por qué?

4. Pablo:_____
He takes her to the movies often.　　(El/lleva mucho al cine)

Luis: ¿Y sus padres?

5. Pablo:_____
Her parents don't know it. (Sus padres no/saben)

Luis: ¡Salúdela Vd. de mi parte mañana!

6. Pablo:_____
I don't want to greet her.　　(No quiero saludar/)

Luis: ¡Claro!

7. Pablo: ¡_____
Greet her yourself! (¡Salude/Vd.!)

Luis: Bueno. Si Vd. lo desea.

8. Pablo:_____
No. Don't greet her!　　(No. ¡No/salude Vd.!)

_____
I will, tomorrow.　　(Yo voy a saludar/mañana)

9. Luis: _____
Let us greet her together, then!　　(Entonces, ¡saludemos/juntos!)

VIII. Oral Proficiency: Respond orally to the situation described. (You may *later* write your responses for more practice.)

Situation: You and your friend are daydreaming about the ideal home for your future. Your friend says:—*Mi casa ideal es muy bonita. ¿Como es tu casa ideal?* You tell your friend about the future home of *your* dreams.

In **five** Spanish sentences describe the neighborhood, the house, and the garden. You may use your own ideas or ideas suggested by the following: *vecindario, cuartos de la casa, construcción de la casa, el jardín, familia en la casa.*

¡No vaya tan de prisa! ¡Espéreme!

*Some people never trust anyone. Have you
ever met a person like Ernesto?*

Un hombre moral

Ernesto Cenicero es un hombre de alta moralidad. El cree, como su padre y su abuelo, que la cosa más importante en esta vida es el trabajo.

— El hombre nace para trabajar — él les dice muchas veces a sus amigos. — Tengo sesenta años y todo el dinero que tengo es de mi propia labor. En este mundo, nada es gratis. Es necesario sudar para poder vivir.

Ernesto, un viejo solterón, trabaja en la oficina de un abogado. Trabaja largas horas, los seis días de la semana. El abogado le da varios papeles legales y Ernesto tiene que clasificarlos, ponerlos en orden, y llevarlos a la corte. Un día Ernesto está en la oficina hasta las siete y media de la noche. Quiere volver a casa lo más pronto posible para comer. Cuando pasa por una calle, nota en la esquina a un hombre pobre y mal vestido. — Ah, otro vago — dice Ernesto. — Esos vagos nunca trabajan. Todo el mundo les da dinero. Pero yo no. Yo tengo que trabajar como un perro para vivir —. Decide sacar la cartera de su chaqueta y la mete en el bolsillo del pantalón.

Nota que el vago lo mira. — Ajá — piensa Ernesto y empieza a andar más rápido.

— Señor, señor, — le grita el vago. — ¡Espere, un momento!

Ernesto dobla la esquina para perderlo. Pero el vago dobla la esquina también y lo sigue.

— Señor, señor, — grita el vago. — Por favor, ¡espere!

Ernesto corre ahora. El vago corre también.

— Señor, señor. ¡No corra Vd.! ¡Espéreme!

Ernesto no puede más. Está cansado.

— Bueno, bueno. ¿Qué quiere Vd? ¿Por qué no trabaja Vd. en vez de molestar a la gente decente?

— Perdone la molestia, señor. Pero Vd. dejó caer su cartera. Aquí la tiene —. Y le da la cartera a Ernesto.

Palabras Nuevas

SUBSTANTIVOS

el abogado   *the lawyer*
el bolsillo   *the pocket*
el cenicero   *the ashtray*
la chaqueta   *the jacket*
la corte   *the court*
Ernesto   *Ernest*
la esquina   *the corner*
la gente   *the people*
la labor   *the work*
la molestia   *the bother*
la moralidad   *the morality*
el orden   *the order*
los pantalones   *the trousers*
el solterón   *the bachelor*

el vago   *the tramp, the
   vagabond*

ADJETIVOS

decente   *decent*
gratis   *free*
(mal) vestido,a   *(badly)
   dressed*

VERBOS

clasificar   *to classify, to file*
dejar caer   *to drop*
doblar la esquina   *to turn the
   corner*
meter   *to put in*

molestar   *to bother*
nacer   *to be born*
no puede más   *he (she) can't
   stand it any longer; you
   (formal sing.) can't stand it
   any longer*
sacar   *to take out*
(lo) sigue   *he (she) follows him;
   you (formal sing.) follow him*
sudar   *to sweat*

OTRAS PALABRAS

en vez de   *instead of*
muchas veces   *often, many
   times*

EJERCICIOS

I. Complete the sentences according to the story.

1. Ernesto cree que la cosa más importante es _____.
2. Ernesto trabaja en el _____ de un _____.
3. El abogado le da _____ _____ y Ernesto tiene que _____.
4. Nota en la _____ a un hombre pobre y _____ _____.
5. Toma la _____ y la mete en el _____ del _____.
6. Ernesto ha _____ _____ la cartera.

II. Place the following sentences in the order in which they occurred.
1.   Está en la oficina hasta las siete y media.
2.   Nota a un hombre pobre en la esquina.
3.   —Aquí tiene Vd. su cartera.
4.   —Señor, señor ¡Espere un momento!
5.   Quiere volver a casa para comer.

1. _____

2. _____

3. _____

4. _____

5. _____

III. Antónimos — Next to column A write the word selected from column B that has the *opposite* meaning.

A.		B.
1 . ahora	_____ a.	joven
2 . más	_____ b.	la derecha
3 . mal	_____ c.	voy
4 . viejo	_____ d.	bajo
5 . meter	_____ e.	lejos
6 . la izquierda	_____ f.	después
7 . vengo	_____ g.	algo
8 . siempre	_____ h.	sacar
9 . allí	_____ i.	menos
1 0 . alto	_____ j.	comprar
1 1 . el vago	_____ k.	la mujer
1 2 . el hombre	_____ l.	aquí
1 3 . cerca	_____ m.	bien
1 4 . vender	_____ n.	el trabajador
1 5 . nada	_____ o.	nunca

IV. Compositions: Oral or written.

(A) Look at the picture at the beginning of this Work Unit. Describe the scene in Spanish to a friend.

(B) Tell about something you lost. Include the following:

Una cosa perdida

1. You are looking for your _____.   2. You want to find it because it is very important to you.
3. It is not worth much money.   4. For the _____ you are going to give five dollars.   5. Your telephone number is _____.

ESTRUCTURAS DE LA LENGUA

Indirect Object Pronouns

A. The *indirect object pronoun* represents the noun *to whom* and *for whom*, *to which* and *for which*, the action is intended.

1. Yo **le** doy el libro.	1. I give the book *to him.*
2. Yo **le** compro el libro.	2. I buy the book *from him.*
3. Yo **no le** escribo el libro.	3. *I don't* write the book *for him.*

Rules:

1. The indirect object pronoun **le** is placed directly *before* the conjugated verb.

2. When **no** is present, it *precedes* the indirect object pronoun **le.**

Yo les doy el dinero.

B. All forms of indirect object pronouns.

María **me** da el libro (a mí).		Mary gives the book *to me.*
te da	(a ti).	*to you* (fam. sing.).
le da	(a él).	*to him.*
le da	(a ella).	*to her.*
le da	(a Vd.).	*to you* (formal sing.).
María **nos** da el libro (a nosotros).		Mary gives the book *to us.*
os da	(a vosotros).	*to you* (fam. pl.).
les da	(a ellos).	*to them* (masc.).
les da	(a ellas).	*to them* (fem.).
les da	(a Vds.).	*to you* (formal pl.).

231

Rules:

1. All indirect object pronouns are placed directly *before* the conjugated verb.

2. Note all the meanings of **le:** *to him; to her; to you* (formal sing.); and of **les:** *to them* (masc. and fem.); *to you* (formal pl.)

3. **A mí, a ti, a él,** etc., are omitted under ordinary circumstances. They are used to *emphasize* the indirect object pronoun.

El me escribe **a mí**; no te escribe **a ti**.
He writes *to me;* he does not write *to you*.

---

4. **Le** (to him, to her, to you *formal sing.*) is clarified by adding **a él, a ella,** or **a Vd.; les** (to them, to you *formal pl.*) is clarified by adding **a ellos, a ellas, a Vds.**

C. Indirect object pronouns in the attached position

---

1. Señorita, **¡escríbale** Vd. una carta!
   Miss, write a letter to him!

2. **¡No le escriba** una tarjeta!
   Don't write a card to him!

3. Para **escribirle** necesito papel.

4. Si Vd. no **le quiere escribir,**
   yo voy a escribirle.

   To write to him I need paper.

   If you don't want to write to him
   I will write.

Rules:

1. The indirect object pronouns are attached to AFFIRMATIVE COMMANDS like the **direct** object pronouns. A written accent mark is then placed over the vowel of the syllable that was stressed in speech, frequently the next to last before attachment of the pronoun.

2. Indirect object pronouns are placed *before* NEGATIVE COMMANDS as well as before conjugated verbs, like direct object pronouns.

3. If an infinitive *follows* a *conjugated verb*, the indirect object pronoun may be placed *either before the conjugated verb* or *attached to the end of the infinitive*. No accent mark is needed when attaching one object pronoun to the infinitive.

Anita no **le quiere hablar.**   Anita no **quiere hablarle.**
Anita does not want to talk to him.

STUDY THE RULES, EXAMPLES, AND MODELS BEFORE BEGINNING THE EXERCISES!

Exercises

I. Rewrite the sentence, using the indirect object pronoun *suggested* by the words in parentheses. (Do *not* write the words in parentheses.)

A. Model: El muestra el lápiz. (a mí) **El me muestra el lápiz.**
             He shows the pencil.   He shows the pencil to me.

1. El enseña la lección.

   (a mí)_____

2. Ellos dan la cartera.

   (a él)_____

3. Nosotros decimos todo.

   (a Vd.)_____

4. El ofrece el automóvil.

   (a ti)_____

5. Vds. no muestran las flores.

   (a ella)_____

6. Da los papeles.

   (a nosotros)_____

7. Enseña la regla.

   (a ellos)_____

8. Vendo la fruta.

   (a ellas)_____

9. No traen el paquete.

   (a Vds.)_____

10. Leo el cuaderno.

   (a él y a ella)_____

II. Write an answer in a complete Spanish sentence using the appropriate indirect object pronoun. *Include* the word cues in parentheses.

A. Model: –¿A quién vende Vd. el perro? (a Juan) **–Le vendo el perro a Juan.**
             To whom do you sell the dog?   I sell the dog to John.

1. ¿A quién lee Vd. la novela?

   (a Tomás)_____

    2. ¿A quién muestra Vd. la casa?

      (a la señora)_____

    3. ¿A quién enseña Vd. el abrigo?

      (a Vd.)_____

    4. ¿A quién escribe Vd. la carta?

      (a ti)_____

    5. ¿A quién canta Vd. esa canción?

      (a mí)_____

B. Model: –¿A quiénes vende él la casa?   To whom does he sell the house?

           (A Juan y a María)

           –El les vende la casa a Juan y a María.   He sells the house to John and Mary.

    1. ¿A quiénes da él el violín?

      (a Pedro y a Anita)_____

    2. ¿A quiénes dice ella la frase?

      (a los alumnos)_____

    3. ¿A quiénes escriben ellos sus ideas?

      (a Ana y a María)_____

    4. ¿A quiénes traen ellas el regalo?

      (a nosotros)_____

    5. ¿A quiénes explica la profesora esa regla?

      (a Elisa y a Vd.)_____

III. Write an affirmative answer. Substitute the appropriate phrase **a él, a ella, a ellos, a ellas** for the expression in *italics*.

    Model: –¿Le mandan ellos el dinero *a Juan*?   –Sí, ellos le mandan el dinero **a él.**
              Do they send the money *to John*?   Yes, they send the money *to him*.

    1. ¿Le muestran ellos el examen *al profesor*?_____

    2. ¿Le escribe él las cartas *a Inés*?_____

    3. ¿Les enseñan ellas la historia *a sus hermanitas*?_____

    4. ¿Les lee ella el periódico *a Miguel y a su hermano*?_____

    5. ¿Les explica la profesora las palabras *a Luisa y a Luis*?_____

IV. Rewrite the sentence changing the position of the indirect object pronoun, according to the models.

A. Model: No quiero hablarle.
No le quiero hablar.
I don't want to speak to him.

1. No deseo leerles._____

2. No quieren hablarnos._____

3. No puede mostrarte._____

4. ¿No van a cantarme?_____

5. ¿No debemos decirle?_____

B. Model: No le debo hablar.
No debo hablarle.
I must not speak to him.

1. No les quiero hablar._____

2. No le deseo cantar._____

3. No me espera escribir._____

4. No te pueden explicar._____

5. No nos van a cantar._____

V. Rewrite the command in the appropriate AFFIRMATIVE form. Make all necessary changes.

Model:	¡No les hable Vd.!	¡No les hablen Vds.!	¡No les hablemos!
	Don't speak to them!	Don't speak to them!	Let's not speak to them!
	¡Hábleles Vd.!	¡Háblenles Vds.!	¡Hablémosles!
	Speak to them!	Speak to them!	Let's speak to them!

1. ¡No me hable Vd.!_____

2. ¡No nos escriba Vd.!_____

3. ¡No nos respondan Vds.!_____

4. ¡No nos lean Vds.!_____

5. ¡No le vendamos!_____

VI. Rewrite the command in the appropriate NEGATIVE form. Make all necessary changes. [Study the affirmative models seen in Exercise V.]

1. ¡Muéstrenos Vd.!_____

2. ¡Léanos Vd.!_____

3. ¡Enséñenme Vds.!_____

4. ¡Escríbanles Vds.!_____

5. ¡Respondámosle!_____

VII. Write a *question*, in Spanish, using the appropriate indirect object pronoun.

    Model: /Dan un regalo a Juan.   –¿**Le** dan un regalo a Juan?
                                                        Are they giving John a present?

1. /Dan una carta a María._____

2. /Mandan dinero a Pablo y a Juan._____

3. /Enseñan el libro a los chicos._____

4. /Dicen la verdad a Juan y a la chica._____

5. /Escriben la carta a Pablo y a Vd._____

VIII. Complete the dialogue using the Spanish vocabulary provided in parentheses. Be sure to supply the missing indirect object pronoun where indicated by the slash.

    Model: He tells *me* the story. (El/dice el cuento.)
              El **me** dice el cuento.

    Pablo: Hermanita, ¡tengo una sorpresa para ti!

1. Ana: ¡_____!
           Please tell *me*. What is it? (Favor de decir/ ¿Qué es?)

    Pablo: ¡Es un reloj de oro!

2. Ana: _____
           Of course! Dad always gives *you* (*fam.*) money. (¡Claro! Papá siempre / da dinero)

    Pablo: No, chica. Yo me gano dinero en un supermercado.

3. Ana: ¿_____?
           And you give presents *to me*? (Y tú / das regalos)

    Pablo: Me gusta dar regalos a la familia.

4. Ana: _____
           Yes, that does give *us* joy. (Sí, eso es dar / alegría)

    Pablo: ¡Y a nuestros padres también!

5. Ana: ¡_____!
           Please give something fantastic *to them*. (Favor de dar / algo fantástico)

    Pablo: ¡Claro, hermanita!

IX. Oral Proficiency. Respond orally to the situation described. (You may *later* write your responses for intensive practice.)

Situation: You are *el hombre moral* of the story in this Work Unit. The tramp returns your wallet and wants to know why you run from him:—*¿Por qué corre Vd., señor?* You explain.

Thank him, and in **four** Spanish sentences give your reasons. You may use your own ideas or the ideas suggested by the following: *what you lost without knowing it (sin saberlo); why you have to work late; what you are afraid of when returning home late (the streets, the night); why you are happy that he is a decent man.*

Dicen en el menú que la paella
es la especialidad de la casa.

Julio wants to impress his girlfriend. The only
problem is that he has no money.

No me gustan las hamburguesas

Es sábado por la noche y Julio y Beatriz salen del cine. Julio está muy contento porque le gusta Beatriz. Ésta es la primera cita. Naturalmente, Julio quiere causar una buena impresión y dice:

— Bueno, Beatriz. No es muy tarde. No son todavía las diez. ¿Tienes hambre? ¿Quieres ir a tomar algo? ¿Un refresco, un helado? (En realidad Julio no tiene much dinero.)
— Pues sí, tengo hambre Julio. Vamos a ese restaurante "La Paella."

Los dos entran en el restaurate y toman asiento. El camarero les trae la lista de platos. Julio mira el menú. ¡Qué precios! Y la paella es el plato más caro. ¡Cuesta doce dólares! Julio tiene solamente diez dólares en el bolsillo y menciona otros platos menos caros.

— Beatriz, dicen que las hamburguesas y las papas fritas son muy buenas aquí.
— No, no me gustan las hamburguesas. Dicen en el menú que la paella es la especialidad de la casa. ¿De qué es?
— Oh, es un plato de arroz, pollo, mariscos y legumbres. Personalmente prefiero comida más sencilla. ¿No te gustan los huevos? Preparan excelentes huevos duros aquí.

En ese momento entra el camarero.

Camarero:	¿Están Vds. listos para ordenar?
Julio:	Sí, yo quiero una tortilla a la española y una Coca Cola.
Beatriz:	Y yo quiero la paella.
Julio:	Ay, Beatriz, tengo una confesión.
Camarero:	Lo siento, señorita, pero no hay más paella.
Beatriz:	No importa. ¿Qué confesión, Julio?
Julio:	Nada, nada. ¿No hay más paella? Oh, ¡qué lástima!

Palabras Nuevas

SUBSTANTIVOS

el arroz *the rice*
Beatriz *Beatrice*
el camarero *the waiter*
la confesión *the confession*
la especialidad *the specialty*
la hamburguesa *the hamburger*
los huevos duros *the hard-boiled eggs*
Julio *Julius*
la legumbre *the vegetable*
la lista de platos *the menu*
el marisco *the shellfish*
la paella *the paella (a Spanish specialty of rice, seafood, chicken, and vegetables)*
las papas fritas *the french fries*
el pollo *the chicken*
la tortilla (a la española) *the (Spanish) omelette*

ADJETIVOS

caro,a *expensive*
sencillo,a *simple*

VERBOS

(no) me gusta(n) *I do (not) like*
¿No te gusta(n)? *Don't you like?*
(no) importa *it does (not) matter*
mencionar *to mention*
ordenar *to order*
lo siento *I am sorry about it*

OTRAS PALABRAS

causar una buena impresión *to create a good impression*
¿De qué es? *What is it made of?*
menos *less*
¡Qué lástima! *What a pity!*

EJERCICIOS

I. (A) Preguntas. Write your answer in a complete Spanish sentence.

1. ¿Por qué está contento Julio?
2. ¿Qué le pregunta Julio a Beatriz?
3. ¿Por qué no quiere ordenar Julio la paella?
4. ¿De qué es la paella?
5. ¿Cuál es la confesión de Julio?

1. _____

2. _____

3. _____

4. _____

5. _____

(B) Preguntas personales y generales. Write your answer in a complete Spanish sentence.

1. ¿Cuál es su comida favorita?
2. ¡Mencione Vd. algunos refrescos!
3. ¿Qué come Vd. generalmente con una hamburguesa?
4. ¿Cuánto dinero necesita Vd. para comprar una comida buena en un restaurante?

1. _____

2. _____

3. _____

4. _____

II. Word Hunt

Find the words in Spanish.

1. shell fish		9. Saturday
2. rice		10. movie
3. waiter		11. more
4. egg		12. year
5. plate		13. very
6. hard (boiled)		14. what
7. expensive		15. a (masc.)
8. night		16. eye

M	A	R	I	S	C	O	S
A	R	C	P	L	A	T	O
B	R	M	U	Y	M	A	S
N	O	C	H	E	A	D	A
Q	Z	I	C	A	R	O	Ñ
U	N	N	H	U	E	V	O
E	F	E	D	U	R	O	S
S	A	B	A	D	O	J	O

III. Compositions: Oral or written.

(A) Look at the picture at the beginning of this Work Unit. Describe the scene in Spanish to a friend.

(B) Tell about going to a restaurant. Include the following:

En el restaurante
1. Where you like to eat. 2. Who brings the menu. 3. What three things you order.
4. Whom you go with. 5. Why it is necessary to have a great deal of money for the restaurant.

ESTRUCTURAS DE LA LENGUA

Gustar *to be pleasing, to like* is not like other verbs. It is *generally used only in the third persons:* **gusta** or **gustan**.

A. **Gustar** really means *to be pleasing,* but it is often used to convey the meaning of the English verb *to like.*

B. **Gustar**'s subject *is the thing(s) that is (are) pleasing.* It's subject generally appears *after* **gustar.**

C. The indirect *personal* object pronouns (**me, te, le, nos, os, les**) *tell to whom* the thing is pleasing and always stand *before* **gustar.**

Gusta before a *singular* subject	**Gustan** before a *plural* subject
Me gusta la flor. The flower is pleasing to me. I like the flower.	**Me gustan las flores.** The flowers are pleasing to me. I like the flowers.
Te gusta la flor. The flower is pleasing to you (fam. sing.). You (fam. sing.) like the flower.	**Te gustan** las flores. The flowers are pleasing to you. You (fam. sing.) like the flowers.
Le gusta la flor. The flower is pleasing to you (to him, to her). You (formal sing.) like the flower. He (she) likes the flower.	**Le gustan** las flores. The flowers are pleasing to you (to him, to her). You (formal sing.) like the flowers. He (she) likes the flowers.
Nos gusta la flor. The flower is pleasing to us. We like the flower.	**Nos gustan** las flores. The flowers are pleasing to us. We like the flowers.
Os gusta la flor. The flower is pleasing to you. You like the flower (fam. pl. in Spain).	**Os gustan** las flores. The flowers are pleasing to you. You like the flowers (fam. pl. in Spain).
Les gusta la flor. The flower is pleasing to them (to you). You (formal pl.) like the flower. They (masc., fem.) like the flower.	**Les gustan** las flores. The flowers are pleasing to them (to you). You (formal pl.) like the flowers. They (masc., fem.) like the flowers.

Rules:

1. The noun(s) *after* **gusta** and **gustan** are the subjects of **gusta** and **gustan**. **Gusta** stands *before a singular subject.* **Gustan** stands *before a plural subject.*

2. **Me, te, le, nos, os,** or **les** must always precede **gustar.** They indicate *who* "likes" or "is pleased" and are called indirect object pronouns. (See Unit 23 for a review of indirect object pronouns.)

D. **Gustar's** Spanish subject pronouns for *it* and *them (they)* are generally *not expressed*.

Me gusta. I like *it*. (It is pleasing to me.)	**Me gustan.** I like *them*. (They are pleasing to me.)
Les gusta. They like *it*. (It is pleasing to them.)	**Les gustan.** They like *them*. (They are pleasing to them.)

E. Interrogative **gustar** and negative **gustar. Gustar** before infinitives, used as subjects.

1. ¿**No** te gusta estudiar? Don't you like to study?	—**No** me gusta mucho. I don't like it very much.
2. ¿**No** le gustan las ensaladas? Don't you like salads?	—**No** me gustan mucho. I don't like them very much.

Rules:

1. To form the question simply place question marks both *before and after* the sentence. No change in word order is necessary.

2. To form the negative place **no** before **me, te, le, nos, os,** or **les.**

3. Infinitives (see **estudiar E. 1.** above) denoting actions that are liked or not liked will be the *subjects* of **gusta.**

F. Emphatic or clarifying expressions before **me, te, le, nos, os, les,** give clarity and emphasis to "the person(s) who likes (like)."

Emphatic or Clarifying Expressions	
A mí me gustan.	*I* like them. (They are pleasing *to me*.)
A ti te gustan.	*You* (fam. sing.) like them.
A Vd. le gustan. [Clarifies **le.**]	*You* (formal sing.) like them.
A él le gustan. [Clarifies **le.**]	*He* likes them.
A ella le gustan. [Clarifies **le.**]	*She* likes them.
A nosotros-as nos gusta.	*We* like it. (It is pleasing *to us*.)
A vosotros-as os gusta.	*You* (fam. pl.) like it.
A Vds. les gusta. [Clarifies **les.**]	*You* (formal pl.) like it.
A ellos les gusta. [Clarifies **les.**]	*They* (masc.) like it.
A ellas les gusta. [Clarifies **les.**]	*They* (fem.) like it.

Rules:

1. **A mí, a ti, a él, a ella, a Vd., a nosotros-as, a vosotros-as, a ellos-as, a Vds.,** are the forms that appearing before **me, te, le, nos, os, les,** emphasize or clarify them.

2. **Me, te, le, nos, os,** or **les** must stand before **gustar** even when the emphatic expressions are used.

G. Gustar with personal *object* nouns.

A María le gustan las flores.	Mary likes the flowers.
A la chica le gustan las flores.	The girl likes the flowers.
A Juan y a Pedro les gusta.	John and Peter like it.
A los chicos les gusta.	The boys like it.

Rules:

1. **A** precedes the person who likes, who is pleased (the objective form). Note that **a** precedes *each* person when there are more than one.

2. The corresponding indirect object pronoun, **le** or **les,** for example, must continue to stand before the forms of **gustar,** but it is *not* translatable, even when the noun — the person(s) who is (are) pleased — is stated.

STUDY THE RULES, EXAMPLES, AND MODELS BEFORE BEGINNING THE EXERCISES!

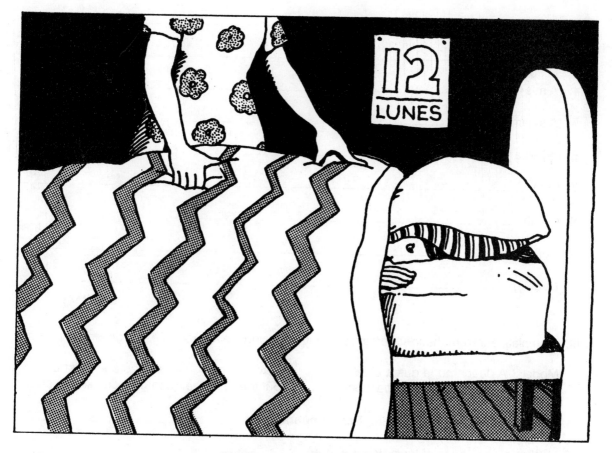

Al niño no le gustan los lunes.

Exercises

I. Rewrite the **model sentence** *replacing the subject after* **gustar** with the new Spanish subject given in parentheses. Make the necessary change in the form of **gustar.**

Model: **No le gustan los lunes.**   (la clase) **No le gusta la clase.**
He does not like Mondays.   He does not like the class.

1. (el cereal)_____

2. (los baños)_____

3. (la escuela)_____

4. (los estudios)_____

5. (la leche)_____

6. (los lunes y los martes)_____

II. Rewrite the model sentence *replacing the person before* **gustar** with the one given in parentheses. Make the necessary change in the indirect object *pronoun*.

Model: *A mí* no me gustan las peras.   (A Juan) **A Juan no le gustan las peras.**
I don't like pears.   John doesn't like pears.

1. (A nosotros)_____

2. (A Vd.)_____

3. (A Vds.)_____

4. (A mis hermanas)_____

5. (A su amigo)_____

6. (A Luisa y a Juan)_____

7. (A ti)_____

8. (A mí)_____

9. (A Pedro)_____

10. (A Lola)_____

III. Complete each emphatic statement affirmatively using the appropriate indirect object pronoun.

Model: A Juana no le gusta el béisbol.   Pero a ellos . . . sí **les** gusta el béisbol.
Joan does not like baseball.   But *they* . . . *they* certainly do like baseball.

1. A María no le gusta tomar café. **Pero a nosotras** _____

2. A ellos no les gusta el tenis. **Pero a Juan** _____

3. A Ana no le gustan las clases. **Pero a las maestras** _____

4. A nosotros no nos gusta ir al cine. **Pero a mi amiga** _____

5. A los chicos no les gustan los sábados. **Pero a mí** _____

6. A la chica no le gustan las fiestas. **Pero a ti** _____

7. A mí no me gustan las rosas. **Pero a Vd.** _____

8. A ti no te gusta el helado. **Pero a los chicos** _____

9. A Vd. no le gustan las comedias. **Pero a nosotros** _____

10. A ella no le gusta bailar. **Pero a Vds.** _____

IV. Write an appropriate affirmative response *replacing the words after* **gustar** with the expression **mucho.**

Models: —¿A Vds. les gusta el pan?   **—Nos gusta mucho.** We like it very much.
           Do you (pl.) like bread?

           —¿A Vd. le gustan los perros?   **—Me gustan mucho.** I like them very much.
           Do you (sing.) like dogs?

1. ¿A Vd. le gusta la playa?_____

2. ¿A Vds. les gusta aprender?_____

3. ¿A ti te gustan aquellos zapatos?_____

4. ¿A Vds. les gustan las películas?_____

5. ¿A ti te gusta este sombrero?_____

V. Write a NEGATIVE answer omitting all nouns. Use the appropriate emphatic expressions and **gusta** or **gustan** as needed.

Model: —¿A Ana y a Vd. les gusta eso?   **—A nosotros no nos gusta.**
          Do Ann and you like that?   We don't like it.

1. ¿A Luis y a Vd. les gusta la clase? _____

2. ¿A Juan le gusta ir al centro?_____

3. ¿A Elsa le gustan las frutas?_____

4. ¿A los alumnos les gustan los exámenes?_____

5. ¿A las chicas les gusta estudiar?_____

VI. Complete each sentence of the dialogue in Spanish.

1. What do you like to do? —A Vd. ¿qué_____ _____hacer?

2. I like to walk. —A mí_____ _____caminar.

3. Do your friends like to walk, too? —¿_____sus amigos_____ _____
   caminar también?

4. *He* (emphatic) doesn't like to walk but *she* (emphatic) does. —A_____no_____ _____

   caminar pero a_____sí_____gusta.

5. Fine. *I* (emphatic) like it, too. —Bueno. A_____ _____ _____ _____también.

VII. Oral Proficiency. Respond orally to the situation described. (You may *later* write your responses for intensive practice.)

Situation: You are in a Spanish restaurant. The waiter asks:—¿*Qué desea Vd. ordenar?* You give the waiter a complete dinner order.

Begin with *por favor.* In **five** Spanish statements or questions order salad, main course, side dishes, and a beverage. You may use your own ideas or ideas suggested by the following: ¿*especialidad?*; ¿*hay?*; *me gusta(n)*; *deseo*; ¿*cómo es?*; *quiero*; ¿*tiene Vd.?*.

GANA CON WELCH
A MILLON

MOTORA, BICICLETAS, JUEGOS
COLECO VISION, T-SHIRTS
Y MUCHO MAS.

REGLAS DEL CONCURSO:

1. Los representantes de Welch Foods Inc. estarán recorriendo los diferentes pueblos de Puerto Rico durante las semanas del 12 de febrero al 12 de mayo de 1984.

2. Cuando uno de los representantes llegue a tu residencia y diga "Gana con Welch A Millón" muéstrale uno de los productos Welch o facsímil razonable y él te entregará una T-Shirt de Welch, un juguete, jugo de uva Welch y un boleto de participación que debes llenar con nombre y dirección y depositarlo en una pequeña urna que llevan los representantes. Este boleto participará en el sorteo de la semana siguiente a la visita y en el sorteo final del concurso.

3. Comenzando el 18 de febrero de 1984 y durante 13 semanas consecutivas se sorteará una bicicleta para niño o niña de 20 pulgadas, en el programa "A Millón" que se transmite por WAPA-TV, Canal 4. El sábado 12 de mayo de 1984, en adición al sorteo de la bicicleta, se sorteará entre todos los participantes del concurso, una motora de playa Suzuki y cuatro equipos Coleco Vision. Todos los sorteos se llevarán a cabo ante la presencia de un

notario público en el programa "A Millón" televisado por WAPA-TV, Canal 4.

4. Los ganadores, además de ser anunciados en el programa "A Millón", recibirán notificación de sus premios por correo certificado. La carta certificada y una identificación razonable deberán ser presentadas al momento de reclamar los premios.

5. Los ganadores están sujetos a ser fotografiados y ser utilizadas sus fotos y nombres en anuncios de prensa sin cobrar por ello.

6. Podrán participar todos los residentes de Puerto Rico, excepto los empleados, familiares cercanos y las agencias de publicidad de Welch Foods Inc., Magna Trading, V. Suárez y Cía. y WAPA-TV, Canal 4.

7. Los premios estarán sujetos a las garantías que ofrece su manufacturero o distribuidor. Welch Foods Inc. no se hace responsable por cualquier accidente que ocurra como resultado de la obtención de los premios.

8. Los premios no reclamados en/o antes del 13 de julio de 1984, caducarán.

9. El concurso está sujeto a todas las leyes estatales y federales que se apliquen.

 # Gana con Welch's en sabor.

Faltaba un gran número
de palabras.

Nowadays the news is often confusing;
especially if many of the words are missing!

Una noticia confusa

Todas las noches, cuando regresa del trabajo, Antonio toma asiento en el sillón más cómodo de la casa, fuma su pipa, y lee las últimas noticias en el periódico. Pero esta noche ¿qué pasa? Cuando empieza a leer el artículo más importante de la primera página, nota que falta un gran número de palabras. Teresita, su niña de dos años, encontró un par de tijeras y cortó una docena de palabras del artículo. Ahora es casi imposible leerlo. Afortunadamente, la niña guardó todas las palabras y Antonio tiene que ponerlas en los espacios apropiados. ¿Puede Vd. ayudarlo? Aquí tiene Vd. el artículo.

Se escaparon tres [____1.____] **peligrosos. Los Angeles,** [__2.__] **de septiembre 1989.**

El jefe de policía reveló hoy que tres hombres se escaparon de la [____3.____]

anoche. Estos hombres están armados y [____4.____]. Los tres salieron ayer del

garaje de la prisión vestidos de mecánicos. (Más tarde [____5.____] a tres mecánicos

atados en [____6.____].) El departamento de policía envió fotos y [____7.____]

a todas las estaciones. El jefe del grupo tiene [__8.__] años y debe servir una sentencia de

[__9.__] años por asesinato. Los otros dos son [____10.____] y deben estar en

la prisión por cometer robo armado. Salieron del garaje en un viejo coche Chevrolet. Pero las

autoridades creen que robaron otro [____11.____] más tarde. Los periódicos recibieron

muchas llamadas telefónicas con información pero hasta ahora el trío está en [____12.____].

Selection:
desesperados	descubrieron	21	el garaje
libertad	criminales	la prisión	ladrones
36	cien	descripciones	automóvil

Palabras Nuevas

SUBSTANTIVOS

el artículo   *the article*
el asesinato   *the murder*
el automóvil   *the automobile*
el coche   *the car*
el departamento   *the department*
el espacio   *the space*
la estación   *the station*
la foto   *the snapshot*
el garaje   *the garage*
el jefe   *the chief, the leader*
el ladrón   *the thief*
la libertad   *the freedom, the liberty*
la llamada telefónica   *the telephone call*
el mecánico   *the mechanic*
el par   *the pair*

la prisión   *the prison*
el robo armado   *armed robbery*
la sentencia   *the sentence*
el sillón   *the armchair*
Teresita   *Tessie, little Theresa*
las tijeras   *the scissors*

ADJETIVOS

apropiado,a   *appropriate*
atado,a   *tied up*
cómodo,a   *comfortable*
desesperado,a   *desperate*
peligroso,a   *dangerous*
último,a   *last*

VERBOS

cometer   *to commit*

cortó   *he (she) did cut; you (formal sing.) did cut*
encontró   *he (she) found, met; you (formal sing.) found, met*
envió   *he (she) sent; you (formal sing.) sent*
se escaparon   *they escaped; you (formal pl.) escaped*
faltar   *to be missing, to lack*
fumar   *to smoke*
guardó   *he (she) kept; you (formal sing.) kept*
recibieron   *they received; you (formal pl.) received*
robaron   *they stole; you (formal pl.) stole*
salieron   *they left; you (formal pl.) left*

EJERCICIOS

I. Preguntas. Write your answer in a complete Spanish sentence.

1. ¿Qué hace Antonio todas las noches?
2. ¿Qué nota en la primera página del periódico?
3. ¿Qué cortó Teresita?
4. ¿Qué tiene que hacer Antonio ahora?
5. En el artículo, ¿cómo se escaparon los tres criminales?

1. _____

2. _____

3. _____

4. _____

5. _____

II. Match the two columns to form sentences. Write the correct letter.

A		B
1. Toma asiento en el sillón _____		a) vestidos de mecánicos.
2. Nota que falta _____		b) a todas las estaciones.
3. Los tres criminales salieron _____		c) un gran número de palabras.
4. El jefe envió fotos _____		d) de cien años.
5. Debe servir una sentencia _____		e) más cómodo de la casa.

III. Emiliano has just seen a robbery. He is being questioned later by the police. What would you say in Spanish if you were Emiliano?

Policía: ¿Qué pasó aquí?

1. *Emiliano:* _____

Policía: ¿Cuándo ocurrió el robo?

2. *Emiliano:* _____

Policía: ¿Puede Vd. darnos una descripción del criminal?

3. *Emiliano:* _____

Policía: ¿Quién es Vd.? ¿Cuál es su nombre y dirección?

4. *Emiliano:* _____

Policía: Muchas gracias. Vd. nos ayudó mucho.

ESTRUCTURAS DE LA LENGUA

The Preterite Indicative: Regular Verbs

A. The preterite tense denotes an action or actions that were begun in the past or that were completed in the past.

B. Learn the *two sets* of regular endings.

AR	**ER** and **IR** share one set of preterite endings	

cantar *to sing*	**comer** *to eat*	**escribir** *to write*
I sang yesterday. I did sing yesterday.	I ate last night. I did eat last night.	I wrote last Saturday. I did write last Saturday.
Cant**é** ayer. cant**aste** cant**ó**	Com**í** anoche. com**iste** com**ió**	Escrib**í** el sábado pasado. escrib**iste** escrib**ió**
Cant**amos** ayer. cant**asteis** cant**aron**	Com**imos** anoche. com**isteis** com**ieron**	Escrib**imos** el sábado pasado. escrib**isteis** escrib**ieron**.

Rules:

1. The characteristic vowel in the endings of the regular **ar** preterite is **a** except for the first person singular, which is **é,** and the third person singular, which is **ó.**

2. The characteristic vowel in the endings of the regular **er** and **ir** preterite is **i.**

3. Written accent marks appear on the final vowels of the first and third persons singular of the regular preterite tense except for **vi** and **vio** of the verb **ver.**

C. Use of the Preterite Tense

1. **Anoche en la fiesta María cantó pero Pablo sólo comió.**
   Last night at the party Mary sang, but Paul only ate.

2. **Ellas bailaron ayer pero Vd. no las vio.**
   They danced yesterday, but you did not see them.

Rule:

When expressions of completed past time such as **ayer** *yesterday,* **anoche** *last night,* **el año pasado** *last year* appear in the sentence, they are additional cues to indicate the use of the preterite tense, because they show that the action was begun or was terminated in the past.

STUDY THE RULES, EXAMPLES, AND MODELS BEFORE BEGINNING THE EXERCISES!

Exercises

I. Rewrite the MODEL sentence in the *preterite* tense substituting the subject in parentheses for the one in *italics*. Make the necessary changes in the verbs.

Model: *Yo* **entré** a las tres y **salí** a las cuatro.   (El) **El entró** . . . **y salió** . . .
I entered at 3:00 and left at 4:00.   He entered at 3:00 and left at 4:00.

1. (Juan)_____

2. (Tú)_____

3. (Tú y yo)_____

4. (Vd.)_____

5. (Vds.)_____

6. (Mis amigos)_____

7. (Yo)_____

II. Rewrite the MODEL sentence in the *preterite* tense substituting the appropriate form of the verb in parentheses for the expression in *italics*.

Model: *Yo escribí* la carta anoche.   (El / enviar) **El envió** la carta anoche.
I wrote the letter last night.   He sent the letter last night.

1. (Vd. / recibir)_____

2. (Yo / cortar)_____

3. (Yo / romper)_____

4. (Nosotros / encontrar)_____

5. (María / buscar)_____

6. (Vds. / terminar)_____

7. (Pedro y Juan / escribir)_____

8. (Tú / responder)_____

9. (El y yo / perder)_____

10. (Tú / describir)_____

III. Write an affirmative answer in a complete Spanish sentence in the *preterite*. See models.

Model: a. —¿Comprendiste el libro?   **—Sí, comprendí el libro.**
           Did you understand the book?   Yes, I understood the book.

         b. —¿Y Elisa?   **—Elisa comprendió el libro también.**
            And Elisa?   Elisa understood the book, too.

1. a. ¿Usaste el sombrero?_____

   b. ¿Y tu madre?_____

2. a. ¿Aprendiste el pretérito?_____

   b. ¿Y tu hermano?_____

3. a. ¿Invitó Vd. al amigo?_____

   b. ¿Y los padres?_____

4. a. ¿Recibió Vd. el paquete?_____

   b. ¿Y yo?_____

5. a. ¿Bailaron ellos el tango anoche?_____

   b. ¿Y tu prima?_____

6. a. ¿Bebieron Vds. café ayer?_____

   b. ¿Y las chicas?_____

7. a. ¿Visitó Juan el museo?_____

   b. ¿Tú y yo?_____

8. a. ¿Lo comió todo?_____

   b. ¿Y ellas?_____

¿Lo comió todo?

9. a. ¿Saludaron los primos a la tía?_____

   b. ¿Y tú?_____

10. a. ¿Recibí yo el regalo?_____

   b. ¿Y Vds.?_____

IV. Rewrite each sentence in the *preterite* telling what happened yesterday.

1. Juan *entra* en la cocina._____

   _____

2. *Toma* pan y un vaso de leche._____

   _____

3. *Come* el pan y *bebe* la leche despacio._____

   _____

4. Pedro y Jorge *llegan* a su casa._____

   _____

5. *Comen* un poco de pan con Juan._____

   _____

6. Luego todos *salen* para la escuela donde *aprenden* mucho._____

   _____

7. *Escuchan* a la maestra en la clase y *practican* mucho en casa._____

   _____

8. Juan y yo *contestamos* muy bien._____

   _____

9. *Aprendemos* mucho cuando *escribimos* ejercicios._____

   _____

10. Yo también *estudio* y *asisto* a las clases._____

   _____

V. Oral Proficiency. Respond orally to the situation described. (You may *later* write your responses for intensive practice.)

Situation: You return home to find that a robbery occurred. The police ask for a complete report:—¿*Cómo pasó?*

In **five** Spanish statements tell them about the robbery. You may use your own ideas or ideas suggested by the following: *when you left the house, whether you closed the doors and the windows, where you kept your money, what or whom you found in the house, whether you received threatening telephone calls.*

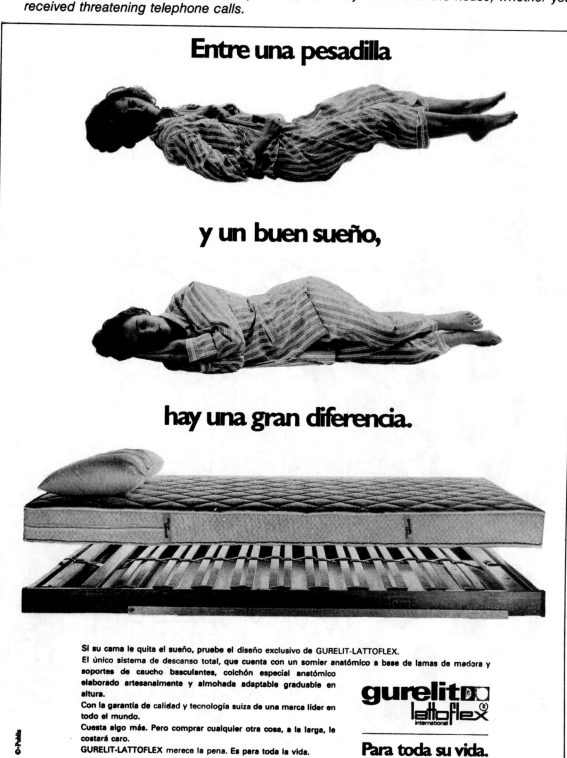

Nadie quiso
darle un asiento a la anciana.

*Is today's generation really as bad as some
say? See if you agree with the article.*

¡Los muchachos de hoy son horribles!

Gregorio entra en la sala donde su padre lee una revista. Tiene un artículo en la mano y está muy excitado.

—Papá, ¡la semana pasada Vd. nos dijo que la generación de hoy es terrible! Pues tengo algo aquí que seguramente va a ser interesante para Vd.

—Bueno, hijo. A ver si ese artículo expresa mis opiniones.

—Pues, ¡escuche Vd.! El artículo comienza así:

Ayer, en el tren, vi algo que me molestó. Esa noche no pude dormir. Cinco o seis jóvenes tomaron asiento en el coche cuando entró una señora de unos setenta años. Nadie quiso darle el asiento a la anciana. ¡Absolutamente nadie! ¿Qué hicieron? Pues sacaron sus periódicos y empezaron a leer. Y la pobre señora tuvo que estar de pie. Pero el incidente de ayer es típico. Todo fue muy diferente antes. Ya no hay respeto; ya no hay consideración para los ancianos como en los tiempos de nuestros padres. Los jóvenes de hoy vinieron a este mundo con todo. No necesitan nada y no quieren trabajar. Cuando vi el incidente de ayer, di las gracias a mis padres porque me enseñaron el respeto y la responsabilidad, y soy mejor hombre por eso.

—Bueno, papá, ¿qué piensa Vd. de este artículo? ¿No cree Vd. que es un poco exagerado?

—De ninguna manera. Ese escritor tiene razón. ¿De qué periódico es? Él conoce bien la generación de hoy.

—Él sabe mucho de la generación de Vd. también. Esto fue escrito en 1950. Encontré este viejo periódico en el sótano.

Palabras Nuevas

SUBSTANTIVOS

la anciana   *the old woman*
los ancianos   *the old people*
la consideración   *the consideration, the kindness*
el escritor   *the writer*
la generación   *the generation*
Gregorio   *Gregory*
el incidente   *the incident*
los jóvenes   *the young people, the youths*
la opinión   *the opinion*
el papá   *the daddy*
el respeto   *the respect*
la responsabilidad   *the responsibility*
la revista   *the magazine*
el sótano   *the attic*
los tiempos   *the times*

ADJETIVOS

exagerado,a   *exaggerated*
excitado,a   *excited*
horrible   *horrible*

VERBOS

comenzar (ie)   *to begin*
dar las gracias   *to thank, to give thanks*
di   *I gave*
dijo   *he (she) said; you (formal sing.) said*
encontrar   *to find*
fue escrito   *it was written*
hicieron   *they did, made; you (formal pl.) did, made*
(no) pude   *I could (not)*

quiso   *he (she) wanted; you (formal sing.) wanted*
tener razón   *to be right*
tuvo que   *he (she) had to; you (formal sing.) had to*
vinieron   *they came; you (formal pl.) came*

OTRAS PALABRAS

¡A ver!   *Let us see!*
de ninguna manera   *by no means*
de pie   *standing*
por eso   *for that reason, because of that*
ya no   *no longer*

EJERCICIOS

I. (A) ¿Cierto (true) **o falso** (false)?

1. El padre de Gregorio lee un libro en la sala. _____
2. Gregorio le trae a su padre un artículo sobre un robo. _____
3. En el artículo setenta jóvenes molestaron a una vieja. _____
4. Los jóvenes de hoy no quieren trabajar porque lo tienen todo. _____
5. El padre de Gregorio expresa la opinión del escritor del artículo. _____

(B) Preguntas personales y generales. Write your answer in a complete Spanish sentence.

1. ¿Qué piensa Vd. de la generación de hoy? ¿Tiene respeto y consideración?
2. ¿Da Vd. su asiento a un anciano en el autobús o en el tren?
3. ¿Qué periódico lee Vd.?
4. ¿Tienen siempre razón sus padres?

1._____

2._____

3._____

4._____

II. Change the verbs of the following sentences from the present to the preterite.

1. Gregorio *entra* en la sala.   _____
2. *Veo* algo en los trenes que me *molesta*.   _____
3. Nadie *quiere* darle asiento.   _____
4. Todos *sacan* sus periódicos y *empiezan* a leer.   _____
5. Los jóvenes no *necesitan* nada.   _____

III. ¿Cómo se dice en español?

1. He comes into the living room.
2. I have something here that is going to be interesting to you.
3. Nobody wanted to give her a seat.
4. The poor woman had to stand.
5. I'm a better man because of that .
6. Don't you think it is a bit exaggerated?

1._____

2._____

3._____

4._____

5._____

6._____

IV. Compositions: Oral or written.

(A) Look at the picture at the beginning of this Work Unit. Describe the scene in Spanish to a friend.

(B) Tell about a considerate act that you have read about. Include the following:

Una cortesía

1. Where you saw the article.   2. Who gave a seat to another person.   3. Why the seat was given.   4. What the other person said.   5. Where and when this happened.

ESTRUCTURAS DE LA LENGUA

The Preterite Indicative: Irregular Verbs

A. *Irregular preterite stems* require only *one set of irregular endings.*

1. **UV** is characteristic of these stems.　　2. **US** and **UP** are characteristic of these stems.

estar *to be*	tener *to have*	poner *to put*	saber *to know*
estuv: Pret. stem	**tuv:** Pret. stem	**pus:** Pret. stem	**sup:** Pret. stem
I was there.	I had a letter.	I put (did put) that there.	I knew (learned about) that.
Estuve allí.	Tuve una carta.	Puse eso allí.	Supe eso.
estuviste	tuviste	pusiste	supiste
estuvo	tuvo	puso	supo
estuvimos	tuvimos	pusimos	supimos
estuvisteis	tuvisteis	pusisteis	supisteis
estuvieron	tuvieron	pusieron	supieron

3. **I** is characteristic of these stems.　　4. **J** is characteristic of these stems.

venir *to come*	hacer *to do, make*	traer *to bring*	decir *to say, tell*
vin: Pret. stem	**hic:** Pret. stem	**traj:** Pret. stem	**dij:** Pret. stem
I came home.	I did (made) that.	I brought this.	I said the truth.
Vine a casa.	Hice eso.	Traje esto.	Dije la verdad.
viniste	hiciste	trajiste	dijiste
vino	hizo	trajo	dijo
vinimos	hicimos	trajimos	dijimos
vinisteis	hicisteis	trajisteis	dijisteis
vinieron	hicieron	trajeron	dijeron

Rules:

1. The one set of endings for **ar, er,** or **ir** verbs that have irregular preterite stems is **e, iste, o, imos, isteis, ieron.** After **j** (Group 4) the third person plural ending is **eron.** Irregular preterites bear *no accent marks.*

2. The following additional irregular preterites are similar to some of the above verbs.

UV like **estar**	**U** like **poner** and **saber**	**i** like **venir** and **hacer**
andar　*to walk*	**poder**　*to be able*	**querer**　*to want*
anduv:　*Pret. stem*	**pud:**　*Pret. stem*	**quis:**　*Pret. stem*
Anduve　*I walked*	**Pude**　*I was able, could*	**Quise**　*I wanted*
(etc.)	(etc.)	(etc.)

259

B. Identical special preterite forms for **ser** *to be*, **ir** *to go*.

C. Dar: An **ar** verb has regular **er/ir** preterite endings.

D. Leer: Y replaces **i** in the third persons.

ser *to be*	ir *to go*	dar *to give*	leer *to read*
fu: Pret. stem	**fu:** Pret. stem	**d:** Pret. stem	**le:** Pret. stem
I was a soldier.	I went home.	I gave thanks.	I did read that.
Fui soldado.	Fui a casa.	Di las gracias.	Leí eso.
fu**iste**	fu**iste**	d**iste**	le**íste**
fu**e**	fu**e**	d**io**	le**yó**
fu**imos**	fu**imos**	d**imos**	le**ímos**
fu**isteis**	fu**isteis**	d**isteis**	le**ísteis**
fu**eron**	fu**eron**	d**ieron**	le**yeron**

Rules:

1. **Ser** and **ir** being exactly alike in the preterite, can be distinguished only according to their use in the sentence.

2. **Leer** keeps its regular **le** stem, adds regular **er** endings, but changes the **ió** and **ieron** endings to **yó** and **yeron** in the third persons singular and plural. An accent mark is written on the **í** of the other personal endings. Conjugate **caer** *to fall*, **creer** *to believe* and **oír** *to hear* like **leer** (D, above).

STUDY THE RULES, EXAMPLES, AND MODELS BEFORE BEGINNING THE EXERCISES!

Exercises

I. Rewrite the sentence in the *preterite* substituting the subject in parentheses. Make necessary changes in each of the two verbs.

> Model: La nieve *vino* y *cayó* todo el día.
> (Las lluvias) **Las lluvias vinieron
> y cayeron todo el día.**

The snow came and fell all day.
The rains came and fell all day.

A. Ellos *tuvieron* la carta ayer y la *pusieron* en la mesa.

1. (Yo) _____

2. (Pedro) _____

3. (Pedro y yo) _____

4. (Vd.) _____

5. (Los chicos) _____

B. Juan *hizo* la tarea y la *trajo* a la clase.

1. (Vds.) _____

2. (Vd.) _____

3. (Yo)_____

4. (La alumna)_____

5. (Nosotros)_____

C. Ellos *dijeron* que sí y *dieron* las gracias.

1. (Mi madre)_____

2. (Vd.)_____

3. (Yo)_____

4. (Nosotros)_____

5. (Los abuelos)_____

D. Los chicos *fueron* buenos cuando *vinieron* a la clase.

1. (La niña)_____

2. (Yo)_____

3. (Tú)_____

4. (Ellas)_____

5. (Ellas y yo)_____

E. Los tíos *fueron* al teatro donde *vieron* una buena comedia.

1. (Yo)_____

2. (Diego)_____

3. (Diego y yo)_____

4. (Mi amiga)_____

5. (Tú)_____

F. María *leyó* la frase y la *creyó*.

1. (Los primos)_____

2. (Nosotras)_____

3. (Yo)_____

4. (Tú)_____

5. (Vd.)_____

G. Yo *oí* los gritos cuando *estuve* allí.

1. (María)_____

2. (Ellos)_____

3. (María y yo)_____

4. (Tú)_____

5. (Yo)_____

H. *Anduve* mucho y *supe* que *pude* hacerlo porque *quise* hacerlo.

1. (Juan)_____

2. (Juan y yo) _____

3. (Juan y Ana) _____

4. (Yo) _____

5. (Tú) _____

II. Rewrite the sentence in the *plural* using the word cues.

1. La piedra cayó. (Las piedras)_____

2. La niña vino. (Las niñas)_____

3. Yo tuve razón. (Nosotros)_____

4. Yo hice el viaje. (Nosotros)_____

5. El hizo el viaje. (Ellos)_____

6. Ella trajo la revista. (Ellas)_____

7. Vd. fue al cine. (Vds.)_____

8. Yo fui excelente. (Nosotros)_____

9. Vd. dijo la frase. (Vds.)_____

10. Vd. dio ayuda. (Vds.)_____

11. Yo leí mucho. (Nosotros)_____

12. Yo oí gritos. (Nosotros)_____

13. El oyó el disco. (Ellos)_____

14. Vd. creyó el artículo. (Vds.)_____

15. Ella leyó el cuento. (Ellas)_____

16. Yo dije que sí. (Nosotros)_____

17. Yo di dinero. (Nosotros)_____

18. Ella fue bonita. (Ellas)_____

19. Yo fui al mercado. (Nosotros)_____

20. Yo lo creí. (Nosotros)_____

III. Write an affirmative answer in a complete Spanish sentence using the cue words.

1. ¿Quiénes estuvieron allí? (Mis amigos)_____

2. ¿Adónde fue Vd.? (a la tienda)_____

3. ¿Cuánto dinero trajo Vd.? (tres dólares)_____

4. ¿Quién hizo las compras? (Yo)_____

5. ¿Dónde pusieron Vds. las compras? (en la mesa)_____

IV. Rewrite each sentence in the *preterite* tense telling what happened yesterday.

1. Vengo a la casa de Anita._____

2. Es su cumpleaños._____

3. Ella tiene regalos de los amigos._____

4. Ellos le dicen : — Feliz cumpleaños._____

5. Luego oyen discos en su casa._____

6. Pueden oír mucho. _____

7. Yo quiero escuchar más. _____

8. Pero tengo que volver a casa. _____

9. Ando a casa. _____

10. Sé que es una buena fiesta._____

V. **Oral Proficiency.** Respond orally to the situation described. (You may *later* write your responses for intensive practice.)

Situation: You visit your grandparents who are interested in hearing how you spent your recent birthday, which they could not attend. They ask:—*¿Cómo pasaste tu cumpleaños?* You tell them how you spent the day.

First, thank them for the present they sent you. Then, in **four** Spanish sentences tell them the events of the day. You may use your own ideas or ideas suggested by the following: *who gave you the party, who came, what gifts they brought, where you went in the evening, how old you now are.*

263

En mi opinión el señor Ramírez
no es culpable.

Guilty or innocent? It's a tough decision to make.

La justicia siempre triunfa

Drama policíaco en un acto

Escena   Tribunal de la corte civil. Hay una docena de espectadores, más o menos. El juez está sentado al frente del salón. Todo el mundo escucha atentamente. Ahora llaman a los testigos.

Personajes   El juez
El abogado defensor
El fiscal
El primer testigo

Abogado: Llamo como primer testigo de la defensa, al señor Ángel Alpargata. Señor Alpargata, como ya sabe usted, el fiscal dice que el acusado, Ramiro Ramírez, cuando borracho, chocó su carro contra la bicicleta de un muchacho. ¿Qué puede Vd. decirnos en la defensa del señor Ramírez?

Testigo: Eso no es verdad. El señor Ramírez es un hombre honrado. No es un borracho y por eso nunca conduce un coche en ese estado. En mi opinión no es culpable.

Fiscal: Protesto, protesto, Aquí en una corte de justicia no importan las opiniones. ¿Estuvo usted allí cuando ocurrió el accidente?

Testigo: No, señor. Nadie estuvo allí. Pero me dicen . . .

Fiscal: No importa eso. ¿Vio o no vio usted el accidente?

Testigo: No señor, el accidente ocurrió a las diez de la noche. ¿Verdad? Y a esa hora, yo estuve en mi cama cansado de trabajar todo el día.

Juez (muy enojado): — ¿Cómo? ¿En la cama? Pero esto es ridículo. ¿Por qué está Vd. aquí como testigo por el señor Ramírez? Vd. nunca vio nada.

Testigo: Pues. . . .Mi mujer dijo que. . . . Señor juez, Ramiro es mi cuñado.

Palabras Nuevas

SUBSTANTIVOS

el abogado defensor   *the defense attorney*
el accidente   *the accident*
el acusado   *the defendent*
la alpargata   *the slipper*
la bicicleta   *the bicycle*
el carro   *the car*
la corte civil   *the civil court*
el cuñado   *the brother-in-law*
la defensa   *the defense*
el drama policíaco   *the detective drama*

el espectador   *the spectator*
el fiscal   *the district attorney*
el juez   *the judge*
la mujer   *the wife*
el testigo   *the witness*
el tribunal   *the courtroom*

ADJETIVOS

borracho,a   *drunk*
culpable   *guilty*
honrado,a   *honest*
ridículo,a   *ridiculous*

VERBOS

conducir   *to drive*
chocar   *to crash*
protestar   *to protest*

OTRAS PALABRAS

atentamente   *attentively*
contra   *against*
¿verdad?   *right?*

EJERCICIOS

I. Preguntas. Write your answer in a complete Spanish sentence.

1. ¿Cuántos espectadores hay en la corte?
2. ¿Con qué chocó Ramiro Ramírez?

265

3. ¿Qué dice Angel sobre el carácter de Ramírez?
4. ¿Por qué protesta el fiscal?
5. ¿Por qué está enojado el juez?

1. _____

2. _____

3. _____

4. _____

5. _____

II. Unscramble the sentences in the boxes.

1.
¿qué	defensa?	en
decirnos	su	puede

2.
es	hombre	señor
el	un	honrado

3.
nos	las	no
opiniones	importan	aquí

4.
accidente	a	ocurrió
las	diez	el

1. _____

2. _____

3. _____

4. _____

III. Find the following words in the boxes.

1. lawyer
2. accused
3. drama
4. car
5. judge
6. witness (word is backward)
7. drunk
8. D.A.
9. less
10. act
11. all
12. as
13. 10

A	B	O	G	A	D	O	J
C	O	C	H	E	F	G	U
U	T	O	D	O	I	I	E
S	M	E	N	O	S	T	Z
A	C	O	M	O	C	S	A
D	R	A	M	A	A	E	C
O	D	I	E	Z	L	T	T
B	O	R	R	A	C	H	O

IV. Compositions: Oral or written.

(A) Look at the picture at the beginning of this Work Unit. Describe the scene in Spanish to a friend.

(B) Tell about a court scene. Include the following:

¿Culpable o no culpable?

1. The lawyer enters the court. 2. There are several witnesses. 3. They all saw the accident.
4. The judge listens attentively. 5. Everyone thinks that the defendant is guilty.

ESTRUCTURAS DE LA LENGUA

| ¡Nadie! | ¡Nunca! | ¡Nada! |

Nunca, nada, nadie in Emphatic Negation. The Tag Question, **¿verdad?**

A. **¡Nunca!** never!; **¡nada!** nothing!; **¡nadie!** nobody!; when used emphatically precede the verb, like **no.**

Questions	*Statements*
1. **¿No** tienen los chicos libros? Don't the boys have any books?	1. Ellos **no** tienen libros. They have no books. (haven't any)
2. **¿Nunca** escuchan ellos? Don't they ever listen?	2. ¡Ellos **nunca** escuchan! They never listen!
3. **¿Nada** estudian? Don't they study anything?	3. ¡Ellos **nada** estudian! They study nothing!
4. **¿Nadie** contesta? Doesn't anybody (anyone) answer?	4. **¡Nadie** contesta! Nobody (no one) answers.

267

Rules:

1. **Nunca, nada, nadie,** precede the verb for emphasis both in questions and in statements, like **no.**

2. Summary of English equivalents for the negative words.

nunca:	never	not . . . ever
nada:	nothing	not . . . anything
nadie:	nobody; no one	not . . . anybody

B. The Spanish speaker requests agreement with a statement by adding **¿no es verdad?** or **¿verdad?**

1. Son españoles, ¿no es verdad?
   They are Spaniards, aren't they?

2. Es domingo, ¿no es verdad?
   It is Sunday, isn't it?

3. No hablan espānol, ¿verdad?
   They don't speak Spanish, do they?

4. No estudian el francés, ¿verdad?
   They don't study French, right?

Rules:

1. **¿No es verdad?** or **¿verdad?** usually follows the statement.

2. Both forms can be translated according to the meaning of the sentence to which they are added: *isn't it (so)?*; *aren't they?*; *isn't that right?*; etc.

STUDY THE RULES, EXAMPLES, AND MODELS BEFORE BEGINNING THE EXERCISES!

Exercises

I. Write a NEGATIVE answer in a complete Spanish sentence according to the model.

Model: –¿Sabe **alguien** todos los idiomas?   –**Nadie** sabe todos los idiomas.
Does anyone know all (the) languages?   *Nobody* (no one) knows all (the) languages.

1. ¿Comprende alguien todos los idiomas?_____

2. ¿Estudia alguien todos los días?_____

3. ¿Lee alguien todos los periódicos?_____

4. ¿Visita alguien todos los países?_____

5. ¿Hace alguien todo el trabajo?_____

II. Write an emphatically NEGATIVE answer in a complete Spanish sentence according to the model.

Model: –¿**Siempre** tienes clases hasta las cinco?
Do you *always* have classes until five o'clock?

–**Nunca** tengo clases hasta las cinco.
I *never* have classes until five.

1. ¿Siempre comes despacio?_____

2. ¿Siempre estás triste después de un examen?_____

3. ¿Siempre tienes hambre a las cuatro?_____

4. ¿Siempre lees en la cama antes de dormir?_____

5. ¿Siempre ayudas a lavar los platos?_____

III. Write an emphatically NEGATIVE answer in a complete Spanish sentence according to the model.

Model: –¿Preparan los chicos **algo** para el desayuno?
Are the boys preparing *something* for breakfast?

–Los chicos **nada** preparan para el desayuno.
The boys are preparing *nothing* for breakfast.

1. ¿Compraron los chicos algo para el viaje?_____

_____

2. ¿Reciben ellos algo para pagar el billete?_____

_____

3. ¿Comió Juan algo antes de salir de la casa?_____

_____

4. ¿Tuvieron ellos que contestar algo a la carta de invitación?_____

_____

5. ¿Deben ellos llevar algo a la casa del amigo?_____

_____

IV. Write an emphatically NEGATIVE answer, in a complete Spanish sentence, according to the negative used in each question. Begin with **Verdad.**

Model: –¿**Nunca** desea asistir él al teatro?   –**Verdad.** El **nunca** desea asistir al teatro.
Doesn't he *ever* want to attend the theater?   *True.* He *never* wants to attend the theater.

1. ¿Nada pueden recibir las niñas pobres para la Navidad?_____

_____

2. ¿Nadie va a comprender la lección hoy?_____

_____

3. ¿Nada quiso escribir el chico perezoso en la pizarra? _____

_____

4. ¿Nadie desea asistir a la fiesta el lunes?_____

_____

5. ¿Nunca debe trabajar un hombre cansado los sábados?_____

_____

V. Rewrite the following in the emphatic NEGATIVE using the word in parentheses.

Model: Los alumnos estudian mucho.   (nunca) Los alumnos **nunca** estudian mucho.
The students study a great deal.   The pupils never study a great deal.

1. María y yo leímos. (nada)

_____

2. Escucha la radio cuando come. (nadie)

_____

3. María tomó sopa. (nunca)

_____

4. ¿Está buena la sopa? (nunca)

_____

5. ¿Está en casa. (nadie)

_____

VI. Write the word in *italics* as a separate QUESTION. Then write a contradicting NEGATIVE response using **nunca, nada** or **nadie,** according to the model.

A. Model: Tú *siempre* lees mucho.   ¿**Siempre?** Yo **nunca** leo mucho.
You always read a great deal.   Always? I never read a great deal.

1. Tú *siempre* cantas en casa._____

_____

2. Vd. *siempre* toma el desayuno temprano._____

_____

3. Laura y Antonio *siempre* pasan el verano en la escuela._____

_____

B. Model: —*Juan* está cansado.   —**¿Juan? Nadie** está cansado.
            John is tired.   John? Nobody is tired.

1. *María* vino a mi casa._____

_____

2. *La familia* fue a esquiar en el invierno._____

_____

3. *Ese zapatero* tiene zapatos excelentes hoy._____

_____

C. Model: —El lee *algo* de eso.   —**¿Algo?** Él **nada** lee de eso.
            He reads something about that.   Something? He reads nothing about that.

1. El sabe *algo* de México. _____

_____

2. El alumno contestó *algo* a la profesora. _____

_____

3. Los niños oyen *algo* en la cocina. _____

_____

4. Los turistas necesitan *algo* para el viaje. _____

_____

VII. Rewrite the sentence as a request for agreement by adding **¿no es verdad?** *Translate* the
complete answer appropriately.
Model: Tus padres van a viajar a Puerto Rico.
         Tus padres van a viajar a Puerto Rico, ¿no es verdad?
         Your parents are going to travel to Puerto Rico, aren't they?

1. Tus padres salieron para Puerto Rico. _____

_____

2. Siempre pasan un mes allí. _____

_____

3. Tú tienes una prima puertorriqueña. _____

_____

4. Se llama Laura y es muy bonita. _____

_____

5. Su casa está en el campo. _____

_____

VIII. Write a complete Spanish sentence using the vocabulary provided.

1. *Nobody* prepares a breakfast like my mother.

_____

/ prepara / desayuno como / madre

2. My father and I *never* prepare breakfast.

_____

/ padre / preparamos / desayuno

3. But my sister takes *nothing* for breakfast.

_____

pero / hermana / toma para / desayuno

4. Your sister takes coffee, doesn't she?

_____

/ hermana toma café /

5. But your brother is still in bed, isn't he?

_____

/ hermano está todavía / cama /

IX. Oral Proficiency. Respond orally to the situation described. (You may *later* write your responses for intensive practice.)

Situation: A friend telephones. She is very upset. She gave a party in your honor but *you* did not appear. She says:—*¡Estoy muy enojada contigo!* You explain the misunderstandings that led to your not being at the party.

Say that you are sorry. In **four** Spanish sentences explain the misunderstandings. You may use your own ideas or ideas suggested by the following: *you never received the invitation; you knew nothing about the party; nobody called you; you are innocent not guilty, right?*

Part Two
IDIOMS AND DIALOGUES

Part Two:
Idioms and Dialogues

Unit 1. Fórmulas de cortesía :

Conversación entre el maestro, su nuevo alumno y una señorita, hermana del alumno, la cual lo lleva a la escuela. Es el primer día de la escuela.

Expressions of Courtesy

Conversation among the teacher, his new pupil, and a young lady who is the pupil's sister, who takes him to school. It is the first day of school.

Greetings

Maestro: —Hola, amigo.	Hi, (hello) friend.	Familiar: **Hola.** *Hello.* Formal: **Buenos días.** *Hello.* **Buenas tardes.** *Good after-noon* or *early evening.* **Buenas noches.** *Good evening* (late); *good night.* **Señora** *m'am, Mrs.* **Señorita** *Miss.* **Señor** *Mr.*
Alumno: —Buenos días, señor.	Good day (good morning), sir.	
Señorita: —Buenos días, señor.		

Please. Thanks

M: —¡Pasen Vds., por favor!	Come in, please.	**Por favor** may follow the request, which is in the COMMAND form. **Haga(n) Vd.(s) el favor de** . . . (formal) and **haz el favor de** . . . (fam. sing. **tú**) precede the request, which is in the INFINITIVE form.
—¡Haga Vd. el favor de pasar, señorita!	Please come in, miss.	
—¡Haz el favor de pasar, niño!	Please come in, child.	
A: —(Muchas) gracias, señor profesor.	Thank you (very much), teacher.	**Maestro** in grade-school **Señor profesor** courtesy form
Srta: —Mil gracias.	Many thanks.	

Welcome (to my house etc.)

M: —Bienvenido, niño.	Welcome, child.	**Bienvenido-a** agrees in gender and number with the person(s) welcomed.
—Bienvenida, señorita.	Welcome, miss.	
—Bienvenidos, todos.	You are all welcome.	

Introductions

M: —Me llamo José López. ¿Cómo te llamas tú, niño?

My name is Joseph López. What is your name, child?

A: —Me llamo Pepe, servidor.

My name is Joey, at your service.

M: —¿Y cómo se llama tu hermana?

And what is your sister's name?

A: —Mi hermana se llama Rosa.

My sister's name is Rose.

M: —Dispense, señorita. ¿Se llama Vd. Rosa?

Excuse me, miss. Is your name Rose?

Srta: —Me llamo Rosa Ortiz, servidora.

My name is Rose Ortiz, at your service.

M: —Mucho gusto.

Great pleasure. (Pleased to meet you.)

Srta: —El gusto es mío.

The pleasure is mine.

Llamarse *to be named, to be called*

me llamo
te llamas
se llama

nos llamamos
os llamáis
se llaman

Servidor-a *At your service.* Courtesy form used after giving one's name in introductions.

To Shake Hands. Of Course

M: —¿Me das la mano, Pepe?

Will you shake hands, Joe?

A: —¡Cómo no! Le doy la mano, señor.

Of course, I'll shake hands, sir.

Dar la mano *to shake hands*

doy	damos
das	dais
da	dan

Polite Inquiries

M: —¿Qué tal, niño?

How are things, child?

A: —Sin novedad.

Nothing new.

M: —Pero, ¿cómo estás tú, Pepe?

But how are you, Joe?

A: —(Estoy) muy bien. ¿Y cómo está Vd., señor?

(I am) very well. And how are you sir?

M: —Así, así. No estoy enfermo. ¿Y Vd., señorita?

So, so. I am not sick. And you, miss?

Srta: —No estoy muy bien. Estoy enferma.

I am not very well. I am ill.

Estar *to be* (health)

estoy	estamos
estás	estáis
está	están

¿Qué tal?

Taking Leave

Srta:	—Con permiso. Hasta mañana.	Excuse me. Until tomorrow.
M:	—Le doy las gracias por la visita.	I thank you for the visit.
Srta:	—De nada, señor profesor. (No hay de qué.)	You are welcome, teacher. (You are welcome.)
M:	—Hasta luego. (Hasta la vista.)	Until later. (See you later.)
Srta:	—Adiós.	Good-bye.

Con permiso *Excuse me:* courtesy form when leaving early or upon inconveniencing a person; also, **dispense.**

Dar las gracias *to thank*

doy	damos
das	dais
da	dan

Farewells: fam.: **Hasta luego (hasta la vista);** *formal:* **Adiós.**

STUDY THE IDIOMS BEFORE BEGINNING THE EXERCISES!

Exercises

I. Write the expression that best completes the sentence, and circle the letter.

1. Cuando mi amigo entra en mi casa, yo le digo:_____
   a. —Bienvenido. b. —Adiós. c. —Dispense. d. —Sin novedad.

2. Si mi amigo me presenta a su profesor, le doy_____
   a. dinero. b. una revista. c. la mano. d. un beso.

3. Cuando mi madre me da la comida, yo le doy_____
   a. la mano. b. las gracias. c. un vaso de leche. d. un dólar.

4. Acepto la invitación a la casa de un amigo cuando le digo:_____
   a. —Con mucho gusto. b. —Hola. c. —Con permiso. d. —Así, así.

5. Si *no* puedo aceptar una invitación digo:_____
   a. —De nada. b. —Mucho gusto. c. —Dispense. d. —Servidor.

6. Si yo visito a una persona en el hospital le digo:_____
   a. —¿Cómo está Vd.? b. —¿Cómo se llama Vd.? c. —Dispense. d. —Bienvenido.

7. Cuando una persona me da las gracias, le contesto:_____
   a. —Hasta luego. b. —Bienvenido. c. —De nada. d. —Buenas noches.

8. Si quiero conocer a una persona le pregunto:_____
   a. —¿Cómo se llama Vd.? b. —¿Qué es esto? c. —¿Dónde estás? d. —¿Adiós?

9. Antes de interrumpir una conversación digo:_____
   a. —Sin novedad. b. —Con permiso. c. —Gracias. d. —No hay de qué.

10. Si mi amigo necesita un favor de mí, yo le respondo:_____
    a. —¡Cómo no! b. —¡Pase Vd.! c. —¡Por favor! d. —Gracias.

II. Write *two* appropriate rejoinders in Spanish from the selection given. Circle the letters.

1. —Te doy las gracias:_____ / _____
   a. —No hay de qué. b. —De nada. c. —Buenas tardes. d. —Así, así.

2. —Te doy el dinero que necesitas:_____ / _____
   a. —Te doy las gracias. b. —No muy bien. c. —De nada. d. —Muchas gracias.

3. —¿Cómo estás?:_____ / _____
   a. —No hay de qué. b. —Adiós. c. —No estoy bien. d. —Estoy enfermo.

4. —¿Entro ahora?: _____ / _____
   a. —De nada. b. —¡Entre Vd. por favor! c. —Así, así. d. —¡Haz el favor de pasar!

5. —¿Qué tal?: _____ / _____
   a. —Por favor. b. —Sin novedad. c. —Muy bien. d. —¿Cómo te llamas?

6. —Hola:_____ / _____
   a. —Buenos días. b. —Buenas tardes. c. —Así, así. d. —De nada.

7. —Adiós:_____ / _____
   a. —Hasta luego. b. —Bienvenido. c. —Hasta la vista. d. —Sin novedad.

8. —¡Dispense!_____ / _____
   a. —Hola. b. —Así, así. c. —¡Cómo no! d. —Con mucho gusto.

III. Write the appropriate rejoinder, and then circle the letter.

1. Vds. llegan a mi casa por la mañana.

   Yo digo: —_____
   a. Buenos días. b. Buenas tardes.
   c. Buenas noches.

2. Yo pregunto: —¿Cómo está tu familia?

   Tú respondes: —_____
   a. Buenas tardes. b. Adiós.
   c. Así, así.

3. Yo pregunto: —¿Cómo se llama Vd.?

   Vd. responde: —_____
   a. Mi amigo se llama Juan. b. Buenas
   tardes. c. Me llamo Juan, servidor.

4. Yo digo: —¡Haga Vd. el favor de entrar!

   Vd. responde: —_____
   a. Le doy las gracias. b. De nada.
   c. Estoy bien.

5. Vd. dice: —Buenas tardes.

   Yo respondo: —_____
   a. Hola. b. Servidor. c. No muy bien.

6. Vd. pregunta: —¿Se llama Vd. Laura?

   Yo respondo: —_____
   a. Sí, muchas gracias. b. Sí, servidora.
   c. Sí, buenas noches.

7. Yo digo: —Adiós.

   Vd. responde: —_____
   a. Hasta la vista. b. Dispense.
   c. Mucho gusto.

8. Yo digo: —Me llamo Juan.

   Vd. responde: —_____
   a. Mucho gusto. b. Dispense.
   c. Hasta la vista.

9. Yo digo: —Yo te doy la mano.

   Tú dices: —_____
   a. Bien. b. De nada. c. Mucho
   gusto.

10. Yo digo: —Gracias.

   Tú respondes: —_____
   a. ¿Cómo está? b. Buenos días.
   c. No hay de qué.

IV. Rewrite the following sentences *with their letters* in the logical order of sequence.
   Model: a. Hasta luego b. Sin novedad. c. ¿Qué tal? d. Buenos días.

       1. (d.) *Buenos días.*   3. (b.) *Sin novedad.*
       2. (c.) *¿Qué tal?*   4. (a.) *Hasta luego.*

A. a. Dices: —No hay de qué. b. Te doy las gracias. c. Tú me das un regalo.

   1._____2._____

   3._____

B. a. Yo te doy la mano y digo: —Mucho gusto. b. Tú respondes: —Me llamo Víctor, servidor. c. Yo pregunto: —¿Cómo te llamas?

   1._____2._____

   _____3._____

C. a. —Entonces, lo invito para mañana. b. —Haga Vd. el favor de venir a mi casa esta tarde. c. —Muchas gracias. d. —Dispense. Estoy enfermo hoy.

   1._____

   2._____3._____

   _____4._____

V. Rewrite the sentence, using the correct expression for *how* or *what*: **¿Cómo?** or **¿Qué?**

   1. ¿_____? 3. ¿_____?
        (se llaman ellos)   (está Vd.)

   2. ¿_____? 4. ¿_____?
         (tal)   (te llamas)

       5. ¿_____?
            (está tu familia)

VI. Complete from the selection below. (See DIALOGUES, pp. 274–276.)

Juan: —_____ tardes, _____ profesor.
                                   1   2

El profesor: —Bienvenido, Juan Gómez: ¡Haga Vd. el _____ de entrar!
                                                                      3

¿Me _____ Vd. la mano?
                    4

Juan: —Sí, ¡_____ no! ¿Cómo _____ Vd.?
                        5   6

El profesor: —Estoy bien; no estoy _____
                                                              7

Juan: —Deseo darle las _____ por la ayuda con el trabajo.
                                      8

El profesor: —No hay de _____. ¿_____ tal, Juan? ¿Y la familia?
                                  9   10

Juan: —_____ novedad. La familia _____ bien. Yo _____
                11   12   13

bien. Tengo que regresar a casa ahora. _____ permiso. Buenas _____
                                                  14   15

El profesor: —_____, Juan.
                              16

Selection: **adiós, buenas, cómo, con, da, enfermo, está, estoy, favor, gracias, está, tardes, qué, señor, sin, qué.**

VII. Copy the Spanish sentence. Then rewrite the sentence, substituting the expressions in parentheses for the appropriate words in *italics*. Make all necessary changes in the verb.
Model: *Él* le da las gracias por *la comida.*   **He thanks him for the meal.**
        (Tú / dinero)   **Tú le das las gracias por el dinero.**
                                                     (You thank him for the money.)

A. *Yo* le doy las gracias por *la visita.*_____

1. (Nosotros/el favor)_____

2. (El maestro/la bienvenida)_____

3. (Sus amigos/su invitación)_____

4. (Tú/los regalos)_____

B. *Ella* le da la mano a *Juan.*_____

1. (Yo/al profesor)_____

2. (Nosotros/a la vecina)_____

3. (Tú/mi padre)_____

4. (Los oficiales/al astronauta)_____   **279**

C. *Señorita, ¡haga Vd. el favor de pasar!*_____

1. (Señora,/responder a la carta)_____

2. (Caballeros,/entrar)_____

3. (Señor,/salir ahora)_____

4. (Señoritas,/poner la mesa)_____

D. *Niño, ¡haz el favor de dar la mano!*_____

1. (Ana,/escuchar al maestro)_____

2. (Chico,/leer el cuento)_____

3. (Prima,/llegar a tiempo)_____

4. (Hijo,/dar las gracias a mamá)_____

E. ¡Pasen Vds., *por favor!*_____

1. (¡Den Vds. la mano!)_____

2. (¡Escriba Vd.!)_____

3. (¡Conteste Vd. en español!)_____

4. (¡Vengan Vds. acá!)_____

VIII. Replace **por favor** by the appropriate form of **hacer el favor de**. Make necessary changes in the verb form and in the word order.

A. Model: ¡Trabajen Vds. menos, por favor!   **¡Hagan Vds. el favor de trabajar** menos!
        Work less, please! (*pl.*)   Please work less! (*pl.*)

1. ¡Den Vds. la mano, por favor!_____

2. ¡Tomen Vds. asiento, por favor!_____

3. ¡Salgan Vds. más tarde, por favor!_____

4. ¡Escriban Vds. su dirección, por favor!_____

5. ¡Hablen Vds. menos aquí, por favor!_____

B. Model: ¡Trabaje Vd. menos, por favor!   **¡Haga Vd. el favor de trabajar** menos!
                Work less, please!   Please work less!

1. ¡Dé Vd. las gracias, por favor!_____

2. ¡Tome Vd. café, por favor!_____

3. ¡Ponga Vd. el libro aquí, por favor!_____

4. ¡Reciba Vd. este dinero, por favor!_____

5. ¡Coma Vd. más, por favor!_____

IX. Write a complete Spanish sentence supplying the missing words for the expressions given below the line.

Model: Les doy/mano/profesores.

Les doy la mano a los profesores.   I shake hands with the teachers.

1. ¡_____!
      Haz/favor/aprender/lección

2. ¡_____!
      Haz/favor/abrir/ventana

3. ¡_____!
      Hagan/favor/no hablar/en/clase

4. ¡_____!
      Pasen/al otro cuarto/favor

5. _____.
      Les doy/gracias/padres

Picasso, Pablo.
Guernica. (1937, May-early June).
Oil on canvas. 11'5½" x 25'5¾"
El Museo del Prado, Madrid, España.

El tiempo, la edad, las sensaciones

Unit 2: Conversaciones breves sobre el tiempo, la edad y unas sensaciones.

Little conversations about the weather, age, and some sensations.

A. El tiempo — *The Weather*

Hace . . .	It is . . . (idiomatic)	**Hace** expresses *what kind of weather it is. It* is understood.
1. —¿Qué tiempo hace?	What kind of weather is it? How is the weather?	
2. —Hace (muy) buen tiempo.	It is (very) good weather.	**Muy** emphasizes the adjectives **buen** and **mal.**
3. —¿Hace calor?	Is it warm?	
4. —Hace sol pero no hace calor.	It is sunny but it is not hot.	**No** appears before **hace** in the negative sentence.
5. —Entonces hace fresco.	Then it is cool.	
6. —Sí, hace fresco pero no hace frío.	Yes, it is cool but it is not cold.	
Muy — Mucho; Poco.	*Very; Slightly*	
1. —¿Hace muy mal tiempo?	Is it very bad weather?	
2. —Sí, hace mucho calor. (Hace mucho frío.)	Yes, it is very hot. (It is very cold.)	**Mucho** emphasizes the nouns: **calor, fresco, frío, sol, viento**
3. —¿Hace mucho viento?	Is it very windy?	
4. —Hace poco viento pero hace mucho sol.	It is slightly windy but it is very sunny.	
1. —¿Está nevando ahora?	Is it snowing now?	Weather verbs that do not need **hace:**
2. —No. Está lloviendo.	No. It is raining.	**llover** (ue) to rain and
3. —¿No nieva aquí?	Doesn't it snow here?	**nevar** (ie) to snow
4. —Nieva poco, pero llueve mucho.	It snows a little, but it rains a great deal.	

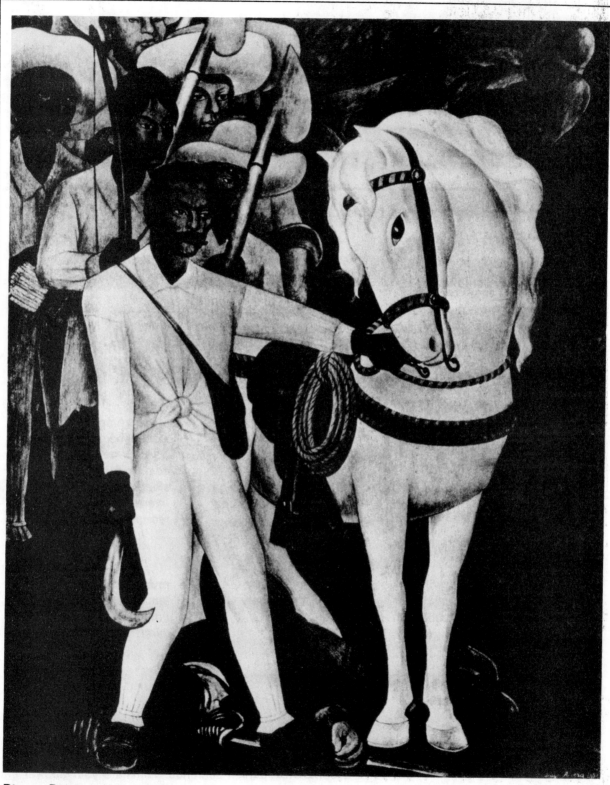

Rivera, Diego
Agrarian Leader Zapata. 1931
Fresco, 7'9¾" x 6'2".
Collection, The Museum of Modern Art, New York
Abby Aldrich Rockefeller Fund

B. Tener_____años (meses)   *Idiomatic: to be _____ years (months) old.*

1. —¿Cuántos años tienes tú?	How old are you? (*fam.*)	
(¿Cuántos años tiene Vd.?)	How old are you? (*formal*)	
2. —Tengo (catorce) años.	I am (fourteen) years old.	Age in numbers:
		tener . . . **años**
3. —¿Y tu hermanito?	And your little brother?	**tener** . . . **meses**
		tengo, tienes, tiene
4. —Él tiene dos meses.	He is two months old.	tenemos, tenéis, tienen

C. Tener sensaciones   *Idiomatic: to be*   *Sensations:*

1. —¿Qué tienen Vds.?	What is the matter with you? (*pl.*)	**tener** *to be the matter with*
2. —Tenemos (mucho) dolor de cabeza (dolor de muelas; dolor de estómago)	We have a (bad) headache. (toothache; stomachache)	**tener dolor de** . . . *to have a pain in* . . .
1. —¿Tienen Vds. calor?	Are you warm?	
2. —Tenemos (mucho) calor.	We are (very) warm.	**mucho** emphasizes the masculine nouns:
. . . . frío	. . . . cold	*warmth:* **calor**
. . . . sueño	. . . . sleepy	*cold:* **frío**
. . . . interés	. . . . interested	*sleepiness:* **sueño**
. . . . miedo	. . . . afraid	*interest:* **interés**
		fear: **miedo**
3. —¿Tienen Vds. hambre?	Are you hungry?	
4. —Yo no tengo mucha hambre pero mi hermano tiene mucha sed.	I am not very hungry, but my brother is very thirsty.	**mucha** *emphasizes the feminine nouns:* *hunger:* **hambre** *thirst:* **sed**

STUDY THE IDIOMS BEFORE BEGINNING THE EXERCISES!

Exercises

I. Write an affirmative answer in a complete Spanish sentence. Translate your answer into English.

1. ¿Hace mucho fresco en el otoño?_____

2. ¿Hace mucho frío y mucho viento en el invierno?_____

_____

3. ¿Hace mucho calor en el verano?_____

_____

4. ¿Hace mucho sol en Puerto Rico?_____

_____

5. ¿Llueve mucho en abril?_____

_____

6. ¿Está lloviendo mucho ahora?_____

_____

7. ¿Nieva mucho en diciembre?_____

_____

8. ¿Está nevando hoy?_____

_____

9. ¿Hace muy buen tiempo en mayo?_____

_____

10. ¿Hace muy mal tiempo en noviembre?_____

_____

II.

A. Write an affirmative answer in a complete Spanish sentence, using the appropriate word for *very*: **muy** or **mucho.**

Model: ¿Hace calor?   Hace **mucho** calor.
         Is it warm?   It is very warm. (hot)

1. ¿Hace frío en el invierno?_____

2. ¿Hace calor en el verano?_____

3. ¿Hace fresco en el otoño?_____

4. ¿Llueve en abril?_____

5. ¿Hace buen tiempo en la primavera?_____ **285**

6. ¿Hace mal tiempo en febrero?_____

7. ¿Nieva en enero?_____

8. ¿Hace viento en marzo?_____

B. Write an affirmative answer using **poco** according to the model.

Model: ¿Hace mucho calor hoy? Hace **poco** calor.
Is it very warm today? It is slightly (hardly) warm.

1. ¿Hace mucho sol hoy?_____

2. ¿Hace mucho frío hoy?_____

3. ¿Hace mucho fresco hoy?_____

4. ¿Hace mucho viento hoy?_____

5. ¿Llueve mucho hoy?_____

6. ¿Nieva mucho hoy?_____

7. ¿Hace mucho calor hoy?_____

III. Write a factual answer in a complete Spanish sentence. Place **no** before the verb *if* your answer is negative.

Model: ¿Hace buen tiempo en el desierto? No hace buen tiempo en el desierto.
Is it good weather in the desert? It is not good weather in the desert.

1. ¿Nieva mucho en la Florida?_____

2. ¿Llueve mucho en el desierto?_____

3. ¿Está lloviendo dentro de la casa?_____

4. ¿Hace fresco en la primavera?_____

5. ¿Está nevando dentro de la casa?_____

6. ¿Hace mucho calor en Alaska?_____

7. ¿Hace mucho frío en Africa?_____

8. ¿Hace mucho sol en Puerto Rico?_____

9. ¿Hace buen tiempo en Londres?_____

10. ¿Hace mal tiempo en California?_____

IV. Write an affirmative answer in a complete Spanish sentence, using the expression in parentheses. Be sure each sentence has a verb.

Model: ¿Qué tiempo hace en la Florida?

_____   **Hace mucho sol en la Florida.**
                    (mucho sol)   It is very sunny in Florida.

1. ¿Qué tiempo hace en el verano?_____
                                              (mucho calor)

2. ¿Qué tiempo hace en el invierno?_____
                                               (mucho frío)

3. ¿Qué tiempo hace en abril?_____
                                        (llueve mucho)

4. ¿Qué tiempo hace en diciembre?_____
                                               (nieva mucho)

5. ¿Qué tiempo hace en marzo?_____
                                          (mucho viento)

6. ¿Qué tiempo hace entre el frío de invierno y el calor de verano?_____

_____
                    (mucho fresco)

7. ¿Qué tiempo hace ahora?_____
                                      (nevando mucho)

8. ¿Qué tiempo hace en este momento?_____
                                                   (lloviendo mucho)

9. ¿Qué tiempo hace en mayo?_____
                                         (muy buen tiempo)

10. ¿Qué tiempo hace en noviembre?_____
                                                 (muy mal)

V. Write a sentence, using the expressions in parentheses and the _appropriate form_ of **tener.**

Model: (el chico/ interés en eso)   El chico tiene interés en eso.
                                                          The boy is interested in that.

1. (Nosotros/sueño aquí)_____

2. (Tú/frío sin abrigo)_____

3. (Juan y Carlos/calor ahora)_____

4. (Vd./dolor de cabeza hoy)_____

5. (Anita/sed y bebe)_____

6. (Yo/hambre y como)_____

7. (Vds./miedo del agua)_____

8. (Luis/dolor de muelas hoy)_____

9. (Vd. y yo/dolor de estómago)_____

10. (Luis y Vd. / interés en ella)_____

VI. Write an affirmative answer in a complete Spanish sentence beginning with **Ella tiene** and using the cue words in parentheses.

Model: ¿Si no duerme?

_____ **Ella tiene sueño si no duerme.**
(sueño)   She is sleepy if she does not sleep.

1. ¿Si no come?_____
(hambre)

2. ¿Si no bebe?_____
(sed)

3. ¿Si no estudia?_____
(miedo)

4. ¿Y si no va al lago?_____
(calor)

5. ¿Y si no va al dentista?_____
(dolor de muelas)

6. ¿Y si no toma aspirinas?_____
(dolor de cabeza)

7. ¿Y si abre la puerta?_____
(frío)

8. ¿Y si come mucho?_____
(dolor de estómago)

9. ¿Y si hoy es su cumpleaños?_____
(quince años)

10. ¿Y si no duerme?_____
(sueño)

VII. Write an affirmative answer in a *short* complete sentence using the appropriate word for *very*: **mucho, mucha,** or **muy,** according to the model.

Model: ¿Tienes hambre por la mañana?   Sí, tengo **mucha** hambre.
Are you hungry in the morning?   Yes, I'm very hungry.

1. ¿Tienes frío en el invierno?_____

2. ¿Tenemos calor en el verano?_____

3. ¿Tienen ellos interés en eso?_____

4. ¿Tiene María hambre cuando no come?_____

5. ¿Tiene Pepe sed cuando no bebe?_____

6. ¿Tengo yo miedo cuando hay un examen?_____

7. ¿Tienes sueño cuando estás cansado?_____

8. ¿Tienes dolor de cabeza si no estás bien?_____

9. ¿Hace buen tiempo si hace fresco?_____

10. ¿Hace mal tiempo cuando llueve?_____

VIII. Complete with the *appropriate form* of **hacer, tener, estar,** or a dash if no addition is necessary.

1. ¿Qué tiempo _____?

2. Yo _____ dolor de cabeza.

3. Ya no _____ mucho viento.

4. Pero _____ fresco.

5. Nosotros _____ dolor de dientes.

6. Hoy _____ mal tiempo.

7. No _____ buen tiempo.

8. ¿Cuántos años _____ ella?

9. Ellos _____ mucha hambre.

10. Siempre _____ nevando.

11. ¿Estás enfermo? ¿Qué _____?

12. No _____ lloviendo ahora.

13. Aquí _____ nieva poco.

14. No _____ llueve mucho.

15. Pero _____ calor, no hace frío.

IX. Write the letter of the expression that best completes the sentence, and circle the letter.

1. Cuando hace mucho sol _____
   a. tenemos frío b. tenemos hambre c. hace frío d. tenemos calor

2. En el cumpleaños de mi amiga, le pregunto: — _____
   a. ¿Tienes frío? b. ¿Qué tienes? c. ¿Cuántos años tienes? d. ¿Qué tiempo hace?

3. Cuando está enferma, María _____
   a. tiene dolor b. tiene quince años c. hace calor d. hace frío

4. Cuando visita al dentista, el niño _____
   a. hace viento b. tiene miedo c. tiene sed d. hace buen tiempo

5. Si no bebo varios vasos de agua _____
   a. nieva b. tengo sed c. tengo frío d. llueve

6. Cuando ella no toma el almuerzo _____
   a. es hombre b. tiene hambre c. hace mal tiempo d. hace fresco

7. Si ella no duerme ocho horas _____
   a. tiene sed b. está lloviendo c. hace fresco d. tiene sueño

8. Si Juan tiene veinte años y yo tengo quince, él _____
   a. tiene cinco años más b. tiene un mes más c. hace viento d. nieva

9. Para saber si hace frío, pregunto: — _____
   a. ¿Qué tiempo hace? b. ¿Cuántos años tiene? c. ¿Qué tiene? d. ¿Está nevando?

10. Si Ana está enferma le pregunto: — _____
    a. ¿Está lloviendo? b. ¿Qué tienes? c. ¿Cuántos años tienes? d. ¿Qué tiempo hace?

X. Write a rejoinder in a complete Spanish sentence using the *appropriate verb* and the expressions in parentheses.

1. Vd. dice: —Voy a comer.

   Yo respondo: —_____
   (Vd./mucha hambre)

2. Tú dices: —Bebo mucha agua fría.

   Yo respondo: —_____
   (Tú/mucha sed)

3. Él dice: —Vas a la cama temprano.

   Yo respondo: —_____
   (Yo/mucho sueño)

4. La madre dice: —Hace mucho viento hoy.

Respondemos: —_____
   (Nosotros no/mucho frío)

5. María dice: —Hace mucho frío.

Su padre responde: —_____
   (Y/nevando mucho)

6. Juan dice: —Tengo mucho calor hoy.

Su amigo responde: —_____
   (Claro,/mucho sol)

7. Mi madre dice: —Debes llevar el paraguas.

Yo respondo: —_____
   (¡No quiero porque no/lloviendo mucho!)

8. El médico dice: —Tu hermano debe tomar aspirinas y no puede comer hoy.

Yo pregunto: —_____
   (¿ /él/dolor/estómago y/cabeza?)

9. La maestra pregunta: —¿Tiene Vd. hermanos menores?

Yo respondo: —_____
   (Yo/quince años/y mis hermanos/quince meses)

10. La vecina dice: —¿Qué tiempo hace hoy?

Mi madre responde: —_____
   (Siempre/muy mal/en noviembre)

Palacio Torre Tagle.
Ministerio de Relaciones Exteriores
Lima, Peru

Segovia, Spain: (r.) The Alcazar Castle built in the 15th century

La hora, la fecha

Unit 3: Conversaciones entre una niña
y su madre.

Conversations between a child
and her mother.

A. La hora *Telling Time*

---

1. —¿Qué hora es?	What time is it?	Time is feminine.
2. —Es la una.	It is one o'clock.	**Una** is the *only* number in *feminine* form. **La** *precedes* **una.**
3. —¿Qué hora es ahora?	What time is it now?	**Las** *precedes all other hours.*
4. —Son las dos. No es la una.	It is two o'clock. It isn't one.	**No** is placed *before* **es** or **son** in a negative sentence.

---

1. —¿Son las cuatro?	Is it four o'clock?	**En punto** *on the dot*; *exactly.*
2. —Son las cuatro en punto.	It is four exactly.	

---

1. —¿Son las cinco *y treinta*?	Is it five *thirty*?	*Add the minutes after the hour. Use* **y** (plus, and).
2. —Sí, son las cinco *y media.*	Yes, it is *half past* five.	**Media** *half* (past)

---

1. —¿Son las ocho y *quince*?	Is it eight *fifteen*?	
2. —Sí, son las ocho y *cuarto.*	Yes, it is a *quarter* past eight.	**Cuarto** *quarter* (past)

---

1. —¿No son las doce *menos cuarto*?	Isn't it a *quarter to* twelve?	*Use* **menos** (minus, less) *to subtract the minutes from the hour.*
2. —No. Es la una *menos cuatro.*	No. It is *four* minutes *to* one.	
3. —Siempre salimos a almorzar entre las doce y media y la una menos veinte y cinco.	We always go out to lunch between half past twelve and twelve thirty-five.	*Add minutes only up to thirty. Past the half hour, name the next hour, and subtract the required minutes. Use* **menos.**

293

1. —¿Cuándo comes más: por la mañana, por la tarde, o por la noche? — When do you eat more: in the morning, in the afternoon, or at night? — **Por la mañana, por la tarde, por la noche** *in the morning, afternoon, evening, are used* when *no hour is stated.*

2. —A las 8 de la mañana no tengo tiempo. A la una de la tarde y a las seis de la tarde como más. — At 8 A.M. I have no time. At 1 P.M. and at 6 P.M. I eat more. — **De la mañana** *A.M.,* **De la tarde** *P.M.* (afternoon and *early* evening, are used when *the hour is stated.*

3. —¿A qué hora vas a dormir? — At what time do you go sleep? — **A la, a las** mean *at* when telling time.

4. —Voy a la cama a las once de la noche. — I go to bed at eleven P.M. — **¿A qué hora?** is *at what time?* **De la noche** is *P.M.* for late evening and night.

B. La fecha — *The Date*

1. —¿Qué día es hoy? — What day is it today? — Days and months are *not usually capitalized.*

2. —Hoy es viernes. — Today is Friday.

3. —¿A cuántos estamos? — What is the date? — The day and date *precede* the month.

4. —Estamos a doce de octubre. — It is October 12.

5. —¿Cuál es la fecha completa? — What is the complete date? — *Except* after **estamos a, el** is used before the date: **El doce de octubre** *Oct. 12.*

6. —Hoy es viernes el doce de octubre. — Today is Friday, October 12.

7. —¿Qué celebramos el doce de octubre? — What do we celebrate on October 12? — *On* is understood when **el** *precedes the date:* **El doce de octubre** *On* October 12th.

8. —Celebramos el **Día de la Raza** el doce de octubre. — We celebrate Columbus Day on October 12.

9. —Y el **Día de las Américas** cae el catorce de abril. — And Pan American Day falls on April 14th.

10. —¿Y el dos de mayo? — And on May 2?

11. —El dos de mayo es el **Día de la Independencia** de España. — May 2 is Spain's Independence Day.

12. —¿Y el cuatro de julio? — And the fourth of July?

13. —El cuatro de julio es el **Día de la Independencia** de los Estados Unidos. — July 4 is the United States' Independence Day.

14. —¿Cuándo celebramos la **Navidad?**	When do we celebrate Christmas?	Simple cardinal numbers express the date *except* for the first of the month.
15. —Celebramos el **Día de la Navidad** el veinte y cinco de diciembre.	We celebrate Christmas on December 25.	
16. —¿Qué fiestas caen el primero del mes?	What holidays fall on the first of the month?	**Primero** expresses the *first* day of the month.
17. —**El Año Nuevo** cae el primero de enero. El **Día de los Inocentes** cae el primero de abril.	New Year's falls on January first. April Fools' Day falls on April first.	

STUDY THE IDIOMS *BEFORE* BEGINNING THE EXERCISES!

Exercises

I. **Write the translation of the Spanish sentence.** Then (1) rewrite the Spanish sentence, substituting the expression in parentheses for the words in *italics*; (2) translate each Spanish sentence you write.

Model: ¿A qué hora *salen*? **At what time do they leave?**

(regresan) (1) **¿A qué hora regresan?** (2) **At what time do they return?**

1. ¿A qué hora *almuerzas*?_____

    a. (vas a la cama) (1)_____

    (2)_____

    b.. (comemos) (1)_____

    (2)_____

    c. (estudian) (1)_____

    (2)_____

2. Salimos *a las seis de la tarde*._____

    a. (a las once de la noche) (1)_____

    (2)_____

    b. (a las ocho de la mañana) (1)_____

    (2)_____

    c. (a la una de la tarde) (1)_____

    (2)_____

3. Estudian *por la noche.*_____

    a. (por la mañana) (1)_____

    (2)_____

    b. (por la tarde) (1)_____

    (2)_____

    c. (por la noche) (1)_____

    (2)_____

4. *¿Cuál es la fecha de* hoy?_____

    a. (¿A cuántos estamos?) (1)_____

    (2)_____

    b. (¿Qué fiesta cae?) (1)_____

    (2)_____

    c. (¿Qué día es?) (1)_____

    (2)_____

5. Hoy es *el primero de mayo.*_____

    a. (el dos de junio) (1)_____

    (2)_____

    b. (el veinte y uno de noviembre) (1)_____

    (2)_____

    c. (el veinte de octubre) (1)_____

    (2)_____

6. *Hoy es el* primero de abril._____

    a. (Estamos a) (1)_____

    (2)_____

    b. (La fiesta cae) (1)_____

    (2)_____

    c. (Mañana es) (1)_____

    (2)_____

II. ¿Qué hora es? Write an answer in a complete Spanish sentence.

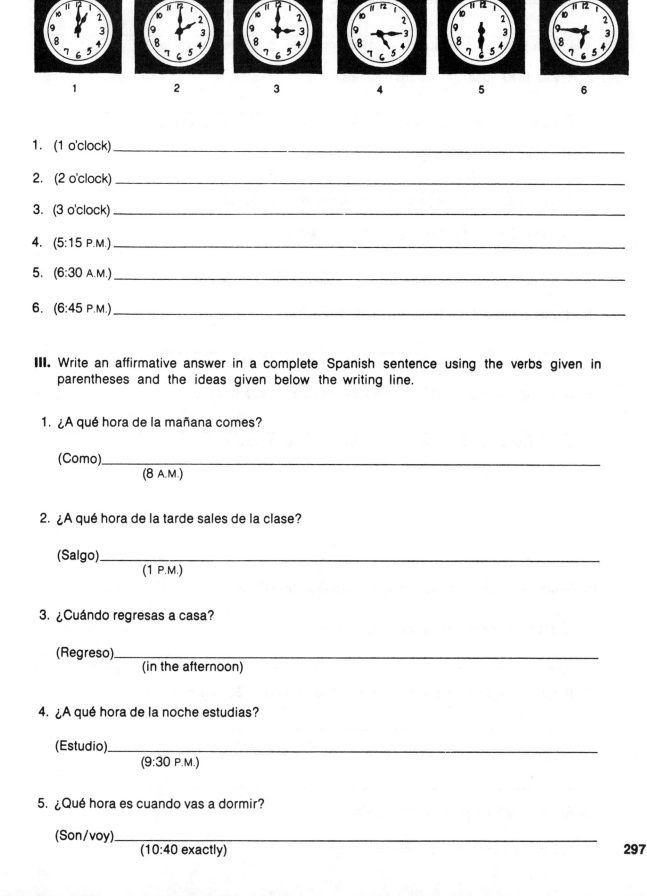

1. (1 o'clock) _____

2. (2 o'clock) _____

3. (3 o'clock) _____

4. (5:15 P.M.) _____

5. (6:30 A.M.) _____

6. (6:45 P.M.) _____

III. Write an affirmative answer in a complete Spanish sentence using the verbs given in parentheses and the ideas given below the writing line.

1. ¿A qué hora de la mañana comes?

(Como)_____
        (8 A.M.)

2. ¿A qué hora de la tarde sales de la clase?

(Salgo)_____
         (1 P.M.)

3. ¿Cuándo regresas a casa?

(Regreso)_____
           (in the afternoon)

4. ¿A qué hora de la noche estudias?

(Estudio)_____
           (9:30 P.M.)

5. ¿Qué hora es cuando vas a dormir?

(Son/voy)_____
           (10:40 exactly)

IV. Write an affirmative answer in a complete Spanish sentence, selecting the correct date. (Write out the numbers in Spanish in your answer.)

1. Hoy celebramos el Día de la Independencia norteamericana. ¿Cuál es la fecha?

_____

a. 4 de julio   b. 1 de enero   c. 12 de octubre   d. 25 de diciembre

2. Hoy es la Navidad. ¿A cuántos estamos?

_____

a. 2 de mayo   b. 1 de enero   c. 25 de diciembre   d. 12 de febrero

3. Hoy es el Día de la Raza. ¿Cuál es la fecha?

_____

a. 4 de julio   b. 14 de julio   c. 12 de octubre   d. 12 de febrero

4. Hoy es el Día de Año Nuevo. ¿A cuántos estamos?

_____

a. 25 de diciembre   b. 4 de julio   c. 1 de enero   d. 1 de abril

5. Hoy es el Día de los Inocentes. ¿Cuál es la fecha?

_____

a. 1 de abril   b. 14 de abril   c. 2 de mayo   d. 12 de octubre

6. Hoy celebramos el Día de las Américas. ¿A cuántos estamos hoy?

_____

a. 4 de julio   b. 14 de abril   c. 2 de mayo   d. 1 de abril

V. Rewrite each sentence, correcting the expressions in _italics_.

1. La Navidad cae _el primero de enero._

_____

2. Pregunto: —¿Cuál es la fecha de hoy? Tú respondes: —_Son las dos._

_____

3. Pregunto: —¿Qué hora es? Tú respondes: —_Es el_ dos.

_____

4. El Día de la Raza es _el cuatro de julio._

_____

5. El Día de la Independencia norteamericana cae *el doce de octubre.*

_____

6. El Día de Año Nuevo cae *el veinte y cinco de diciembre.*

_____

7. El Día de las Américas cae *el dos de mayo.*

_____

8. El Día de la Independencia española cae *el catorce de abril.*

_____

VI. Write the question suggested by each statement. Use the cues in parentheses and question marks.

    Model: Ana es linda.   (Quién) **¿Quién es linda?** Who is pretty?

1. _____
   Hoy es martes el tres de marzo.   (Cuál)

2. _____
   Estamos a jueves el trece de abril.   (A cuántos)

3. _____
   Son las diez de la mañana.   (Qué)

4. _____
   Comen a la una de la tarde.   (A qué)

5. _____
   Celebramos La Navidad el veinte y cinco de diciembre.   (Cuándo)

VII. Complete using the appropriate equivalent of ''*what*'': **¿cómo?, ¿cuál?, ¿qué?** or **¿cuántos?**

1. ¿ _____ hora es?   3. ¿ _____ se llama Vd.?

2. ¿ _____ es la fecha de hoy?   4. ¿A _____ estamos?

          5. ¿A _____ hora comes?

VIII. Complete the sentence, using the appropriate verb: **es, estamos, llama,** or **son.** (The same verb may be used appropriately more than once.)

1. ¿A cuántos _____ hoy?

2. ¿Qué hora _____ ?

3. ¿Cómo se _____ su padre?

4. ¿Cuál _____ la fecha de hoy?

5. Hoy _____ lunes.

6. Hoy _____ martes.

7. _____ la una menos cuarto.

8. _____ las diez y media.

IX. Complete with the appropriate article **el, los, la, las.** Write a dash if *no* article is needed.

1. Hoy es _____ dos de junio.

2. Estamos a _____ diez de junio.

3. ¿Cuál es _____ fecha de hoy?

4. Hoy es _____ viernes.

5. Es _____ una de _____ tarde.

6. Son _____ ocho de _____ mañana.

7. Comemos a _____ cinco.

8. Miramos la televisión por _____ noche, o a _____ cuatro de _____ tarde.

X. Write the Spanish equivalent adapted from the DIALOGUES, pages 293–295.

1. What time is it?_____

2. It is one P.M. _____

3. What time is it now?_____

4. It is two. It is not one._____

5. Is it four o'clock exactly?_____

6. It is four forty._____

7. Is it five thirty now?_____

8. Yes, it is half past five._____

XI. Complete in Spanish. (Consult DIALOGUES, pp. 385–387, for review.)

A.

Luis: —¿Son las ocho?

Ana: —Sí, _____ _____ ocho.
            1   2

Luis: —¿Y ahora?

Ana: —Y ahora son_____ocho y cinco.
                      3

B.

Pepe: —Siempre almuerzo antes de

      _____ una. Como siempre,
        1
      hoy salgo a _____ una
                2
      _____ cuarto.
        3

Lola: —Es todavía temprano. Es
          solamente el mediodía.

      _____ _____ doce
        4   5

      _____ punto.
        6

C.

Ana: —¿A _____ hora comes más,
        1

     a _____ ocho _____ la
       2   3

     mañana o a _____ una de
               4

     _____ tarde?
       5

Paco: —A _____ una de _____ tarde
        6   7

     como más. A _____ ocho de
             8

     _____ mañana corro a la escuela.
       9

Ana: —¿ _____ _____ hora vas a dormir,
        10   11

     a _____ seis _____ _____
       12   13   14

     tarde o _____ las once _____
          15   16

     _____ noche?
       17

Juan: —Voy a dormir _____ _____
                18   19

     once _____ la noche.
          20

D.

María: —¿Cuándo estudias, _____ la
                    1

     mañana, _____ la tarde
             2

     o _____ la noche?
       3

Pablo: —Estudio _____ la tarde o por
               4

     _____ noche. No tengo tiempo
       5

     para estudiar más temprano.

En la clase

Unit 4: En la clase: Conversación entre el maestro y una alumna.

In class: A conversation between the teacher and a student.

¿De quién? Whose?

Maestro:	—¿De quién es la clase?	Whose class is it?
Alumna:	—Es mi clase.	It is my class.

La clase de español The Spanish class

M: —¿Qué clase es?
A: —Es la clase de español.

What class is it?
It is the Spanish class.

De meaning *about;* **La clase de español; la lección de español; el maestro de español.** The class *about* the Spanish language, etc.

Es verdad It is true. That's right.

M: —¿Estudias la lec-
ción de español?
A: —Sí, es verdad.

Are you studying the Spanish lesson?
Yes, that's right. (True, so)

Prestar atención to pay attention

M: —¿Prestas atención?
A: —Presto atención en la clase.

Do you pay attention?
I pay attention in class.

prestar	
présto	prestamos
prestas	prestáis
presta	prestan

Querer a to love

M: —¿Quieres al pro-
fesor de español?
A: —Sí, quiero al pro-
fesor.

Do you love the Spanish teacher?
Yes, I love the teacher.

querer	
quiero	queremos
quieres	queréis
quiere	quieren

Querer decir to mean

M:	—¿Qué quiere decir **'chica'?**	What does **chica** mean?	In **querer decir, querer** is conjugated; **decir** does *not* change its infiniitve form.
A:	—**'Chica'** quiere decir **'muchacha'.**	**Chica** means **muchacha.**	

¿Cómo se dice? How do you say?, how does one say?

M:	—¿Cómo se dice **'chico'** en inglés?	How do you say **chico** in English?	**Se** represents impersonal *"you"* or *"one"*
A:	—Se dice **'boy'.**	One says "boy." (You say "boy.")	

Estar de pie to be standing

M:	—¿Para qué estás de pie?	Why are you standing?		**estar**
			estoy	estamos
A:	—Estoy de pie para contestar.	I'm standing in order to answer.	estás	estáis
			está	están

Saber *before an infinitive* to know how (can)

M:	—¿Sabes escribir español?	Do you know how to write Spanish?		**saber**
			sé	sabemos
A:	—Sí, sé leer también.	Yes, I know how to read, too.	sabes	sabéis
			sabe	saben

Salir bien en to pass (a test, a course, etc.)
Salir mal en to fail (a test, a course, etc.)

M:	—¿Sales mal o bien en el examen?	Do you fail or pass a test?		**salir**
			salgo	salimos
A:	—No salgo mal en el examen. Salgo bien porque es fácil.	I don't fail the test. I pass because it is easy.	sales	salís
			sale	salen

Creer que sí (**no**) to believe so (not)

M:	—¿Hay que estudiar para salir bien?	Is it necessary to study in order to pass?		**creer**
			creo	creemos
A:	—Creo que no.	I don't think so.	crees	creéis
M:	—Yo creo que sí. Si no estudias no sabes contestar.	I think so. If you do not study you cannot answer.	cree	creen

¡Concedido! Agreed!
Por eso Therefore

A:	—¡Concedido! Por eso, hay que estudiar.	Right! (Agreed!) Therefore, one must study.

STUDY THE IDIOMS BEFORE BEGINNING THE EXERCISES!

Exercises

I. **Write the translation of the Spanish sentence.** Then (1) rewrite the Spanish sentence, substituting the expressions in parentheses for the words in *italics*; (2) translate each Spanish sentence you write.

Model: *Ellos* prestan atención *al circo.*   **They pay attention to the circus.**
a. (Tú/al tigre) (1) **Tú prestas atención al tigre.**   (2) **You pay attention to the tiger.**

1. *Yo* quiero a *mi madre.*_____

   a. (Tú/a la maestra) (1)_____

      (2)_____

   b. (Nosotros/a los amigos) (1)_____

      (2)_____

   c. (Juan/a la chica) (1)_____

      (2)_____

   d. (Ana y Pepe / a sus hermanos) (1)_____

      (2)_____

   e. (Yo/al compañero de clase) (1)_____

      (2)_____

2. *Ellos* saben *tocar el piano.*_____

   a. (Yo/cantar la canción) (1)_____

      (2)_____

   b. (María/bailar la bamba) (1)_____

      (2)_____

   c. (Tú/hablar español) (1)_____

(2)_____

   d. (Tú y yo/jugar al tenis) (1)_____

(2)_____

   e. (Ellos/tocar el violín) (1)_____

(2)_____

3. *Luis y Pedro* están *de pie.*_____

   a. (Yo/de pie) (1)_____

(2)_____

   b. (Vd. y yo/levantados) (1)_____

(2)_____

   c. (Vd./sentado) (1)_____

(2)_____

   d. (Tú/de pie) (1)_____

(2)_____

   e. (Los chicos/de pie) (1)_____

(2)_____

4. *Yo salgo bien en el examen.*_____

   a. (Tú/mal en la clase) (1)_____

(2)_____

   b. (Juan y yo/bien en el examen) (1)_____

(2)_____

   c. (Los alumnos/mal en sus estudios) (1)_____

(2)_____

   d. (Yo/bien en los exámenes) (1)_____

(2)_____

5. ¿Qué quiere decir *la palabra*?_____

   a. (¿Qué/decir las frases?) (1)_____

(2)_____

   b. (¿Qué/decir tú?) (1)_____

(2)_____

305

c. (¿Qué/decir Juan?) (1)_____

(2)_____

6. Yo creo *que sí.*_____

a. (Él y yo/que no) (1)_____

(2)_____

b. (La madre/que no) (1)_____

(2)_____

c. (Tú/que sí) (1)_____

(2)_____

II. Complete the response.

1. —¿Estás sentado cuando contestas?
   —No. Estoy _____ pie.

2. —¿Es tu pluma?
   —No. No sé _____ quién es la pluma.

3. —¿Sabes el inglés?
   —Sí, Yo _____ el inglés.

4. —¿Sabes escribir el chino?
   —No. No _____ _____ el chino.

5. —¿Sales mal en el examen de español?
   —No. Salgo bien _____ el examen.

6. —¿Quieres a tu profesora?
   —Sí, _____ _____ mi profesora.

7. —¿Quieres decir que ella es bonita?
   —Quiero _____ que es una buena maestra.

8. —¿Cómo se dice **maestra** en inglés?
   —Se _____ "teacher" o _____ dice "instructor".

9. ¿Hay que prestar atención en la clase de español?
   —Sí, _____ _____ prestar atención.

10. —¿Es verdad?
    —Sí, es _____

11. —¿Cree tu profesora que sí?
    — _____ verdad. Mi profesora cree _____
    _____.

12. —¿Cree tu amigo que sí?
    —No. Mi amigo _____ que _____.

13. —¿Crees que sí?
    —Sí. Yo _____ _____ sí.

14. —¿Por eso prestas atención?
    —Sí, _____ eso, _____ atención.

15. —¿Concedido?
    —Sí ¡ _____ !

III. Write the appropriate rejoinder in Spanish, and circle the letter.

1. Vd. dice: —Sé escribir muy bien el español.

   Yo respondo: —_____

   a. ¿Cree Vd. que sí?   b. ¿A cuántos estamos hoy?   c. ¿Cómo se llama Vd.?

2. Vd. pregunta: —¿De quién es el libro?

Yo respondo: —_____
a. Creo que no.   b. Queremos al alumno.   c. No sé de quién es.

3. Vd. dice: —¡Tome Vd. esta silla, por favor!

Yo respondo: —Gracias pero_____
a. quiero estar de pie.   b. quiero salir bien.   c. quiero hablar español.

4. Vd. dice: —Hay que salir bien en el examen.

Yo respondo: —_____
a. ¡Concedido!   b. Sabemos bailar.   c. Estamos de pie.

5. Vd. dice: —Quiero a mi maestra.

Yo respondo: —_____
a. ¿Cómo se dice **maestro?**   b. ¿Qué quiere decir **maestro?**   c. ¡Por eso prestas atención!

IV. Write an affirmative response in a complete Spanish sentence, using the cue word in parentheses at the beginning of the answer. Then translate your answer.
Model: ¿Hay que estudiar?

_____   **¡Concedido! Hay que estudiar.**
(¡Concedido!)   *Agreed! One must study.*

1. ¿Está Vd. en una clase de español?_____
(Estoy)

_____

2. ¿Está la maestra de pie?_____
(La maestra)

_____

3. ¿Sabe Vd. cómo se dice "*book*" en español?_____
(Sí, sé)

_____

4. ¿Sabe Vd. de quién es el libro?_____
(Yo)

_____

5. ¿Sabe Vd. leer el español?_____
(Yo)

_____

6. ¿Presta Vd. atención?_____
(Sí, yo)

_____   **307**

7. ¿Hay que trabajar en la clase de historia?_____
   (Hay)

   _____

8. ¿Sale Vd. bien en los exámenes?_____
   (Salgo)

   _____

9. ¿Quieres mucho a la maestra?_____
   (Quiero)

   _____

10. ¿No es verdad que la maestra cree que sí?_____
    (Es)

    _____

V. Write the expression that best completes the sentence, and circle the letter.

1. Cuando el maestro enseña yo_____
   a. estoy de pie   c. toco la guitarra
   b. presto atención   d. creo que sí

2. Cuando leo para la clase_____
   a. quiero a mi padre   c. creo que no
   b. creo que sí   d. estoy de pie

3. Cuando el maestro es simpático yo_____
   a. lo quiero mucho   c. salgo mal
   b. se dice: —chico   d. pienso que hay que salir

4. Para salir bien en la clase de español_____
   a. hay que escuchar   c. sé tocar el piano
   b. hay que salir mal   d. aprendo el inglés

5. Para saber el dueño del lápiz pregunto: —_____
   a. ¿A quién quieres?   c. ¿De quién es esto?
   b. ¿Cómo se dice lápiz?   d. ¿Qué es esto?

6. Para aprender una palabra le pregunto a la profesora: —_____
   a. ¿Qué quiere decir eso?   c. ¿Hay que aprender?
   b. ¿Sales bien en el examen?   d. ¿Sabes leer?

7. Para saber una pronunciación yo pregunto: —_____
   a. ¿Hay que estudiar?   c. ¿De quién es?
   b. ¿Cómo se dice esto?   d. ¿A quién quieres?

8. Practico la guitarra porque quiero_____
   a. estar de pie   c. bailar a la música
   b. salir bien en inglés   d. saber tocar música

9. Estudio mucho en casa para_____
    a. creer que sí   c. prestar atención
    b. salir bien   d. estar de pie

10. Si es verdad yo digo: —_____
    a. Creo que sí   c. Por eso
    b. Creo que no   d. Hay que estudiar

VI. Write the entire expression from the second column that means the *same* as the word in *italics*. Before each expression write its corresponding letter.

1. *Escucho* _____   a. ¿Qué quiere decir?

2. *¿Qué significa?*_____   b. de pie

3. *¿A quién amas?*_____   c. ¡Concedido!

4. *¡Cómo no!*_____   d. Presto atención.

5. *levantado*_____   e. ¿A quién quieres?

Registration — Universidad de Puerto Rico, Río Piedras.

309

Un sâbado en el parque

Unit 5:   **Un sábado en el parque.**   A Saturday in the park.

Conversación entre una vecina y un
alumno sobre qué va a hacer el alumno
el sábado en el parque.

Conversation between a neighbor and a pupil
about how he plans to spend his Saturday
in the park.

Asistir a to attend

Sra.: —¿No asistes a la escuela hoy?	Don't you attend school today?	**asistir**	
		asisto	asistimos
		asistes	asistís
Alumno: —No asisto hoy. Es sábado.	I don't today. It's Saturday.	asiste	asisten

---

Ir a + *noun* to go to

S: —¿Adónde vas?	Where are you going?	**ir**	
		voy	vamos
A: —Voy al parque.	I'm going to the park.	vas	vais
		va	van

Ir de paseo to go for a walk

S: —¿Por qué vas al parque?	Why are you going to the park?
A: —Voy de paseo allí.	I'm going for a walk there.

Subir a to get on (*vehicle*)

S: —¿Cómo vas a llegar al parque?	How are you going to get to the park?	**subir**	
		subo	subimos
		subes	subís
A: —Primero, subo al tren.	First, I get on the train.	sube	suben

---

Bajar de to get off (*vehicle*)
Entrar en to enter

bajar

bajo	bajamos
bajas	bajáis
baja	bajan

S: —¿Y luego? And then?

entrar

A: —Luego, bajo del Then, I get off the train and
tren y entro en el enter the park.
parque.

entro	entramos
entras	entráis
entra	entran

Ir a + *infinitive* to be going to (do); **Dar un paseo a pie** to take a walk; **Dar un paseo a caballo** to ride horseback; **Dar un paseo en bicicleta** to take a ride on a bicycle; **Dar un paseo en automóvil** to take a ride in a car.

S: —¿Qué vas a hacer What are you going to do in
en el parque? the park?

dar

doy	damos
das	dais
da	dan

A: —Voy a dar un paseo I'm going to take a walk, or go
a pie o en bicicleta. bicycle riding.

S: —¿No das un paseo a Don't you go horseback riding?
caballo?

A: —Sí, doy un paseo a Yes, I ride when I have
caballo cuando money.
tengo dinero.

S: —¿Por qué no das un Why don't you take a ride in
paseo en automóvil? a car?

A: —No doy paseos en I don't go riding in a car
automóvil porque because I have no car.
no tengo automóvil.

Por todas partes everywhere
Todo el mundo everyone, everybody

S: —¿Quién está en el Who is in the park?
parque?

A: —Todo el mundo está Everyone is there.
allí.
Por todas partes Everywhere there are people
hay gente y flores. and flowers.

Poner la mesa to set the table
Salir de to leave
Regresar a casa to go home
Estar en casa to be at home
Tocar el piano, el violín, la guitarra
to play the piano, violin, guitar

To express "home" use
1. **a casa** after a verb of
   locomotion: **correr, volver**
2. **en casa** after **estar**

S: —¿Cuándo sales del parque?

When do you leave the park?

A: —Salgo del parque temprano para volver a casa.

I leave the park early to return home.

A: —¿Qué haces en casa?

What do you do at home?

S: —En casa, primero pongo la mesa. Después de comer, toco el piano y mis hermanos tocan el violín y la guitarra.

At home, first I set the table. After eating, I play the piano, and my brothers play the violin and the guitar.

poner

pongo	ponemos
pones	ponéis
pone	ponen

STUDY THE IDIOMS BEFORE BEGINNING THE EXERCISES!

Exercises

I. Write the translation of the sentence. Then (1) rewrite the Spanish sentence, substituting the expressions in parentheses for the words in *italics*; (2) translate each Spanish sentence you write.

Model: *Me* gusta la clase *de historia.*   **I like the history class.**
    a. (Les/de inglés)   (1) **Les gusta la clase de inglés.**
                          (2) **They like the English class.**

1. Yo doy un paseo *a caballo.*_____

   a. (Tú/a pie) (1)_____

      (2)_____

   b. (Vds./en automóvil) (1)_____

      (2)_____

   c. (Nosotros/en bicicleta) (1)_____

(2)_____

2. *Nosotros* bajamos *del tren.*_____

   (a) (El piloto/del avión) (1)_____

       (2)_____

   b. (Los amigos/del coche) (1)_____

       (2)_____

   c. (Yo/del autobús) (1)_____

       (2)_____

3. *Todo el mundo* asiste *al teatro.*_____

   a. (Yo/a la escuela) (1)_____

       (2)_____

   b. (Ellos/al cine) (1)_____

       (2)_____

   c. (Nosotros/a las fiestas) (1)_____

       (2)_____

4. *Yo* pongo la mesa *con el mantel.*_____

   a. (Tú/la mesa con vasos) (1)_____

       (2)_____

   b. (Ana y yo/la mesa con cucharas) (1)_____

       (2)_____

   c. (Marta/la mesa con cuchillos) (1)_____

       (2)_____

   d. (Yo/la mesa con servilletas) (1)_____

       (2)_____

5. *Tú y yo* entramos *en el cine.*_____

   a. (Vd./en la casa) (1)_____

       (2)_____

   b. (Vd. y Juan/en la clase) (1)_____

       (2)_____

    c. (Yo/en la escuela) (1)_____

        (2)_____

6. Yo voy de paseo *por todas partes.*_____

    a. (Yo/de paseo al parque) (1)_____

        (2)_____

    b. (Tú/de paseo a casa) (1)_____

        (2)_____

    c. (Ellos/de paseo al cine) (1)_____

        (2)_____

    d. (Tú y yo/de paseo al centro) (1)_____

        (2)_____

II. Write an affirmative answer in a complete Spanish sentence. Begin with the cue in parentheses. *Then translate your answers.*

1. ¿Asistes a la escuela los lunes?_____
               (asisto)

  _____

2. ¿Vas de paseo al parque?_____
          (voy)

  _____

3. ¿Subes al tren para ir al parque?_____
             (subo)

  _____

4. ¿Bajas del tren y entras en el parque?_____
             (bajo)

  _____

5. ¿Primero das un paseo a pie y luego en bicicleta?_____
                  (primero doy)

  _____

6. ¿Sabes tocar un instrumento como el violín?_____
             (sé tocar)

  _____

7. ¿Está todo el mundo por todas partes del parque?_____
(todo el mundo)

_____

8. ¿Sales del parque para ir a casa?_____
(salgo)

_____

9. ¿Pones la mesa antes de comer?_____
(pongo)

_____

10. ¿Tocas la guitarra, el piano y el violín en casa?_____
(toco)

_____

III. Write a *logical* or factual answer in a complete Spanish sentence.

1. ¿Quién asiste a la escuela *todo el mundo* o *nadie*?

_____

2. ¿Qué sabe Vd. tocar bien *las paredes* o *la guitarra*?

_____

3. ¿Hay mucha gente por todas partes *del campo* o *de la ciudad*?

_____

4. ¿Antes de comer pones la mesa con *un mantel* o con *una manta*?

_____

5. ¿Cuándo das un paseo en bicicleta a la playa *el lunes* o *el sábado*?

_____

6. ¿De dónde sales a las tres *del cine* o *de la escuela*?

_____

7. ¿A qué subes para llegar al piso del vecino *al ascensor* o *al avión*?

_____

8. ¿Cómo regresas a casa *a caballo* o *a pie*?

_____

9. ¿Por dónde das un paseo a caballo por *la calle* o por *el parque*?

_____

10. ¿En dónde entras a las ocho de la mañana en *el dormitorio* o en *la clase*?

_____

IV. Write the appropriate response or rejoinder, and circle the letter.

1. —Vamos a la escuela todos los días.

_____

   a. —Todo el mundo da paseos.   b. —Siempre asistimos a las clases.
              c. —Entramos en casa.

2. —Vamos a comer.

_____

   a. —Voy a poner la mesa.   b. —Voy a dar un paseo.
              c. —Voy a bajar del tren.

3. —Son las ocho de la mañana.

_____

   a. —Es hora de entrar en la escuela.   b. —Es hora de poner la mesa.
              c. —Es hora de ir a dormir.

4. —Voy al parque.

_____

   a. —¿Va Vd. a pie?   b. —¿Sale Vd. del cine?
              c. —¿Entra Vd. en la tienda?

5. —¿Dónde hay alumnos?

_____

   a. —Hay muchos maestros.   b. —Están por todas partes.
              c. —Todo el mundo es alumno.

V. Write the expression that best completes the sentence, and circle the letter.

1. Cuando doy un paseo al centro_____
   a. voy a pie   b. subo al avión   c. voy a caballo   d. asisto a la clase

2. Voy al parque porque deseo_____
   a. tocar el piano   b. salir mal   c. ir de paseo   d. poner la mesa

3. Cuando hace buen tiempo_____va de paseo.
   a. el automóvil   b. todo el mundo   c. la guitarra   d. la bicicleta

4. En la primavera todo el mundo da paseos_____
   a. en las escuelas   b. por todas partes   c. en los edificios   d. en los museos

5. Prestamos atención al maestro cuando_____
   a. asistimos   b. salimos   c. estamos de pie   d. damos paseos

---

VI. Rewrite the following sentences *with their letters* in a *logical sequence.*

Para llegar a la escuela: *To reach my school.*

a. Entro en la clase.   1._____

b. Bajo del tren.   2._____

c. Subo al tren.   3._____

d. Salgo de mi casa.   4._____

e. Veo que todo el   5._____
   mundo asiste.

VII. Complete in Spanish.

1. Voy _____ casa.

2. Estoy _____ casa.

3. Doy un paseo _____ bicicleta.

4. Pedro baja _____ automóvil.

5. Él va _____ paseo al centro.

6. Doy un paseo _____ pie.

7. Subimos _____ tren.

8. Asisto _____ la clase.

9. Damos un paseo _____ automóvil.

10. Entras _____ la clase.

VIII. Complete, using an appropriate expression from the selection provided below.

1. La tía: —¿No asistes _____
   la escuela hoy, Paco?

2. Paco: —Yo no _____ hoy
   porque es sábado.

3. La tía: —Entonces, ¿adónde _____?

4. Paco: —Voy _____ paseo al parque.
   Allí doy un paseo_____ pie o_____
   bicicleta. Si tengo dinero_____ un
   paseo_____ caballo.

5. La tía: —Aquí tienes dinero para_____
   un_____ a caballo.
   Paco: —Mil gracias.

Selection: a, asisto, dar, de, doy, en, paseo, vas

La cita

Unit 6: La cita

En el supermercado. Juan quiere salir con Alicia, quien trabaja en el supermercado. Alicia decide finalmente no salir con él porque él le hace muchas preguntas.

The Appointment (The Date):

At the supermarket. John wants to go out with Alice, who is working in the supermarket. She finally decides not to go out with him because he asks so many questions.

Juan: —¿Asistes al cine a menudo?

Alicia: —Asisto muchas veces con mis amigos.

Do you go to the movies often?

I go often with my friends.

Sinónimos
a menudo often
muchas veces often

J: —¿Deseas ir de nuevo hoy?

A: —¿Otra vez? Sí. Gracias.

Do you want to go again today?

Again? Yes. Thanks.

Sinónimos
de nuevo again
otra vez again

J: —¿Deseas ir conmigo en seguida?

A: —No. Más tarde. Tengo mucho trabajo.

How about going with me right away?

No. Later. I have a great deal of work.

Antónimos
en seguida right away (immediately)
más tarde later

J: —¿No terminas en seguida?

A: —No. Termino poco a poco hoy.

Won't you be finishing at once?

No. I'll be finishing little by little (gradually) today.

Antónimos
en seguida at once
poco a poco little by little (gradually)

J: —¿Así no llegamos tarde?

A: —No. Llegamos a tiempo.

Won't we arrive late this way?

No. We'll arrive on time.

Antónimos
tarde late
a tiempo on time

J: —¿Trabajaste también el sábado pasado?

A: —Sí, y trabajé toda la semana pasada, el mes pasado y el año pasado.

Did you work last Saturday, too?

Yes, and I worked all last week, last month, and last year.

"Last _____"
el sábado pasado last Saturday
la semana pasada last week
el año pasado last year
el mes pasado last month

J: —¿Y trabajas el sábado que viene?

A: —El sábado próximo, la semana próxima, el mes próximo, y el año próximo.

And *next* Saturday?

Next Saturday, next week, next month, and next year.

Next *"Sinónimos"*
el año que viene next year
el año próximo next year
Antónimos
_____ pasado-a last
_____ próximo-a (que viene) next

J: —Así trabajas mucho pero estudias pocas veces como yo.	Then you work a great deal, but you study rarely like me.	*Antónimos* **pocas veces** rarely **a menudo** (muchas veces) often
A: —No. Estudio a menudo (muchas veces).	No. I often study.	

J: —Entonces ¿vas conmigo al cine todas las semanas?	Then will you go with me to the movies every week?	*Antónimos* **todas las semanas** every week
A: —No voy ni esta noche, ni esta semana, ni este mes, ni este año.	No, I'm not going tonight, or this week, or this month, or this year.	**esta semana** this week **todas las noches** every night **esta noche** tonight

J: —¿Por qué no deseas salir conmigo ahora?	Why don't you want to go out with me now?	**todos los días** every day **hoy** today **todos los meses** every month
A: —No tengo tiempo para hablar contigo hoy ni todos los días, ni todos los meses, ni todos los años.	I don't have time to chat with you today, or every day, or every month, or every year.	**este mes** this month **todos los años** every year **este año** this year

---

STUDY THE IDIOMS BEFORE BEGINNING THE EXERCISES!

I. (1) Write an affirmative answer in a complete Spanish sentence beginning your answer with the cue words in parentheses. (2) Translate your answer into English.

1. ¿Asistes a fiestas a menudo? (1) _____
(Asisto)

(2) _____

2. ¿Fuiste a muchas fiestas el mes pasado? (1) _____
(Fui)

(2) _____

3. ¿Llegas muchas veces a tiempo? (1) _____
(Llego)

(2) _____

4. ¿Deseas ir de nuevo? (1) _____
(Deseo)

(2) _____

5. ¿Quieres ir en seguida? (1) _____
(Quiero)

(2) _____

6. ¿Terminas el trabajo para la clase más tarde? (1)_____
   (Termino)

   _____

   (2)_____

7. ¿Estudias pocas veces este año como el año pasado? (1)_____
   (Estudio)

   _____

   (2)_____

8. ¿Luego aprendes poco a poco? (1)_____
   (Aprendo)

   (2)_____

9. ¿Pero trabajaste mucho toda la semana pasada? (1)_____
   (Trabajé)

   _____

   (2)_____

10. Entonces ¿vas a México el año próximo como todos los años? (1)_____
    (Voy)

    _____

    (2)_____

11. ¿Celebras el cumpleaños la semana próxima? (1)_____
    (Celebro)

    _____

    (2)_____

12. ¿Vas al campo otra vez el mes que viene? (1)_____
    (Voy)

    (2)_____

13. ¿Das una fiesta esta semana como todas las semanas? (1)_____
    (Doy)

    _____

    (2)_____

14. ¿Sales esta noche como todas las noches? (1)_____
    (Salgo)

    (2)_____

15. ¿Asistes a las clases hoy como todos los días? (1)_____
(Asisto)

_____

(2)_____

II. Write the expression that best completes the sentence, and circle the letter.

1. Para ver todas las buenas películas hay que ir al cine_____
   a. a menudo   b. sin dinero   c. a caballo   d. con dolor

2. Conocen muchos países porque viajan a Europa_____
   a. todos los días   b. todos los años   c. más tarde   d. en seguida

3. Ayer tuvimos un examen, y hoy hay un examen_____
   a. a tiempo   b. de nuevo   c. poco a poco   d. muchas veces

4. La escuela se abre a las ocho y nosotros entramos en la clase_____
   a. todos los sábados   b. el domingo que viene   c. a tiempo   d. el año pasado

5. Si no podemos salir en seguida, vamos a salir_____
   a. más tarde   b. anoche   c. el mes pasado   d. otra vez

III. Write the expression that best completes the answer, and circle the letter.

1. —¿Cómo aprendes el español?

   —Lo aprendo_____
   a. el año pasado   b. todos los meses   c. poco a poco

2. —¿Hay que estudiar hoy?

   —Siempre hay que estudiar_____
   a. todos los días   b. el mes pasado   c. el año pasado

3. —¿Presta la clase atención a menudo?

   —Sí, _____
   a. escucha muchas veces   b. presta atención en seguida   c. estudia pocas veces

4. —¿Cuándo celebramos un cumpleaños?

   —Lo celebramos_____
   a. todos los años   b. todos los meses   c. todas las semanas

5. —¿Pones la mesa de nuevo?

   —Sí, la pongo_____
   a. pocas veces   b. otra vez   c. el mes pasado

321

IV. Write the expression that means the *opposite* of the expression in *italics*. Circle the letter.

1. Estudian *pocas veces.*_____
   a. poco a poco   b. a menudo   c. más tarde   d. la próxima semana

2. Van *la semana próxima.*_____
   a. la semana pasada   b. antes   c. tarde   d. la semana que viene

3. Aprenden *en seguida.*_____
   a. en punto   b. a tiempo   c. poco a poco   d. a menudo

4. Viene *más tarde.*_____
   a. muchas veces   b. en seguida   c. pocas veces   d. el año pasado

5. Llega *a tiempo.*_____
   a. en seguida   b. tarde   c. en punto   d. a menudo

V. Complete in Spanish with the appropriate expression from the selection below.

1. Pepe: —¿Sales _____ menudo?

2. Lola: —Sí, salgo muchas _____.

3. Pepe: —¿Tienes tiempo para salir _____ noche?

4. Lola: — _____ seguida no tengo tiempo, pero _____ tarde sí.

5. Pepe: —Entonces salgamos temprano para llegar al cine _____ tiempo.

6. Lola: —Salimos todas _____ semanas y nunca llegamos tarde. ¡No lo repitas

   _____ nuevo la semana _____!

   Selection: **a, de, en, esta, las, más, a, próxima, veces**

SPANISH

SPANISH

SPANISH

ENGLISH

ENGLISH

Vocabulary

Spanish-English

A

a at, in, to, on; **a causa de** because of; **a la derecha** on the right; **a menudo** often; **a veces** at times

abajo below

abierto, -a open

abogado *m.* lawyer; **abogado defensor** defense attorney

abrigo *m.* overcoat

abuelo *m.* grandfather; **abuela** *f.* grandmother; **abuelita** *f.* grandma; **abuelos** *m. pl.* grandparents, grandfathers

abril *m.* April

abrir to open

aburrido, -a bored

acá here, around here

acabar de (regresar) to have just (returned)

accidente *m.* accident

aceptar to accept

acerca de about, concerning

acostarse (ue) to go to bed

actividad *f.* activity

activo, -a active

actor *m.* actor

actriz *f.* actress

actual present day

además besides, moreover

adivinanza *f.* riddle

adiós good-bye

admirar to admire

¿adónde? where?

aeroplano *m.* airplane

aeropuerto *m.* airport

afortunadamente fortunately

afuera outside

agencia de viajes *f.* travel agency

agosto August

agradable agreeable

agua *f.* water

ahora now; **ahora mismo** right now; **por ahora** for now

aire *m.* air; **al aire libre** in the open air

ajá aha

a las doce (at) 12:00

a las once (at) 11:00

a las siete (at) 7:00

al to the, at the, in the **al aire libre** outdoors; **al fin** finally, at last; **al + inf.** upon __ing; **al dar** upon striking

Alberto Albert

alcoba *f.* bedroom

aldea *f.* town

alegre happy, lively, cheerful; **me alegro mucho;** I'm very happy, I'm glad

alegremente happily

alemán, -a German

Alemania *f.* Germany

alfombra *f.* carpet

Alfredo Alfred

algo something

algodón *m.* cotton

alguien someone, somebody

algún (o) -a some; **algunas veces** sometimes

Alicia Alice

alimentos *m. pl.* food

allá there, around there

allí there

almacén *m.* department store

almorzar (ue) to lunch

almuerzo *m.* lunch; **tomar el almuerzo** to have lunch

alquiler *m.* rent

alto, -a tall, high

alumno, -a *m./f.* student

amable friendly, pleasant

amarillo, -a yellow

americano, -a American

amigo, -a *m./f.* friend

amiguito, a *m./f.* little friend

amor *m.* love

Ana Ann

anaranjado, -a orange

ancho, -a wide

anciano *m.* old man

andar to go, to walk; **andar en bicicleta** to go bicycle riding

animal *m.* animal

anoche last night

ansioso, -a anxious, worried

antes (de) before

antiguo, -a ancient, former

antipático, -a unpleasant

Antonio Anthony, Tony

año *m.* year; **Año Nuevo (el)** New Year; **el año pasado** last year; **tener ____ años** to be ____ years old; **¿cuántos años tiene Vd.?** how old are you?

apendicitis *f.* appendicitis

apetito *m.* appetite

aplicado, -a studious

apreciar tó appreciate

aprende he, she, you learn(s)

aprender to learn

aprisa in a hurry

aquel *m.* that; **aquella** *f.* that; **aquellas** *f. pl.* those;

aquellos *m. pl.* those
aquí here
árbol *m.* tree
arbusto *m.* bush
aritmética *f.* arithmetic
armario *m.* closet
arriba above, up
arroz *m.* rice
artículo *m.* article
artista *m./f.* artist
Arturo Arthur
asa *f.* handle
ascensor *m.* elevator
asesinato *m.* murder
así so, (in) this way; **así, así** so, so
asiento *m.* seat
asistir (a) to attend
aspirina *f.* aspirin
astronauta *m.* astronaut
atados tied up
atención *f.* attention; **prestar atención** to pay attention; **con atención** attentively
atentamente attentively
atleta *m./f.* athlete
atractivo, -a attractive
aún even
aunque although
autobús *m.* bus; **autobús turístico** sightseeing bus
automóvil *m.* automobile
autor *m.* author
avenida *f.* avenue
aventura *f.* adventure
aviador *m.* aviator
avión *m.* airplane
ayer yesterday
ayuda *f.* aid, help
azúcar *m.* sugar
azul blue

B

bailar to dance
baile *m.* dance
bajar to go down, to put down; **bajar (de)** to get down (from)
bajito, -a short

bajo, -a low, short
balcón *m.* balcony
banco *m.* bank, bench
bandera *f.* flag
banquero *m.* banker
bañarse to bathe
baño *m.* bath; **cuarto de baño** *m.* bathroom
barato, -a cheap
barbería *f.* barber shop
barco *m.* ship, boat
barra *f.* bar, rod
barrio *m.* district
bastante enough
beber to drink
bebida *f.* drink
béisbol *m.* baseball
bello, -a pretty
beso *m.* kiss
biblioteca *f.* library
bicicleta *f.* bicycle
bien well, good
bienvenido, -a welcome
billete *m.* ticket
blanco, -a white
blusa *f.* blouse
boca *f.* mouth
bodega *f.* grocery store
bola *f.* ball
bonito, -a pretty
borracho, -a drunk
borrador *m.* eraser
bolsillo *m.* pocket
bosque *m.* woods
bote *m.* boat
botella *f.* bottle
brazo *m.* arm
breve brief
brillante brilliant
bueno, -a good, well; all right
burro *m.* donkey
buscar to look for

C

caballo *m.* horse; **a caballo** on horseback
caballero *m.* gentleman
cabello *m.* hair
cabeza *f.* head
cada each

caer to fall; **caerse** to fall down; **se cayó** he fell down
café *m.* coffee, café (informal restaurant)
cafetería *f.* cafeteria
caja *f.* box
calabaza *f.* pumpkin
calcetines *m. pl.* socks
caliente warm, hot
calor *m.* heat; **hacer (mucho) calor** to be (very) warm (weather); **tener calor** to be warm (persons)
calle *f.* street
cama *f.* bed; **guardar cama** to stay in bed
camerero, -a waiter, waitress
cambiar to change, exchange
caminar to walk, to go
camino *m.* road
camisa *f.* shirt
campamento *m.* camp; **campamento de verano** summer camp
campo *m.* field, country
Canadá (el) *m.* Canada
canal *m.* channel
canción *f.* song
cansado, -a tired
cantar to sing
Caperucita Roja Little Red Riding Hood
capital *f.* capital
capitán *m.* captain
capítulo *m.* chapter
cara *f.* face
cárcel *f.* jail
cariñosamente affectionately
Carlos Charles
Carlota Charlotte
carnaval *m.* carnival
carne *f.* meat
carnicería *f.* butcher shop
carnicero *m.* butcher
caro, -a expensive, dear
carro *m.* car
carta *f.* letter
cartera *f.* wallet, purse

cartero *m.* letter carrier

cartón *m.* cardboard

casa *f.* house; **en casa** at home; **casa particular** private house; **casa de apartamientos (pisos)** apartment house; **Casa Blanca (la)** the White House

casarse (con) to marry

casi almost

caso *m.* case

castañuela *f.* castenet

castellano *m.* Spanish, Castilian

Castilla *f.* Castile

católico, -a Catholic

catorce fourteen

causa *f.* cause

caverna *f.* cave

cayó he, she, you fell

cebolla *f.* onion

celebrar to celebrate

celo *m.* zeal

cena *f.* supper; **tomar la cena** to have supper

centavo *m.* cent

central central

centro *m.* downtown

Centro América Central America

cerca (de) near

cercano, -a nearby

ceremonias *f.* ceremonies

cereza *f.* cherry

cero *m.* zero

cerrado, -a closed

cerrar (ie) to close

cesto, -a *m./f.* basket

cielo *m.* sky; **mi cielo** my darling

ciencia *f.* science

científico *m.* scientist

cien (to) a hundred

cierto, -a (a) certain

cinco five

cincuenta fifty

cine *m.* movie(s)

circo *m.* circus

cita *f.* date, appointment

ciudad *f.* city

claro, -a clear

¡claro! of course!

clase *f.* **sala de clase** classroom

clavel *m.* carnation

clima *m.* climate

coche *m.* car; **en (por) coche** by car; **coche patrullero** patrol car

cocina *f.* kitchen; **clase de cocina** *f.* cooking class

cocinar to cook

cocinero, -a *m./f.* cook

coleccionista *m.* collector

colegio *m.* high school, private boarding secondary school

Colón Columbus

color *m.* color

comedor *m.* dining room

comenzar (ie) to begin

comer to eat

comercial commercial

comerciante *m.* merchant

comestibles *m. pl.* groceries

cometer faltas to make errors

comida *f.* meal, dinner, food

como like, as

¿cómo? how? what do you mean? **¡cómo no!** of course! **¡cómo qué no?** what do you mean, "no"?

cómodo, -a comfortable; **cómodamente** comfortably

compañero, -a *m./f.* companion, friend

compañero, -a de clase *m./f.* classmate

comparar to compare

compra *f.* purchase; **ir de compras** to go shopping

comprador *m.* buyer

comprar to buy

comprender to understand

con with **conmigo** with me;

contigo with you *(fam.)*; **con ella** with her

¡concedido! agreed!

concierto *m.* concert

concurso *m.* contest

conducir to drive, to lead

congelado, -a frozen

conocer to know (acquainted)

consejo *m.* advice

consejero *m.* counselor

conservar to conserve

construir to construct

consultorio *m.* clinic

consultorio sentimental *m.* advice to the lovelorn

consumir to consume

contar (ue) to tell, to count; **cuenta** he tells

contento, -a happy; **contentamente** happily

contestar to answer

contra against

conversación *f.* conversation

conversar to converse, to chat

copa *f.* (wine) glass

copiar to copy

corbata *f.* tie

corona *f.* crown

correcto, -a *correct;* **correctamente** correctly

correr to run

cortar to cut

cortés polite(ly)

cortina *f.* curtain

corto, -a short

cosa *f.* thing

cosméticos *m. pl.* cosmetics

costa *f.* coast

costar (ue) to cost; **cuesta** it costs; **me costó** it cost me

crecer to grow

creer to believe, to think; **creer que sí (no)** to believe so (not)

crema *f.* cream

creo I believe

criado, -a *m./f.*

maid, servant

criminal *m.* criminal

crudo, -a raw

cruzar to cross

cuaderno *m.* notebook

cuadro *m.* picture

¿cuál? which (one)?, what?

cuando when; **¿cuándo?** when?

¿cuánto, -a? how much? **¿cuánto tiempo?** how long?; **¿cuántos, -as?** how many?; **¿cuántos años tiene?** How old is he (she)?; **¿a cuántos estamos hoy?** what's today's date?

cuarto *m.* room, quarter; **cuarto de baño** bathroom

cuatro four

cuatrocientos four hundred

Cuba *f.* Cuba, **cubano, -a** Cuban

cubrir to cover

cuchara *f.* spoon

cucharita *f.* teaspoon

cuchillo *m.* knife

cuello *m.* collar, neck

cuenta he tells

cuento *m.* story

cuerpo *m.* body

cuesta it costs

culpable guilty

cultivar to grow

cultural cultural

cumpleaños *m.* birthday

cuñado *m.* brother-in-law

curar to cure

CH

chal *m.* shawl

chaqueta *f.* jacket

charlar to chat

cheque *m.* check

chica girl; **chico** boy

chicle *m.* chewing gum

Chile South American country

chino, -a Chinese; **damas chinas** *f. pl.* checkers

chocar to crash

chocolate *m.* chocolate

chófer *m.* driver

D

dale give him

da(n) he, she, (they) (give)s

dar to give; **doy** I give; **dar la mano** to shake hands; **dar las gracias** to thank; **dar un paseo** to take a walk; **dar un paseo a caballo, a pie, en automóvil** to go horseback riding, to take a walk, to take a drive

de of, from; than; **de acuerdo** in agreement; **de compras** shopping; **de día** by day; **de la mañana** A.M.; **de la noche** P.M.; **de la tarde** P.M.; **de nada** you're welcome; **de ninguna manera** by no means; **de niño** as a child; **de noche** at night; **de nuevo** again; **de pie** on foot; **de repente** suddenly

debajo (de) below, underneath

deber to owe, must; ought to

deberes *m. pl.* duties, homework

débil weak

decidir to decide

decir to say, to tell; **dice(n)** he, she, you, (they) (tell)s; **¿cómo se dice...?** how do you say...?

decisión *f.* decision

defender (ie) to defend

dejar to leave, to let; **dejar caer** to drop

del of the, in the

delante (de) in front (of)

delgado, -a slender, thin

delito *m.* offense, crime

demás *m. pl.* others

demasiado, -a too much

democracia *f.* democracy

dentro inside

dependiente, -a *m./f.* clerk

derecho *m.* straight ahead; **a la derecha** to the right

desafortunadamente unfortunately

desayuno *m.* breakfast; **desayunar (se)** to eat breakfast; **tomar el desayuno** to have breakfast

descansar to rest

describir to describe

descubrir to discover

desde from, since

desear to wish, to want

desesperado, -a desperate

desierto, -a deserted

despacio slowly

despertarse (ie) to wake up

después (de) after(wards)

detestar to detest

detrás de behind

día *m.* day; **al día siguiente** the next day; **buenos días** good morning; **de día** by day; **todos los días** everyday

día de entrevistas entre los padres y maestros Open School Day

Día de la Raza Columbus Day (October 12)

Día de los Reyes Magos Day of the Epiphany (January 6)

Día de los Inocentes April Fool's Day (April 1)

diario, -a daily

diciembre December

dice(n) he says (they say)

dictado *m.* dictation

dictadura *f.* dictatorship

diente *m.* tooth

diferencia *f.* difference

diferente different

difícil difficult

difícilmente with difficulty

dificultad f. difficulty

digo I say, I tell **(decir)**

dígame tell me

dijo he, she, you said **(decir)**

dile tell him (fam.)

diligente diligent

dinero m. money

Dios m. God; **¡Dios mío!** My God!

director, -a m./f. principal

dirigir to direct; **dirigirse** to go toward

disco m. record

dispense Vd. excuse me

disputa f. dispute

distinto, -a different

doblar la esquina to turn the corner

docena f. dozen

doctor m. doctor

dólar m. dollar

doler to hurt

dolor m. ache, pain; **dolor de cabeza (muelas, estómago)** headache (toothache, stomach-ache)

domingo m. Sunday, Dominic

dominó m. dominoes

donde where; **¿dónde?** where?

dormir (ue) to sleep

durmiendo sleeping

dormitorio m. bedroom

Dorotea Dorothy

dos two

dote m. dowry

doy (dar) I give; **doy las gracias** I thank; **doy un paseo** I take a walk; I take a ride

drama m. drama, play

ducha f. shower

duelo m. duel

duermo I sleep

dulce sweet; **dulces** m. pl. candy

durante during; for (time)

duro, -a hard

E

e and

edad f. age

edificio m. building

ejercicio m. exercise

el m. the

él he, it

eléctrico, -a electric

elefante m. elephant

elegante elegant

elemental elementary

Elena Elaine

ella she, it; **ellas** they, them

empezar (ie) to begin

empieza (n) he, she, begins (they begin)

empiezo I begin

empleado m. employee, clerk

empleo m. job, employment

en in, on, at; **en casa** at home; **en punto** sharp, exactly; **¿en qué puedo servirle?** what can I do for you?; **en seguida** immediately; **en vez de** instead of; **en voz baja** in a whisper

enamorado, -a in love

encontrar (ue) to meet, to find

enero January

enfermedad f. illness

enfermera f. nurse

enfermo, -a sick, ill

enfermo m. sick person

enojado, -a angry

enorme enormous, large

Enrique Henry

ensalada f. salad; **ensalada de papas** potato salad

enseñanza f. teaching

enseñar to show, to teach

entender (ie) to understand

entero, -a entire, all

entonces then

entrada f. ticket, entrance

entrar (en) to enter

entre between, among

entrevista f. interview

enviar to send

equipo m. team

equivocado, -a mistaken

eran they were

eres you are (fam. s.) **(ser)**

error m. error

es is **(ser)**

esa f. that; **esas** f. pl. those

escape m. escape

escribir m. to write

escritor m. writer

escritorio m. desk

escuela f. school; **escuela de cocina** cooking school; **escuela superior** high school

escuchar to listen to

ese m. that; **esos** m. pl.

esencial essential

eso that (neut.) **por eso** therefore

esos m. pl. those

espacio m. space

España f. Spain

español, -a Spanish m./f. Spaniard

especialmente specially

esperanza f. hope

esperar to hope, to wait for

espléndido, -a splendid

esposa f. wife

esposo m. husband

esposos m. pl. husbands, husband and wife, Mr. and Mrs.

esquiar to ski

esta f. this; **esta noche** tonight

estación f. season, station

estado m. state

Estados Unidos (los) m. pl. the United States

estante m. shelf

estar to be; **estar bien (mal)*** to be well (ill); **está**

*also: **malo, -a**

bien O.K.; **¿cómo está usted?** how are you?; **estar de pie** to be standing
estas f. pl. these
estás you are (fam. s.)
este m. this
este m. east
esto this (neut.)
estómago m. stomach
estos m. pl. these
estoy I am **(estar)**
estrecho, -a narrow
estrella f. star
estudia he, she studies
estudiante m./f. student
estudiar to study
estudios m. pl. studies
estudioso, -a studious
estufa f. stove
estupendo, -a stupendous
etiqueta f. label
Europa f. Europe
evento m. event
exactamente exactly
examen m. examination
examinar to test
excursión f. trip
exhausto, -a exhausted
experiencia f. experience
explicar to explain
explorador m. explorer, Boy Scout
explorar to explore
extraño, -a strange
extraordinario, -a extraordinary
extravagante extravagant

F

fábrica f. factory
fácil easy
fácilmente easily
falda f. skirt
falta f. mistake
faltar to be missing
familia f. family; **toda la familia** the whole family

familiar m./f. family member
famoso, -a famous
fantasma m. ghost
fantástico, -a fantastic
farmacia f. pharmacy
fatigado, -a tired
favor m. favor; **hacer el favor de** + inf. please; **por favor** please
favorito, -a favorite
fecha f. date; **¿cuál es la fecha de hoy?** what is today's date?; **¿a cuántos estamos hoy?** what is today's date?
felicidades f. congratulations
Felipe Phillip
feliz happy, content
felizmente happily
feo, -a ugly
ferrocarril m. railroad
fiebre f. fever
fiesta f. party
fin m. end; **al fin** at last; **fin de semana** m. weekend; **por fin** finally
fiscal m. district attorney
flaco, -a thin, skinny
flojo, -a lazy
flor f. flower
flotar to float
forma f. form
foto (grafía) f. photo(graph)
francés m. French, Frenchman; **francesa** Frenchwoman (girl)
Francia f. France
Francisco Frank, Francis
frase f. sentence
frecuentemente frequently
frente m. front; **al frente** in front
fresco, -a fresh, cool; **hacer fresco** to be cool (weather)
frío, -a cold, cool; **hacer frío** to be cold (weather); **tener frío** to be cold (persons)
frito, -a fried
fruta f. fruit

fuerte strong
fumar to smoke
fútbol m. football, soccer

G

gallina f. hen
gallo m. rooster
ganar to earn, to win
garganta f. throat
gaseosa f. soda
gastar to spend
gatito m. kitten
gato m. cat
generalmente generally
generoso, -a generous
gente f. people
geografía f. geography
Gertrudis Gertrude
gimnasia f. gymnastics
gimnasio m. gymnasium
golpe m. blow
goma f. rubber
gordo, -a fat
gorra f. cap
gota f. drop
gozar to enjoy
grabado m. picture
gracias f. pl. thanks; **dar las gracias** to thank; **muchas gracias** thank you very much
gramática f. grammar (book)
gran great
grande big, large
gratis free
grave serious
gris gray
gritar to shout
grito m. shout
guante m. glove; **guante de béisbol** baseball glove
guapo, -a handsome
guardar to keep; **guardar cama** to stay in bed
guía m. guide
Guillermo William
guitarra f. guitar
guitarrista m./f. guitarist

gustar to like, to be pleasing; **me, te, le gusta** I, you, (he), (she), you like(s); **nos, os, les gusta** we, you, they, you like.

gusto *m.* pleasure; **con mucho gusto** gladly, with much pleasure

H

ha conocido has known
había there was, were
habitación *f.* room
hablando speaking
hablar to speak; **¡hable!** speak!
hacer to do, to make; **hacer buen (mal) tiempo** to be good (bad) weather; **hacer frío (calor, sol, viento, fresco)** to be cold (warm, sunny, windy, cool) weather; **hacer el favor de + *inf.*** please; **hacer preguntas** to ask questions; **hace una semana (un mes, etc.)** (a month ago, etc.)
haga el favor de + *inf.* please
hago I do, I make **(hacer)**
hallar to find
hambre *f.* hunger; **tener hambre** to be hungry
hasta until, up to
hasta la vista until I see you again; **hasta luego** until then; **hasta mañana** until tomorrow
hay there is, there are; **no hay de qué** you're welcome; **hay que + *inf.*** one must
hebreo *m.* Hebrew
helado *m.* ice cream
hermana *f.* sister; **hermano** *m.* brother; **hermanos** *m. pl.* brother(s) and sister(s)
hermoso, -a beautiful

hice I made, did **(hacer)**
hierba *f.* grass
hierro *m.* iron
hija *f.* daughter; **hijo** *m.* son; **los hijos** *m. pl.* son(s) and daughter(s)
hispánico, -a Hispanic
hispano, -a Hispanic, Spanish-speaking
hispanoamericano, -a Spanish-American
historia *f.* story, history
histórico, -a historic
hoja *f.* leaf
hola hello
hombre *m.* man
honor *m.* honor
honrado honorable
hora *f.* hour, time; **¿a qué hora?** at what time?; **a la una** at one o'clock; **a las dos** at two o'clock; **a esta(s) hora(s)** at this time; **por hora** by the hour; **¿qué hora es?** what time is it?; **es la una** it's one o'clock; **son las dos** it's two o'clock
hormiga *f.* ant
hospital *m.* hospital
hotel *m.* hotel
hoy today
hueso *m.* bone
huevo *m.* egg; **huevos duros** hard-boiled eggs
huir to flee

I

idea *f.* idea
idioma *m.* language
iglesia *f.* church
imaginario, -a imaginary
importante important
imposible impossible
impresión *f.* impression
independencia *f.* independence
indio, -a *m./f.* Indian
Inés Agnes, Inez

información *f.* information
Inglaterra *f.* England; **Inglés** *m.* English, Englishman; **Inglesa** Englishwoman
inmediatamente immediately
inquieto, -a restless
insistir to insist
instrumento *m.* instrument
inteligencia *f.* intelligence
inteligente intelligent
interés *m.* interest
interesante interesting
interesar to interest
interrumpir to interrupt
invierno *m.* winter
invitado, -a *m./f.* guest; invited
invitación *f.* invitation
invitar to invite
ir go **voy, vas, va** I, you, (he), (she), you, (it) go(es); **vamos, vais, van** we, you, they, you go; **ir a casa (a la escuela, de paseo)** to go home (to school, for a walk); **ir de compras** to go shopping
isla *f.* island
Isabel Elizabeth
Italia *f.* Italy
italiano, -a Italian
izquierdo *m.* left; **a la izquierda** to the left

J

Jaime James
jardín *m.* garden
Jorge George
José Joseph
jota *f.* j (letter)
joven *m./f.* young person
Juan John
Juana Jane, Joan
juega (n) he, she, (you), (they) (play)s; **juegas** you play *(fam.)*
juego *m.* game

jueves *m.* Thursday
juez *m.* judge
jugador *m.* player
jugar (ue) (a) to play
jugo *m.* juice; **jugo de naranja** orange juice
julio July
junio June
junto together
juvenil juvenile

K

kilómetros *m. pl.* kilometers

L

la (las) *f. pl.* the; **las (veo)** (I see) them
labio *m.* lip
laboratorio *m.* laboratory
lado *m.* side; **al lado de** beside, next to; **por otro lado** on the other hand
ladrar to bark
ladrón *m.* thief
lago *m.* lake
lámpara *f.* lamp
lana *f.* wool
lápiz *m.* pencil
largo, -a long
las *f. pl.* the, them
lástima pity; **¡qué lástima!** what a shame!
latín *m.* Latin
latinoamericano, -a Latin-American
lavar (se) to wash (oneself)
La Paz Bolivian capital
le him, you *in Spain*
le to him, to her, to you, to it
le gusta he, she, (you), it (like)s
le gustaron he, she, you, it liked
lección *f.* lesson
lectura *f.* reading
leche *f.* milk

leer to read
legumbres *f. pl.* vegetables
lejos de far from
lengua *f.* language, tongue
lento, -a slow; **lentamente** slowly
león *m.* lion
les to them, to you
les gusta they, you like
letrero *m.* sign
levantado, -a up, standing
levantarse to get up
leve light
liberal liberal
libra *f.* pound
libre free
libro *m.* book
Lima Peru's capital
limón *m.* lemon
lindo, -a pretty
lista *f.* list; **lista de platos** menu
listo, -a ready
lo *m.* him, it, you; **los** *m. pl.* the, them, you; **lo siento (mucho)** I'm (very) sorry; **lo que** what
lobo *m.* wolf
loco, -a crazy
locutor *m.* announcer
Londres London
luego next, then; **hasta luego** until then, see you later
lugar *m.* place
Luis Louis
Luisa Louise
luna *f.* moon
lunes *m.* Monday
luz *f.* light

LL

llamar to call; **llamar a la puerta** to knock at the door; **llamar(se)** to (be) called; to (be) name(d); **¿cómo se llama Vd?** what's your name?

llave *f.* key
llegar to arrive
llenar to fill
llevar to carry, to wear, to take
llorar to cry
llover (ue) to rain
lloviendo raining
llueve it rains, it's raining
lluvia *f.* rain

M

madera *f.* wood; **de madera** wooden
madre *f.* mother
maestro, -a *m./f.* teacher; **maestro de ceremonias** master of ceremonies
magnífico, -a magnificent
maíz *m.* corn
mal badly, ill
maleta *f.* suitcase
malo, -a bad, ill
mamá *f.* mom, mommy
mandar to order, to send
manejar to drive
mano *f.* hand; **dar la mano** to shake hands; **entre las manos de** in the hands of
mantel *m.* tablecloth
mantequilla *f.* butter
mantilla *f.* lace shawl
manzana *f.* apple
mañana *f.* morning, tomorrow; **de la mañana** A.M.; **por la mañana** in the morning; **hasta mañana** until tomorrow
mapa *m.* map
máquina de coser *f.* sewing machine
máquina de escribir *f.* typewriter
mar *m.* sea
marchar to walk
María Mary
marido *m.* husband
marisco *m.* shellfish
Marta Martha

martes *m.* Tuesday

más most, more; **más tarde** later; **lo más pronto posible** as soon as possible

material *m.* material

mayo May

mayor older, larger

me (to) me, myself

me gusta (n) I like

me presento I introduce myself

mecanismo *m.* mechanism

medianoche *f.* midnight

medias *f. pl.* stockings

médico *m.* doctor

medio, -a half; **en medio de** in the middle of; **media hora** half an hour

mediodía *m.* noon

mejor better; **el mejor** best

melodía *f.* melody

memoria *f.* memory

menor younger, smaller

menos few, less, minus; **al menos** at least

menudo, -a small; **a menudo** often

mercado *m.* market

mes *m.* month; **el mes pasado** last month

mesa *f.* table; **poner la mesa** to set the table

mesita *f.* small table, end table

meter to put (in)

método *m.* method

mexicano, -a Mexican

México Mexico

mezcla *f.* mixture

mi, mis my

mí me

micrófono *m.* microphone

miedo *m.* fear

mientras while

miércoles Wednesday

Miguel Michael; **Miguelito** Mike

mil one thousand

mineral mineral

minuto *m.* minute

mío, -a (of) mine, my

mirar to look (at)

misa *f.* mass

mismo, -a same; **lo mismo** the same

mitad *f.* half

moderno, -a modern

molestar to bother

momento *m.* moment

mono *m.* monkey

montaña *f.* mountain

monte(s) *m. (pl.)* mountain(s)

monumento *m.* monument

moreno, -a dark-haired, dark-eyed, brunette

morir to die

mostrar (ue) to show

mover (ue) to move

mozo *m.* boy, waiter

muchacha *f.* girl; **muchacho** *m.* boy

mucho, -a much, a lot

muchos, -as many

muebles *m. pl.* furniture

muerto, -a dead

mujer *f.* woman, wife

mundo *m.* world; **todo el mundo** everyone

muñeca *f.* doll

museo *m.* museum

música *f.* music

músico *m.* musician

muy very; **muy bien** very well

N

nacer to be born

nación *f.* nation

nacional national

Naciones Unidas *f. pl.* (ONU) United Nations

nada nothing; **de nada** you're welcome

nadar to swim

nadie no one, anyone

naranja *f.* orange

nariz *f.* nose

natación *f.* swimming

naturalmente naturally

navaja *f.* razor

Navidad *f.* Christmas; **Feliz Navidad** Merry Christmas; **Día de Navidad** Christmas Day

neblina *f.* fog

necesario, -a necessary

necesitar to need

negocio *m.* business

negro, -a black

nene *m.* infant

nervioso, -a nervous

nevado, -a snowy, snowcapped

ni nor, not even

ni . . . ni neither . . . nor

nieta *f.* granddaughter; **nieto** *m.* grandson; **nietos** *m. pl.* grandchildren

nieva it snows, it's snowing

nieve *f.* snow

nilón *m.* nylon

ninguno, -a none

niño, -a *m./f.* child

¿no? really?, no?

no importa it doesn't matter

noche *f.* night; **buenas noches** good night, good evening; **de noche** at night; **de la noche** P.M.; **esta noche** tonight; **por la noche** in the evening, at night

nombre *m.* name

normal normal

norteamericano, -a North American

nos us, to us, ourselves

nos gusta we like

nosotros, -as we, us

nota *f.* grade, note

notar to note, to comment on

noticia *f.* news

novedad *f.* novelty; **sin novedad** as usual

novela *f.* novel

noventa ninety

noviembre November

nube *f.* cloud

nuestro, -a (of) our(s)

Nueva York New York
nueve nine
nuevo, -a new; **de nuevo** again
Nuevo Mundo New World
número m. number
numeroso, -a numerous
nunca never

O

o or
obedecer to obey
obra f. work
observar to observe
Océano Atlántico m. Atlantic Ocean
octubre October
ocupado, -a (en) busy (with)
ochenta eighty
ocho eight
oeste m. west
oficina f. office
ofrecer to offer
¡oiga! I hear
oigo I hear
oír to hear; **oye** he, she, (you) (hear)s; **se oyen** are heard; **oyó** he, she, you heard
ojo m. eye
olor m. odor
olvidar to forget
ómnibus m. bus
once eleven; **a las once** (at) 11:00
operación f. operation
operar to operate
opinión f. opinion
ordenar to order
oreja f. ear
Organización de Estados Americanos f. (OEA) Organization of American States
oro m. gold
otoño m. autumn
otro, -a (an) other; **otros, -as** other(s); **otras veces** on other occasions
oyó he heard **(oír)**

P

Pablo Paul
Paco Frank
paciencia f. patience
paciente m./f. patient
padre m. father; **padres** m. pl. parents, mother(s) and father(s)
pagar to pay (for)
página f. page
país m. country
pájaro m. bird
palabra f. word
palacio m. palace
pálido, -a pale; **se puso pálido** he turned pale
pan m. bread
panadería f. bakery
panadero m. baker
pantalones m. pl. pants
pañuelo m. handkerchief
papá m. dad, father
papas f. pl. potatoes; **papas fritas** French fries
papel m. paper
paquete m. package
par m. pair
para for, in order to; **para que** in order that; **¿para qué?** why?
parada f. stop, military parade
paraguas m. umbrella
paralítico, -a paralyzed
pardo, -a brown
parecer to look like, seem; **¿qué te parece?** what do you think of it?
pared f. wall
pareja f. pair, couple
pariente m./f. relative; **parientes** pl. relatives
parque m. park; **parque zoológico** m. zoo
párrafo m. paragraph
parte f. part; **por todas partes** everywhere
participar to participate
particular private
partido m. game, match

partir to leave
pasado m. past
pasado, -a past; **el año pasado** last year; **el mes pasado** last month; **la semana pasada** last week
pasajero, -a passenger
pasar to spend (time), to happen; **pasar un buen (mal) rato** to have a good (bad) time; **¡pase Vd.!** come in!; **¿qué le pasa a Vd.?** what's the matter with you? **¿qué pasa?** what's going on?
Pascua Florida f. Easter
paseo m. walk; **dar un paseo** to take a walk; **ir de paseo** to go for a walk
pasión passion
pasta f. dough, paste
pasta dentífrica f. toothpaste
pastel m. cake, pie
patatas f. pl. potatoes
patio m. yard
patria f. country
patrón, -a m./f. boss
payaso m. clown
pedazo m. piece
pedir (ie) to ask for
Pedro Peter
película f. movie
peligroso, -a dangerous
pelo m. hair
pelota f. ball
pensar (ie) to think; **pensar en** to think of; **pensar +** inf. to intend
pensión f. boarding house
pequeño, -a small
pera f. pear
perder (ie) to lose
perdóneme excuse me
perezoso, -a lazy
perfecto, -a perfect
periódico m. newspaper
permiso m. permission; **con permiso** excuse me
pero but
perro m. dog; **perrito** m. puppy

persona *f.* person
personaje *m.* character
personalidad *f.* personality
pescado *m.* fish
peseta *f.* Spanish money
peso *m.* Mexican money
piano *m.* piano
pie *m.* foot; **a pie** on foot; **al pie de** at the bottom of; **estar de pie** to be standing
piedra *f.* stone
piensa he, she (you) (think)s **(pensar)**
pierna *f.* leg
piloto *m.* pilot
pimienta *f.* pepper
pintar to paint; **pintado, -a** painted
pintura *f.* painting
pipa *f.* pipe
piso *m.* floor, story, apartment; **piso de arriba (abajo)** upstairs (downstairs)
pizarra *f.* blackboard
planchar to iron
planta *f.* plant
plata *f.* silver
platillo *m.* saucer
plato *m.* dish (of food)
playa *f.* beach
plaza *f.* square, plaza
pluma *f.* pen
pobre poor
poco, -a few, little; **pocas veces** few times; **poco a poco** little by little; **poco después** shortly afterward **un poco de** *m.* a little of
poder (ue) to be able; **puede** he, she, (you) can, is (are) able; **no poder más** not to be able to go on
poesía *f.* poetry
policía *m.* policeman
polvo *m.* dust
pollitos *m. pl.* chicks
pollo *m.* chicken

poncho woolen blanket pulled overhead and worn as an overgarment
poner to put, to place; **poner la mesa** to set the table; **ponerse** to become, to put on; **me pongo** I put on; **se pone** he becomes
por for, through, by, times (multiply); **por ahora** for now; **por eso** therefore; **por favor** please; **por fin** at last; **por hora** per hour; **por la mañana (tarde, noche)** in the morning (afternoon, evening); **por otro lado** on the other hand; **por supuesto** of course; **por todas partes** everywhere
porque because
¿por qué? why?
portugués *m.* Portuguese
postre *m.* dessert
practicar to practice
práctico, -a practical
preceder to go before
precio *m.* price
preferido, -a favorite
preferir (ie) to prefer
prefiero I prefer
pregunta *f.* question; **hacer preguntas** to ask questions
preguntar to ask; **preguntar por** to ask about
prehistórico, -a prehistoric
preocupado, -a worried
preparar to prepare
presentar to present
presente *m.* present; **los presentes** those present; **me presento** I introduce myself
presidente *m.* president
prestar to lend; **prestar atención** to pay attention; **prestar juramento** to be sworn in

pretérito *m.* preterite
primavera *f.* spring
primero, -a first
primo, -a *m./f.* cousin
principal main
prisa *f.* speed, haste; **de (con) prisa** in a hurry
privilegio *m.* privilege
problema *m.* problem
procesión *f.* procession
produce you produce
producto *m.* product
profesor, -a *m./f.* teacher
programa *m.* program
prometer to promise
pronto soon
pronunciar to pronounce
propio, -a own
próximo, -a next
público *m.* public
pudieron they could, were able **(poder)**
pueblo *m.* town
puede(n) he, she can; (they can) **(poder)**
puedo I can **(poder)**
puente *m.* bridge
puerco *m.* pig
puerta *f.* door
puertorriqueño, -a Puerto Rican
pues well
puesto *m.* job, position
pulso *m.* pulse; caution
punto *m.* period; **en punto** on the dot (on time)
pupitre *m.* desk
puro, -a pure
puso he, she put **(poder)**; **se puso pálido** he turned pale

Q

que that, than, who; **¡qué!** how . . .!, what a . . .!, what!; **¿qué?** what?, which?; **¿qué hay?** what's the matter?, what's up?; **¿qué le pasa a Vd.?** what's the matter with you?; **¿qué pasa?** what's going on?; **¿qué tal?** how's everything?; **que viene** next, that is coming; **lo que** what

quedar to remain

querer (ie) to want, to love; **querer a** to love; **querer decir** to mean; **¿qué quiere decir…?** what does … mean?

querido, -a dear

queso m. cheese

quien(es) who; **¿quién(es)?** who?; **¿a quién(es)?** to whom?; **¿de quién(es)?** whose?, of whom?; **¿para quién?** for whom?

quieres you (fam. s.) want

quince fifteen

quinientos, -as five hundred

quitarse to remove, to take off

R

rabo m. tail

radio f. radio

Ramón Raymond

rancho m. ranch

rápido, -a rapid; **rápidamente** rapidly

raro, -a strange

rascacielos m. skyscraper

rato m. a while; **pasar un buen (mal) rato** to have a good (bad) time

real real

recibir to receive

recién recently

recordar (ue) to remember

recuerda he, she, (you) (remember)s

recuerdo I remember

refrescarse to refresh oneself

refresco m. cool drink, refreshment

regalo m. gift

regla f. rule

regresar to return

regreso m. return

reír (í) to laugh

reloj m. watch

remoto, -a far away

repite he, she, (you) (repeat)s (**repetir**)

representar to represent

resfriado m. cough, cold

respectivamente respectively

respirar to breathe

responder to answer

respuesta f. answer

restaurante m. restaurant

reunión f. get-together, meeting

revista f. magazine

Reyes Magos m. pl. Wise Men

Ricardo Richard

rico, -a rich; **¡qué rico!** how delicious!

rincón m. corner

río m. river

risa f. laughter

ritmo m. rhythm

robar to steal, to rob

Roberto Robert

rojo, -a red

romántico, -a romantic

ropa f. clothes; **ropa interior** f. underwear

rosa f. rose

rosado, -a rose-colored

rubio, -a blond

ruido m. noise

ruso, -a Russian

S

sábado m. Sunday

sabe know(s)

saber to know; **saber + inf.** to know how to

sabor m. flavor

sacar to take out, to stick out (fam.); **sacar fotos** to take pictures; **sacar una nota** to get a mark

sal f. salt

sala f. living room; **sala de clase** classroom

¡salgan Vds.! leave!

salgo I leave (**salir**)

salir (de) to leave, to go out; **salir bien (mal)** to make out well (badly), to pass (fail), (unsuccessfully); **salir el sol** sunrise

saltar to jump

salud f. health

saludar to greet

Santiago Chile's capital

santo, -a m./f. saint

sastre m. tailor

satisfecho, -a satisfied

se (reflex.) himself, herself, yourself, itself, themselves, yourselves; **se + 3rd person vb.** one, they, you (in a general sense)

se cayó (del avion) he fell (out of the plane); **se levanta** he, she, (you) (get)s up; **se oyen** they are heard; **se puso pálido** he turned pale; **se sienta** he, she, (you) (sit)s down

sé I know (**saber**)

secretaria f. secretary

secreto m. secret

secundario, -a secondary

sed f. thirst; **tener sed** to be thirsty

seda f. silk

seguida; en seguida at once

seguir (i) to follow

seguro, -a sure, certain

seis six

semana f. week; **todas las semanas** every week

sencillo, -a simple

sentarse (ie) to sit down; **sentado, -a** seated; **se sienta** he, she, (you) (sit)s; **¡siéntese Vd.!** sit down!

sentido *m.* sense, feeling

sentir (ie) to feel, to regret; **lo siento (mucho)** I'm (very) sorry

señor *m.* Mr., sir, gentleman

señora *f.* Mrs., lady

señorita *f.* Miss, lady

septiembre September

ser to be; **ser la hora de + *inf.*** to be time to

serio, -a serious

serpiente *f.* serpent

servicio *m.* service

servidor, -a at your service

servilleta *f.* napkin

servir (i) to serve; **sirve para** is used for

sesenta sixty

setenta seventy

si if, whether

sí yes; **sí que** indeed

siempre always

sienta seats

¡siéntese Vd.! sit down!

siento I'm sorry

siesta *f.* nap, short rest

significar to mean; **esto significa** this means

siguiente following, next

silencio *m.* silence

silla *f.* chair

sillón *m.* armchair

simbolizar to symbolize

similar similar

simpático, -a nice, pleasant

sin without; **sin parar** without stopping

sincero, -a sincere

sirve para is used for

sirven they serve

sitio *m.* place

sobre on, over, about

sobre todo especially

sobrina *f.* niece; **sobrino** *m.* nephew; **sobrinos** *m. pl.* nephew(s) and niece(s)

sofá *m.* couch, sofa

sol *m.* sun; **hacer sol** to be sunny; **salir el sol** sunrise

solamente only

soldado *m.* soldier

solitario, -a lonely

solo, -a alone

sólo only

solterón *m.* bachelor

solución *f.* solution

sombrero *m.* hat

somos we are **(ser)**

son they are **(ser)**

sonar to ring

sonido *m.* sound

sonreír to smile

sopa *f.* soup

soplar to blow (out)

sorprendido, -a surprised

sorpresa *f.* surprise

sótano *m.* basement

soy I am **(ser)**

su, sus his, her, their, your, its

subir to go up; **subir a** to get into, go up to; **subir en avión** to go up in a plane

subterráneo *m.* subway

suburbio *m.* suburb

sudar to sweat

sueldo *m.* salary

suelo *m.* ground

suena rings

sueño *m.* dream; **tener sueño** to be sleepy

suerte *f.* luck

sufrimiento *m.* suffering

sufrir to suffer

supermercado *m.* supermarket

supo he found out **(saber)**

sur *m.* south

Susana Susan

suyo, -a (of) his, (of) her(s), (of) your(s), (of) their(s)

T

tal such (a); **¿qué tal?** how are things?

talento *m.* talent

también also

tan so

tan . . . como as . . . as

tango *m.* Argentine dance

tanto, -a so much, as much

tapa *f.* cover

tarde *f.* afternoon, late; **buenas tardes** good afternoon; **de la tarde** P.M.; **más tarde** later; **por la tarde** in the afternoon; **tarde o temprano** sooner or later

tarea *f.* task, homework

tarjeta *f.* card

taxi *m.* taxi

taxista *m.* taxi driver

taza *f.* cup

te you, to you, yourself

te gusta you *(fam.)* like

té *m.* tea

teatro *m.* theater

techo *m.* ceiling, roof

telefonear to telephone

teléfono *m.* telephone

televidente *m.* TV viewer

televisión *f.* television

televisor *m.* television set

temperatura *f.* temperature

templo *m.* temple

temprano early

tendero *m.* storekeeper

tenedor *m.* fork

tener to have;

tener . . . años to be . . . years old; **tener calor** to be warm; **tener hambre** to be hungry; **tener interés** to be interested; **tener miedo** to fear; **tener prisa** to be in a hurry; **tener que + *inf.*** to have to; **tener razón** to be right; **tener sed** to be thirsty; **tener sueño** to be sleepy; **¿qué tiene Vd.?** what's the matter with you?

tengo I have; **tengo que + *inf.*** I have to, must **(tener)**

tenis *m.* tennis

tercer third

Teresa Teresa

terminar to end, to finish

tertulia *f.* chat, social gathering

testigo *m.* witness

ti you

tiempo *m.* time, weather; **a tiempo** on time; **hacer buen (mal) tiempo** to be good (bad) weather; **mucho tiempo** for a long time; **al mismo tiempo** at the same time

tienda *f.* store; **tienda de ropa** clothing store; **tienda de comestibles** grocery store

tiene(n) he, she, (you, they) has (have); **tiene(n) que** he, she, (you, they) has (have) to, must; **¿qué tiene?** what is the matter with him?

tierra *f.* earth

tigre *m.* tiger

tijeras *f. pl.* scissors

timbre *m.* bell

tinta *f.* ink

tío *m.* uncle; **tía** *f.* aunt; **tíos** *m. pl.* aunt(s) and uncle(s)

tirar to throw

tiza *f.* chalk

tocadiscos *m.* record player

tocar to play (an instrument); to touch, to knock

todo, -a all, everything; **todo el día** *m.* all day; **todo el mundo** everybody

todos, -as every, all; **todos los días** everyday; **todas las semanas** every week

toldo *m.* awning

tomar to take, to drink; **tomar el almuerzo** to have lunch; **tomar la cena** to have supper; **tomar el desayuno** to have breakfast; **tomar asiento** to get seated

Tomás Thomas

tonto, -a silly, stupid, dumb

tópico *m.* topic

torero *m.* bullfighter

toro bull

torpe dull, stupid

torta *f.* cake

tortilla *f.* omelet

tostado *m.* toast

trabajar to work

trabajador hardworking

trabajo *m.* work

traer to bring

traficante *m.* dealer

tráfico *m.* traffic

traigo I bring **(traer)**

traje *m.* suit; **traje de baño** bathing suit

treinta thirty

tren *m.* train

tres three

triste sad

tristemente sadly

tristeza *f.* sadness

tu, tus your *(fam.)*

tú you

tulipán *m.* tulip

turista *m./f.* tourist

tuyo, -a (of) your(s) *(fam.)*

U

un(o), una *m./f.* a, an, one; **unos, -as** some, a few; **un poco de** . . . a bit of . . .

único, -a only

Unión Soviética *f.* Soviet Union

universidad *f.* university

usar to use, to wear

usted (es) you *(pl.)*

utensilio *m.* utensil

útil useful

V

va he, she, you go (es) **(ir)**

vaca *f.* cow

vacaciones *f. pl.* vacation; **las vacaciones de verano** summer vacation

vago *m.* vagrant, bum

valer to be worth; **vale** it costs

vamos we go, we're going; let's go **(ir)**

van they go **(ir)**

vapor *m.* steamship

varios, -as several

vaso *m.* glass

¡vaya! go! **(ir)**

Vd(s). you (abbrev.)

veces times; **a veces** at times; **algunas veces** sometimes; **otras veces** other times

vecindario *m.* neighborhood

vecino, -a *m./f.* neighbor, *(adj.)* neighboring

vegetal *m.* vegetable

veinte twenty

vela *f.* candle

vendedor *m.* seller

vender to sell

¡venga! come **(venir)**

vengo I come

venir to come; **viene** he, she, (you) (come)s

venta sale; **a la venta** for sale

ventana *f.* window

ventanilla *f.* window (of a car or bus)

veo I see **(ver)**

ver to see; **a ver** let's see; **veo** I see

verano *m.* summer

verdad *f.* truth; **¿no es verdad?** isn't it so?; **¿verdad?** right?

verde green

vestíbulo *m.* vestibule

vestido *m.* dress, suit

vestido, -a(de) dressed (in)

vez *f.* time; **por primera vez** for the first time; **a veces** at times; **algunas veces** sometimes; **muchas**

veces many times, often;
otra vez again; **otras
veces** on other occasions;
pocas veces a few times

viajar to travel

viaje *m.* trip

viajero *m./f.* traveler

Vicente Vincent

vida *f.* life; **mi vida** my darling

vidrio *m.* glass

viejo, -a old; **el viejo** old man

viene he, she, (you) (come)s

viento *m.* wind; **hacer
viento** to be windy

viernes *m.* Friday

vino *m.* wine

violeta *f.* violet

violín *m.* violin

visita *f.* visit

visitar to visit

Víspera *f.* **de Todos los
Santos** Halloween

vista *f.* view, sight; **hasta la
vista** until I see you again

vivir to live

volar (ue) to fly

volumen *m.* volume, book

volver (ue) to return; **vuelve
a casa** he, she, (you)
(return)s home; **volver a
mirarlo** to see something
again

votar to vote

voy I go; **va** he, she, (you)
(go)es; **van** they, you go **(ir)**

voz *f.* voice; **en voz baja** in a
whisper

vuela he, she flies **(volar)**

vuestro, -a (of) your(s) *(fam.)*

Y

y and

ya now, already

ya no no longer

¡ya lo creo! I should say so!

yo I

yo no not I

Z

zapatería *f.* shoestore

zapatero *m.* shoemaker

zapatos *m.* shoes

ENGLISH

ENGLISH

SPANISH

SPANISH

SPANISH

Vocabulary

English - Spanish

A

a, an **un, -a**
able, can **poder (ue)**
above **arriba, sobre**
absent **ausente**
advice **consejo;** to the lovelorn **consultorio sentimental**
affectionately **cariñosamente**
after **después (de)**
afternoon **la tarde;** good afternoon **buenas tardes;** in the afternoon **por la tarde;** P.M. **de la tarde**
again **de nuevo, otra vez**
against **contra**
agreed! **¡concedido!** in agreement **de acuerdo**
air **el aire;** in the open air **al aire libre**
airplane **el avión**
all **todo, -a**
all day **todo el día**
all right **bueno, -a**
always **siempre**
A.M. **de la mañana**
angry **enojado, -a**
animal **el animal**
announcer **el locutor**
another **otro, -a**
answer **la respuesta;** to answer **contestar, responder**
ant **la hormiga**
apartment **el piso, el apartamiento**
apple **la manzana**
appointment **la cita**

April **abril**
arm **el brazo**
armchair **el sillón**
to arrive **llegar**
as **como;** as . . . as **tan . . . como**
to ask for **pedir**
at **a, en;** at once **en seguida;** at the **al, a la, en el, en la;** at last **al fin;** at least **al menos**
to attend **asistir (a)**
attention **la atención;** to pay attention **prestar atención**
attentively **con atención**
August **agosto**
aunt **la tía**
automobile **el automóvil**
autumn **el otoño**
avenue **la avenida**

B

bad **malo, -a**
bachelor **el solterón, el soltero**
baker **el panadero**
bakery **la panadería**
barber shop **la barbería**
basement **el sótano**
basket **el cesto, la cesta**
bathroom **el cuarto de baño**
to be **estar;** to be standing **estar de pie;** to be well (ill) **estar bien (mal)**
to be **ser;** to be time to **ser hora de + *inf.*;** to be afraid **tener miedo;** be cold **tener frío;** be hungry

tener **hambre;** be in a hurry **tener prisa;** be sleepy **tener sueño;** be thirsty **tener sed;** be warm **tener calor;** be . . . years old **tener . . . años**
beach **la playa**
beautiful **hermoso, -a**
because **porque;** because of **a causa de**
bed **la cama**
bedroom **el dormitorio**
before **antes (de)**
behind **detrás (de)**
to believe **creer;** believe so (not) **creer que sí (no)**
bell **el timbre**
below **abajo**
between **entre**
better **mejor**
best **el mejor**
bicycle **la bicicleta**
big **grande**
bird **el pájaro**
birthday **el cumpleaños**
bit of **un poco de . . .**
blackboard **la pizarra**
blond **rubio, -a**
blouse **la blusa**
blow **el golpe**
to blow (out) **soplar**
blue **azul**
boat **el barco, el bote**
body **el cuerpo**
bone **el hueso**
book **el libro**
bored **aburrido, -a**
to be born **nacer**
to bother **molestar**

boy **el chico, el muchacho**

bread **el pan**

breakfast **el desayuno**; to breakfast **tomar el desayuno**

bridge **el puente**

to bring **traer**

brother **el hermano**; brother-in-law **el cuñado**

brown **pardo, -a**

brunette **moreno, -a**

building **el edificio**

bus **el autobús, la guagua (Carib.)**

butcher **el carnicero**

butchershop **la carnicería**

butter **la mantequilla**

to buy **comprar**

by **por**; by no means **de ninguna manera**

C

cake **la torta**

camp **el campamento**; summer camp **el campamento de verano**

can **poder (ue)**

Canada **el Canadá**

candle **la vela**

cap **la gorra**

captain **el capitán**

car **el carro, el coche**

cardboard **el cartón**

carnation **el clavel**

carnival **el carnaval**

carpet **la alfombra**

to carry **llevar**

Castillian **el castellano**

cat **el gato**

cave **la caverna**

chair **la silla**

chalk **la tiza**

to change **cambiar**

channel **el canal**

character **el personaje**

cheerful **alegre**

cheese **el queso**

cherry **la cereza**

Chinese **el chino**

Christmas **la Navidad**

church **la iglesia**

class **la clase**

classsroom **la sala de clase**

clinic **el consultorio**

closet **el armario**

clothes **la ropa**; clothing store **la tienda de ropa**

cloud **la nube**

coffee (house) **el café**

cold **el frío** (weather); **el resfriado** (illness); to be cold (persons) **tener frío**; to be cold weather **hacer frío**

color **el color**

Columbus **Colón**

Columbus Day **el Día de la Raza**

to come **venir**

comfortable **cómodo, -a**

concert **el concierto**

congratulations **felicidades, felicitaciones**

to conserve **conservar**

to construct **construir**

to consume **consumir**

contest **el concurso**

cool **fresco, -a**; to be cool **hacer fresco**

cotton **el algodón**

country **el país, la patria** (nation)

cousin **el primo, la prima**

cover **la tapa**

cow **la vaca**

to crash **chocar**

crazy **loco, -a**

cup **la taza, la copa**

curtain **la cortina**

to cut **cortar**

D

to dance **bailar**

dangerous **peligroso, -a**

date **la fecha**; what's today's date? **¿cuál es la fecha de hoy? ¿a cuántos estamos hoy?**

daughter **la hija**

day **el día**; the next day **al día siguiente**; everyday **todos los días**

December **diciembre**

defense attorney **el abogado defensor**

democracy **la democracia**

department store **el almacén**

desk **el escritorio, el pupitre**

dessert **el postre**

dictation **el dictado**

dictatorship **la dictadura**

to die **morir**

different **diferente**

difficult **difícil**

to dine **cenar, comer**; dining room **el comedor**; dinner **la cena, la comida**

dish **el plato**

district **el barrio**

district attorney **el fiscal**

divided by **dividido por**

to do **hacer**; to do well (on an examination) **salir bien**; to do poorly **salir mal**

doctor **el doctor, el médico**

dog **el perro**

doll **la muñeca**

door **la puerta**

downstairs **piso de abajo**

dozen **la docena**

dreaming **soñando**

dress **el vestido**

to drink **beber, tomar**

driver **el chófer**

to drive **conducir, manejar, guiar**

to drop **dejar caer**

drunk **borracho, -a**

duty **el deber**

E

ear **la oreja, el oído**

early **temprano**

to earn **ganar**

earth **la tierra**

east **el este**
Easter **la Pascua Florida**
easy **fácil**
to eat **comer**
egg **el huevo;** hard-boiled
  eggs **huevos duros**
eight **ocho**
eighteen **diez y ocho**
elephant **el elefante**
elevator **el ascensor**
eleven **once**
to end **terminar**
England **Inglaterra;** English
  el inglés; Englishman **el
  inglés**
to enjoy **gozar**
enough **bastante**
to enter **entrar**
equals **son**
eraser **el borrador**
error **la falta**
evening **la noche;** in the
  evening **por la noche;**
  P.M. **de la noche**
ever **aún**
every **todo, -a;** everybody
  todo el mundo; every
  Sunday **todos los
  domingos;** everything
  todo; every week **todas
  las semanas;** everywhere
  por todas partes
examination **el examen**
to exchange **cambiar**
excuse me! **¡dispense Vd.!,
  ¡perdón!**
exercise **el ejercicio**
exhausted **exhausto, -a**
expensive **caro, -a**
to explain **explicar**
eye **el ojo**

F

face **la cara**
factory **la fábrica**
to fall **caer**
fall **el otoño**
family **la familia**

far (from) **lejos (de)**
farmer **el campesino**
father **el padre**
to fear (be afraid) **tener
  miedo de**
February **febrero**
feeling **el sentido**
few **poco, -a**
field **el campo**
fifteen **quince**
to fill **llenar**
finger **el dedo**
five **cinco**
flag **la bandera**
to flee **huir**
floor **el piso**
flower **la flor**
to fly **volar (ue)**
fog **la neblina**
to follow **seguir**
foot **el pie**
for **para, por**
fork **el tenedor**
fortunately **afortunadamente**
four **cuatro**
fourth **(el) cuarto**
France **Francia**
free **libre;** (for) free **gratis**
French **el francés;**
  Frenchman **el francés**
Friday **viernes**
friend **la amiga, el amigo**
from **de, desde**
front **el frente**
frozen **congelado, -a**
fruit **la fruta**
furniture **los muebles**

G

garden **el jardín**
gentleman **el señor**
Germany **Alemania;** German
  el alemán
Gertrude **Gertrudis**
to get off, down (from) **bajar
  de**
to get on **subir a**
to get seated **tomar asiento**

ghost **el fantasma**
girl **la chica, la muchacha**
to give **dar;** give thanks **dar
  las gracias**
glass **el vaso** (for drinking);
  el vidrio
gloves **los guantes**
to go **ir;** go down **bajar;** go
  for a walk **ir de paseo,
  dar un paseo;** go home **ir
  a casa;** go on foot **ir a
  pie;** go out **salir;** go
  shopping **ir de compras;**
  go to school **ir a la
  escuela;** go up **subir**
gold **el oro**
good **bien, bueno, -a**
goodbye **adiós**
granddaughter **la nieta**
grandfather **el abuelo**
grandmother **la abuela**
grandparents **los abuelos**
grandson **el nieto**
grass **la hierba**
gray **gris**
green **verde**
groceries **los comestibles**
grocery store **la bodega
  (Carib.), la tienda de
  comestibles**
ground **el suelo**
guide **el guía**
guilty **culpable**
gymnasium **el gimnasio**

H

hair **el pelo, el cabello**
half **medio, -a;** (one) half **la
  mitad;** half an hour **media
  hora**
Halloween **la Víspera de
  Todos los Santos**
hand **la mano;** to shake
  hands **dar la mano**
handkerchief **el pañuelo**
to happen **pasar**
happy **alegre, contento, -a,
  feliz**

hardworking **trabajador, -a**

hat **el sombrero**

to have **tener;** to have to **tener que;** to have just **acabar de**

head **la cabeza;** headache **el dolor de cabeza**

health **la salud**

to hear **oír**

heat **el calor;** to be warm (weather) **hacer calor;** to be warm (persons) **tener calor**

Hebrew **el hebreo**

hello **hola**

help **la ayuda**

to help **ayudar**

hen **la gallina**

her **su, sus, la (para) ella**

here **aquí**

high **alto, -a**

him **lo, le, (para) él**

his **su, sus**

home **la casa;** at home **en casa**

homework **la tarea, el trabajo**

horse **el caballo**

hospital **el hospital**

hotel **el hotel**

hour **la hora**

house **la casa;** private house **una casa particular**

how? **¿cómo?;** how are you? **¿cómo está Vd.?;** how are things? **¿qué tal?**

how many? **¿cuántos, -as?**

how much? **¿cuánto, -a?**

how old is he (she)? **¿cuántos años tiene?**

hunger **el hambre** *(fem.);* to be hungry **tener hambre**

hurry **la prisa;** in a hurry **de (con) prisa**

to hurt **doler**

husband **el marido**

I

illness **la enfermedad**

imaginary **imaginario, -a**

important **importante**

in **a, en**

in a hurry **a prisa**

infant **el nene**

in front **al frente**

in front of **delante de**

ink **la tinta**

in order to **para**

inside **dentro**

intelligent **inteligente**

interview **la entrevista**

invitation **la invitación**

iron **el hierro**

Italian **el italiano**

Italy **Italia**

J

jacket **la chaqueta**

January **enero**

jail **la cárcel**

job **el empleo, el puesto**

judge **el juez**

July **julio**

to jump **saltar**

K

to keep **guardar**

key **la llave**

kitchen **la cocina**

knife **el cuchillo**

to know **conocer;** (acquainted), **saber;** to know how **saber** + *inf.*

L

label **la etiqueta**

lamp **la lámpara**

language **la lengua**

large **grande**

late **tarde**

later **más tarde**

Latin **el latín**

lawyer **el abogado**

lazy **perezoso, -a**

to learn **aprender**

at least **a lo menos**

to leave **salir (de)**

left **el izquierdo;** to the left **a la izquierda**

leg **la pierna**

lemon **el limón**

lesson **la lección**

letter-carrier **el cartero**

life **la vida**

to like (be pleasing) **gustar**

lion **el león**

lips **los labios**

to listen (to) **escuchar**

little **poco, -a;** little by little **poco a poco**

to live **vivir**

living room **la sala**

loafer **el holgazán**

long **largo, -a**

to look (at) **mirar**

love **el amor**

to love **querer (a)**

luck **la suerte**

lunch **el almuerzo;** to have lunch **almorzar (ue), tomar el almuerzo**

M

magazine **la revista**

to make **hacer**

many **muchos, -as**

map **el mapa**

March **marzo**

mark **la nota;** to get a mark **sacar una nota**

market **el mercado**

to marry **casarse (con)**

master of ceremonies **maestro de ceremonias**

May **mayo**

meal **la comida**

to mean **querer decir, significar;** what does . . . mean? **¿qué quiere decir . . . ?**

meat **la carne**

menu **la lista de platos**

merchant **el comerciante**

343

Merry Christmas **Feliz Navidad**
method **el método**
Mexico **México**
Michael **Miguel**
microphone **el micrófono**
midnight **la medianoche**
in the middle **en medio de**
milk **la leche**
minus **menos**
minute **el minuto**
Miss **(la) señorita**
to be missing **faltar**
mistaken **equivocado, -a**
mixture **la mezcla**
Monday **lunes**
money **el dinero**
monkey **el mono**
month **el mes**
moon **la luna**
more **más**
morning **la mañana;** good morning **buenos días;** in the morning **por la mañana**
mother **la madre**
mountain **el monte**
mouth **la boca**
movie **la película**
movies **el cine**
Mr. **(el) señor**
much **mucho, -a**
murder **el asesinato**
museum **el museo**
music **la música**
my **mi, mis; mío, -a**

N

name **el nombre;** what is your name? **¿cómo se llama Vd.?, ¿cómo te llamas?;** to be called **llamarse**
napkin **la servilleta**
narrow **estrecho, -a**
near **cerca (de)**
to need **necesitar**

neighbor **el vecino, la vecina**
neighborhood **el vecindario, el barrio**
nephew **el sobrino**
never **nunca**
new **nuevo, -a;** nothing's new **sin novedad**
New York **Nueva York**
newspaper **el periódico**
niece **la sobrina**
night **la noche;** good night (evening) **buenas noches;** last night **anoche;** at night **de noche**
nine **nueve**
nineteen **diez y nueve**
no? **¿no?**
noise **el ruido**
none **ninguno, -a**
noon **el mediodía**
no one **nadie**
north **el norte**
nose **la nariz**
not I **yo no**
notebook **el cuaderno**
nothing **nada**
November **noviembre**
now **ahora**
number **el número**
nurse **la enfermera**
nylon **el nilón**

O

October **octubre**
of **de;** of course **por supuesto**
office **la oficina**
often **a menudo**
O.K. **está bien**
old **viejo, -a**
to be ____ years old **tener ____ años**
older **mayor**
omelet **la tortilla**
on **en, sobre**
one **un, una, uno**

only **solamente, sólo; único, -a**
to open **abrir**
or **o, u**
orange **la naranja**
orange (color) **anaranjado, -a**
orange juice **jugo de naranja**
other(s) **otro(s)**
our **nuestro, -a**
outside **afuera**
over **sobre**
overcoat **el abrigo**
to owe **deber**
own **propio, -a**

P

package **el paquete**
page **la página**
pair **el par, la pareja**
palace **el palacio**
pants **los pantalones**
paper **el papel**
paragraph **el párrafo**
parents **los padres**
park **el parque**
party **la fiesta**
past **el pasado**
patrol car **el coche patrullero**
pear **la pera**
pen **la pluma**
pencil **el lápiz**
people **la gente**
pepper **la pimienta**
permission **el permiso;** excuse me **con (su) permiso**
pharmacy **la farmacia**
picture **el cuadro, el grabado**
pig **el puerco**
pilot **el piloto**
pity **lástima;** what a pity! **¡qué lástima!**
place **el lugar, el sitio**
plant **la planta**
to play a game **jugar a (ue)**
to play the piano **tocar el piano**

pleasant **simpático, -a**
please **hacer el favor de +**
  inf. **por favor**
plus **y**
P.M. **de la tarde, de la noche**
pocket **el bolsillo**
poor **pobre**
Portuguese **el portugués**
potatoes **las patatas, las**
  papas (Latin-American)
pound **la libra**
prehistoric **prehistórico, -a**
to prepare **preparar**
to present **presentar**
present **el regalo**
president **el presidente**
pretty **bonito, -a, lindo, -a**
price **el precio**
principal **el director, la**
  directora
privilege **el privilegio**
program **el programa**
to put **poner**

Q

quarter **el cuarto**
question **la pregunta;** to
  question **preguntar**

R

radio **la radio, el radio**
railroad **el ferrocarril**
rain **la lluvia;** to rain **llover**
  (ue)
raw **crudo, -a**
razor **la navaja**
to read **leer**
ready **listo, -a**
record **el disco**
record player **el tocadiscos**
red **rojo, -a**
relative **el pariente, la**
  pariente; relatives **los**
  parientes
rent **el alquiler**

republic **la república**
restaurant **el restaurante**
to return **regresar, volver**
  (ue)
rich **rico, -a**
riddle **la adivinanza**
right? **¿verdad?**
right **el derecho;** to the right
  a la derecha; to be right
  tener razón
to ring **sonar;** it rings **suena**
river **el río**
road **el camino**
romantic **romántico, -a**
roof **el techo**
room **el cuarto, la**
  habitación
rooster **el gallo**
rose **la rosa**
rule **la regla**
Russian **el ruso**

S

sad **triste;** sadness **la**
  tristeza
salad **la ensalada**
salary **el sueldo**
salt **la sal**
same **mismo, -a**
Saturday **sábado**
saucer **el platillo**
to say, tell **decir;** how do you
  say . . .? **¿cómo se**
  dice . . .?
scientist **el científico**
scissors **las tijeras**
sea **el mar**
season **la estación**
seat **el asiento**
secret **el secreto**
to see **ver**
to send **enviar**
sentence **la frase**
September **septiembre**
serpent **la serpiente**
seven **siete**
seventeen **diez y siete**

sharp **en punto**
shellfish **el marisco**
shirt **la camisa**
shoes **los zapatos**
shoestore **la zapatería**
short **bajo, -a, bajito, -a,**
  corto, -a
sick **enfermo, -a; mal (o, -a)**
sightseeing bus **el autobús**
  turístico
sign **el letrero**
silver **la plata**
similar **similar**
simple **sencillo, -a**
to sing **cantar**
sir **(el) señor**
six **seis**
sixteen **diez y seis**
skirt **la falda**
sky **el cielo**
sleep **dormir (ue);** to be
  sleepy **tener sueño**
slender **delgado, -a**
small **pequeño, -a**
smile **la sonrisa**
to smoke **fumar**
snow **la nieve;** to snow
  nevar (ie); it snows **nieva**
so **tan;** so much **tanto**
so, so **así, así**
socks **los calcetines**
soda **la gaseosa**
sofa **el sofá**
soldier **el soldado**
solution **la solución**
son **el hijo**
song **la canción**
soon **pronto;** as soon as
  possible **lo más pronto**
  posible; sooner or later
  tarde o temprano
south **el sur**
South America **la América**
  del Sur, Sudamérica;
  South American
  sudamericano, -a
Spain **España;** Spaniard **el**
  (la) español, (-a)
to speak **hablar** **345**

speed **la prisa**

to spend (time) **pasar;**
(money) **gastar**

spoon **la cuchara**

spring **la primavera**

star **la estrella**

to stay in bed **guardar cama**

steamship **el vapor**

to stick out **sacar**

stockings **las medias**

store **la tienda**

story **el cuento**

stove **la estufa**

strange **extraño, -a**

street **la calle**

strong **fuerte**

student **el alumno, la alumna**

to study **estudiar**

stupid **tonto, -a**

subway **el subterráneo**

such (a) **tal**

suddenly **de repente**

suffering **el sufrimiento**

sugar **el azúcar**

suit **el traje**

summer **el verano**

summer vacation **las vacaciones de verano**

sun **el sol;** to be sunny **hacer sol**

Sunday **domingo**

supermarket **el supermercado**

supper **la cena**

surprised **sorprendido, -a**

to sweat **sudar**

swimming **la natación**

T

table **la mesa;** to set the table **poner la mesa**

tablecloth **el mantel**

tailor **el sastre**

to take **tomar;** to take a walk **dar un paseo;** take a horseback ride **dar un**

paseo a caballo; to go on foot **ir a pie;** to take a car ride **dar un paseo en automóvil;** to take out **sacar,** to take pictures **sacar fotos**

tall **alto, -a**

taxi **el taxi**

tea **el té**

to teach **enseñar;** teaching **la enseñanza**

teacher **el maestro, el profesor; la maestra, la profesora**

team **el equipo**

teaspoon **la cucharita**

telephone **el teléfono**

television **la televisión;** T.V. viewer **el televidente**

temple **el templo**

ten **diez**

thank you (very much) **(muchas) gracias**

that **ese, esa, aquel, aquella** (dem. adj.), **que** (rel. pro.)

the **el, los** (masc.), **la, las** (fem.)

theater **el teatro**

their **su, sus**

them **los, las, (para) ellos, -as,**

then **luego**

there **allí**

therefore **por eso**

there is, are **hay;** there was, were **había**

these **estos, -as**

thin **delgado, -a; flaco, -a**

to think (of) **pensar (en)**

third **tercer**

thirst **la sed;** to be thirsty **tener sed**

thirteen **trece**

thirty **treinta**

those **aquellos, -as; esos, -as**

thousand **mil**

three **tres**

throat **la garganta**

to throw **tirar**

Thursday **jueves**

tie **la corbata**

tiger **el tigre**

time **el tiempo;** at the same time **al mismo tiempo;** on time **a tiempo** (instance) few times **pocas veces;** many times **muchas veces**

time **la hora;** at what time? **¿a qué hora?;** at one o'clock **a la una;** at two o'clock **a las dos;** what time is it? **¿qué hora es?;** it's one o'clock **es la una;** it's two o'clock **son las dos;** on the dot **en punto**

times (multiply) **por**

tired **cansado, -a; fatigado, -a**

to **a, en**

today **hoy**

together **junto**

tomorrow **mañana;** until tomorrow **hasta mañana**

tongue **la lengua**

too much **demasiado**

tooth **el diente**

to the **al, a la, a los, a las**

town **el pueblo, la aldea**

train **el tren**

to travel **viajar;** travel agency **la agencia de viajes**

tree **el árbol**

trip **la excursión, el viaje**

truth **la verdad**

Tuesday **martes**

tulip **el tulipán**

twelve **doce**

twenty **veinte**

two **dos**

U

ugly **feo, -a**

umbrella **el paraguas**

uncle **el tío**

under **debajo (de)**
to understand **comprender, entender (ie)**
underwear **la ropa interior**
unfortunately **desafortunadamente**
United Nations **las Naciones Unidas**
United States **los Estados Unidos**
until I see you again **hasta la vista**
until then **hasta luego**
up **arriba;** upstairs **piso de arriba**
us **nos, para nosotros, -as**
to use **usar**
useful **útil**

V

vacation **las vacaciones**
vagrant **el vago**
vegetables **las legumbres, los vegetales**
very **muy**
violet **la violeta**
to visit **visitar**
voice **la voz;** in a low voice **en voz baja**

W

waiter **el mozo, el camerero**
walk **el paseo;** to walk **caminar;** to take a walk **dar un paseo**
wall **la pared**
wallet **la cartera**
to want **desear, querer (ie)**
watch **el reloj**
water **el agua** *(fem.)*

we **nosotros, -as**
weak **débil**
to wear **llevar, usar**
weather **el tiempo;** to be good (bad) weather **hacer buen (mal) tiempo;** to be warm (cold) **hacer calor (frío);** to be sunny (windy) **hacer sol (viento);** to be cool **hacer fresco**
Wednesday **miércoles**
week **la semana;** last week **la semana pasada;** next week **la semana próxima, que viene**
welcome **bienvenido, -a;** you're welcome **de nada, no hay de qué**
well **bien, bueno, -a**
west **el oeste**
what? **¿qué?, ¿cuál?;** what's going on? **¿qué pasa?;** what's the matter? **¿qué hay?;** what's the matter with him? **¿qué tiene él?**
when **cuando**
when? **¿cuándo?**
where **donde**
where? **¿dónde?**
which **que** *(rel. pro.)*
which? **¿qué + *noun*?**
which (one)? **¿cuál?;** which (ones)? **¿cuáles?**
white **blanco, -a**
White House **la Casa Blanca**
who **que** *(rel. pro.);* who? **¿quién?;** of whom? **¿a quién?;** whose? **¿de quién?**
why? **¿por qué?, ¿para qué?**
wide **ancho, -a**
wind **el viento;** to be windy **hacer viento**
window **la ventana, la**

ventanilla *(car or bus)*
wine **el vino**
winter **el invierno**
to wish **desear, querer**
with **con;** with me **conmigo;** with you *(fam.)* **contigo**
without **sin;** without stopping **sin parar**
witness **el testigo**
wolf **el lobo**
woman **la mujer**
wood **la madera**
wooden **de madera**
woods **el bosque**
wool **la lana**
word **la palabra**
work **el trabajo**
to work **trabajar**
worried **preocupado, -a; ansioso, -a**
to be worth **valer**
to write **escribir**

Y

year **el año**
yellow **amarillo, -a**
yesterday **ayer**
you **tú** *(fam.)*
you **usted (es)** *(formal);* **Vd(s).** (abbrev.)
young man (woman) **el (la) joven**
younger **menor**
your **tu, tus** *(fam.)*
your **su, sus** *(formal)*

Z

zoo **el parque zoológico**

Answer Key

Lesson 1: La casa

1. No señor (señorita, señora), no es la puerta. Es el teléfono. 2. No señor (señorita, señora), no es la radio. Es la puerta. 3. Sí señor, es la lampara. 4. No señor, no es el padre. Es el hermano. 5. No señor, no es la madre. Es la hermana. 6. No señor, no es el disco. Es la mesa. 7. Sí señor, es la ventana. 8. No señor, no es el teléfono. Es el disco. 9. No señor, no es la cocina. Es el televisor. 10. No señor, no es la sala. Es la flor.

Lesson 2: La escuela

Exercise A. 1. Es un libro. 2. Es un cuaderno. 3. Es un pupitre. 4. Es una mesa. 5. Es una pizarra. 6. Es una pluma. **Exercise B.** 1. Sí señor (señorita, señora), es un papel. 2. Sí señor, es un cuaderno. 3. No señor, es una mesa. 4. No señor, es una pluma. **Exercise C.** 1. Es un lápiz. 2. Es un libro. 3. Es una pizarra. 4. Es un mapa. 5. Es un televisor. 6. Es una ventana. 7. Es una puerta. 8. Es un gato.

Lesson 3: La ciudad

Exercise A. 1. Es una revista. 2. Es un policía. 3. Es un edificio. 4. Es un coche. 5. Es una mujer. **Exercise B.** 1. No es una revista. Es un periódico. 2. Es un hombre. 3. No es un coche. Es un autobús. 4. Es el cine. 5. No es un profesor. Es un policía. **Exercise C.** 1. El muchacho está en la clase. 2. El policía está en la calle. 3. La madre está en la cocina. 4. La radio está en la mesa. 5. El hombre está en la puerta.

Lesson 4: Los alimentos

Exercise A. 1. Compro una botella de leche. 2. Compro un pan. 3. Compro jugo de naranja. 4. Compro helado (de chocolate). 5. Compro queso. **Exercise B.** 1. No compro helado. Compro mantequilla. 2. No compro naranjas. Compro manzanas. 3. No compro dulces. Compro huevos. 4. Compro flores. 5. No compro una Coca-Cola. Compro una botella de leche.

Lesson 5: Acciones

Exercise A. 1. El profesor escribe en la pizarra. 2. La muchacha come el pan. 3. El alumno sale de la escuela. 4. El policía bebe la Coca-Cola. 5. El hombre lee el periódico. **Exercise B.** 1. La mujer no mira la televisión. Escucha la radio. 2. La hermana canta. 3. El policía no corre. El policía descansa. 4. Carlos no estudia. Mira la televisión. 5. María no come el queso. Bebe la leche.

Lesson 6: Descripciones

Exercise A. 1. El hombre es grande. 2. La lección es difícil. 3. El profesor es perezoso. 4. El alumno es tonto. 5. La madre es trabajadora. **Exercise B.** 1. El elefante no es pequeño. Es grande. 2. No hay pocos alumnos en la clase. Hay muchos. 3. La casa no está aquí. Está allí. 4. La manzana está deliciosa. 5. El hombre come mucho.

Part One: Structures and Verbs

Work Unit 1:

Answers to Reading Exercises: ¡La televisión es muy importante!

Exercise I. A. 1. estudiosa 2. lección de español 3. papel (cuaderno) 4. periódico…sala 5. radio, cocina 6. hermano 7. importante 8. mirar 9. mañana 10. amor, pasión **Ex. I. B.** 1. cuaderno 2. español 3. lápiz 4. televisión. 5. español. **Ex. II. B.** 1. Yo necesito estudiar. 2. Esta noche hay programas interesantes. 3. Es muy fácil. 4. Es mi programa favorito. 5. No es necesario estudiar el español. **Exercise III.** 1. lápiz 2. sala 3. libro 4. cuaderno 5. frase 6. hermano 7. también 8. con 9. fácil 10. ahora 11. hay 12. mira 13. noche 14. lee 15. esta **Exercise IV.** Compositions are Ad Lib.

Answers to Grammar Exercises: The Noun and the Definite Article (Singular)

Exercise I. A. 1. La escuela es interesante. 2. El libro… 3. La alumna… 4. La señorita… 5. El periódico… **Ex. I. B.** 1. El padre estudia mucho. 2. La madre… 3. El hombre… 4. La mujer… 5. El señor… **Ex. I. C.** 1. El examen es importante. 2. La lección… 3. El día… 4. La noche… 5. La televisión… 6. La nación… 7. El programa… 8. La ciudad… 9. La frase… 10. El idioma… 11. El mapa… 12. La cocina… 13. La calle… 14. El español… 15. La clase… **Exercise II.** 1. El señor Moreno mira el programa de televisión. 2. La profesora Mendoza lee el mapa de la ciudad. 3. El presidente Guzmán entra en la capital de la nación. 4. La señorita Gómez estudia el idioma toda la noche. 5. La señorita Molina escucha la radio todo el día. **Exercise III.** 1. Habla español. Pronuncia bien el español. 2. …francés…el francés. 3. …italiano…el italiano. 4. …inglés…el inglés. 5. …alemán…el alemán. **Exercise IV. A.** 1. El alumno estudia en el hotel. 2. …la clase de español. 3. …el edificio. 4. la sala de inglés. 5. …la escuela. **Ex. IV. B.** 1. La alumna escucha la música. 2. …el disco. 3. …el inglés. 4. …el reloj. 5. …la radio. **Ex. IV. C.** 1. El profesor toma el lápiz. 2. …la pluma. 3. …el papel. 4. la casa. 5. …el libro. 6. …el cuaderno. 7. …la gramática. 8. …el avión. 9. …el tren. 10. …el coche. **Exercise V.** 1. La 2. la 3. la 4. la 5. el 6. el 7. La 8. la 9. — 10. el 11. la 12. la 13. el 14. — 15. el 16. — 17. el 18. el 19. — 20. la

Answers to Oral Proficiency Exercises. Sample answers are provided. Your variations are encouraged.

A. El español es fácil. Es también interesante, importante y necesario.
B. Yo necesito el libro de gramática. El diccionario también es importante.
C. Por favor, esta noche, no. Mañana es posible. Yo necesito estudiar. Mi hermana también estudia la lección de español. Mi hermano pone la televisión. Mi madre escucha música y lee el libro. Mi padre lee el periódico y mira su programa favorito con mi hermano.
D. — El examen de español es muy fácil.
  — Es posible estudiar mañana.
  — Quiero mirar "El amor y la pasión."
  — " . . . ." es también mi programa favorito.

Work Unit 2:

Answers to Reading Exercises: Todo es rápido en la ciudad.

Exercise I. A. 1. c 2. d 3. b 4. d **Ex. I. B.** 1.Nueva York es una ciudad grande. 2. Los edificios … 3. …las calles. 4. …las aldeas. 5. …ahora (hoy). **Exercise II.** 1. d 2. e 3. a 4. c 5. b **Exercise III.** 1. lápiz 2. amor 3. cine(s) 4. importante 5. una 6. dinero 7. ahora 8. descansar **Exercise IV.** Compositions are Ad Lib.

Answers to Grammar Exercises: The Noun and the Definite Article (Plural)

Exercise I. 1. Los chicos son estudiosos 2. Las muchachas… 3. Los hombres… 4. Las madres… 5. Las lecciones… 6. Los lápices… 7. Los papeles… 8. Las mujeres… 9. Los profesores… 10. los cines… 11. Las frases… 12. Los trenes… 13. Las ciudades…

14. Los días... 15. Las flores... **Exercise II.** 1. No. Solamente el restaurante grande. 2. ...el museo... 3. ...la aldea... 4. ...la clase... 5. ...el periódico... 6. ...la gramática... 7. ...el edificio... 8. ...el hotel... 9. ...el parque... 10. ...la calle... **Exercise III.** 1. Sí. todos los libros. 2. Sí, todos los papeles. 3. Sí, todas las gramáticas. 4. Sí, todas las canciones. 5. Sí, todos los trenes. 6. Sí, todos los idiomas. 7. Sí, todas las universidades. 8. Sí, todos los mapas. 9. Sí, todas las lecciones de español. 10. Sí, todos los programas de televisión. **Exercise IV.** 1. las 2. los 3. el 4. los 5. Los 6. la 7. el 8. los 9. la 10. la 11. las 12. el 13. los 14. las 15. las 16. los 17. la 18. la 19. Los 20. los.

Answers to Oral Proficiency Exercises. Sample answers are provided. Your variations are encouraged.

Primo(a), en la ciudad es necesario trabajar mucho. Es importante vivir rápido y ganar mucho dinero. En la pequeña aldea es posible descansar y respirar aire fresco. Es fácil vivir en la aldea. En la ciudad as interesante visitar los museos y los teatros. Pero también es muy tonto vivir con mucha prisa.

Work Unit 3:

Answers to Reading Exercises: El cumpleaños de Joselito.

Exercise I. A. 1. cumpleaños, años. 2. mundo, ocupado 3. trabajar, ayudar 4. cantar, bailar 5. refrescos, torta. **Ex. I. B.** 1. Joselito está solo en su cuarto. 2. Los padres compran la magnífica piñata típica. 3. Los amiguitos llevan regalitos. 4. Los vecinos caminan a la casa Hernández. 5. Joselito va a soplar las velas, cortar la torta y tomar el pedazo más grande. Va a ayudar en la fiesta. **Ex. I. C.** 1. Los niños necesitan soplar las velas, cortar la torta y tomar el pedazo más grande. 2. Los hermanos preparan los juegos y las actividades. 3. Yo quiero un regalo, una piñata, etc.... 4. Todo el mundo está contento. 5. Todos gritan:—¡Felicidades! ¡Feliz cumpleaños! **Exercise II.** 1. d 2. e 3. a 4. b 5. c. **Exercise III.** 1. feliz 2. escuchar 3. llegar 4. invitar 5. cumpleaños 6. importante 7. dulces 8. abuela 9. desear 10. escuela 11. soplar.

Answers to Grammar Exercises: Present Indicative Tense of Regular Verbs, AR Conjugation

Exercise I. A. 1. Él... 2. Ella... 3. Ellos... 4. Ellas... 5. Nosotros -as. **Ex. I. B.** 1. Yo bailo. 2. Él baila. 3. Vd. baila. 4. Tú bailas. 5. Vds. bailan. 6. Tú y yo bailamos. 7. Ella baila. 8. Ellas bailan. 9. Ellos bailan. 10. Nosotros bailamos. **Ex. I. C.** 1. a. Sí, ella canta... b. Nosotros cantamos... 2. a. Sí, ellos contestan... b. Pedro contesta... 3. a. Sí, los amigos escuchan... b. Tú y yo escuchamos... 4. a. Sí, yo deseo... b. Juanita y Pablo desean... 5. a. Sí, ellos andan... b. Yo ando... **Ex. I. D.** 1. Sí yo compro... 2. Sí, yo visito... 3. Sí, nosotros estudiamos... 4. Sí, Vds. necesitan... 5. Sí, Vd. (tú) respira(s)... **Ex. I. E.** 1. ¿Escucho yo...? 2. ¿Visita Carlos...? 3. ¿Desean los niños...? 4. ¿Andamos él y yo...? 5. ¿Tomamos café Pedro y yo?

Answers to Oral Proficiency Exercise. *This is the last of the sample answer guides for Oral Proficiency.* Your variations are encouraged here and in the remaining Work Units.

Sí, ¡vamos a gozar! Nosotros compramos regalos y piñatas. Preparamos la torta y juegos. Entramos y gritamos: —¡Felicidades! Bailamos y cantamos con la radio. Cortamos la torta y tomamos pedazos deliciosos.

Work Unit 4:

Answers to Reading Exercises: La carta misteriosa.

Exercise I. A. 1. recibe (lee); comprende. 2. sabe; escribe. 3. sale; corre. 4. abre; vive. 5. asisten; comen. **Ex. I. B.** 1. Juanita lee la invitación. 2. Es muy tarde. 3. Ella no sabe quién escribe la carta (qué reunión es; por qué es a las once; es tarde; no hay nadie en las calles; está loca de curiosidad). 4. Es a las once de la noche. 5. No hay luz. Un fantasma abre la puerta. **Ex. I. C.** 1. Es necesario escribir invitaciones para (invitar a los amigos á) las fiestas. 2. Hay tortas, helados y dulces. 3. Necessitamos música. 4. Todo el mundo escribe cartas a los amigos. 5. El treinta y uno de octubre es misterioso porque es la Víspera de Todos Los Santos y hay fantasmas con máscaras en las calles a las once de la noche. **Exercise II.** 1. fiesta 2. aquí 3. nerviosa 4. tarde 5. abre 6. sorprendida 7. misteriosa 8. amigo.

Answers to Grammar Exercises: Present Indicative Tense of ER and IR Conjugations

Exercise I. A. 1. Ella... 2. Él... 3. Ellas... 4. Nosotros... 5. Ellas... **Ex. I. B.** 1. Yo respondo... 2. Vd. responde... 3. Tú respondes... 4. Ella responde... 5. Vds. responden... 6. Vd. y yo respondemos... 7. Ellos responden... 8. Él responde... 9. Nosotras respondemos... 10. Él y ella responden... **Ex. I. C.** 1. a. Sí, nosotros comemos... b. La niña come... 2. a. Sí, yo respondo... b. María responde... 3. a. Sí, ellos aprenden... b. Nosotros respondemos... 4. a. Sí, José lee... b. Yo leo... 5. a. Sí, nosotros comprendemos... b. Los muchachos comprenden... **Ex. I. D.** 1. Sí, yo corro... 2. Sí, nosotros vendemos... 3. Sí, María y yo creemos... 4. Sí, las primas ponen... 5. Sí, yo como... **Exercise II. A.** 1. Ella... 2. Vds.... 3. Ellas... 4. Ellos... 5. Nosotros -as... **Ex. II. B.** 1. Tú asiste... 2. Vd. asiste... 3. Ellos asisten... 4. Vds. asisten... 5. Ella y yo asistimos... 6. Ellas asisten... 7. Yo asisto... 8. Él asiste... 9. Ella asiste... 10. Nosotras asistimos... **Ex. II. C.** 1. a. Sí, Carlos recibe... b. Las hermanas reciben... 2. a. Sí, los amigos escriben... b. Nosotros escribimos... 3. a. Sí, yo vivo... b. Los primos viven... 4. a. Sí, Vd. cubre... b. Nosotros cubrimos... 5. a. Sí, nosotros subimos... b. Luis sube... **Ex. II. D.** 1. Sí, Ana y Vd. abren los periódicos. 2. Sí, yo cubro... 3. Sí, nosotros partimos... 4. Sí, yo describo... 5. Sí, el profesor omite... 6. Sí, yo asisto... 7. Sí, Juanita recibe... 8. Sí, yo vivo... 9. Sí, Vds. escriben... 10. Sí, ellos suben... **Ex. III A.** 1. Señor López, Vd. entra... 2. Señora Gómez, Vd. cree... 3. Profesor Ruiz, Vd. vive... 4. Señorita Marín, Vd. toca... 5. Doctor Muñoz, Vd. escribe... **Ex. III. B.** 1. Pepe, tú trabajas... 2. Ana, tú contestas... 3. Carlos, tú aprendes... 4. Niño, tú corres... 5. Niña, tú describes... **Ex. III. C.** 1. ¿Comprendo yo...? 2. ¿Corre Carlitos...? 3. ¿Desean los niños...? 4. ¿Asistimos él y yo...? 5. ¿Tomamos Pedro y yo...?

Work Unit 5:

Answers to Reading Exercises: ¿Conoce usted historia?

Exercise I. A. 1. historia 2. inteligente, aplicado 3. estudia, aprende 4. muerto 5. enfermo **Ex. I. B.** 1. El señor... es presidente de los Estados Unidos. 2. Una persona que está enferma va al hospital. 3. Debo ir a la escuela para aprender. 4. No hay (Hay...) alumnos perezosos en la clase de español. 5. Aprendo mucho de los Estados Unidos en la clase de historia. **Exercise II.** 1. El profesor decide usar otros métodos. 2. Jaimito va a contestar primero. 3. Estoy en esta clase de historia tres años. 4. ¿Dónde vive el presidente? 5. ¿Quién es el presidente de los Estados Unidos?

Answers to Grammar Exercises: Simple Negative; Interrogative Words

Exercise I. 1. a. Ellos no hablan de la chica. b. ¿No hablan ellos de la chica? 2. a. Vd. no canta en la fiesta b. ¿No canta Vd. en la fiesta? 3. a. Tú no escribes mucho. b. ¿No escribes tú mucho? 4. a. Nosotros -as no vendemos periódicos b. ¿No vendemos nosotros periódicos? 5. a. Yo no vivo en la ciudad. b. ¿No vivo yo en la ciudad? **Exercise II.** 1. a. Yo no como mucho en el café. b. Los amigos no comen mucho en el café. 2. a. Yo no estudio... b. Luis no estudia 3. a. Nosotros -as no comprendemos... b. Las alumnas no comprenden... 4. a. Rosa y yo no asistimos... b. Jorge y Elisa no asisten... 5. a. Juan y Vd. no abren... b. Nosotros -as no abrimos... **Exercise III.** 1. a. ¿Cómo escribe Ana la lección? b. Ana escribe la lección de prisa. 2. a. ¿Cuándo toma Luis el tren? b. Luis toma el tren ahora. 3. a. ¿Cuántos alumnos leen la pregunta? b. Tres alumnos leen la pregunta. 4. a. ¿Dónde escuchan la niña y su madre al Doctor Solar? b. La niña y su madre escuchan al médico en el hospital. 5. a. ¿Qué leemos mi amigo y yo? b. Mi amigo y yo leemos la pregunta. 6. a. ¿Quién recibe la invitación? b. El chico recibe la invitación. 7. a. ¿Quiénes preguntan mucho? b. Las chicas preguntan mucho. 8. ¿A quién escribimos Marta y yo? b. Marta y yo escribimos al padre. 9. a. ¿Por qué aprende la alumna muchas cosas? b. La alumna aprende muchas cosas porque escucha bien. 10. a. ¿Para qué compra Luis fruta? b. Luis compra fruta para la fiesta de Ana. **Exercise IV. A.** 1. ¿Cómo preparas tú la lección? 2. ...prepara Vd... 3. ...preparan ellos... 4. ...preparamos nosotros... **Ex. IV. B.** 1. ¿Qué canto yo? 2. ...cantan Vds.? 3. ...cantamos Juan y yo? **Ex. IV. C.** 1. ¿Dónde bebe el animal? 2.

. . . bebemos nosotros? 3. . . . bebes tú? 4. bebe Vd.? **Ex. IV. D.** 1. ¿Cuántas papas fritas come Ana? 2. . . . comen ellos? 3. . . . comemos tú y yo? **Ex. IV. E.** 1. ¿A quién escribe Pepe? 2. . . . escribimos Vd. y yo? 3. . . . escriben las niñas? 4. . . . escribe Vd.? **Ex. IV. F.** 1. ¿No vivimos nosotros en Los Ángeles? 2. ¿Quién no vive . . . 3. ¿Quiénes no viven . . . **Ex. IV. G.** 1. ¿Cuándo toma ella el tren? 2. . . . toma su familia . . . 3. . . . tomamos nosotras . . . **Ex. IV. H.** 1. ¿Para qué aprendemos nosotros el español? 2. . . . aprendo yo . . . 3. . . . aprenden él y ella . . . **Ex. IV. I.** 1. ¿Por qué partimos Vd. y yo? 2. . . . partes tú? 3. . . . parten Vds.? **Exercise V. A.** 1. a. Él no anda a la escuela. b. Nosotros no andamos a la clase. c. ¿Quién no anda a la clase? 2. a. ¿Cuándo corro yo a casa? b. Juanito, ¿cuándo corres a casa? c. ¿Cuándo corre bien el señor Torres? 3. a. ¿A quién escribe ella? b. ¿A quiénes escribimos nosotros -as? c. ¿A quiénes escriben ellos -as? **Ex. V. B.** 1. a. Aquí no compran periódicos. b. Aquí no leemos periódicos. c. Aquí no recibes periódicos. 2. a. ¿Cómo contestas tú, Juan? b. ¿Cómo comprende María? c. ¿Cómo partimos? 3. a. ¿Dónde escuchamos? b. ¿Dónde aprendes tú, Ana? c. ¿Dónde asisten ellos? 4. a. ¿Por qué abre Vd. la ventana? b. ¿Por qué cubrimos la ventana? 5. a. ¿Cuánto dinero deseamos? b. ¿Cuánta fruta vendemos? c. ¿Cuántos libros necesitan? 6. a. ¿Quién no vive en casa? b. ¿Quién(es) no trabaja(n) en casa? c. ¿Quién(es) no responde(n) en casa? 7. a. ¿Qué no pregunto yo? b. ¿Qué no escribimos nosotros? c. ¿Qué no practica ella?

Work Unit 6:
Answers to Reading Exercises: El trabajo de la mujer es fácil

Exercise I. 1. Alicia no va de compras hoy porque está enferma. 2. Alicia necesita unas cosas de la tienda de comestibles. 3. Antonio va a la tienda de comestibles. 4. Antonio compra una docena de huevos, una botella de leche, un pan, una libra de mantequilla, queso, jugo de naranja y unas manzanas. 5. Todo eso es cinco dólares, cincuenta centavos. 6. Es inteligente porque compra todo sin lista. **Exercise II.** 1. docena 2. huevos 3. queso 4. dólares 5. centavos 6. jugo 7. leche 8. fruta 9. pan 10. tres 11. libra 12. ¿cuánto? 13. cosas 14. sale 15. sé **Exercise III.** Personalized answers: Ad Lib.

Answers to Grammar Exercises: The Indefinite Articles: Un, Una, Unos, Unas

Exercise I. 1. Un diccionario interesante. 2. Una revista . . . 3. Un profesor . . . 4. Un periódico . . . 5. Una ciudad . . . 6. Una lección . . . 7. *Una pensión . . . 8. Un programa . . . 9. Un día . . . 10. Una música . . . **Exercise II.** 1. No, solamente un cuaderno. 2. una palabra. 3. . . . una frase. 4. . . . un lápiz. 5. . . . un idioma. **Exercise III.** 1. No. Solamente unos periódicos. 2. . . . unas revistas. 3. . . . unas lecciones. 4. . . . unos programas. 5. . . . unas ciudades. **Exercise IV.** 1. una 2. unos 3. una 4. un 5. unas. **Exercise V.** 1. una 2. unas 3. unos 4. un 5. unas. **Exercise VI.** 1. un 2. una 3. un 4. un 5. unos 6. la 7. una 8. el 9. un 10. una 11. la 12. la 13. unas 14. los 15. las.

Work Unit 7:
Answers to Reading Exercises: Vamos a un país tropical

Exercise I. A. 1. Marta desea descansar en una playa bonita. 2. Miguel prefiere pasar las vacaciones donde no hace calor. 3. Quieren nadar y tomar el sol en Chile en junio. 4. Es el invierno en Chile en junio. 5. Es posible esquiar en junio en Chile, cuando hace calor aquí. **Ex. I. B.** 1. Hoy hace . . . 2. Quiero ir a . . . 3. Hace sol y calor en . . . 4. Todo el mundo va a la playa. 5. Hace mucho frío en diciembre, enero y febrero. **Exercise II.** 1. primavera 2. mes 3. amor 4. mayo 5. invierno 6. sol **Exercise III.** 3, 5, 1, 4, 2 **Exercise IV.** Compositions are Ad Lib.

Answers to Grammar Exercises: Cardinal Numbers 1–31; Times, Days, Months, Seasons

Exercise I. 1. nueve 2. veinte y tres (veintitrés) 3. diez 4. doce 5. veinte y uno (veintiuno) 6. treinta 7. diez y seis (dieciséis) 8. ocho 9. quince 10. veinte y siete (veintisiete) 11. diez y siete (diecisiete) 12. catorce 13. seis 14. cuatro 15. treinta. **Exercise II.** 1. Si hoy es lunes, mañana es martes. 2. . . . sábado, . . . domingo. 3. . . . miércoles, . . . jueves. 4. . . . jueves, . . . viernes. 5. . . . viernes, . . . sábado. **Exercise III.** 1. abril 2. mayo 3. junio 4. agosto 5. septiembre 6. octubre 7. diciembre 8. enero 9. diciembre 10. primero. **Exercise IV.** 1. Es la . . . (1:15) 2. Son las . . . (2:30). 3. Son las . . . (12:15). 4. Es la . . . (12:35). 5. Son las . . . (10:45). **Exercise V.** 1. . . . tres y media de la tarde. 2. . . . una menos cuarto (quince) de la mañana. 3. . . . cuatro menos veinte de la tarde. 4. . . . hora es? 5. . . . a la una y cuarto (quince). **Exercise VI.** 1. Sí, estudiamos a las cinco de la tarde. 2. Sí, tomamos el almuerzo a la una de la tarde. 3. Sí, dormimos a las once menos veinte de la noche. 4. Sí, toman el desayuno a las nueve y media de la mañana. 5. Sí, estudian a la una menos cuarto de la tarde. **Exercise VII.** 1. a. Hoy no es miércoles el treinta y uno de diciembre. b. Hoy es jueves el primero de enero. 2. a. No es todavía la primavera en el mes de junio. b. Tenemos . . . el verano en el mes de julio. 3. a. No son las doce del mediodía. b. Es la una de la tarde. 4. a. No llegamos el miércoles el treinta de septiembre. b. Llegamos el jueves el primero de octubre. 5. a. No celebramos el día de la Navidad el veinte y cuatro de noviembre. b. Celebramos . . . el veinte y cinco de diciembre. **Exercise VIII.** 1. . . . lunes, martes, miércoles, jueves y viernes. 2. El sábado . . . 3. El domingo . . . 4. . . . siete . . . 5. . . . treinta y un . . . 6. . . . veinte y cuatro . . . 7. . . . a las ocho y media de la mañana. 8. . . . veinte y una . . . 9. a las tres y veinte y cinco de la tarde. 10. . . . a las once menos veinte de la noche.

Work Unit 8:

Answers to Reading Exercises: Así es la vida

Exercise I. A. 1. . . sale 2. ve . . . cita 3. cae . . . pone 4. cine . . . fin . . . semana 5. equipo . . . fútbol **Ex. I. B.** 1. Este sábado voy . . . 2. (No) Estoy ocupado(a). 3. Dan . . . 4. Voy . . . después de la clase de español. 5. Cuando tengo unos momentos libres . . . **Exercise II.** 1. Perdone, señorita, ¿es éste su libro? 2. Voy a mi clase de álgebra. 3. Ve a Josefina delante de él. 4. Este sábado dan una película buena. **Exercise III.** 1. Paco invita a Josefina al cine. 2. Josefina no tiene tiempo libre. 3. Alejandro invita a Josefina a ver una película. 4. Josefina no está ocupada y sale. 5. Alejandro es el capitán del equipo de fútbol.

Answers to Grammar Exercises: Irregular Verbs of the Present Tense

Exercise I. 1. Yo veo la tarea. 2. Yo traigo . . . 3. Yo tengo . . . 4. Yo hago . . . 5. Yo digo . . . 6. Yo sé . . . **Exercise II.** 1. —Yo salgo ahora. 2. Yo conozco . . . 3. Yo vengo . . . 4. Yo le traigo . . . 5. Yo caigo . . . 6. Yo hago . . . 7. Yo pongo . . . 8. Yo voy . . . 9. Yo oigo . . . 10. Yo le doy . . . **Exercise III. A.** 1. Tú vienes a papá, le dices hola, y le das un beso. 2. Él viene . . . dice . . . da . . . 3. Ellos vienen . . . dicen . . . dan . . . 4. Nosotros venimos . . . decimos . . . damos . . . 5. Vd. viene . . . dice . . . da . . . 6. Yo vengo . . . digo . . . doy . . . **Ex. III. B.** 1. Tú vas a casa y oyes la canción que tienes que aprender. 2. El chico va . . . oye . . . tiene . . . 3. Las chicas van . . . oyen . . . tienen . . . 4. Tú y yo vamos . . . oímos . . . tenemos . . . 5. Vds. van . . . oyen . . . tienen . . . 6. Yo voy . . . oigo . . . tengo . . . **Exercise IV.** 1. a. Sí, voy a la escuela. b. Ellos también van a la escuela. 2. a. Sí, oyen . . . b. Yo . . . oigo . . . c. Vds. . . . oyen . . . (Nosotros oímos . . .). 3. a. Sí, digo . . . b. Nosotros . . . decimos . . . c. Luisa . . . dice . . . 4. a. Sí, viene . . . b. Yo . . . vengo . . . c. Nosotros . . . venimos . . . (Vds. vienen) 5. a. Sí, Vds. tienen . . . (nosotros tenemos) b. Yo . . . tengo c. Ellos . . . tienen . . . 6. a. Sí, veo . . . b. Ellos . . . ven 7. a. Sí, doy . . . b. Vd. . . . da . . . (tú das . . .) 8. a. Sí, Juan . . . trae . . . b. Yo . . . traigo . . . 9. a. Sí, conozco . . . b. Juan y yo . . . conocemos . . . 10. a. Sí, sé . . . b. Ellas . . . saben . . . 11. a. Sí, salgo . . . b. Salimos . . . (Vds. salen . . .) 12. a. Sí, pongo . . . b. Tú y yo . . . ponemos . . . 13. a. Sí, hago . . . b. Lola y yo hacemos . . . **Exercise V.** 1. (Yo) salgo de la casa ahora. 2. (Yo) traigo . . . 3. (Yo) vengo . . . 4. (Yo) veo . . . 5. (Yo) pongo . . . 6. (Yo) doy . . . 7. (Yo) hago . . . 8. (Yo) digo . . . 9. (Yo) sé . . . 10. (Yo) tengo . . . 11. (Yo) conozco . . . 12. (Yo) oigo . . . 13. (Yo) voy . . . 14. (Yo) (me) caigo . . . 15. (Yo) digo . . .

Work Unit 9:

Answers to Reading Exercises: Una excursión por la ciudad

Exercise I. A. 1. Diego y Hortensia visitan a los Estados Unidos. 2. El primer autobús sale a las doce en punto. 3. Tienen veinte pisos. 4. En el parque es posible mirar los animales, sacar fotos o tomar un helado. 5. Ella tiene billetes para todos los cabarets. **Ex. I. B.** 1. Hay hoteles, museos y grandes almacenes. 2. El subterráneo corre debajo de la tierra. 3. Hay muchos rascacielos en el barrio comercial. 4. Es bueno tomar un autobús turístico. 5. Es bueno descansar en un hotel o en casa. **Exercise II.** 1. Bienvenidos a esta excursión. 2. Vds. ven los edificios de la universidad a la izquierda. 3. A la derecha . . . la Biblioteca Central. 4. Esta es una ciudad famosa por sus rascacielos. 5. Es posible caminar y tomar un helado. **Exercise III.** 1. c 2. e 3. d 4. a 5. b **Exercise IV.** Compositions are Ad Lib.

Answers to Grammar Exercises: Uses of the Preposition "a"

Exercise I. 1. —Sí, camino al centro. 2. . . .viajo al campo. 3. . . .corro a la tienda 4. . . .hablo a la chica. 5. . . .corro a los museos. 6. . . .camino a los parques. 7. . . .regreso a las clases. 8. . . .hablo a María. 9. . . .viajo a España. 10. . . .regreso al amigo pronto. **Exercise II.** 1. Regreso a la oficina. 2. . . .al subterráneo 3. . . .a las escuelas. 4. . . .a los parques. 5. . . .a la casa. 6. . . .a la biblioteca. 7. . . .al centro. 8. . . .al autobús 9. . . .al museo. 10. . . .a Pedro. **Exercise III.** 1. Escucho el piano con atención. 2. . . .al alumno. . . 3. . . .las guitarras. . . 4. . . .a las amigas. . . 5. . . .los discos. . . 6. . . .a Luis. . . 7. . . .a los señores. . . 8. . . .la música. . . 9. . . .a la madre. . . 10. . . .a Ana. . . **Exercise IV.** 1. a. Necesito el lápiz. b. Necesito al amigo. 2. a. Visito los países. b. . . .a los primos. 3. a. Escucho la radio. b. . . .a la madre. 4. a. Prefiero las melodías. b. . . .a las niñas. 5. a. Miro el programa. b. . . .al chico. **Exercise V.** 1. Tienen un profesor. 2. comprendo el libro. 3. Escucho a las profesoras. 4. Miras el cuadro. 5. Miran la ciudad. **Exercise VI.** 1. a la 2. el. . .la 3. — . . .al 4. — 5. a. . .a la 6. — . . .a. . .a 7. a los 8. al 9. al 10. — **Exercise VII.** 1. A las nueve miramos el reloj. 2. Vamos a la clase y escuchamos al profesor. 3. Tenemos un amigo allí y hablamos a Luis. 4. Escuchamos las respuestas y copiamos las palabras. 5. Estudiamos las lecciones y comprendemos a los profesores.

Work Unit 10:

Answers to Reading Exercises: ¿De quién es este hueso?

Exercise I. A. 1. regalos 2. etiquetas 3. un día 4. cambiar 5. un hueso **Ex. I. B.** 1. Uso "Feliz Navidad". 2. Un buen regalo para un abuelo es una navaja o. . . 3. Es para Rosalía. 4. Un buen regalo es una falda. 5. No quiero recibir un hueso. Quiero. . . **Exercise II.** *Horizontales:* 1. Navidad 6. al 7. va 9. nene 12. el 14. Yo 15. sorpresas 16. viejo 17. hay. *Verticales:* 1. navajas 2. ve 3. dar 4. al 5. abuelos 7. lee 10. perro 11. ir 13. le 14. ya **Exercise III.** 1. d 2. c 3. a 4. b 5. e

Answers to Grammar Exercises: Use of the Preposition "de"

Exercise I. 1. Los sombreros son del chico. 2. . . .de la abuela 3. . . .del abuelo 4. . . .de Juan. 5. . . .de mi padre. 6. . . .de los hermanos. 7. . . .de María y de Pedro. 8. . . .de sus amigos. 9. . . .de las primas. 10. . . .del hermano y de la hermana **Exercise II.** 1. Las casas son del profesor. 2. Ella es la madre de la muchacha. 3. Somos los profesores del chico. 4. Es el padre de la alumna. 5. Es la clase del alumno de español. **Exercise III.** 1. Es el libro de la prima. 2. Son las flores de los muchachos. 3. Son los cuadernos del chico. 4. Es. . .de mis padres. 5. Es. . .del primo. 6. Son. . .de Juan y de Luisa. 7. Son. . .del hombre. 8. Es. . .de las hermanas. 9. Es. . .de los chicos. 10. Son. . .del muchacho. **Exercise IV.** 1. Soy de los Estados Unidos. 2. Estoy en la clase de historia. 3. Mi casa es de piedra. 4. Las cortinas son de algodón. 5. Mi abuelo es del otro país. 6. Mi reloj es de plata y de oro. 7. Mi hermanito hable del parque. 8. Mi hermanita va a la clase de inglés. 9. Mi blusa y mi falda son de lana y de seda. 10. La profesora de español enseña aquí. **Exercise V.** 1. De 2. de 3. del 4. de la 5. de 6. del 7. de los 8. de las 9. de 10. de 11. De 12. de 13. de 14. de 15. de 16. De 17. de 18. del 19. de 20. de los. **Exercise VI.** 1. el coche de su (tu) padre? 2. la casa de la chica. 3. mi clase de historia. 4. ¿De qué es su blusa? 5. de algodón y de seda. 6. ¿De quién es la revista? 7. la revista del chico. 8. las revistas de Roberto. 9. el cuaderno de los niños. 10. mi profesora de español.

Work Unit 11:

Answers to Reading Exercises: ¿Quién soy yo?

Exercise I. 1. Virgilio no presta atención a la profesora. 2. Lee un libro de adivinanzas. 3. La ventana deja entrar aire en la clase. Es de vidrio. 4. Uso una tiza para escribir en la pizarra. Uso una pluma y un lápiz para escribir en el cuaderno. 5. Una puerta es útil para entrar y salir. Generalmente es de madera. **Exercise II.** 1. alumno 2. diente 3. inteligente 4. ventana 5. información 6. negro 7. atención 8. norteamericano 9. pizarra 10. abrir **Exercise III.** Compositions are Ad Lib.

Answers to Grammar Exercises: "Ser" to be

Exercise I. 1. La chica es de los Estados Unidos. 2. Yo soy. . . 3. Tú eres. . . 4. Vd.

es . . . 5. Ella es . . . 6. Roberto es . . . 7. Nosotros somos . . . 8. Tú y yo somos . . . 9. Vds. son . . . 10. Eduardo y Pablo son . . . **Exercise II.** 1. Yo soy bonito -a. 2. Vd. es actor. 3. Tú eres un chico aplicado. 4. ¿Es el reloj . . . ? 5. Él no es . . . **Exercise III.** 1. Ellas son cubanas. 2. ¿Son las dos? 3. ¿Son sábado y domingo los días? 4. Juan y yo no somos . . . 5. Vd. y Luis son mis primos. **Exercise IV.** 1. a. Soy de los Estados Unidos. b. El chico es de los Estados Unidos también. 2. a. Somos americanos. b. Ellos son . . . 3. a. Tú y yo somos personas. b. Los hermanos son . . . 4. a. Yo soy alumno, -a b. La chica es alumna . . . 5. a. Vd. y el Sr. Delibes son maestros. b. La señora es maestra. **Exercise V.** 1. Hoy no es domingo. 2. Los días son largos. 3. Juan y María son inteligentes. 4. ¿Soy yo inteligente? 5. ¿Por qué no somos (nosotros) aplicados? 6. La chica es de los Estados Unidos. 7. Vd. es mi amigo. 8. Vds. son generosos. 9. ¿De qué color son los libros? 10. No es la una. 11. ¿Quién eres tú? 12. Ellos son franceses. 13. ¿De quién son las casas? 14. ¿No somos altos tú y yo? 15. ¿De qué es su sombrero? **Exercise VI.** 1. — Soy alumno -a. 2. — Sí, soy norteamericano -a. 3. — Mis ojos son negros. 4. — Soy inteligente y hermoso -a. 5. — Mis padres son de los Estados Unidos. 6. — Mi padre es capitán 7. — Mi casa es azul. 8. — Somos alumnos del Sr. López. 9. — Mi mesa y mi silla son de madera. 10. — Deseo ser profesor -a.

Work Unit 12:

Answers to Reading Exercises: Una enfermedad imaginaria

Exercise I. A. 1. No sale porque dice que está enfermo. 2. Ella está muy preocupada. 3. El muchacho está sentado en la cama. 4. Tiene dolor de cabeza y garganta. 5. No hay examen de matemáticas mañana. **Ex. I. B.** 1. Mi madre está preocupada por mi salud. 2. Guardo cama cuando estoy enfermo. 3. Digo — Aaaaah. 4. Sufro en la clase de . . . 5. Cuando tengo hambre, (yo) tomo una fruta, etc. **Exercise II.** 1. Su madre está triste y preocupada. 2. Estoy mejor; tengo hambre; quiero comer. 3. Ay cómo sufre mi pobre hijo. 4. En ese momento suena el teléfono. **Exercise III.** Compositions are Ad Lib.

Answers to Grammar Exercises: "Estar" to be; contrasting uses of "Estar" and "Ser"

Exercise I. 1. (Yo) estoy muy bien hoy. 2. María está . . . 3. El chico está . . . 4. Tú estás . . . 5. Vd. está . . . 6. Nosotros estamos . . . 7. Los chicos están . . . 8. Ellas están . . . 9. Juan y Pedro están . . . 10. Tú y yo estamos . . . **Exercise II.** 1. La puerta está abierta. 2. El profesor está triste. 3. Felipe y Pedro están contentos hoy. 4. Elisa y su prima están sentadas. 5. Tú y yo no estamos ausentes. **Exercise III.** 1. — No estoy en la luna. Estoy en la tierra. 2. — No estoy triste cuando recibo dinero. Estoy alegre. 3. — Mis amigos y yo no estamos presentes en la clase los sábados. Mis amigos y yo estamos ausentes. 4. — Los alumnos no están de pie cuando escriben en sus cuadernos. Los alumnos están sentados. 5. — Las escuelas no están abiertas los domingos. Las escuelas están cerradas. 6. — Los profesores no están sentados todo el día. Los profesores están ocupados. 7. — La gente en el hospital no está bien. La gente en el hospital está enferma. 8. — La gente allí no está descansada al fin del día. — La gente está cansada al fin del día. 9. — No estoy contento -a en el hospital. Estoy triste en el hospital. 10. — No deseo estar en el hospital. Deseo estar en casa. **Exercise IV.** 1. Estoy bien. 2. Estoy sentado -a porque escribo. 3. Vd. está (Tú estás) en la calle ahora. 4. Las tiendas están abiertas los sábados. 5. Sí, los amigos y yo (nosotros) estamos alegres los sábados. **Exercise V.** 1. Los niños están sentados. 2. Mi madre es mexicana. 3. Nosotros somos inteligentes. 4. Yo soy médico. 5. Ahora son las tres. 6. Las mesas son de madera. 7. Hoy es el primero de junio. 8. La casa es de mi abuela. 9. Tú y yo estamos en San Francisco. 10. Tú eres de Chicago. 11. La escuela está abierta. 12. Yo estoy aquí. 13. ¿Estás tú cansada? 14. Juana está enferma (mal, mala). 15. Los alumnos están ausentes.

Work Unit 13:

Answers to Reading Exercises: El consultorio sentimental

Exercise I. 1. La chica española es alta y delgada, interesante y simpática, con pelo negro y ojos verdes. 2. El "querido desesperado" es bajito y gordo, pero generoso, con pelo como un mono. 3. Va a llevar un sombrero alto para parecer más alto y para cubrir su pelo. 4. Va a estar tan flaco como la chica. 5. Es . . . **Exercise II.** 1. querido 2. flaco 3. alto 4. gordo 5. ojos 6. además 7. pelo 8. mono 9. barbería 10. comer 11. todo 12. un 13. sus 14. dice 15. si **Exercise III.** 1. Un muchacho está enamorado de una chica española. 2. La chica tiene el pelo negro y los ojos verdes. 3. Ella dice que no quiere salir con él. 4. El muchacho no desea ir a la barbería. 5. No tiene apetito y no quiere comer. **Exercise IV.** Compositions are Ad Lib.

Answers to Grammar Exercises: Descriptive Adjectives and Limiting Adjectives

Exercise I. 1. María es una chica alta y elegante. 2. . . .inglesa y rubia. 3. . . .española y morena. 4. . . .sincera y agradable. 5. . . .alemana y práctica. **Exercise II.** 1. Los niños son alumnos aplicados. 2. Los primos son chicos ingleses. 3. Las ciencias son estudios fáciles. 4. Las cosas son tizas azules. 5. Las abuelas son señoras españolas. 6. Las madres son mujeres inteligentes. 7. Las tías son personas liberales. 8. Los señores son profesores alemanes. 9. Las muchachas son chicas francesas. 10. Los tíos son hombres españoles. **Exercise III.** 1. Es un hombre inteligente. 2. Es una mujer triste. 3. Es un maestro español. 4. Es un cine alemán. 5. Es un periódico francés. **Exercise IV.** 1. a. Muchas contestan bien. b. Muchas alumnas contestan bien. c. Muchas alumnas lindas contestan bien. d. Muchas alumnas lindas y amables contestan bien. 2. a. Los muchachos hablan hoy. b. Todos los muchachos hablan hoy. c. Todos los muchachos españoles hablan hoy. d. Todos los muchachos españoles hablan inglés hoy. e. Todos los muchachos españoles hablan poco inglés hoy. 3. a. Mi amiga lee aquí. b. Mi amiga lee revistas aquí. c. Mi amiga lee varias revistas aquí. d. Mi amiga lee varias revistas interesantes aquí. e. Mi amiga lee varias revistas interesantes y cómicas aquí. 4. a. El muchacho escribe ahora. b. El mismo muchacho escribe ahora. c. El mismo muchacho bueno escribe ahora. d. El mismo muchacho bueno y aplicado escribe ahora. e. El mismo muchacho bueno y aplicado escribe ruso ahora. f. El mismo muchacho bueno y aplicado escribe bastante ruso ahora. **Exercise V.** 1. Todos los chicos españoles trabajan. Todas las chicas españolas trabajan también. 2. Ellas compran sombreros bonitos y baratos. Ellas compran también muchas faldas bonitas y baratas. 3. La familia tiene otro coche nuevo y lindo. La familia tiene también otra casa nueva y linda. 4. Los chicos ven pocas ciudades grandes y hermosas. Los chicos ven también pocos países grandes y hermosos. 5. Varios señores ingleses visitan bastantes ciudades interesantes. Varias señoras inglesas visitan también bastantes ciudades interesantes.

Work Unit 14:

Answers to Reading Exercises: El hombre más viejo del mundo.

Exercise I. A. 1. entrevista 2. cuatro mil años 3. come. . .duerme. . .mira 4. pelo largo 5. las comidas congeladas T.V. **Ex. I. B.** 1. La persona más famosa es. . . 2. Hoy tenemos la televisión, la luz eléctrica, etc. 3. Mi comida favorita es el bistec con papas fritas etc. 4. Tengo. . .años. 5. Tengo una cita con mi amigo. . . **Exercise II.** 1. c 2. e 3. a 4. d 5. b **Exercise III.** Personalized answers: Ad Lib.

Answers to Grammar Exercises: Cardinal Numbers 31–100

Exercise I. 1. Es setecientos. 2. Es quinientos. 3. Es novecientos. 4. Es sesenta y siete. 5. Es ciento cincuenta. 6. Es mil quinientos. 7. Es novecientos ocho. 8. Es trescientos treinta. 9. Es ciento quince. 10. Es quinientos cinco. **Exercise II.** 1. Treinta y diez son cuarenta. 2. Ochenta menos veinte son sesenta. 3. Ciento por dos son doscientos. 4. Mil dividido por dos son quinientos. 5. Treinta y cinco y treinta y seis son setenta y uno. 6. Trescientos menos ciento cincuenta son ciento cincuenta. 7. Seiscientos dividido por tres son doscientos. 8. Cuatrocientos cuarenta y cuatro menos cuarenta son cuatrocientos cuatro. 9. Setecientos menos doscientos son quinientos. 10. Setecientos y doscientos son novecientos. **Exercise III.** 1. Cuarenta y un. . . 2. Cincuenta y una. . . 3. Ciento una. . . 4. Cien. . . 5. Ciento quince. . . 6. Seiscientas noventa y una. . . 7. Doscientas. . . 8. Doscientos sesenta y un. . . 9. Trescientos setenta y un. . . 10. Cuatrocientas ochenta y una. . . **Exercise IV.** 1. Cuentan quinientas cincuenta y cinco personas. 2. . . .setecientas setenta y siete. . . 3. . . .novecientas noventa y una. . . 4. . . .mil 5. . . .mil setecientas diez y siete. . . **Exercise V.** 1. Hoy es el primero de marzo de mil novecientos noventa y nueve. 2. . . .el treinta y uno de enero de mil ochocientos ocho. 3. Mañana es el once de agosto de mil seiscientos sesenta y seis. 4. Estamos a quince de octubre de mil quinientos cincuenta y cinco. 5. . . .catorce de diciembre de mil setecientos setenta y siete. **Exercise VI.** 1. catorce 2. el treinta y uno de mayo 3. ciento quince 4. mil ciento setenta y uno (once setenta y uno) 5. cuarenta 6. cincuenta 7. novecientos noventa y nueve 8. cien 9. una 10. mil novecientos. . .

Work Unit 15:

Answers to Reading Exercises: Queridos mamá y papá

Exercise I. 1. No tiene nada que hacer. 2. Va a un campamento de verano. 3. Escribe una carta a sus padres todos los días. 4. Quiere volver a casa. **Exercise II.** 1. Van a pasar las vacaciones lejos de la ciudad. 2. Vamos a hacer cosas nuevas todos los días. 3. Siempre come de día y de noche. 4. Todo el mundo grita y tira cosas.

Exercise III.

Querid**o** Federic**o**

V**a**m**o**s **a**l l**a**g**o** **e**sta n**o**che. P**o**dem**o**s ir **a la** isla c**o**n un**o** de l**o**s b**o**tes. Si el c**o**nsejer**o** s**a**be, v**a a** estar muy en**o**jad**o**.

Tu **a**mig**o**,
In**o**cenci**o**.

Exercise IV. Compositions are Ad Lib.

Answers to Grammar Exercises: Ordinal Numbers; Shortening of Adjectives "bueno," "malo"

Exercise I. 1. Veo el buen sombrero. 2. Ahí va la buena alumna. 3. Paso el primer día aquí. 4. Leo durante la primera hora. 5. Tiene el mal pensamiento. 6. Cuenta la mala cosa. 7. Ocupan el tercer asiento. 8. . . .la tercera línea. **Exercise II.** 1. Francisco tiene un buen padre. 2. . . .unas buenas ideas. 3. . . .un mal cuento. 4. . . .una mala comida. 5. . . .unos malos errores. **Exercise III.** 1. No. Es la décima canción. 2. No. Es el sexto piso. 3. No. Es la octava avenida. 4. No. Es el tercer alumno. 5. No. Es la quinta casa. **Exercise IV.** 1. Sí, es su cuarta visita. 2. . . .segunda blusa. 3. . . .séptimo viaje. 4. . . .tercera falta. 5. . . .primer helado. **Exercise V.** 1. Deseo el primer dólar. 2. Quiero ver un buen drama. 3. Deseo un buen examen fácil. 4. Es más fácil la tercera hora. 5. Escribo la quinta frase. **Exercise VI.** 1. séptima 2. sexta 3. buen 4. malas 5. primeros 6. buenas 7. tercer 8. primer 9. buenos 10. segunda.

Work Unit 16:

Answers to Reading Exercises: Si está perdido, llame a un policía.

Exercise I. A. 1. las ocho. . .jefe 2. sentado. . .coche 3. derecho. . .cuadras 4. tren. . .esquina . . .norte 5. reunión. . .ciudad **Ex. I. B.** 1. Llamo a un policía. 2. Hay. . .cuadras entre la escuela y mi casa. 3. Una avenida es más grande (larga, importante.) 4. Hay una tienda de comestibles, un edificio alto, etc. 5. El alumno a mi izquierda es. . . **Exercise II.** 1. Tiene una cita con su jefe. 2. En ese momento pasa un policía. 3. Si estás (está) perdido, llama (llame) a un policía. 4. Puede tomar el tren en la esquina. 5. ¡Pregunte a ese hombre que vende periódicos! **Exercise IV.** Compositions are Ad Lib.

Answers to Grammar Exercises: Formation and Use of Direct Commands

Exercise I. 1. ¡Escuche Vd. bien! 2. ¡Escuchemos bien! 3. ¡Coman Vds. poco! 4. ¡Comamos poco! 5. ¡Viva Vd. mucho tiempo! 6. ¡Vivamos mucho tiempo! 7. ¡Salgan Vds. pronto! 8. ¡Salgamos pronto! 9. ¡Vaya Vd. al mercado! 10. ¡Vamos al mercado! 11. ¡Sean Vds. diligentes! 12. ¡Seamos diligentes! 13. ¡Esté Vd. contento! 14. ¡Estemos contentos! 15. ¡Den Vds. las gracias! 16. ¡Demos las gracias! **Exercise II. A.** 1. – Sí, ¡cante Vd. ahora! 2. – Sí, ¡responda Vd. ahora! 3. – Sí, ¡escriba Vd. ahora! 4. – Sí, ¡compre Vd. ahora! 5. – Sí, ¡lea Vd. ahora! **Ex. II. B.** 1. – Sí, ¡hablen Vds. ahora! 2. – Sí, ¡aprendan Vds. ahora! 3. – Sí, ¡coman Vds. ahora! 4. – Sí, ¡anden Vds. ahora! 5. – Sí, ¡corran Vds. ahora! **Ex. II. C.** 1. – ¡Estudiemos ahora mismo! 2. – ¡Bebamos . . .! 3. – ¡Asistamos. . .! 4. – ¡Entremos. . .! 5. – ¡Leamos. . .! **Exercise III. A.** 1. – Bueno, ¡venga Vd. tarde! 2. . . .oiga Vd. . . . 3. . . .conozca Vd. . . . 4. . . .haga Vd. . . . 5. . . .ponga Vd. . . . 6. . . .sea Vd. . . . 7. . . .dé Vd. . . . **Ex. III. B.** 1. – Bueno, ¡sepan Vds. la verdad! 2. . . .digan Vds. . . . 3. traigan Vds. . . . 4. estén Vds. . . . 5. . . .tengan Vds. . . . 6. . . .vean Vds. . . . 7. . . .salgan Vds. . . . 8. . . .oigan Vds. . . . **Exercise IV.** 1. Estudie Vd. 2. Haga Vd. 3. Asista Vd. 4. Sea Vd. 5. Traiga Vd. 6. Sepa Vd. 7. Venga Vd. 8. Vaya Vd. 9. Conozca Vd. 10. Dé Vd.

Work Unit 17:

Answers to Reading Exercises: Su hija es una alumna excelente

Exercise I. A. 1. vez...hablar...profesores 2. primer...enseñanza 3. biología 4. buena nota 5. Sonia **Exercise I. B.** 1. Voy a sacar una... 2. Ellos dicen que soy un alumno... 3. Mi padre viene...veces al año. 4. ...siempre sale bien en los exámenes. 5. Debo hacer mi tarea para aprender bien. **Exercise II.** 1. enseñar 2. nota 3. tarea 4. gracias 5. examen 6. vez 7. siempre 8. sacar 9. tantos 10. aparecer **Exercise III.** Compositions are Ad Lib.

Answers to Grammar Exercises: Possessive Adjectives

Exercise I. 1. Tengo mis cuadernos. 2. ...sus casas. 3. ...nuestras clases. 4. ... mis respuestas. 5. ...tus tíos? 6. ...sus cuartos. 7. nuestros periódicos. 8. tus comidas. 9. ... sus lecciones. 10. ...sus programas... **Exercise II.** 1. No. Es nuestra pluma. 2. ...nuestro sombrero. 3. No. Son nuestros zapatos. 4. ...nuestras hijas 5. ...nuestros amigos **Exercise III.** 1. Sí, Uso tu abrigo. 2. ...sus pantalones 3. ...Abro mi puerta 4. ...Deseo mis lecciones. 5. ...Necesito tus radios. **Exercise IV.** 1. No son los lápices de él. Son de ella. 2. ...las camisas de él. Son de ella. 3. No es la amiga de él. Es de ella. 4. ...el reloj de él. Es de ella. 5. No son los hermanos de él. Son de ella. **Exercise V.** 1. No es el coche de Vds. Es el coche de ellos. 2. ...la pelota de Vds. Es la pelota de ellos. 3. No son las chaquetas de Vds. Son las chaquetas de ellos. 4. ...los abrigos de Vds. Son los abrigos de ellos. 5. No es la familia de Vds. Es la familia de ellos. **Exercise VI.** 1. Vendo mis coches. 2. ...nuestras cartas. 3. ...sus lecciones. 4. ...sus cuartos. 5. ...tu casa. 6. ...su examen. 7. ...nuestro mapa. 8. ...su respuesta. 9. ...su casa. 10. ...sus preguntas. **Exercise VII.** 1. mi 2. tu 3. nuestras...tus...mis 4. nuestros.

Work Unit 18:

Answers to Reading Exercises: Casa a la venta

Exercise I. A. 1. Carlos ve un letrero delante de una casa. 2. Quiere ver la casa porque está a la venta. 3. en la cocina hay un refrigerador y una estufa. 4. Los dormitorios son grandes y claros. 5. El va a poner su casa a la venta. **Ex. I. B.** 1. Generalmente hay un refrigerador y una estufa en una cocina. 2. Hay...habitaciones en mi apartamiento. Son... 3. Hay casas modernas, trenes y autobuses. Hay muchas tiendas allí etc. 4. pongo las palabras: Casa a la venta 5. Digo: Buenos días, ¿qué tal? **Exercise II.** 1. g 2. e 3. b 4. h 5. f 6. d 7. c 8. a **Exercise III.** 1. Casa a la venta. Pida informes adentro. 2. Toca a la puerta y espera unos momentos. 3. Buenos días, ¿en qué puedo servirle? 4. Mucho gusto en conocerle. 5. Dígame algo del vecindario. **Exercise IV.** Compositions are Ad Lib.

Answers to Grammar Exercises: Demonstrative Adjectives

Exercise I. A. 1. Compro esta tiza 2. ...estas plumas... 3. ...este lápiz... 4. ... estos papeles... 5. ...este diccionario... **B.** 1. ¿Deseas esa silla ahí? 2. ...esas peras... 3. ...esos periódicos... 4. ...esos libros... 5. ...ese sombrero... **C.** 1. Admiramos aquella rosa allí. 2. ...aquellas pinturas... 3. ...aquel coche... 4. aquellos cuadros... 5. ...aquel edificio... **Exercise II.** 1. Reciben este papel y aquel libro. 2. Esta palabra...esa frase. 3. ...ese profesor...aquel alumno. 4. ...esa puerta...aquella ventana. 5. ...este pañuelo... ese zapato? **Exercise III.** 1. Leemos estos periódicos y esos artículos. 2. ...estas sillas... aquellas camas. 3. estos sombreros...aquellos vestidos. 4. ...esas clases...aquellos profesores. 5. ...esos vestidos...aquellas faldas. **Exercise IV.** 1. ¿Este amigo? Sí, gracias. 2. ¿Esta revista?... 3. ¿Estos cuentos?... 4. ¿Estas fotos?... 5. ¿Este papel?... **Exercise V.** 1. ¿Ese postre? No, gracias. 2. ¿Esa gramática?... 3. ¿Esos libros?... 4. ¿Esas manzanas?... 5. ¿Esos amigos?... **Exercise VI.** 1. este...ese 2. aquel 3. estos...esos 4. aquellos 5. aquellas...aquella 6. estas...esta 7. esa... 8. esas.

Work Unit 19:

Answers to Reading Exercises: ¡Qué dientes tan grandes tienes!

Exercise I. A. 1. f 2. f 3. f 4. f 5. f 6. c **Exercise I. B.** 1. Contesto: —Soy yo. 2. Uso una pasta dentífrica. 3. (No) hay mucha diferencia... 4. Un buen nombre es... 5. Un animal que tiene los dientes grandes es el perro, (el elefante, etc.) **Exercise II.** Personalized answers: Ad lib. **Exercise III.** 1. frutas 2. dulces 3. flor 4. huevo 5. helado

Answers to Grammar Exercises: Common Adverbs; Exclamatory "¡Que!"

Exercise I. 1. Entro tarde hoy. 2. Termino temprano y bien. 3. Hablo poco allí. 4. Aprendo mucho ahora. 5. Contesto más después. 6. Como mal aquí. 7. Viajo lejos mañana. 8. Siempre tomo café antes. 9. Nunca llego más tarde. 10. Grito menos cuando Ana está cerca. **Exercise II.** 1. Juan estudia poco. 2. ...ahora. 3. Nunca... 4. menos... 5. ...cerca. 6. Mañana... 7. ...allí 8. después. 9. ...tarde. 10. ...mal. **Exercise III.** 1. ¡Qué bien... 2. ¡Qué mal... 3. ¡Qué tarde... 4. ¡Qué cerca... 5. ¡Qué lejos... **Exercise IV.** 1. ¡Qué tarde llega ella! 2. ¡Qué bien... 3. ¡Qué mal... 4. ¡Qué temprano... 5. ¡Qué lejos... 6. ¡Qué cerca... 7. ¡Qué cansada... 8. ¡Qué pobre... 9. ¡Qué ricos... 10. ¡Qué bonita... **Exercise V.** 1. ¡Qué casas! ¡Qué casas altas! 2. ¡Qué madre! ¡Qué madre buena! 3. ¡Qué niños! ¡Qué niños lindos! 4. ¡Qué cielo! ¡Qué cielo azul! 5. ¡Qué escuela! ¡Qué escuela grande! **Exercise VI.** 1. ¡Qué día interesante! 2. ¡Qué año importante! 3. ¡Qué muchacho simpático! 4. ¡Qué profesores amables! 5. ¡Qué clases buenas!

Work Unit 20:

Answers to Reading Exercises: ¿Qué dice el horóscopo?

Exercise I. A. 1. supersticiosas 2. fortuna 3. las noticias, los deportes 4. Acuario 5. gastar dinero **Ex. I. B.** 1. Leo la sección de... 2. El día de mi nacimiento es... 3. Mi signo del zodíaco es... 4. Puedo ganar... 5. Un cartero trae las cartas. **Exercise II.** SIEMPRE ES IMPORTANTE ESTUDIAR EL ESPAÑOL **Exercise III.** 1. ¡No pierda el tiempo! Su oportunidad está aquí. 2. ¡Defienda sus derechos! ¡No sea tímido! 3. ¡Cambie su fortuna! Vd. tiene suerte. 4. ¡Tenga paciencia! Su signo es favorable. 5. ¡No gaste mucho dinero! 6. 7. Ad lib. **Exercise IV.** Compositions are Ad Lib.

Answers to Grammar Exercises: Stem-Changing Verbs of "ar" and "er" Infinitives

Exercise I. A. 1. Tú piensas ir mañana. 2. Diego piensa... 3. Diego y María piensan... 4. Tú y yo pensamos... 5. Vds. piensan... 6. Yo pienso... **Ex. I. B.** 1. ¿Almuerza Vd. a las doce? 2. ¿Almorzamos...? 3. ¿Almuerzan...? 4. ¿Almuerza...? 5. ¿Almuerzo...? 6. ¿Almuerzas...? **Exercise II.** 1. Ellos comienzan el examen. 2. ¿Encuentras tú...? 3. Ana y él entienden... 4. Él empieza... 5. Vds. no vuelven a... 6. Ella pierde... 7. Vd. no lo cierra... 8. Yo recuerdo... 9. ¿No lo empiezan ellas...? 10. Nosotros contamos... **Exercise III.** 1. Vds. comienzan a las cuatro. 2. Vds. cierran los libros a las diez. 3. Vds. pueden venir temprano. 4. Vds. vuelan a Madrid. 5. Nosotros queremos viajar en coche. 6. Nosotros no entendemos la novela. 7. Nosotras encontramos comida en la cafetería. 8. Yo nunca cuento los dólares. 9. Yo pierdo dos dólares. 10. Tú vuelves a casa con nosotros. **Exercise IV.** 1. Nosotros no empezamos la comida ahora. Ella sí que empieza la comida ahora. 2. ...no almorzamos...... almuerza... 3. ...no entendemos...... entiende... 4. ...no comenzamos a comer... ...comienza a comer... 5. ...no movemos... mueve... 6. ...no cerramos...... cierra... 7. ...no queremos...... quiere... 8. ...no podemos comer...... puede 9. no volvemos... ...vuelve... 10. ...no jugamos... juega... **Exercise V.** 1. ¡No pierda Vd.! 2. ¡No perdamos! 3. ¡No piensen Vds.! 4. ¡No pensemos! 5. ¡No cuente Vd.! 6. ¡No contemos! 7. ¡No defiendan Vds.! 8. ¡No defendamos! 9. ¡No vuelva Vd.! 10. ¡No volvamos! **Exercise VI.** 1. (Yo) pienso en el trabajo. 2. (Yo) comienzo 3. (Yo) no entiendo... 4. (Yo) pierdo... 5. Yo cierro... 6. Yo quiero... 7. Yo almuerzo... 8. Yo recuerdo... 9. Yo vuelvo... 10. Yo muestro...

Work Unit 21:

Answers to Reading Exercises: Quiero ser rico

Exercise I. A. 1. Teodoro va a graduarse. 2. Está allí cinco años. 3. Quiere ser rico. 4. Tiene miedo de los aviones. **Ex. I. B.** 1. Voy a terminar... 2. Quiero ser... 3. Quiero ser rico porque... 4. Como médico (abogado etc.) voy a recibir un buen sueldo. **Exercise II.** 1. Finalmente va a graduarse. 2. Quiere encontrar trabajo lo más pronto posible. 3. Quiero ganar mucho dinero. 4.

Quiero un trabajo fácil para descansar. **Exercise III.** 1. (Yo) busco un trabajo con un buen sueldo. 2. Quiero trabajar este verano. Puedo ir a la universidad en septiembre. 3. Quiero ganar cien dólares por semana, más o menos. 4. Muchas gracias por su ayuda. Hasta mañana.

Answers to Grammar Exercises: The Complementary Infinitive; "ir a . . . ," "tener que . . . ," "para . . ."

Exercise I. 1. (Yo) tengo que comer. 2. (Tú) tienes que . . . 3. Juan tiene que . . . 4. Vds. tienen que . . . 5. Vd. tiene que . . . 6. Ana y yo tenemos que . . . 7. Juan y Ana tienen que . . . **Exercise II.** 1. Los tíos no van a leer esta noche. 2. Susana no va a . . . 3. Tú no vas a . . . 4. Vds. no van a . . . 5. Marta y yo no vamos a . . . 6. Yo no voy a . . . 7. Él no va a . . . **Exercise III.** 1. ¿Estudiamos para comprender? 2. ¿Leemos para saber? 3. ¿Hablamos para practicar? 4. ¿Escuchamos para aprender? 5. ¿Trabajamos para comer? **Exercise IV.** 1. Necesita hacerlo. 2. Deben hacerlo 3. Tiene que hacerlo. 4. Puedes hacerlo. 5. Sé hacerlo. 6. Tengo que hacerlo. 7. Trabaja para hacerlo. 8. Quiero hacerlo. 9. Vamos a hacerlo. 10. Desean hacerlo. **Exercise V.** 1. — 2. para 3. a 4. que 5. — 6. a 7. — 8. a (para) 9. — 10. — **Exercise VI.** 1. tengo que 2. debo 3. voy a 4. para escribir 5. quiero comer 6. no puede 7. tiene que 8. necesitamos . . . para vivir 9. sé escribir 10. estudiar . . . comer. **Exercise VII.** 1. — Tengo que llegar al trabajo a las tres de la tarde. 2. — Sé vender ropa allí. 3. — Tengo que trabajar tres horas después de la escuela. 4. — Voy a casa a comer un poco antes de las seis. 5. — Puedo salir temprano los sábados. 6. — Siempre deseo jugar por la tarde. 7. — Trabajo para tener dinero. 8. — Necesito dinero para ir a estudiar en la universidad. 9. — Sí, mi hermano debe trabajar también. 10. Sí, vamos a estudiar juntos.

Work Unit 22:

Answers to Reading Exercises: ¡Qué vida tan cruel!

Exercise I. A. 1. A las doce todas las mujeres miran un programa en la televisión. 2. Alfonso y Adela llevan una vida triste. 3. Alfonso trae una mala noticia. 4. Raúl y Rodrigo están ahora en la prisión. 5. Gustavo vuelve temprano a la casa. **Ex. I. B.** 1. Mi papá se sienta en el sillón y lee el periódico. 2. Tengo que guardar cama. 3. Hay dinero dentro de mi cartera. 4. Puedo comprar zapatos, ropa, etc. 5. Una persona pierde su empleo, está enfermo, va al hospital, etc. **Exercise II.** 1. Llora constantemente durante toda una hora. 2. Tengo una mala noticia para ti. 3. Nuestros hijos son adorables pero estúpidos. 4. Todos tenemos que buscar otro empleo. **Exercise III.** Compositions are Ad Lib.

Answers to Grammar Exercises: Prepositional Pronouns

Exercise I. 1. Compran el regalo con él y es para él. 2. . . . con ellos . . . para ellos. 3. . . . con ella . . . para ella. 4. . . . con ellas . . . para ellas. 5. . . . conmigo . . . para mí. 6. . . . contigo . . . para ti. 7. . . . con Vds. . . . para Vds. 8. . . . con nosotros . . . para nosotros. 9. . . . con vosotros . . . para vosotros. 10. . . . con Vd. . . . para Vd. **Exercise II.** 1. Vivo cerca de ellos. 2. . . . sin ellos. 3. . . . para ellas. 4. . . . a Vds. 5. . . . con nosotros. **Exercise III.** 1. — Sí, vivo cerca de ella. 2. . . . preparo para ellas. 3. . . . deseo escribir sin él. 4. . . . estoy sentado en él. 5. . . . juego cerca de ellos. **Exercise IV.** 1. ¿Para mí? Gracias. 2. ¿Conmigo? . . . 3. ¿Sin mí? . . . 4. ¿Cerca de nosotros -as? . . . 5. ¿Con Vds? . . . **Exercise V.** 1. Sí. Asisten conmigo. 2. . . . con nosotros. 3. . . . conmigo. 4. . . . con Vds. (con nosotros). 5. . . . contigo (con Vd.). **Exercise VI.** 1. Compran el regalo para mí y para él. 2. El niño juega conmigo y con mi amigo. 3. Ella corre a él, no a Vd. 4. El hombre trabaja sin nosotros y sin ella. 5. Ella vive cerca de ti, Pedro, y cerca de ellos.

Work Unit 23:

Answers to Reading Exercises: Vamos a construir una casa

Exercise I. A. 1. Esmeralda tiene seis años. 2. Está sola y está cansada de jugar con su muñeca. 3. El padre trabaja, los hermanos están en la escuela y la madre está en la casa de una vecina. 4. Hace mal tiempo. Hace frío y llueve. 5. Su muñeca, Pepita, va a estar sola. **Ex. I. B.** 1. Miro la televisión, leo un libro, etc. 2. Estoy aburrido en mi clase de . . . 3. La puerta sirve para entrar y salir. 4. Vivo en . . . 5. Hay mapas, cuadros, etc. en las paredes. **Exercise II.** 1. caja 2. lados 3. paredes 4. techo 5. puerta 6. entran 7. salen 8. puerta 9. ventanas 10. aire 11. árboles **Exercise III.** Compositions are Ad Lib.

Answers to Grammar Exercises: Direct Object Pronouns

Exercise I. 1. Yo no los leo. 2. . . .no lo toman. 3. . . .no la tiene. 4. . . .no las sabe. 5. . . .no lo desean. **Exercise II.** 1. Me necesitan a mí en el jardín. 2. La ven a Vd. . . . 3. Lo visitan a Vd. . . . 4. Lo observan a él . . . 5. Te permiten a ti . . . 6. Los hallan a Vds. . . . 7. Nos describen a nosotros . . . 8. Las miran a ellas . . . 9. La escuchan a ella . . . 10. Los comprenden a ellos . . . **Exercise III. A.** 1. Sí que la invitan a ella. 2. . . .lo prefieren a él. 3. . . .las quieren a ellas. 4. . . . los ven a ellos. 5. . . .los escuchan a ellos. **Ex. B.** 1. Sí, los ven a Vds. (nos ven a nosotros). 2. . . . lo necesitan a Vd. (te necesitan a ti). 3. . . .me comprenden a mí. 4. . . .nos visitan a nosotros 5. . . .me observan a mí. **Exercise IV. A.** 1. No deseo leerlo. 2. ¿No quiere visitarlos? 3. No vamos a comerte. 4. ¿No pueden vernos? 5. No deben mirarme. 6. No voy a construirla. **Ex. IV. B.** 1. No te esperamos ver. 2. ¿No las sabes hacer? 3. No la prefiere contestar. 4. ¿No me pueden comprender? 5. No nos van a escuchar. **Exercise V.** 1. ¡No lo enseñe Vd.! 2. ¡No me llame Vd.! 3. ¡No la visiten Vds.! 4. ¡No nos miren Vds.! 5. ¡No los invitemos! **Exercise VI.** 1. ¡Visítelo Vd.! 2. ¡Mírennos Vds.! 3. ¡ 3. ¡Contestémosla! 4. ¡Úselos Vd.! 5. ¡Imítenme Vds.! **Exercise VII.** 1. Sí, la veo. 2. No, ella no me mira. 3. Sí, lo saluda ella a él. 4. El la lleva mucho al cine. 5. Sus padres no lo saben. 6. No quiero saludarla. 7. ¡Salúdela Vd.! 8. No. ¡No la salude Vd.! Yo voy a saludarla mañana. 9. ¡Entonces, saludémosla juntos!

Work Unit 24:

Answers to Reading Exercises: Un hombre moral

Exercise I. 1. el trabajo 2. despacho. . .abogado 3. varios papeles. . .clasificarlos 4. esquina. . . mal vestido 5. cartera. . .bolsillo. . .pantalón 6. dejó caer. **Exercise II.** 1. 5, 2, 4, 3 **Exercise III.** 1. f 2. i 3. m 4. a 5. h 6. b 7. c 8. o 9. l 10. d 11. n 12. k 13. e 14. j 15. g **Exercise IV.** Compositions are Ad Lib.

Answers to Grammar Exercises: Indirect Object Pronouns

Exercise 1. 1. El me enseña la lección. 2. . . .le dan. . . 3. . . .le decimos. . . 4. . . . te ofrece. . . 5. . . .no le muestran. . . 6. Nos da. . . 7. Les enseña. . . 8. Les vendo. . . 9. No les traen. . . 10. Les leo. . . **Exercise II. A.** 1. —Le leo la novela a Tomás. 2. —Le muestro. . .a la señora. 3. —Le enseño. . .a Vd. 4. —Te escribo. . .a ti. 5. —Me canto. . .a mí. **Ex. II. B.** 1. El les da el violín a Pedro y a Anita. 2. Ella les dice. . .a los alumnos. 3. . . .les escriben. . .a Ana y a María. 4. . . .nos traen. . .a nosotros. 5. . . .les explica. . .a Elisa y a Vd. **Exercise III.** 1. —Sí, ellos le muestran el examen a él. 2. . . .le escribe. . .a ella. 3. . . .les enseñan. . .a ellas. 4. . . .les lee. . .a ellos 5. . . .les explica. . .a ellos. **Exercise IV. A.** 1. No les deseo leer. 2. No nos quieren hablar. 3. No te puede mostrar. 4. ¿No me van a cantar? 5. ¿No le debemos decir? **Ex. IV. B.** 1. No quiero hablarles. 2. No deseo cantarle. 3. No espera escribirme. 4. No pueden explicarte. 5. No van a cantarnos. **Exercise V.** 1. ¡Hábleme Vd.! 2. ¡Escríbanos Vd.! 3. ¡Respóndannos Vds.! 4. ¡Léannos Vds.! 5. ¡Vendámosle! **Exercise VI.** 1. ¡No nos muestre Vd.! 2. ¡No nos lea Vd.! 3. ¡No me enseñen Vds.! 4. ¡No les escriban Vds.! 5. ¡No le respondamos! **Exercise VII.** 1. —¿Le dan una carta a María? 2. —¿Les mandan. 3. —¿Les enseñan. . . 4. ¿Les dicen. . . 5. —¿Les escriben. . . **Exercise VIII.** 1. Favor de decirme. 2. ¡Claro! Papá siempre te da dinero. 3. ¿Y tú me das regalos a mí? 4. Sí, eso es darnos alegría. 5. Favor de darles algo fantástico.

Work Unit 25:

Answers to Reading Exercises: No me gustan las hamburguesas

Exercise I. A. 1. Está contento porque sale con Beatriz. 2. Julio pregunta: —¿Quieres ir a tomar algo? 3. Julio tiene solamente diez dólares, y la paella cuesta doce dólares. 4. Es una mezcla de arroz, pollo, mariscos y legumbres. 5. El no tiene bastante dinero. **Ex. I. B.** 1. Mi comida favorita es . . . 2. Algunos refrescos son: la leche, el vino, la Coca-Cola, el té, y el café. 3. Generalmente como papas fritas con una hamburguesa. 4. Necesito. . .dólares **Exercise II.** 1. mariscos 2. arroz 3. camarero 4. huevo 5. plato 6. duro(s) 7. caro 8. noche 9. sábado 10. cine 11. más 12. año 13. muy 14. qùé 15. un 16. ojo. **Exercise III.** Compositions are Ad Lib.

Answers to Grammar Exercises: "Gustar," to be pleasing, to like

Exercise 1. 1. No le gusta el cereal. 2. . . .no le gustan. . . 3. . . .no le gusta. . . 4. . . .no le gustan. . . 5. . . .no le gusta. . . 6. . . .no le gustan. . . **Exercise II.** 1. A nosotros no nos gustan las peras. 2. A Vd. no le gustan. . . 3. A Vds. no les gustan. . . 4. A mis hermanas no les gustan. . . 5. A su amigo no le gustan. . . 6. A Luisa y a Juan no les gustan. . . 7. A ti no te gustan. . . 8. A mí no me gustan. . . 9. A Pedro no le gustan. . . 10. A Lola no le gustan. . . **Exercise III.** 1. A nosotras sí nos gusta tomar café. 2. A Juan sí le gusta el tenis. 3. A las maestras sí les gustan las clases. 4. A mi amiga sí le gusta ir. 5. A mí sí me gustan. . . 6. A ti sí te gustan. . . 7. A Vd. sí le gustan. . . 8. A los chicos sí les gusta. . . 9. A nosotros sí nos gustan. . . 10. A Vds. sí les gusta bailar. **Exercise IV.** 1. —Me gusta mucho. 2. —Nos gusta. . . 3. —me gustan. . . 4. —Nos gustan. . . 5. —Me gusta. . . **Exercise V.** 1. —A nosotros no nos gusta. 2. —A él no le gusta. 3. —A ella no le gustan. 4. —A ellos no les gustan. 5. A ellas no les gusta. **Exercise VI.** 1. le gusta 2. me gusta 3. A. . .les gusta 4. . . .él. . .le gusta. . .ella. . .le 5. . . .mí me gusta.

Work Unit 26:

Answers to Reading Exercises: Una noticia confusa

Artículo: 1. criminales 2. 21 3. prisión 4. desesperados 5. descubrieron 6. garaje 7. descripciones 8. 36 9. cien 10. ladrones 11. automóvil 12. libertad. **Exercise I.** 1. Toma asiento en un sillón, fuma su pipa y lee el periódico. 2. Nota que falta un gran número de palabras. 3. Teresita cortó una docena de palabras del artículo. 4. Tiene que poner las palabras en los espacios. 5. Se escaparon en un viejo coche Chevrolet. **Exercise II.** 1. e 2. c 3. a 4. b 5. d **Exercise III.** Personalized answers: Ad Lib.

Answers to Grammar Exercises: The Preterite Indicative: Irregular Verbs

Exercise I. 1. Juan entró a las tres y salió a las cuatro. 2. Tú entraste. . .saliste. . . 3. Tú y yo entramos. . .salimos. . . 4. Vd. entró. . .salió. . . 5. Vds. entraron. . .salieron. . . 6. Mis amigos entraron. . .salieron. . . 7. Yo entré. . .salí. . . **Exercise II.** 1. Vd. recibió la carta anoche. 2. Yo corté. . . 3. Yo rompí. . . 4. Nosotros encontramos. . . 5. María buscó. . . 6. Vds. terminaron. . . 7. Pedro y Juan escribieron. . . 8. Tú respondiste. . . 9. Él y yo perdimos. . . 10. Tú describiste. . . **Exercise III.** 1. a. —Sí, usé el sombrero. b. —Mi madre usó el sombrero también. 2. a. . . .aprendí. . . b. —Mi hermano aprendió. . . 3. a. . . .invité. . . b. Los padres invitaron. . . 4. a. . . .recibí. . . b. —Vd. recibió (tú recibiste). . . 5. a. . . .bailaron. . . b. —Mi prima bailó. . . 6. a. . . .bebimos. . . b. —Las chicas bebieron. . . 7. a. . . .visitó. . . b. —Tú y yo visitamos. . . 8. a. . . .comió. . . b. —Ellas comieron. . . 9. a. . . .saludaron. . . b. —Yo saludé . . . 10. a. . . .Vd. recibió (tú recibiste). . . b. —Nosotros recibimos. . . **Exercise IV.** 1. Juan entró en la cocina. 2. Tomó. . . 3. Comió. . .bebió 4. . . .llegaron. . . 5. Comieron. . . 6. . . .salieron. . .aprendieron. . . 7. Escucharon. . .practicaron. . . 8. . . .contestamos 9. aprendimos . . .escribimos. . . 10. . . .estudié. . .asistí. . .

Work Unit 27:

Answers to Reading Exercises: ¡Los muchachos de hoy son horribles!

Exercise I. A. 1. F 2. F 3. F 4. C 5. C **Ex. I. B.** 1. La generación de hoy (no) tiene. . . 2. (no) doy mi asiento a un anciano. 3. Yo leo. . . 4. Mis padres (no) tienen siempre razón. **Exercise II.** 1. entró 2. Vi. . .molestó 3. quiso darle 4. sacaron, empezaron 5. necesitaron **Exercise III.** 1. Entra en la sala 2. Tengo algo aquí que va a ser interesante para Vd. 3. Nadie quiso darle el asiento. 4. La pobre señora tuvo que estar de pie. 5. Soy mejor hombre por eso. 6. ¿No cree Vd. que es un poco exagerado? **Exercise IV.** Compositions are Ad Lib.

Answers to Grammar Exercises: The Preterite Indicative: Irregular Verbs

Exercise I. A. 1. Yo tuve la carta ayer y la puse en la mesa. 2. Pedro tuvo. . .puso. . . 3. Pedro y yo tuvimos. . .pusimos. . . 4. Vd. tuvo. . .puso. . . 5. Los chicos tuvieron. . .pusieron . . . **Ex. I. B.** 1. Vds. hicieron la tarea y la trajeron a la clase. 2. Vd. hizo. . .trajo. . . 3. Yo hice. . .

traje... 4. La alumna hizo...trajo... 5. Nosotros hicimos...trajimos... **Ex. I. C.** 1. Mi madre dijo que sí y dio las gracias. 2. Vd. dijo...dio... 3. Yo dije...di... 4. Nosotros dijimos...dimos ... 5. Los abuelos dijeron...dieron... **Ex. I. D.** 1. La niña fue buena cuando vino a la clase. 2. Yo fui bueno...vine... 3. Tú fuiste bueno...viniste... 4. Ellas fueron buenas...vinieron... 5. Ellas y yo fuimos buenos...vinimos... **Ex. I. E.** 1. Yo fui al teatro donde vi una buena comedia. 2. Diego fue...vio... 3. Diego y yo fuimos...vimos... 4. Mi amiga fue...vio... 5. Tú fuiste... viste... **Ex. I. F.** 1. Los primos leyeron la frase y la creyeron. 2. Nosotras leímos...creímos. 3. Yo leí...creí 4. Tú leíste...creíste. 5. Vd. leyó...creyó. **Ex. I. G.** 1. María oyó gritos cuando estuvo allí. 2 Ellos oyeron...estuvieron... 3. María y yo oímos...estuvimos... 4. Tú oíste... estuviste... 5. Yo oí...estuve... **Ex. I. H.** 1. Juan anduvo mucho y supo que pudo hacerlo porque quiso hacerlo. 2. Juan y yo anduvimos...supimos...pudimos...quisimos. 3. Juan y Ana anduvieron...supieron...pudieron...quisieron. 4. Yo anduve...supe...pude...quise. 5. Tú anduviste...supiste...pudiste...quisiste. **Exercise II.** 1. Las piedras cayeron. 2. Las niñas vinieron. 3. Nosotros tuvimos los regalos. 4. Nosotros hicimos los viajes. 5. Ellos hicieron los viajes. 6. Ellas trajeron los libros. 7. Vds. fueron a ios cines. 8. Nosotros fuimos excelentes. 9. Vds. dijeron las frases. 10. Vds. dieron ayuda. 11. Nosotros leímos mucho. 12. Nosotros oímos gritos. 13. Ellos oyeron los discos. 14. Vds. creyeron los artículos. 15. Ellas leyeron los cuentos. 16. Nosotros dijimos que sí. 17. Nosotros dimos dinero. 18. Ellas fueron bonitas. 19. Nosotros fuimos a los mercados. 20. Nosotros los creímos. **Exercise III.** 1. Mis amigos estuvieron allí. 2. Fui a la tienda. 3. Traje tres dólares. 4. Yo hice las compras. 5. Nosotros pusimos las compras en la mesa. **Exercise IV.** 1. Vine a la casa de Anita. 2. Fue... 3. Ella tuvo... 4. Ellos le dijeron... 5. Luego oyeron ... 6. Pudieron... 7. Quise... 8. ...tuve que... 9. Anduve... 10. Supe que fue...

Work Unit 28:

Answers to Reading Exercises: La justicia siempre triunfa

Exercise 1. 1. Hay una docena de espectadores. 2. Chocó contra la bicicleta de un muchacho. 3. Dice que Ramírez es un hombre honrado. 4. Protesta porque el testigo dio su opinión. 5. El juez está enojado porque el testigo no vio el accidente. **Exercise II.** 1. ¿Qué puede Vd. decirnos en su defensa? 2. El señor es un hombre honrado. 3. Aquí no nos importan las opiniones. 4. El accidente ocurrió a las diez. **Exercise III.** 1. abogado 2. acusado 3. drama 4. coche 5. juez 6. testigo 7. borracho 8. fiscal 9. menos 10. acto 11. todo 12. como 13. diez **Exercise IV.** Compositions are Ad Lib.

Answers to Grammar Exercises: "Nunca," "nada," "nadie" in Emphatic Negation; Tag Question "¿verdad?"

Exercise I. 1. Nadie comprende todos los idiomas. 2. Nadie estudia... 3. Nadie lee ... 4. Nadie visita... 5. Nadie hace... **Exercise II.** 1. Nunca como despacio. 2. Nunca estoy ... 3. Nunca tengo... 4. Nunca leo... 5. Nunca ayudo... **Exercise III.** 1. Los chicos nada compraron para el viaje. 2. Ellos nada reciben... 3. Juan nada comió... 4. Ellos nada tuvieron que contestar... 5. Ellos nada deben... **Exercise IV.** 1. Verdad. Las niñas pobres nada reciben para la Navidad. 2. ...Nadie va a comprender... 3. ...El chico perezoso nada quiso escribir... 4. ...Nadie desea asistir... 5. ...Un hombre cansado nunca debe trabajar... **Exercise V.** 1. María y yo nada leímos 2. Nadie escucha... 3. María nunca tomó... 4. La sopa nunca está... 5. Nadie está... **Exercise VI. A.** 1. ¿Siempre? Yo nunca canto en casa. 2. ¿Siempre? Yo nunca tomo... 3. ¿Siempre? Laura y Antonio nunca pasan... **Ex. VI. B.** 1. ¿María? Nadie vino a mi casa. 2. ¿La familia? Nadie fue a esquiar... 3. ¿Ese zapatero? Nadie tiene... **Ex. VI. C.** 1. ¿Algo? Él nada sabe de México. 2. ¿Algo? El alumno nada contestó... 3. ¿Algo? Los niños nada oyen... 4. ¿Algo? Los turistas nada necesitan... **Exercise VII.** 1. Tus padres salen para Puerto Rico, ¿no es verdad? Your parents are leaving for Puerto Rico, aren't they? 2. ...¿no es verdad? They always spend a month there, don't they? 3. ..., ¿no es verdad? You have a Puerto Rican cousin, don't you? 4. ..., ¿no es verdad? Her name is Laura and she's very pretty, isn't she? 5. ..., ¿no es verdad? Her house is in the country, isn't it? **Exercise VIII.** 1. Nadie prepara un desayuno como mi madre. 2. Mi padre y yo nunca preparamos el desayuno. 3. Pero mi hermana nada toma para el desayuno. 4. Tu (su) hermana toma café, ¿no es verdad? 5. Pero tu (su) hermano está todavía en la cama, ¿no es verdad?

Part Two: Idioms and Dialogues

Unit 1. Exercise I. 1. a 2. c 3. b 4. a 5. c 6. a 7. c 8. a 9. b 10. a **Exercise II.** 1. a, b 2. a, d 3. c, d 4. b, d 5. b, c 6. a, b 7. a, c 8. c, d **Exercise III.** 1. a 2. c 3. c 4. a 5. a 6. b 7. a 8. a 9. c 10. c. **Exercise IV. A.** 1. c 2. b. 3. a **B.** 1. c 2. b 3. a **C.** 1. b 2. d 3. a 4. c **Exercise V.** 1. ¿Cómo se llaman ellos? 2. ¿Qué tal? 3. ¿Cómo está Vd.? 4. Cómo te llamas? 5. ¿Cómo está tu familia? **Exercise VI.** 1. Buenas. 2. señor 3. favor 4. da 5. Cómo 6. está 7. enfermo 8. gracias 9. qué 10. Qué 11. Sin 12. está 13. estoy 14. Con 15. noches 16. Adiós **Exercise VII. A.** 1. Nosotros le damos las gracias por el favor. 2. El maestro le da las gracias por la bienvenida. 3. Sus amigos le dan las gracias por su invitación. 4. Tú le das las gracias por los regalos. **Exercise VII. B.** 1. Yo le doy la mano al profesor. 2. Nosotros le damos la mano a la vecina. 3. Tú le das la mano a mi padre. 4. Los oficiales le dan la mano al astronauta. **Exercise VII. C.** 1. Señora, ¡haga Vd. el favor de responder a la carta! 2. Caballeros, ¡hagan Vds. el favor de entrar! 3. Señor, ¡haga Vd. el favor de salir ahora! 4. Señoritas, ¡hagan Vds. el favor de poner la mesa! **Exercise VII. D.** 1. Ana, ¡haz el favor de escuchar al maestro! 2. Chico, ¡haz el favor de leer el cuento! 3. Prima, ¡haz el favor de llegar a tiempo! 4. Hijo, ¡haz el favor de dar las gracias a mamá! **Exercise VII. E.** 1. ¡Den Vds. la mano, por favor! 2. ¡Escriba Vd., por favor! 3. ¡Conteste Vd. en español, por favor! 4. ¡Vengan Vds. acá, por favor! **Exercise VIII. A.** 1. ¡Hagan Vds. el favor de dar la mano! 2. ¡Hagan Vds. el favor de tomar asiento! 3. ¡Hagan Vds. el favor de salir más tarde! 4. ¡Hagan Vds. el favor de escribir su dirección! 5. ¡Hagan Vds. el favor de hablar menos aquí! **Exercise VIII. B.** 1. ¡Haga Vd. el favor de dar las gracias! 2. ¡Haga Vd. el favor de tomar café! 3. ¡Haga Vd. el favor de poner el libro aquí! 4. ¡Haga Vd. el favor de recibir este dinero! 5. ¡Haga Vd. el favor de comer más! **Exercise IX.** 1. ¡Haz el favor de aprender la lección! 2. ¡Haz el favor de abrir la ventana! 3. ¡Hagan Vds. el favor de no hablar en la clase! 4. ¡Pasen Vds. al otro cuarto, por favor! 5. Les doy las gracias a los padres.

Unit 2. Exercise I. 1. Sí, hace mucho fresco en el otoño. Yes, it is very cool in autumn. 2. Sí, hace mucho frío y mucho viento en el invierno. Yes, it is very cold and very windy in winter. 3. Sí, hace mucho calor en el verano. Yes, it is very warm in summer. 4. Sí, hace mucho sol en Puerto Rico. Yes, it is very sunny in Puerto Rico. 5. Sí, llueve mucho en abril. Yes, it rains a lot in April. 6. Sí, está lloviendo mucho ahora. Yes, it is raining hard now. 7. Sí, nieva mucho en diciembre. Yes, it snows a lot in December. 8. Sí, está nevando hoy. Yes, it is snowing today. 9. Sí, hace muy buen tiempo en mayo. Yes, it is very good weather in May. 10. Sí, hace muy mal tiempo en noviembre. Yes, it is very bad weather in November. **Exercise II. A.** Hace mucho frío en el invierno. 2. Hace mucho calor en el verano. 3. Hace mucho fresco en el otoño. 4. Llueve mucho en abril. 5. Hace muy buen tiempo en la primavera. 6. Hace muy mal tiempo en febrero. 7. Nieva mucho en enero. 8. Hace mucho viento en marzo. **Exercise II. B.** 1. Hace poco sol. 2. Hace poco frío. 3. Hace poco fresco. 4. Hace poco viento. 5. Llueve poco. 6. Nieva poco. 7. Hace poco calor. **Exercise III.** 1. No nieva mucho en la Florida. 2. No llueve mucho en el desierto. 3. No está lloviendo dentro de la casa. 4. Hace fresco en la primavera. 5. No está nevando dentro de la casa. 6. No hace mucho calor en Alaska. 7. No hace mucho frío en África. 8. Hace mucho sol en Puerto Rico. 9. No hace buen tiempo en Londres. 10. No hace mal tiempo en California. **Exercise IV.** 1. Hace mucho calor en el verano. 2. Hace mucho frío en el invierno. 3. Llueve mucho en abril. 4. Nieva mucho en diciembre. 5. Hace mucho viento en marzo. 6. Hace mucho fresco entre el frío de invierno y el calor de verano. 7. Está nevando ahora. 8. Está lloviendo mucho en este momento. 9. Hace muy buen tiempo en mayo.

10. Hace muy mal tiempo en noviembre. **Exercise V.** 1. Nosotros tenemos sueño aquí. 2. Tú tienes frío sin abrigo. 3. Juan y Carlos tienen calor ahora. 4. Vd. tiene un dolor de cabeza hoy. 5. Anita tiene sed y bebe. 6. Yo tengo hambre y como. 7. Vds. tienen miedo del agua. 8. Luis tiene dolor de dientes hoy. 9. Vd. y yo tenemos dolor de estómago. 10. Luis y Vd. tienen interés en ella. **Exercise VI.** 1. Ella tiene hambre si no come. 2. Ella tiene sed si no bebe. 3. Ella tiene miedo si no estudia. 4. Ella tiene calor si no va al lago. 5. Ella tiene dolor de muelas si no va al dentista. 6. Ella tiene dolor de cabeza si no toma aspirinas. 7. Ella tiene frío si abre la puerta. 8. Ella tiene dolor de estómago si come mucho. 9. Ella tiene quince años si hoy es su cumpleaños. 10. Ella tiene sueño si no duerme. **Exercise VII.** 1. Sí, tengo mucho frío. 2. Sí, tenemos mucho calor. 3. Sí, ellos tienen mucho interés. 4. Sí, María tiene mucha hambre. 5. Sí, Pepe tiene mucha sed. 6. Sí, Vd. tiene (tú tienes) mucho miedo. 7. Sí, tengo mucho sueño. 8. Sí, tengo mucho dolor de cabeza. 9. Sí, hace muy buen tiempo. 10. Sí, hace muy mal tiempo. **Exercise VIII.** 1. hace 2. tengo 3. hace 4. hace 5. tenemos 6. hace 7. hace 8. tiene 9. tienen 10. está 11. tienes 12. está 13. – 14. – 15. hace. **Exercise IX.** 1. d 2. c 3. a 4. b 5. b 6. b 7. d 8. a 9. a 10. b **Exercise X.** 1. Vd. tiene mucha hambre. 2. Tú tienes mucha sed. 3. Yo tengo mucho sueño. 4. Nosotros no tenemos mucho frío. 5. Y está nevando mucho. 6. Claro, hace mucho sol. 7. ¡No quiero porque no está lloviendo mucho! 8. ¿Tiene él dolor de estómago y de cabeza? 9. Yo tengo quince años y mis hermanos tienen quince meses. 10. Siempre hace muy mal tiempo en noviembre.

Unit 3. Exercise I. 1. At what time do you eat lunch? **a.** (1) ¿A qué hora vas a la cama? (2) At what time do you go to bed? **b.** (1) ¿A qué hora comemos? (2) At what time do we eat? **c.** (1) ¿A qué hora estudian? (2) At what time do they study? 2. We leave at six P.M. **a.** (1) Salimos a las once de la noche. (2) We leave at eleven P.M. **b.** (1) Salimos a las ocho de la mañana. (2) We leave at eight A.M. **c.** (1) Salimos a la una de la tarde. (2) We leave at one P.M. 3. They study in the evening (at night). **a.** (1) Estudian por la mañana. (2) They study in the morning. **b.** (1) Estudian por la tarde. (2) They study in the afternoon. **c.** (1) Estudian por la noche. (2) They study in the evening. 4. What is today's date? **a.** (1) ¿A cuántos estamos hoy? (2) What is today's date? **b.** (1) ¿Qué fiesta cae hoy? (2) What's today's holiday? **c.** (1) ¿Qué día es hoy? (2) What day is today? 5. Today is the first of May. **a.** (1) Hoy es el dos de junio. (2) Today is the second of June. **b.** (1) Hoy es el veinte y uno de noviembre. (2) Today is November 21st. **c.** (1) Hoy es el veinte de octubre. (2) Today is October 20th. 6. Today is April 1st. **a.** (1) Estamos a primero de abril. (2) Today is April 1st. **b.** (1) La fiesta cae el primero de abril. (2) The holiday falls on April 1st. **c.** (1) Mañana es el primero de abril. (2) Tomorrow is April 1st. **Exercise II.** 1. Es la una. 2. Son las dos. 3. Son las tres. 4. Son las cinco y cuarto (quince) de la tarde. 5. Son las seis y media de la mañana. 6. Son las siete menos cuarto (quince) de la nche. **Exercise III.** 1. Como a las ocho de la mañana. 2. Salgo de la clase a la una de la tarde. 3. Regreso a casa por la tarde. 4. Estudio a las nueve y media de la noche. 5. Son las once menos veinte en punto cuando voy a dormir. **Exercise IV.** 1. La fecha es el cuatro de julio. 2. Estamos a veinte y cinco de diciembre. 3. La fecha es el doce de octubre. 4. Estamos a primero de enero. 5. La fecha es el primero de abril. 6. Estamos a catorce de abril. **Exercise V.** 1. La Navidad cae el veinte y cinco de diciembre. 2. Es el dos de . . . 3. Son las dos. 4. El Día de la Raza es el doce de octubre. 5. El Día de la Independencia norteamericana cae el cuatro de julio. 6. El Día de Año Nuevo cae el primero de enero. 7. El Día de las Américas cae el catorce de abril. 8. El Día de la Independencia española cae el dos de mayo. **Exercise VI.** 1. ¿Cuál es la fecha de hoy? 2. ¿A cuántos estamos hoy? 3. ¿Qué hora es? 4. ¿A qué hora comen? 5. ¿Cuándo celebramos La Navidad? **Exercise VII.** 1. Qué 2. Cuál 3. Cómo 4. cuántos 5. qué **Exercise VIII.** 1. estamos 2. es 3. llama 4. es 5. es 6. es 7. Es 8. Son **Exercise IX.** 1. el 2. – 3. la 4. – 5. la; la 6. las; la 7. las 8. la; las; la **Exercise X.** 1. ¿Qué hora es? 2. Es la una de la tarde. 3. ¿Qué hora es ahora? 4. Son las dos. No es la una. 5. ¿Son las cuatro en punto? 6. Son las cinco menos veinte. 7. ¿Son las cinco y treinta ahora? 8. Sí, son las cinco y media. **Exercise XI. A.** 1. son, 2 las, 3 las **B.** 1 la, 2 la, 3 y, 4 Son, 5 las, 6 en **C.** 1 qué, 2 las, 3 de, 4 la, 5 la, 6 la, 7 la, 8 las, 9 la, 10 A, 11 qué, 12 las, 13 de, 14 la, 15 a, 16 de, 17 la, 18 a, 19 las, 20 de **D.** 1 por, 2 por, 3 por, 4 por, 5 la.

Unit 4. Exercise I. 1. I love my mother. **a.** (1) Tú quieres a la maestra. (2) You love the teacher. **b.** (1) Nosotros queremos a los amigos. (2) We love the friends. **c.** (1) Juan quiere a la chica. (2) John loves the girl. **d.** (1) Ana y Pepe quieren a sus hermanos. (2) Ann and Joe lover their brothers (and sisters). **e.** (1) Yo quiero al compañero de clase. (2) I love the class-mate. 2. They know how to play the piano. **a.** (1) Yo sé cantar la canción. (2) I know how to sing the song. **b.** (1) María sabe bailar la bamba. (2) Mary knows how to dance la bamba. **c.** (1) Tú sabes hablar español. (2) You know how to speak Spanish. **d.** (1) Tú y yo sabemos jugar al tenis. (2) You and I know how to play tennis. **e.** (1) Ellos saben tocar el violín. (2) They know how to play the violin. 3. Louis and Peter are standing. **a.** (1) Yo estoy de pie. (2) I am stand-ing. **b.** (1) Vd. y yo estamos levantados. (2) You and I are standing. **c.** (1) Vd. está sentado. (2) You are seated. **d.** (1) Tú estás de pie. (2) You are standing. **e.** (1) Los chicos están de pie. (2) The boys are standing. 4. I do well in (pass) the examination. **a.** (1) Tú sales mal en la clase. (2) You do poorly in (fail) the class. **b.** (1) Juan y yo salimos bien en el examen. (2) John and I do well on (pass) the examination (test). **c.** (1) Los alumnos salen mal en sus estudios. (2) The pupils do poorly (fail) in their studies. **d.** (1) Yo salgo bien en los exámenes. (2) I do well on (pass) the examinations. 5. What does the word mean? **a.** (1) ¿Qué quieren decir las frases? (2) What do the sentences mean? **b.** (1) ¿Qué quieres decir tú? (2) What do you mean? **c.** (1) ¡Qué quiere decir Juan? (2) What does John mean? 6. I believe so. **a.** (1) El y yo creemos que no. (2) He and I believenot. **b.** (1) La madre cree que no. (2) The mother believes not. **c.** (1) Tú crees que sí. (2) You believe so. **Exercise II.** 1. de 2. de 3. sé 4. sé escribir 5. en 6. quiero a 7. decir 8. dice; se 9. hay que 10. verdad 11. Es; que sí 12. cree; no 13. creo que 14. por; presto 15. ¡concedido! **Exercise III.** 1. a 2. c 3. a 4. a 5. c **Exercise IV.** 1. Estoy en una clase de español. I am in a Spanish class. 2. La maestra está de pie. The teacher is standing. 3. Sí, sí cómo se dice *book* en español. Yes, I know how to say "book" in Spanish. 4. Yo sé de quién es el libro. I know whose book it is. 5. Yo sé leer el español. I know how to read Spanish. 6. Sí, yo presto atención. Yes, I pay attention. 7. Hay que trabajar en la clase de historia. One must work in the history class. 8. Salgo bien en los exámenes. I do well in (pass) the examinations. 9. Quiero mucho a la maestra. I love the teacher very much. 10. Es verdad que la maestra cree que sí. It is true that the teacher believes so. **Exercise V.** 1. b 2. d 3. a 4. a 5. c 6. a 7. b 8. d 9. b 10. a **Exercise VI.** 1. d 2. a 3. e 4. c 5. b.

Unit 5. Exercise I. 1. I go horseback riding. **a.** (1) Tú das un paseo a pie. (2) You take a walk. **b.** (1) Vds. dan un paseo en automóvil. (2) You take a car ride. **c.** (1) Nosotros damos un paseo en bicicleta. (2) We take a bicycle ride. 2. We get off the train. **a.** (1) El piloto baja del avión. (2) The pilot gets off the plane. **b.** (1) Los amigos bajan del coche. (2) The friends get out of the car. **c.** (1) Yo bajo del autobús. (2) I get off the bus. 3. Everyone attends the theater. **a.** (1) Yo asisto a la escuela. (2) I attend the school. **b.** (1) Ellos asisten al cine. (2) They attend the movies. **c.** (1) Nosotros asistimos a las fiestas. (2) We attend the parties. 4. I set the table with the tablecloth. **a.** (1) Tú pones la mesa con vasos. (2) You set the table with glasses. **b.** (1) Ana y yo ponemos la mesa con cucharas. (2) Ann and I set the table with spoons. **c.** (1) Marta pone la mesa con cuchillos. (2) Martha sets the table with knives. **d.** (1) Yo pongo la mesa con servilletas. (2) I set the table with napkins. 5. You and I enter the movies. **a.** (1) Vd. entra en la casa. (2) You enter the house. **b.** (1) Vd. y Juan entran en la clase. (2) You and John enter the class. **c.** (1) Yo entro en la escuela. (2) I enter the school. 6. I go for a walk everywhere. **a.** (1) Yo voy de paseo al parque. (2) I go for a walk to the park. **b.** (1) Tú vas de paseo a casa. (2) You go for a walk home. **c.** (1) Ellos van de paseo al cine. (2) They go for a walk to the movies. **d.** (1) Tú y yo vamos de paseo al centro. (2) You and I go for a walk downtown. **Exercise II.** 1. Asisto a la escuela los lunes. I attend school on Mon-days. 2. Voy de paseo al parque. I go for a walk to the park. 3. Subo al tren para ir al parque. I get on the train to go to the park. 4. Bajo del tren y entro en el parque. I get off the train and enter the park. 5. Primero doy un paseo a pie y luego en bicicleta. First, I take a walk and then a bicycle ride. 6. Sé tocar un instrumento como el violín. I know how to play an instrument like the violin. 7. Todo el mundo está por todas partes del parque. Everyone is everywhere in the park. 8. Salgo del parque para ir a casa. I leave the park to go home. 9. Pongo la mesa antes de comer. I set the table before eating. 10. Toco la guitarra, el piano y el violín en casa. I play the guitar, the piano and the violin at home. **Exercise III.** 1. Todo el mundo asiste a la escuela. 2. Sé tocar bien la guitarra. 3. Hay mucha gente por todas partes de la ciudad. 4. Antes de comer pongo la mesa con un mantel. 5. Doy un paseo en bicicleta a la playa el sábado. 6. Salgo de la escuela a las tres. 7. Subo al ascensor para llegar al piso del vecino. 8. Regreso a casa a pie. 9. Doy un paseo a caballo por el parque. 10. A las ocho de la mañana entro en la clase. **Exercise IV.** 1. b 2. a 3. a 4. a 5. b **Exercise V.** 1. a 2. c 3. b 4. b 5. a **Exercise VI.** 1. d 2. c 3. b 4. a 5. e **Exercise VII.** 1. a 2. en 3. en 4. del 5. de 6. a 7. al 8. a 9. en 10. en **Exercise VIII.** 1. a 2. asisto 3. vas 4. de, a, en, doy, a 5. dar, paseo

Unit 6. Exercise I. 1. (1) Asisto a fiestas a menudo. (2) I attend parties often. 2. (1) Fui a muchas fiestas el mes pasado. (2) I went to many parties last month. 3. (1) Llego muchas veces a tiempo. (2) I often arrive on time. 4. (1) Deseo ir de nuevo. (2) I want to go again. 5. (1) Quiero ir en seguida. (2) I want to go right away. 6. (1) Termino el trabajo para la clase más tarde. (2) I finish the work for the class later. 7. (1) Estudio pocas veces este año como el año pasado. (2) I rarely study this year like last year. 8. (1) Aprendo poco a poco. (2) I learn little by little. 9. (1) Trabajé mucho toda la semana pasada. (2) I worked hard all last week. 10. (1) Voy a México el año próximo como todos los años. (2) I'm going to Mexico next year like every year. 11. (1) Celebro el cumpleaños la semana próxima. (2) I'll celebrate the birthday next week. 12. (1) Voy al campo otra vez el mes que viene. (2) I'm going to the country again next month. 13. (1) Doy una fiesta esta semana como todas las semanas. (2) I'm having (giving) a party this week like every week. 14. (1) Salgo esta noche como todas las noches. (2) I leave tonight like every night. 15. (1) Asisto a las clases hoy como todos los días. (2) I attend classes today like every day. **Exercise II.** 1. a 2. b 3. b 4. c 5. a **Exercise III.** 1. c 2. a 3. a 4. a 5. b **Exercise IV.** 1. b 2. a 3. c 4. b 5. b **Exercise V.** 1. a 2. veces 3. esta 4. En, esta 5. a 6. las, de, próxima.

Index

Índice de títulos de los cuentos en español

Numbers refer to pages.